D0757672

am 2/84

DATE DUE

SARA F. YOSELOFF MEMORIAL PUBLICATIONS
In Judaism and Jewish Affairs

This volume is one in a series established in memory
of Sara F. Yoseloff,
who devoted her life to the making of books.

OTHER BOOKS by DAVID S. LIFSON

The Yiddish Theatre in America

EPIC AND FOLK PLAYS
OF THE YIDDISH THEATRE

Translated and Edited by

David S. Lifson

Rutherford • Madison • Teaneck
Fairleigh Dickinson University Press
London: Associated University Presses

Riverside Community College
Library
4800 Magnolia Avenue
Riverside, CA 92506

© 1975 by Associated University Presses, Inc.

Associated University Presses, Inc.
Cranbury, New Jersey 08512

Associated University Presses
108 New Bond Street
London W1Y OQX, England

Library of Congress Cataloging in Publication Data

Lifson, David S   comp.
    Epic and folk plays of the Yiddish theatre.

    CONTENTS: Hirshbein, P.   Farvorfen vinkel.—
Leivick, H.   Hirsh Lekert.—Kobrin, L.   Yankel Boyla.
[etc.] 1. Yiddish drama—Translations into English
2. English drama—Translations from Yiddish.
I. Title.
PJ5191.E5L5   839'.09'2008   73-2899
ISBN 0-8386-1082-X

PRINTED IN THE UNITED STATES OF AMERICA

Dedicated to
Dorothy,
Hank,
Sue,
Jeffrey,
and Amy,
who cherish our immortal cultural heritage.

CONTENTS

Foreword by Charles Angoff   9

Prefatory Note   11

Introduction   13

FARVORFEN VINKEL, by Peretz Hirshbein (translated by David S. Lifson) 25

HIRSH LEKERT, by H. Leivick (translated by David S. Lifson)   65

YANKEL BOYLA, by Leon Kobrin (translated by David S. Lifson)   101

RECRUITS, by Axenfeld-Reznik (translated by David S. Lifson)   141

HAMAN'S DOWNFALL, by Chaim Sloves (translated by Max Rosenfeld) 195

7

FOREWORD
by
Charles Angoff

Yiddish as a language and a literature has one thing in common with the Jewish people as a whole: its demise has been predicted for centuries, yet it survives. All the "facts" point to its "inevitable" extinction: the virtual death of Yiddish writing and Yiddish culture in general in the Soviet Union and in Poland where both had flourished so long; the continued (even though somewhat lessened) hostility of some Israeli officials to Yiddish; the great difficulties of Yiddish journalism in the United States (there is now only one major daily newspaper, the *Forward,* and it has had to combine its Saturday and Sunday editions); and the sorry state of the Yiddish theatre in New York. There are other factors that appear to indicate the end of Yiddish. The one major Yiddish newspaper in Israel, *Die Letzte Neues* is embarrassingly poor, and is getting poorer. The contempt of Israeli Hebrew journalists for Yiddish persists. A reporter for *Maariv,* one of the most influential Israeli dailies, interviewed me not long ago and refused to talk to me in Yiddish, claiming he didn't know the language, even though he clearly understood some of the Yiddish expressions I used. Indeed, so deep is the gloom in certain intellectual quarters that even Abraham Sutskever, the eminent Yiddish poet and editor of *Die Goldene Kayt,* a Yiddish quarterly of outstanding stature, has become pessimistic. I was at his home last summer, and he presented mounting evidence that Yiddish writers are not only dying but are not being replaced, and he added, "In the United States, the Jews have not produced a single American-born Yiddish writer of any significance."

All this is true, but the conclusion is wrong. It used to be said of the late Senator Robert A. Taft, "He is a very brilliant man until he makes up his mind." A similar thing is true about the future of Yiddish. Some things in life are governed by a sort of mystical logic. They who claimed that the American revolutionaries couldn't possibly succeed in their revolt against the mother country in the 1770s had all the facts on their side, except one: the stubborn insistence of the poorly organized, poorly financed, poorly equipped, economically impoverished American colonists on establishing their own nation. Wasn't the same true of Israel? All Dr. Herzl heard from most of the Jewish political theoreticians and historians and economists, those "who really know," was that he was insane, that the reestablishment of a Jewish nation in Palestine was "absolutely impossible on every imaginary ground." But Dr. Herzl insisted that "if you will it, it will be."

They who believe in the persistence of Yiddish literature and general Yiddish culture have "facts" of their own. Yiddish may be declining in some areas in the United States, but it is also revealing amazing life in others. There are more and more courses in Yiddish in the colleges and universities across the land. The popularity of I. B. Singer's Yiddish novels and short stories, even in English translation, is significant. The same with *Fiddler on the Roof,* a musical based upon a small portion of a Sholom Aleichem story. Some maintain that the musical is "false" to Sholom Aleichem. There is some basis to this claim, but it is also true that what millions of Americans and others were attracted to was, in large part, its Jewish esprit as distilled through the Yiddish of a Yiddish master. The popularity of such books as *The Joys of Yiddish* and *The World of Sholom Aleichem* also has significance. But there is a spiritual fact overwhelmingly more significant. The viability of Yiddish is governed by the mystical logic that seems to mock the logic of those practical men who put so much trust in statistics, slide rules, test tubes, and computers. Yiddish is 1,000 years old. It has been, and still is, the *lingua franca,* in one form or another, of the vast majority of the Jewish people. While it has had its ups and downs in acceptability, while it has been sneered at as a mere *jargon,* not a language at all, only the language of the common street folk, it was on the lips of most of the 6,000,000 Jews who were killed by the Nazis and thus has been sanctified by history for all time. It has evolved into a flexible, colorful, evocative language with almost infinite nuances, so much so that the literature that has been produced in it is still the most beautiful that the Jews have produced in the past 100 years. Not that the Israeli literature of the past twenty-five years is not worthy. It is very much so, but it has not the sublimity, insofar as the Jewish soul is concerned, that the Yiddish literature has. After all, 1,000 years is longer than 25 years, and a literature, like wine, needs aging. Indeed, the great masters of modern Hebrew literature have been criticized for the substratum of *Yiddishhert* in their writings. It has been said of no less a person than the late Nobel Prize winner Agnon that, while he wrote in Hebrew, he thought and felt in Yiddish. And the same has been said about his great contemporary, Hazaz.

Yiddish is very much a vital factor in Jewish life all over the world even if only, in some parts of the world, chiefly by the invisible infiltrations of echoes and nuances. Alas, too many pople think of Yiddish literature as being confined to the novel, the short story, and poetry. It also has great riches in the drama and that is where Professor Lifson has once again put us in his debt (he has already done so before with his excellent book, *The Yiddish Theatre in America*) with his fine edition of English translations of five Yiddish plays, including a *Purin shpil,* which has been so enduring a part of Jewish life down the centuries of the *Galut.* His Introduction to the collection is learned and perceptive, as are his running notes and commentaries. *Epic and Folk Plays of the Yiddish Theatre* is an important contribution to the mounting scholarship of Yiddish culture.

CHARLES ANGOFF
Fairleigh Dickinson University
New Jersey

PREFATORY NOTE

After attending the memorable Yiddish production of *Recruits* by the great Artef Troupe, I wanted to share the exciting experience with my friends, with my neighbors, and with everyone who did not understand the Yiddish language. Whereupon I embarked upon its translation with the able and sympathetic editorial assistance of Bronya Neiman. When Nat Kornbluth and his lovely wife learned of the completion of my work on this play, they graciously turned their London home over to me for a reading of it. During that evening I was overwhelmed by the hungry, avid interest in Yiddish drama by their circle of friends among London's intellectuals, artists, writers, and critics. That stirring evening at the Kornbluths' convinced me that the important, immortal plays of the Yiddish theatre should not remain buried in Judaic libraries, but should again come alive, not only for the loyal Yiddishists but for all drama devotees. Thus encouraged, I started upon the project of selecting and translating plays I consider to be epic and folk.

I owe the realization of this work to the perception and unfaltering faith of Thomas Yoseloff and Charles Angoff, who provided for publication. Dina Abramowitz, the indefatigable librarian at Yivo, and Yivo provided the original Yiddish plays. Ruby Radosh gave unstintingly of his time and knowledge in editorial help. When I was worried about the faithfulness of my interpretation of the passionate poetry of H. Leivick, I was fortunate in Nat Lev's guidance and assurance as well as his authoritative literary comments. Monmouth College provided a grant that helped me considerably to meet the expenses of this project.

I am particularly grateful to the copyright owners of the original Yiddish plays for their faith in me as demonstrated by their granting me permission to proceed with this work. Among them are Eleanor Kobrin and Laura Tauben for Leon Kobrin's *Yankel Boila,* Omus Hirshbein for Peretz Hirshbein's *Farvorfen Vinkel,* Daniel Leivick for H. Leivick's *Hirsh Lekert,* and Max Rosenfeld for his admirable translation of Chaim Sloves's *Haman's Downfall.*

To Lou Auerbach I am especially indebted for his expert guidance in the proofreading of the galleys, which, for him, was a labor of love.

Because of the wide and popular reception of my book *The Yiddish Theatre in America* (Yoseloff 1965), I am grateful to all who are dedicated to an undying cultural heritage that lives in the dramatic literature of an epic and folk theatre.

D.L.

INTRODUCTION

As I walked down the cream-colored marble stair, I was reminded of the white marble stairs at the Paris Opéra. Well, not quite, for this Teatrul Evreiesc of Bucharest was much simpler, not so grand—rather, say it was commensurate with the Petit Trianon, whereas the baroque elegance of the Paris Opéra is comparable with the palace at Versailles. Nonetheless, I was thrilled with pride in this glorious temple of an undying art—the Yiddish drama. Here indeed was an answer to the inevitable question that always challenged me after one of my talks back home at a Jewish center's cultural series or at a synagogue's Oneg Shabat. The question usually came from an eager young matron whom the rabbi classified among the "young marrieds"; she would sadly ask, "Is the Yiddish theatre really dead?" No, it is not dead! It is alive and well in Bucharest, a living testament to its continuing glory.

Before I went to Bucharest in 1970, I was as unaware of the living Yiddish theatre, there between the Carpathians and the Danube, as our younger people are unaware of their ancestral theatre, about which they have heard from their elders but have never witnessed on stage. The melancholy story of the moribund Yiddish theatre in America, in Western Europe, and in South America is too well known. The pioneer spirit of Israel rejects vestiges of ghetto culture of the Diaspora as contained in the dramatic works of the Yiddish theatre. To tell the eager young Americans of Jewish descent that a Yiddish theatre is flourishing in Romania cannot satisfy their hunger for partaking in their Jewish cultural heritage. Even there, how long will it bloom? There is a foreboding of inevitable doom in the presence, at the Teatrul Evreiesc, of transistor hearing devices that relay in the Romanian language what is being said in Yiddish on the stage to the young people who come to the theatre but do not understand their *momme loshen* (mother tongue) Yiddish. The hard core of Yiddish theatre devotees in Bucharest, exactly like that at the infrequent Yiddish plays in New York, is composed of middle-aged and old people who are the dwindling remnant of Yiddishists. So, before I went to Bucharest (to study the Yddish theatre there as a Fulbright-Hays Research Scholar), when the rueful question was asked, "Is the Yiddish theatre really dead?" my response was the question, "Is the ancient Greek theatre dead?" Obviously the Greek theatre lives on, and scarcely a day passes but a Greek classic is being presented in translation somewhere in the world.

During its brief history of less than a century, the Yiddish theatre has contributed outstanding dramas that have taken their place in the roster of poetic dramas of the world repertoire, according to prominent critic and authority Allardyce Nicoll. The most successful long-run production in the history of Broadway is the musical *Fiddler on the Roof,* an adaptation of the Yiddish folk drama based on Sholem Aleichem's *Tevye der Milchedicker. Der Dybbuk* has succeeded in an English-language production on the stage in New York and on television. A burgeoning interest in the literature of the Yiddish stage is evident in the publication of Joseph C. Landis's felicitous and brilliant translations of *Der Dybbuk and Other Great Yiddish Plays.* Since Samuel J. Citron's excellent chapter on Yiddish theatre and drama in Clark and Freedley's *A History of Modern Drama* (1947), and since my *Yiddish Theatre in America* (1965), interest in the treasures of the Yiddish theatre has grown so that the latest edition of Freedley and Reeves, *A History of the Theatre* (1968), includes a chapter each on Yiddish and Hebrew theatres; while the forthcoming edition of the *Encyclopedia Britannica* will include a section on the performing arts of the Jews. Growing numbers of scholars are pursuing research on Yiddish theatre and drama in various graduate schools. The nationalizing influence of the Yiddish theatre was excitingly and dramatically demonstrated when, in France, soon after the liberation from the Nazis, Jews in unprecedented numbers flocked to a revival of the Yiddish theatre in Paris, more than to their synagogues. Yiddish plays have found their way into other languages and have made theatrical history thereby. Max Reinhardt produced Pinski's *The Treasure* in German in 1910, and the same play was done in English by the Theatre Guild in New York. Arthur Hopkins produced Hirshbein's *Idle Inn* in English on Broadway. Why, eleven plays from the Yiddish were translated into Japanese as early as 1922!

The success of these translations and productions from the Yiddish in various languages demonstrates the universality of theme and treatment of the plays. The Yiddish theatre also had an enormous impact upon the theatre art of various countries. It served as a bridge over which were brought various innovative European-theatre art forms to America. It also inspired an awakening in the stodgy, predominantly French-classic-style theatre in Romania when the visiting Vilna Troupe electrified the Bucharest theatre world in 1923; since then the Romanian theatre has become one of the most exciting experimental theatre centers in the world.

In Romania, where the modern, professional Yiddish theatre was founded by Abraham Goldfaden in 1876, the valor of the Jewish people also made history behind the scenes of the Yiddish theatre. It was in Bucharest, Romania, where the epic drama of the Jewish theatre people's confrontation with the Fascists (1940–1944) was enacted. The actors, writers, and directors of Jewish origin who were forbidden to appear in the Romanian theatre, and those who had been in the Yiddish theatre, were able to sustain the morale of the beleaguered Jews and to encourage Romanian patriots to throw off the tyrannical yoke that enslaved the nation. The Jewish theatrical fraternity daily risked torture and death in order to keep alive the folk traditions by means of a heroic Yiddish theatre. Aesopean devices were employed in three forms.

There were the dramatizations of great Yiddish classic poems and short stories that were presented at synagogue services despite official prohibition of anything but religious ritual. The Jewish theatre folk circumvented the Argus-eyed secret police by innocently giving their presentations at the synagogues as memorial services or birthday celebrations of prominent Yiddish writers. One suspicious Nazi policeman questioned the celebration of three different birthdays for Goldfaden in one year. Then at the Barasheum Center* two theatres operated, one musical and

---

* The Jewish center of Bucharest and the Yiddish theatre are both known as the Barasheum. They are named for the famous Jewish doctor, Julio Barash, who organized Romanian medicine much as Abraham Flexner did American medicine.

the other dramatic. The dramatic theatre presented officially approved plays like Ossip Dymov's *Singer of His Sorrows,* while the musical theatre offered revues. Romanian patriots recall with pride and enthusiasm when an audience of Romanian army officers (non-Jewish, of course) stood and cheered a song of a scarecrow, the lyrics of which promised that one day a fresh wind will come to blow away the plague of black crows—an obvious reference to the Nazis. Came the heroic days of the summer of 1944 when the Nazi blight was lifted. Since then, a benign and grateful government supports and encourages a continually inspiring Yiddish theatre.

There were Hebrew and Yiddish plays written before Goldfaden's emergence in Romania. In addition to the usual reference to the Song of Songs and the Book of Job as evidence of Biblical drama among the Hebrews, there is evidence of Jewish dramatists going back to 150 B.C. There have been Jewish playwrights who wrote dramas in Hebrew, in Germany, during the seventeenth and eighteenth centuries; their plays occasionally were produced by students. The popular theatre of the Jews through the centuries before that historic date in Romania developed out of the religious traditions of the Jews. B. Gorin, historian of the Yiddish theatre, records a presentation of the story of Esther in 415 C.E. The festivities accompanying the Purim holiday included performances by jesters, tumblers, and mimes. Gradually through the years, a dramatic continuity evolved, with the climax of the burning of Haman in effigy. In 1708, *A Beautiful New Ahasuerus Play,* written anonymously in Hebrew, was the first of plays known as *purim-shpil* to be published. Two years later, one Bermann, of Lemberg, published his *purim-shpil, Mechirat Yosef (The Sale of Joseph).* Among subsequent plays for the Purim merrymaking that became popular were *The Sacrifice of Isaac* and *David and Goliath.*

In addition to the *purim-shpil,* itinerant folk singers, individuals or groups, traveled through eastern Europe, where they offered their songs, in towns or shtetls, in Yiddish. The lyrics, rooted in Jewish life and lore, were set to folk tunes and religious chants, although some were original music. These lyrics make for a considerable Yiddish literature. Among the popular singers during the mid-nineteenth century were Velvel Zbarsher (Wolf Ehrenkrantz, 1826–1883), who reawakened interest in Romanian folk songs among non-Jews even though his lyrics were in Yiddish; Michael Gordon; and Eliokhum Zunzer. The Broder Singers, from Brod, Galicia, were great favorites and became the vehicle for Goldfaden's entrance into the theatre.

Of particular importance to the Yiddish drama was the world of the shtetl, which may be considered the heart of Yiddish culture. Millions of Jews, with one common language, with one religion, with one set of moral values, with similar social mechanisms and institutions, who spread across national boundaries from the Baltic to the Black Sea, through Russia, Poland, Romania, Austria-Hungary, and parts of Germany, had an indentity as a folk. Those first-generation immigrants from the shtetls who settled in the Jewish sections of eastern Europe, England, America, South Africa, and Argentina carried with them the shtetl way of life. Not only was the shtetl the birthplace of the most notable writers in the Yiddish language, it was also the source and substance of their writings; the characters and locale were inextricably the shtetl. Yiddish writers found their inspiration, their themes, their stories, and their most pungent language in the shtetl. The most treasured of Yiddish literature, be it poetry, stories, or drama, overflows with the abundance of the intense microcosm of the shtetl, with the joys and anguish, with the hopes and frustrations of the Jews, who clung faithfully to their folkways as a refuge from oppressive despotism. In the Old World, alas, the shtetl has fallen victim to the depredations of German Nazism and Soviet denationalization—it is no more. In the New World, assimilation, demise of first-generation immigrants, and de-ghettoization by their progeny, who became suburbanites, also took their toll of the shtetl milieu. In the pioneer society of Israel, with its propulsion toward modernism, a shtetl way of life is alien.

The recent crop of plays written in Israel does not include themes, settings, characters, nor stories and plots of the folk and epic style and content of the Yiddish dramatic literature, of the Jewish tradition within the shtetl genre. In Israel, plays are being written, for its vigorous and popular theatres, in Hebrew. There, as elsewhere throughout the world, the decline in the currency of the Yiddish language may be a discouraging factor for playwriting in Yiddish. Israel Bercovici in Romania and Haim Sloves and L. Brookstein in France continue to write significant drama for the Yiddish stage.

The roll call of Yiddish playwrights starts late in the eighteenth century. With the evangelical fervor of the Haskala movement, scholars who had been writing in Hebrew turned to the lingua franca of the masses and sought to reach the people in Yiddish. Among the first was Aaron Halle (Walfsohn, 1754-1835) who sought to elevate the Jews from their provincial medievalism with modern dramas that would relate to actual Jewish life and guide Jewish youth away from Hassidic fanaticism toward enlightenment. Although he did not fancy the "jargon" of Yiddish, he wrote a romantic play in that language, *Leichtsin und Fremmelai* (published in Breslau, 1796). The first significant Yiddish play was Solomon Ettinger's *Serkele* (ca. 1825). Most of the early Yiddish plays were circulated in manuscript form and were not published until many years after they were written. Noteworthy among the early playwrights were Israel Axenfeld (*The First Jewish Recruit in Russia,* 1827, published 1862; *Husband and Wife, Sister and Brother,* published 1862; *The Treasure,* and *Rich Man, Poor Man,* published a few years later); Abraham Ber Gottlober (*The Marriage Veil,* 1838, published 1876); Ludwig Levinsohn (*The Women's Knots,* 1874); Wolf Kamrash (*The Village Council,* n.d.); Gedaliah Belloi (*Jacob and His Son,* 1868, and *Judith,* 1870); J. B. Falkowitch (*Reb Chaim'l the Tycoon,* and *Rachel the Singer,* 1868); and Isaiah Gutman (*The Three Cousins,* n.d., and *The Kol Boi'nik,* n.d.; followed by *Mondrish,* n.d.).

Before he founded the modern Yiddish theatre in 1876, Abraham Goldfaden wrote two plays, *Aunt Sosie* and *The Two Neighbors.* During his colorful life he wrote many plays and operettas, the most prominent of which are still revived: *The Witch, Bar Kochba, Shulamith,* and *The Two Kuni Lemels.* Goldfaden's success was capitalized upon by imitators who tried to emulate his formula, a formula that employed banal plots, sentimental songs, and situations familiar to the simple tastes of his audiences. The most successful of his imitators were Moses Hurwitz and Joseph Lateiner, whose works lacked both Goldfaden's originality and his tender love for the heritage, traditions, and aspirations of the shtetl-rooted Jews. Hurwitz, Lateiner, and their like crudely pandered to primitive tastes.

Favorite writers in those early years of the young Yiddish theatre were J. J. Lerner, R. Katzenellenbogen, M. L. Lillienblum, S. J. Abramowitch (Mendele Mocher Sforim), and Nahum Meier Shaikewitch (Shomer). Although these writers occasionally offered reasonably acceptable plays, for the most part writers like Hurwitz and Lateiner monopolized the theatres of the new center of Jewish culture, New York, with melodramas and operettas that catered to the low tastes of the untutored immigrants. Their plays were corruptions of Jewish history, degraded and corrupted folk tales, and shoddy adaptations from the world repertoire. This insipid and tawdry fare became known as *shund.* Maudlin songs and dialogue in bathetic situations cluttered the offerings that were written as vehicles for the special talents of popular stars.

However, the intelligentsia among the Jews of New York sought to improve their drama. Critics, editors, actors, and writers agitated for a better theatre. Jacob Gordin, a Tolstoyan socialist, turned to the theatre and provided the great Yiddish tragedian, Jacob P. Adler, with a serious play, *Siberia,* which was presented in 1891. This production inaugurated an exciting decade, which has become known as the "first golden epoch of the Yiddish theatre." Gordin, who wrote some seventy plays, reformed the Yiddish theatre and drama by purifying the language and by bringing serious plays to the stage. His problem plays were derivative and still written as vehicles for great stars, but his penchant for realism avoided cheap vulgarity, and he helped develop higher literary standards for the Yiddish drama.

In addition to the playwriting of the Goldfaden genre and the Gordin golden epoch, some Yiddish writers offered a constant flow of banal melodramas, tawdry operettas, derivative social problem plays, and *ihberzetsungs* (translations) from the classic world repertoire and current popular Broadway plays. After Gordin there was a regression to an intensification of the melodramas with lurid sex content, through a period of nationalistic plays, and then to a "second golden epoch," brought about by the Yiddish art theatre movement. Throughout the sequence the Yiddish theatre offered plays that in many ways paralleled the fare in the leading Western capitals, particularly in New York. Coming hard upon the heels of George Bernard Shaw's *Mrs. Warren's Profession,* the more dramatically sexy play by Asch, *God of Vengeance,* may have been inspired by it. A distinguishing feature of the Yiddish theatre was its ever-conscious effort to create and maintain a bond with its audience. In so doing, the playwrights filled their offerings with readily identifiable folk types, sentimental folk music, obligatory ceremonials—a wedding, the sabbath eve feast, the *havdullah* (the close of the sabbath), the bravura moment of a cantor singing a familiar liturgical melody, the naive religious student adrift in a corrupt world, the mother blessing the sabbath candles—all to arouse in the breasts of the responsive audience a nostalgia for *der heim,* for the past, for the little synagogue back in the shtetl, for the loved ones still languishing under the czarist yoke.

Of the nationalistic plays, the word *Jew* in the title had its vogue in such plays as *Dos Pintele Yid* or *The Jewish Heart.* Up to the eve of World War I, a plethora of plays about prostitution, fallen women, illegitimacy, and gangsterism flooded the Yiddish theatre with titles that all-too-obviously reveal their content: *White Slaves, The Sinner, Love for Sale, The Red Light,* and *The Devil's Power.* Isaac Zolotarefsky was the principal writer of these lurid plays. Michael Sharkanski wrote within the formula of the historical operettas, but with a difference that manifested itself in logical continuity and honest dialogue. Meanwhile better plays were being written and produced intermittently in the European Yiddish theatre, although Zalman Liben and Leon Kobrin were attempting to elevate the New York Yiddish theatre with meaningful plays about the Jews in the New World.

Back in Russia and Poland, inspired by the Moscow Art Theatre and encouraged by Jewish intellectuals led by the poet Bialik, Peretz Hirshbein toured (1908–1910) his Hirshbein Troupe with a repertoire of the best of Yiddish dramatic literature, which included not only his own poetic plays, but also the great plays of Sholem Asch and David Pinski. Apparently the Yiddish theatre audience was becoming more sophisticated and was developing better taste. Plays of high artistic merit became popular with all classes and types of audience. The symbolic and mystic folk plays of I. L. Peretz are monumental testaments to a folk literature that cries out for translation so that the world may share its treasures. Sholem Aleichem's stories and his *Tevye der Milchidicker* have enchanted readers and viewers in languages other than Yiddish. His other plays, both those he wrote and those adapted from his stories, make for an entirely delightful theatre by themselves.

His *200,000,* his *Stempenyu the Fiddler,* and his *Bewitched Tailor* were success-fully produced by the art theatre movement. Other important playwrights, all of whom deserve volumes of critical treatment and a place in the hall of fame of the world's great writers, are Ossip Dymov, H. Leivick, Harry Sackler, Jacob Preger, Alter Katzizne, Mark Arnstein, Aaron Zeitlin, Chone Gottesfeld, David Bergelson, and Peretz Markish. In a class all by himself is the creator of *Der Dybbuk,* Sholem Ansky. The challenging task of selecting from the riches of these and other play-wrights is one that I would like to share with the reader and, hopefully, the audi-ence that may see these plays in production.

Among the criteria for selection were considerations of historical importance, poetic content, honest evocation of and insight into the world of the people, the lyric drama of the language and situations, and the theatricality of the staging. This last is not based upon my own taste but upon the judgment of eminent critics who have been enthusiastic about the productions of these plays. The incidence of the selection of each of these plays, however, was accompanied by contributory, per-sonal experiences. Some of these considerations and experiences are as follows:

In Romania, non-Jewish professionals in the theatre remembered the power of Roman's play *Manasse,* about the intermarriage of a Jew and a Christian girl. Many claimed it to be the greatest play written in Romanian. This recalled to me the many times some of my weeping students would seek me out for advice about how to handle parental disapproval of their love for one outside their religion. The prevalence of this problem does not necessarily make its theatrical treatment stageworthy, but when I recently saw a revival of Leon Kobrin's *Yankel Boila* at the Educational Alliance in New York, I was overwhelmed by its valid shtetl types, its compelling drama, its portrayal of genuine folkways and tradition, as well as the ever-recurrent, eternal problem of intermarriage. Kobrin treated the situation with sensitivity and understanding, all expressed in an earthy and spirited language. His style and treatment of characters place him among the immortals of dramatic liter-ature.

Kobrin's individualization of his characters, lifting them thereby above the stereotype of stock characters, recalls the plays of humours in the Jacobean theatre. Just as Ben Jonson individualized his characters with idiosyncratic attributes, so Kobrin creates his—for example, Chatze, the religious fanatic, with his constant protest "I mean, really!" Chekhov used this device ideally in his *Cherry Orchard* when he had Gaev perpetually playing an imaginary billiard game as a key to the character of this frivolous-brained excrescence of a decadent aristocracy. The Yiddish playwrights used this device with sophisticated creativity. Axenfeld and Resnik provide Gavriel Shed in *Recruits* with the repeated phrase "crazy world" as a rubric to his character, a misfit in society. Hirshbein, in *Farvorfen Vinkel,* has old Todros constantly scrounging a pinch of snuff as an indication of a life of deprivation of material things. Thus, not only do these devices give individual di-mensions to the characters, but they also are part of the method by which the dramatists re-created a world. We meet people with their problems and we get to know them, their neighbors, their families, and the earth on which they walk. How poignantly the bedevilment of all mankind confounds the protagonists in these epic folk dramas of the Yiddish theatre! Axenfeld's *Recruits* was one of the earliest Yiddish plays to re-create the world of the shtetl, a world in which the human condition is honestly, compassionately, and dramatically presented. The characters, each with his special "hang-up," or humour, are unforgettable, and set a pattern for modern playwrights, actors, and directors. Each character has what present-day theatre people term "a handle," which sets him apart from all others. Above all, the play captures the drama of innocents caught between the cross fire of forces they cannot comprehend, cannot control, and cannot divert, and to which they must be sacrificed. Consider the little world of Nachman and Frume in *Recruits* to understand why I selected this play.

Long ago and far away, in that part of Russia known as the Pale, was a shtetl known as Nibivayla. Learned scholars tell us that a literal translation of Nibivayla means "never was"; but anyone who comes from this shtetl remembers it with an affection that unfailingly produces a tear, a wan smile, a quickening of the pulse, a reddening of the face, and a faraway look, which can only mean that for a transient moment the expatriot is transported back to *der heim*. For mere strangers, *heim* means home—where one goes to eat, to sleep, to spend time until the urgencies of the next day's business oblige one to leave until nightfall. *Der heim* for a Jew who has wandered from his birthplace means—ah, what does it not mean! Whatever else it may suggest, above all it means a way of life. The worker in the cities of the New World, he who lives in the tenements, or the millionaire who lives in splendor and security, will recall *der heim* with a nostalgia that dispels the urgencies of life in the New World, that overcomes the intense tempo of modern living, that transports him back to the changeless time by *unz in der heim* or in *unzer shtetl*.

The Jews survived there only by some illogical obstinacy, refusing to succumb either to the harassments of the unsympathetic natural elements or to the whimsical demands of a most Christian Czar. In their wisdom, the village elders had made peace with the elements, in a fatalistic deference to the greater wisdom of Him on high Who knew more about the vagaries of nature than is revealed in the Talmud. But, as for the unexpected and catastrophic demands of the more temporal force, even though the Czar was as unapproachable, as far away, as remote as the Almighty, he was a more immediate threat. Millennia of experience with proconsuls, Hamans, and Torquemadas had well prepared the little shtetl for any threat, for any calamity, even from so formidable an oppressor as the Czar, bless him.

As in most plays of the shtetl milieu, in *Recruits* the Jews had found a precarious haven along the western periphery of Russia from the depredations by marauding knights and their armies on their holy mission to secure the Christian Holy Land from the heathen. There, at least, they were not exposed to the auto-da-fé of the Inquisition, and marginal life under the protection of Holy Russia exposed them to only occasional pogroms and to but vague decrees from St. Petersburg. They eked out their existence comforted by their daily prayers in their pathetic little synagogues at the close of day, when they poured out their thanks to the Almighty that they had survived yet another day. The limitations upon a Jew's activities spared him from conscription into the Czar's army, where the period of service was 25 years, years of bondage and alienation from the holy Jewish way of life.

Life went on; generation succeeded generation; but when disaster is imminent, how filled with despair become a young maid and her lover! The Czar, in his bounty, had decreed that Jews might partake in some benefits of citizenship. True, they would still not be allowed to own land, nor travel, nor pursue careers in the professions, but they might serve in the army. This was the Czar's ukase of 1828 —a time when the two young lovers had plans, had hope, shared an idyllic love, had a joyful and innocent faith in their future happiness. Obstacles of the caste system, of religious fanaticism, of the disfavor of a rich father toward the suit of an impoverished tailor aroused fears, anguish, unbearable frustrations. I saw a memorable production of this drama by the renowned Artef Theatre Troupe. Tender love, robust youth, and the forces of evil were in dreadful confrontation. The Artef, acknowledged to have been one of the most important theatre groups in the history of the theatre, won universal critical acclaim with its production of *Recruits*.

Recruits appears to be both epic and folk in its classification as drama. Folk in its true recreation of a world of a people, and epic in its crystallization of the character of Nachman, in whom is embodied the aspirations of Jewish youth, *Recruits* faithfully portrays its world. So does Hirshbein's *Farvorfen Vinkel,* especially in revealing a way of life among the provincial Jews other than that of "handling," for *handling,* or petty trade, was the only source of livelihood for the Jews, who were denied other areas of activity and careers. Hirshbein's simple and lovable characters have a kinship with the uncomplicated people we have met in folk tales of all the world. The rustic lovers have an eternal appeal; the baffled women who cannot cope with the egos and economic drives of their husbands draw us into their dilemmas; the petty competition and conflicts of the men take on the proportions of the dramatic struggle of nations at each other's throats; and the wisdom of accommodation sought by the aged Todros is the lesson of history. Perceptive critics hailed the production of this play in 1918 and proclaimed its presentation as the start of the "second golden epoch" of the Yiddish theatre, and as the start of the art movement in the professional Yiddish theatre. In addition to these endorsements, I like the play. Hence its inclusion in this collection.

Omnipresent by implication in almost all Yiddish folk plays is the villainous power of the anti-Semitic authority of the host nation. It was taken for granted, like the inevitability of death or the changes of the seasons. Symbolically or actually, the dread presence did not make its appearance in the foregoing plays, even though too often it was the dramatic force that determined the course of action. In his *Hirsh Lekert,* the immortal poet H. Leivick has brought us face to face with the monstrous evil that hovered over and crushed the lives of innocent Jews. Although I was familiar with the true life story of the Jewish hero Hirsh Lekert, my interest in the dramatic story of like heroes as fit subject matter for the stage was first aroused at the memorial services for the legendary Mendel Elkin. Mendel had been of incalculable service to me in my research projects at Yivo in New York, where he was its head librarian. I recall that, a few months before his death at the age of 89, when I asked him about a book, he was about to send for it from the theatre collection a few flights above his office. Impatiently, he beckoned to me to follow him; I could barely keep pace with his youthful spring as he ran up the flights of stairs three steps at a time; he seemed as indestructible as the culture over which he stood guard. Thirty days after his death, Yivo, for which he had devised a library card system that in its simplicity rivals the Dewey and Library of Congress systems, held memorial services for him.

The most distinguished of the Jewish literary and theatrical world came to pay tribute to Mendel Elkin, who was, besides being one of the founders and directors of the Vilna Troupe, a dentist, a poet, and an editor. The evening's proceedings included the reading of two selections from Elkin's unpublished memoirs; Celia Adler and Sheftel Zack, two prominent Yiddish actors, presented the dramatic readings. The episode read by Zack concerned the arrest and condemnation to death of a group of militant Jewish workers who had defied the Russian governor of Vilna when they demonstrated against oppressive conditions. At the beginning of the excellent actor's presentation, I was much distracted by an elderly man who stood near the door, bobbing his head obtrusively. The fact that he stood while everyone else sat was odd in itself. But I was soon absorbed in the story Zack so brilliantly read: When the condemned Jewish workers were incarcerated in the fortress to await execution, members of the Jewish community resolved to save them. A secret committee approached the official doctor of the impregnable fortress with instructions that he was to visit the prisoners at once and declare they suffered from a virulent communicable disease and must be removed at once to the hospital. Lacking the numerous military guards and the massive thick walls of the fortress, the hospital was more accessible. When the doctor hesitated, he was informed that he had no choice: unless he cooperated, his family and himself would not witness another dawn. He saw the light and cooperated. The gambit worked and the condemned were soon in the hospital. The next step was to eliminate the two guards at the hospital. Drugged cigarettes were obtained, and a twelve-year-old boy offered them to the guards who, upon smoking them, quickly became unconscious. Zack read that twelve prisoners were rescued from the hospital. At that point, the bobbing old man at the door shouted, "No, it was thirteen, thirteen!" All of us in the auditorium turned upon him and hushed him. He stood his ground as he stubbornly muttered "thirteen." Zack continued his story of how all but two of the prisoners made good their escape.

As we were leaving at the end of the services, I ran into the old man who had interrupted the reading. He stood disgruntled and alone. I tried to befriend him by showing an interest in his assertion. After a brief exchange, I asked, "But how do you know there were thirteen men and not twelve?" He snapped back his response, "What do you mean, how do I know? I was the twelve-year-old boy who gave the *paparushen** to the two soldiers!" Later, the historian Zalmen Zylbercwaig confirmed his claim to have been that boy. I came away exalted, feeling I had rubbed elbows with history. Each of us may recall moments of heroism in the history of our nation or of our people. The recollection makes us proud. H. Leivick recollected the martyrdom of Hirsh Lekert as being the heroic but frightful end that he himself as a youth barely escaped. Leivick found in the robust vitality of the Yiddish theatre a manifold Jewish life in which his poetic expressions of man's everlasting search for the good life would find a place, as indeed they did. His masterpiece, *The Golem,* is a monumental tribute to Yiddish dramatic poetry. His dramatic poem, *Hirsh Lekert,* is his life's blood tribute to the undying heroism of the Jewish workers.

A collection of folk and epic plays, or both, of the Jewish people must include a *purim-shpil.* The *purim-shpil* was the earliest and, for centuries, the only folk theatre of the people. It is based on the epic tale, related in the Megillah, of Esther, bride of King Ahasueras, and her uncle, Mordecai, who saved the Jews from annihilation by the evil Haman. The religious holiday of Purim that celebrates this "historic" event has been accompanied by enactments of the legend by amateurs in almost all Jewish communities. Chaim Sloves, prominent French poet and dramatist, has written *Haman's Downfall,* which joyously reenacts the story that alone, of all the stories of Jewish travail through the millennia, has a happy ending. The story is epic, and its adoption by and popularity among the people have made it authentically folk. Understandably, the production of this play in Paris, when France was liberated from the scourge of German Nazis, became a symbol of the indomitable and eternal spirit of the Jewish people.

These plays do not depend upon gimmicks, fadism, or weird and imaginative concoctions by their authors. The authors seem to say, "Here are my people, for better or worse, truly mine own." The authors' affection for their people infects us: we laugh with them, we weep with them, their joys are ours, their woes make us suffer too. And after we have been exposed to one of these plays, we realize that we have walked with an eternal people, the knowing of whom has enriched our lives. Perhaps, soon, the great wealth of Yiddish dramatic literature will become part of the English-language repertoire as more and more of these wonderful plays are translated and made available to a much larger audience.

The apparent decline in the currency of the Yiddish language in the U.S.A. precludes the possibility of a reestablishment of a successful, continuing Yiddish theatre in the Yiddish language such as is maintained in Romania. In that country

---

*Cigarettes.

the government subsidizes the Teatrul Evreiesc de Stat. Although in recent years our own government and various foundations have done an exemplary job in supporting and encouraging theatre groups of various ethnic and racial origin, rarely if ever have subsidies gone to theatre troupes performing in foreign languages, with the exception of Spanish. In Romania, in addition to the Yiddish theatre, the government supports six Hungarian-language and two German-language troupes as well as numerous Romanian-language theatres. There, the government is dedicated to strengthening the various national and cultural groups that make up the nation, and the Yiddish theatre commands special attention because it was founded in Romania and demonstrably, through the Vilna Troupe, influenced the direction of Romanian theatre art. But, if the Yiddish-language theatre is doomed in the U.S.A. and elsewhere except Romania, the treasures of the Yiddish drama are available for translation to enrich, to elevate, to stimulate, and to fortify the world repertoire of great plays, especially in English. This collection is offered as one more step toward this desired objective.

Those readers who are conversant with Yiddish may think of happier colloquialisms than those I have used in the translations. Many Yiddish expressions have a wide range of interpretation; I trust that my interpretations have been substantially apt. Purists among readers may question inverted word order and a straining of the English for the effect of the periodic sentence. I have followed the original Yiddish in this respect in order to retain the distinctive cadence of spoken Yiddish that provides its life-echoing drama with its rich pungency and color.

EPIC AND FOLK PLAYS
OF THE YIDDISH THEATRE

FARVORFEN VINKEL*
by
Peretz Hirshbein
(1880-1948)

The day after the opening, November 16, 1918, of Peretz Hirshbein's play *Farvorfen Vinkel* at the Irving Place Theatre in New York, the prominent critic of the *Warheit*, Joel Entin, wrote:

> The literary Yiddish drama celebrates its greatest triumph. . . . *Farvorfen Vinkel* [is] a fortunate inspiration . . . the noblest for which the public and artists have aspired . . . the ultimate goal of dramatic art. The suspense, the deep joy in . . . scenes, moments, and characters . . . were proven by the enthusiastic ovations after the final curtain [of] . . . this good, worthy, and tasty drama. . . . *Farvorfen Vinkel* [has] freshness, vitality, and unity, with heartfelt creative joy, taste, and tact. . . . The theatregoer is filled with love and pride [in this] simple, natural, honest tale, . . . a fusion of milieu and people with subtle humor . . . [in] a complete identification.

On the opening night the audience included a group of influential intellectuals that called itself *The Schnorrers* (scroungers). The ovation was without parallel. The critic for *Der Tag*, J. Wortsman, wrote, "The Yiddish theatre was anaemic till last night." The production was hailed as the "foundation stone of the Yiddish art theatre in America." The editor of *Der Tag*, William Edlin, said it was "the sort of play that elevates the theatre to a dramatic art temple. . . . "

Prior to the historic opening night of *Farvorfen Vinkel*, the Yiddish theatre in New York had plodded its dreary route through the years since its first "golden epoch" of the Gordin era with each play selected on the basis of its suitability as a vehicle for the star of a theatre. Literary and other artistic criteria were ignored. Maurice Schwartz had gathered a troupe of excellent actors, at the Irving Place

---

* Like many other Yiddish idiomatic expressions that are difficult to translate into English, *Farvorfen Vinkel* presents a problem. Some possibilities are "Far-Away Corner," "Off the Beaten Track," "Forgotten Corner," "Forsaken Nook," "By Time Forgotten." I favor "Long Ago and Far Away."

Theatre, whose common bond was a desire for and a dedication to better theatre. Schwartz had promised them that he would present a repertoire of plays of literary and artistic worth. When he opened the theatre with new plays that were built on the same weary formulas that his group of dedicated actors had deplored, young Jacob Ben Ami, former actor in Hirshbein's memorable art troupe, prevailed on Schwartz to offer Hirshbein's *Farvorfen Vinkel.* Only after Ben Ami threatened to resign unless the play was done and offered to subsidize the production out of his salary did the new impresario, Schwartz, consent to the production. After the great success of the play, Schwartz claimed credit for bringing this play to New York's Yiddish stage and for launching, thereby, the Yiddish art-theatre movement. However, Yiddish theatre historians suggest that the art movement in the Yiddish theatre started before Schwartz's venture: Director Fishman claimed to have started it earlier that same year when he directed the Folksbuehne production of Hirshbein's bucolic idyll, *Green Fields.* Most authorities suggest that art in the Yiddish theatre started with the Hirshbein Troupe, 1908–1910, in Russia. Thus, P. Hirshbein's name is identified by all with the Yiddish art-theatre movement.

Born near Kletschel, Grodno, White Russia, in 1880, Peretz Hirshbein was raised in the countryside, where his parents owned a mill. After studying at the local religious school, he was sent for further study to the Yeshivas of Brest-Litovsk and Vilna. This gentle poet had an extraordinary vitality that caused him to be interested in and responsive to every facet of life. As a naturalist, he traveled all over the world. But in his writings, he always returned to the soil that nurtured him. He rejected a rabbinical career and turned to writing, in Hebrew. But he soon joined the movement of writers who sought to reach the masses in the Yiddish language. In his early writing he was concerned with style, particularly that of the French imagists and the school of naturalism. He translated his early Hebrew play, *The Other Side of the River*, into Russian, in which language it was produced in the Russian State Theatre in Odessa. One of his memories of that production was a boorish and outrageous anti-Semitic slur by Ivan Bunin. Later, after he bemoaned to the poet Bialik the absence of a Yiddish theatre in Odessa, he resolved to do something about it. Hence, in 1908, he organized a truly Yiddish art-theatre group that traveled through the Russian Pale as the Hirshbein Troupe until it reached Warsaw in 1910, where adversity obliged it to fold.

The year after the demise of his troupe, the poet came to America, where he continued his writing. Hirshbein did not exploit his own theatre troupe and oblige it to be a showcase for his own writings, for he offered plays by Asch, Peretz, and Gordin and most diffidently allowed his own symbolic plays to be included in the repertoire. Similarly, he demurred against producing his own plays at *Unzer Teater* in New York's East Bronx (1924–1925), of which he was one of the directors with Leivick and Pinski, on these grounds: "How would it look if we open a theatre with ourselves as directors and to have our own plays done? It's not ethical. We must produce plays written by other, new writers."

The Hirshbein Troupe left a legacy of high artistic standards for Yiddish drama and for individuals who enriched the world theatre complex by being among the founders of the famous Vilna Troupe and being among those who brought European art-theatre concepts to America by means of the Yiddish theatre. The Hirshbein Troupe brought more literary awareness to the Yiddish theatre of Russia and Poland so that intellectuals found a new affinity with it. It stimulated interest in theatre art, so that young people sought training in schools and studios for careers in theatre. The troupe set standards for ensemble acting, and for the purity of the Yiddish language; it also roused concern for the literary content and style of a play, and encouraged deemphasis of the star system. As writer and managing director, Hirshbein contributed enormously to the improvement of the Yiddish stage which had too long been in bondage to such *shund* writer-managers as Hurwitz and Lateiner, who pandered to the primitive tastes of the uncultured immigrants.

As an author, Hirshbein preferred that the production of his pastoral plays be in the hands of the noncommercial clubs in New York, such as the Progressive Dramatic Club, which presented his *Der Puste Kretchme* (*The Idle Inn*) in 1913 (Arthur Hopkins brought an English translation of this play to Broadway in 1922). Another of his folk plays, *Green Fields,* has been made into a rolicking Yiddish-language film and is available in Joseph C. Landis's superb English-language translation in a collection of other Yiddish plays.* When he died, Hirshbein left many volumes of poetry, children's stories, travel notes on Japan, Palestine, India, South America, and Canada, as well as his many plays. Alas, too few of the works of this talented genius are available in English.

In his folk plays, Hirshbein returns to the idyllic, bucolic, simple life of unpretentious Jewish village folk who lived close to the soil. The plays have the charm of warm humor and reveal the author's unabashed love for his people. In contrast to earlier dramas that featured sinful, illicit love, his plays took innocent, pure love as a motif. After the hiatus of twenty years to 1904, when the Yiddish theatres were again allowed to open in Russia, the style and content of Yiddish drama had undergone a change. The concocted Biblical and shabby operettas and melodramas gave way to the social and realistic dramas of Gordin, Libin, Asch, and Kobrin, and folk dramas such as those by I. L. Peretz, as well as to translations from the world classics and popular successes. Although Hirshbein reveled in humor and pathos, he did not sacrifice his penetrating probing of the depths of his characters, and brought them forth with complete psychological *gestalt* as individuals and not contrived, manipulated, stock puppets. Each character has a life of his own, his personal identity, while being at the same time symbolically representative of his folk, his milieu, and his type. Within a wholesome, earthy, village setting, with the use of a simple and robust folk tongue, a philosophy of human relationships is explored with a lambent, poetic pen. This is the essence of *Farvorfen Vinkel,* a delightful folk drama with universal implications, with a plot of a perennial family feud, and with traditions in conflict with the aspirations of youth, all of which are not exclusive to the Jewish community but are intensely a part of Jewish life.

Isaac Goldberg, in his brilliant *Drama of Transition* said, "The best of Hirshbein's longer plays . . . establishes a restorative contact with the earth that his early years have known, with the simple folk among whom he was reared, with the bumpkins and hoydens of peasant life as he saw it and felt it." *Farvorfen Vinkel* is the story of a Romeo and Juliet in a shtetl setting, but with a triumphant and joyful ending rather than a tragic one, with ebullient youth surmounting the prejudices and obstinacy of middle age. Hirshbein endeared the simple country Jew, the natural man of the soil, to theatre audiences. Thus, Hirshbein's greatness grew out of his love for his people, as shown in his affectionate treatment of his characters, as well as in his dedication to the art of the theatre. He loathed having his beloved characters debased by crude, stock interpretations of commercial troupes; he much preferred production of his plays by perceptive and artistic groups who provided warm understanding and kinship for the ideas and roles.

Like Sean O'Casey, Hirshbein in his plays "presented the language, the customs, the attitudes, and the problems of a particular locale and its people," according to Carl Van Vechten, who ranked the Jewish playwright with Synge and Lady Gregory. Ludwig Lewisohn ranked him with J. M. Barrie. His works, aside from plots and climaxes that grow out of the soil and out of his characters, have a refresh-

---

* Joseph C. Landis, *The Dybbuk and Other Great Yiddish Plays.* New York: Bantam Books, 1966.

ingly natural joy, delightfully robust characterizations, a human point of view, charming episodes, poetic enchantment, and snatches of folk and religious song. Writing of the Jewish peasants in the little Russian villages that huddle close to the soil, Hirshbein showed them living under the sky, far from the ghetto that everlastingly reminded them of their sorrows and released them from their past, making a pagan, joyous gesture. As the Hellenist of Jewish literature, he celebrated the joy, the hope, the unquenchably romantic Jewish spirit that resolutely lives against enormous odds. The prominent Yiddish actress Celia Adler said that no other playwright understood the Jewish girl in love—her flirtations, her impishness, her maturing bloom—as did Hirshbein, who presented her with ineffable charm.

When the curtain rose for *Farvorfen Vinkel* on that memorable 1918 fall evening, the audience found itself once again back in *der heim* among the folk who spoke the *momme loschen* of their unforgettable past. The scene is a forsaken corner in a far away shtetl, a part of the cemetery, the house of the gravedigger who lives there with his wife, his father, his nubile daughter, and his goat. The frost-hardened Lithuanian field provides little sustenance for the goat from the sparse grass growing among the graves. Close by are the mill and the household of the miller, his wife, and his son. The miller's son and the gravedigger's daughter woo each other without the knowledge of their parents—but the girl's grandfather happily knows. The young man teasingly warns the girl that the spirit of a ghost will possess her because she drinks the milk of the goat that grazes on the graves. The girl's father, the gravedigger, aspires to leave his meagre, miserable calling to open a mill, with the aid of a rich suitor for his daughter's hand. This intensifies the feud between the gravedigger and the miller, whose livelihood is thus threatened. The womenfolk remain friendly and comfort each other in the face of their feuding men, whose bitter struggle is accompanied by blows and stone throwing. The theme indicates how the escape of one from his bitter livelihood undermines the existence of the other. The crazed, bereaved mother of five dead children, Dobe, appears throughout the play. In her phantasy world, her children still live in the cemetery where she comes to comfort and care for them. She is a symbol to remind the quarreling parents to count their blessings—their living children. Blindly clinging to their hatreds the embattled parents almost crush the young people's love. Reluctant reconciliation shows life's joyful possibilities.

The presentation of Hirshbein's *Farvorfen Vinkel* opened one of the finest chapters in the history of the Yiddish theatre, for it offered a literature of a folk's life, a folk's philosophy, a folk's morals—a folk's theatre of the highest artistic calibre.

FARVORFEN VINKEL

by

Peretz Hirshbein

A Play in Four Acts

Translated from the Yiddish by David S. Lifson

CHARACTERS

NOTE,* a Gravedigger
KREINE, his wife
TZIRL, his daughter
TODROS, his father
HAIM HERSH, owner of a neighboring flour mill
KREISEL, his wife
HAYEH, his daughter
NOAH, his son
HATZKEL, a wealthy manipulator, Tzirl's suitor
DOBE, a woman who has lost her five children

Act I takes place in a corner of a cemetery near Note's house; a wooden fence
  circles the area that has no graves, although graves appear in the background.
  It is dawn of an early spring day.
Act II takes place in the home of the miller, Haim Hersh; later that morning.
Act III takes place in the home of the gravedigger, Note, on a summer evening.
Act IV takes place in the home of the miller, Haim Hersh, on an autumn night.

---

* Esther Shumiatcher Hirshbein, distinguished poet and widow of Peretz Hirshbein, has
  challenged my spelling of certain names and a few idiomatic expressions. She suggests
  that Note should be spelled Nohte (I might offer Noteh or Nutteh); for *Der Tag* she
  suggests *Der Tog* (different pronunciations are found in various European areas: *Der
  Tugg, Der Tohg,* and *Der Toog*). Dobe is pronounced Dobeh. Ed.

29

ACT I

A cemetery corner. Apparently this spot is close to the home of the poor gravedigger, Note, for his wooden house projects from the upper right. Off in the distance is seen the melancholy vista of graves that illogically brighten in the sunlight. A section of a wooden fence that circles the cemetery does not succeed in holding out an early spring dawn with its bright sunlight. The earth itself refuses to mourn for its guests and proudly shows its happy green grass.

No sooner does the curtain rise than the gentle old Todros enters. We first see the stooped back of this rather tall ancient when he appears; he is talking to an unseen person.

TODROS. Nah, nah. You mustn't during the daytime. What will people say if they see you among the graves! At night . . . then it is all right, but in the daytime, no. (*Noah, a handsome young man, in work clothes that are heavily dusted with white flour, comes up to the fence and hails the old man.*)

NOAH. Good morning, Reb Todros.

TODROS. Who . . . what . . . ah, is that you, Noah? What are you doing, standing over there like a stranger? Come, come over already.

NOAH. I look like a ghost with all this flour all over me. I might frighten the dead.

TODROS. (*Laughs.*) Nothing disturbs the dead. But I don't know about the goat. The goat you can really scare.

NOAH. You've taken on quite a job, dragging that goat around.

TODROS. Don't you say anything against the goat. This goat is really smart, has the brains of a man. Just look, that goat knows where to feed; around the graves the grass is more delicious. So, why are you standing there? Come on over already. You have enough time. Jump over. (*As Noah jumps over the fence.*) Aha, that's it. Who needs a door or a gate when you're young! Ho ho, you really are covered with flour.

NOAH. What a night! I didn't close my eyes for a minute.

TODROS. You're telling me! What a wind! It howled around without any letup. It roared from the north to the east. I heard the sails from the mill whirling all night.

NOAH. It really was a strong wind. Not even a wink of sleep. I'm telling you, when that wind blows from the northwest, spirits jump and frolic. Up with the stone, down with the stone. It's like hurling a dog to the devil.

TODROS. Who's tending the mill now?

NOAH. Papa is up.

TODROS. I've been thinking of going over to the mill.

NOAH. Why? Something you need there?

TODROS. I've been thinking . . . there's something I ought to talk over with your father.

NOAH. Say, did you hear the women wailing in the cemetery yesterday? They were going at it strong. We heard them all the way over at the mill.

TODROS. Ah, the women, may God bless them. They've got nothing else to do, so they weep and wail. At least, if it were their own flesh and blood! Strangers . . . they come, the tears flow . . .

NOAH. How many funerals were there yesterday?

TODROS. Two. The widows have cried their eyes out at home, so when they come here they're quiet. Then, when the first clods of earth echo on the boards of the coffin, their wounds are cut open as if with a sharp knife. They see the others crying, and that starts them off crying again. (*The old Todros has seated himself on a bench near the fence. Noah joins him and sits.*)

NOAH. How many years have you lived here?

TODROS. How many years? Who can remember so far back? I came here before my son, Note, was born. Why, your mill wasn't even standing yet.

NOAH. It's an old mill. We should have

torn it down years ago and built a new one. When a wind like last night's comes along, I'm afraid to let the the the sails go at full swing.

TODROS. She groans, croaks, and protests, hah?

NOAH. Ho ho, does she groan! You'd think the old mill was a living thing.

TODROS. Once upon a time, windmills were surrounded by magic.

NOAH. Papa claims that the millstones in his grandfather's mill were surely stolen away by magic.

TODROS. An old story! Let me tell you what I saw with my own eyes. A mill turned over, and then, what do you think happened? The millstones rolled by themselves, side by side, as far as the eye could see, and then disappeared on the other side of the mountain.

NOAH. Honestly? Tsk, tsk. Were they big, heavy millstones?

TODROS. Big? Heavy? Let me tell you something. I took four pair of oxen to haul back each stone, one at a time.

NOAH. Side by side, all the way?

TODROS. Both of them, by themselves, rolled straight out of the mill.

NOAH. Was it really done by magic?

TODROS. What a question, was it done by magic? Of course it was—how else? And you know something, it was a German trick. There was a German laborer wandering around the vicinity. He had an axe and a saw strapped on his back and he was looking for work. We know that kind, they're thieves, so we didn't take him in. That's why he played this trick on us.

NOAH. And you didn't break his head?

TODROS. Who wanted to start up with him?

NOAH. (*Stretching and yawning.*) Oh ho, if it happened to me, I'd fix him, that German!
(*Yawns again.*)
Gosh, I'm sleepy!

TODROS. Have you said your morning prayers?

NOAH. Not yet. I've just come from the mill.

TODROS. You'll say your prayers, then eat something, and go to bed. It's a good thing to be a help to your father when you grow up. You're a fine young scamp. (*He nudges Noah.*) Ho ho! If Tzirl only knew you were here!

NOAH. (*With clumsy bravado that does not fool anyone.*) What if she knows?

TODROS. Just look at him! We know a thing or two . . . we know where the dog is buried . . . we know that a calf loses its milk teeth!

NOAH. (*With pretended casualness.*) Is she still sleeping?

TODROS. (*Mimicking Noah's transparent indifference.*) Is she still sleeping? Just like that he asks! She's asleep.

NOAH. I wonder how long this wind will keep up.

TODROS. Maybe till nighttime, but it'll get warmer.

NOAH. It was cold enough last night, good and cold.

TODROS. Have you got a sheepskin pelt?

NOAH. Of course. But last night I kept warm without it. Work . . . why, I didn't get a single minute's rest.

TODROS. That's good. (*A woman's voice is heard singing a sad, melancholy air in the cemetery.*)

NOAH. Who's that? Who's singing?

TODROS. Probably Dobe. She must have spent the night here again. She hid from me.

NOAH. You mean she spent the whole night here, in the cemetery?

TODROS. She's made herself at home among the children's graves. She even made a place for herself to sleep there. She's pretty lucky that my son, Note, isn't here. He'd . . .

NOAH. What's it to him if she sleeps there?

TODROS. We have our hands full putting up with the dead; do we have to put up with the living, too?

NOAH. (*Sighing.*) Every one of her five children is buried here.

TODROS. She simply went out of her mind when her last child died. She won't stay away; she says this is her home now, with her children. (*Dobe enters. She is middle-aged. She stares off into the distance with a look of frozen ecstasy. Todros speaks to her with feigned anger.*) You were told not to come here. Don't you know you're not to come here? It's a good thing my son, Note, isn't here to catch you.

DOBE. If I don't come here, who will watch over my children?

TODROS. So-o-o-o, did you talk with them?

DOBE. Yes, I talked with them.

NOAH. Come, Dobe, come over to our house by the mill. Mamma will give you something to eat.

DOBE. Haven't I got my own home?

TODROS. So why don't you go there, to your own home?

DOBE. This place, here, is my home. You know, soon, when it's warmer, I'll uncover my children and we'll all go for a walk together.

TODROS. (*To Noah.*) When she says it, you can believe her! If we don't watch out, one of these nights she'll actually dig up the graves. (*He turns to Dobe.*) Now listen to me. Don't get any ideas of doing any digging around here! You'll get yourself a good beating. What has been given to the earth we cannot take back from the earth. (*Dobe stands silently, with tears streaming from her eyes.*)

NOAH. Look, just look how she's crying.

TODROS. (*With compassion, to Dobe.*) Why don't you take hold of yourself and be sensible? You'll get well and God will be merciful; you'll see, you'll have more children. (*Still silent, Dobe turns and leaves in the direction from which she entered. Todros calls after her.*) If you don't want trouble, watch out. When Note wakes up soon, he'll show you where the gate is! (*Note, the grave-digger, enters from the direction of the house. He carries a pick and shovel.*)

NOTE. Good morning. Is that Dobe you're yelling at?

NOAH. She was just here.

NOTE. I don't know what can be done with her. We can't keep her away. Ah, it's going to be a warm day, no?

NOAH. See how green the grass is growing already. I think we can let the horses out to graze now.

NOTE. But the earth is still frozen pretty deep. If I didn't have this pick I couldn't turn over a shovelful.

NOAH. Do you still have to lay a fire on the ground to soften the earth?

NOTE. The frost goes down around three fingers deep yet. It's nothing to worry us anymore. But I haven't got anyone to help me . . . I can't catch up no matter how much I tear my guts out. Yesterday I dug two graves, and already today I have to dig two more and maybe another one. Where's your father? What's he doing?

NOAH. I left him at the mill.

NOTE. You can tell him for me—he's no damn good . . .

NOAH. Why . . . ?

NOTE. He knows why all right . . .

TODROS. That's enough. Just keep quiet and don't say another word . . .

NOTE. Just don't butt in, papa. If he won't agree in a peaceful way to what I say, we'll fix him. We'll put a fire under him—he'll burn like a candle.

NOAH. If he hasn't been set on fire by now . . .

NOTE. It's never too late . . . he'll burn plenty yet.

NOAH. I suppose you'll do it all by yourself, huh?

NOTE. Don't you worry who's going to do it. If I'd felt like it, your father's old mill would have nothing left but burnt-out ashes long ago. You can tell him from me!

NOAH. Me tell him? I'm not mixing in.

NOTE. Come now, papa. You'll help me roll away a stone. Just where there's a pile of stones, there only, it came into Reb Yona's head that he must have his father buried. What does he care if I tear out my guts, the devil take it. Come, papa.

(*Note walks off toward the graves.*)

TODROS. (*To Noah*) Don't worry. He's not setting fire to anything. Just a lot of talk. But your father shouldn't be such a fool.

NOAH. He simply doesn't want to see another mill around here. You can't blame him for that, can you?

TODROS. He has me to thank that he has a mill at all—even after he got married. He couldn't afford a mill.

NOAH. Papa intends to build a new mill soon.

TODROS. That's up to him; it's his own business.

NOTE. (*Offstage.*) Papa! Papa!

TODROS. All right, already, all right . . . I'm coming already! (*Tzirl enters. She's a pretty girl, slightly younger than Noah. Todros cautions Noah.*) Here's Tzirl. Don't say anything to her.

TZIRL. (*Overhears.*) What shouldn't he tell me?

TODROS. (*As he leaves.*) The less you know, the better.

TZIRL. Tell me, Noah. What is he talking about?

NOAH. You really got up early today!

TZIRL. Don't change the subject. What were you two talking about?

NOAH. (*Attempting to embrace her.*) Come here, I'll cover you with flour!

TZIRL. (*Slipping from him.*) First tell me what you and my grandfather were talking about . . . then maybe I'll let you.

NOAH. Honest?

TZIRL. You think I don't know what it's about?

NOAH. Your father threatens to set our mill on fire.

TZIRL. Ridiculous. I don't believe it.

NOAH. Ask him yourself. He really said it.

TZIRL. When did he say it?

NOAH. I heard him . . . with my own ears. He sounded like he meant it. He even told me to tell my father.

TZIRL. You're making it up. It's a lie.

NOAH. So it's a lie if you say so . . . it's a lie!

TZIRL. My father is fed up with being a gravedigger. He's had enough. He just wants to get away from this . . . this . . . and I'm fed up with living in a cemetery too.

NOAH. Oh yes. I know what's on your mind. You think if you get away from the cemetery you'll be a fancy lady. Why? I know all right. Then you think Hatzkel will want to marry you!

TZIRL. Really! If you came here at the crack of dawn to taunt me, you might just as well not have come and stayed home in your old mill.

NOAH. Who said I came to see you. It's a beautiful morning, so I decided to go for a stroll.

TZIRL. (*After a pause.*) You don't sleep at night and you look pale as a ghost.

NOAH. You might try visiting me at the mill at night . . . it wouldn't hurt you to try . . .

TZIRL. I did. And what did I find? There you were, sound asleep on a sack of flour!

NOAH. That's not so. I . . .

TZIRL. Oh yes I did. I came up to the steps and peeked in.

NOAH. Oh yes, I can believe it. You . . . You're afraid of your shadow to come alone at night.

TZIRL. I am not afraid! I saw you, sprawled over a sack.

NOAH. What was I wearing? Did I have my sheepskin on?

TZIRL. I . . . I don't remember. But you were asleep all right.

NOAH. Well . . . so you were there, that's that.

TZIRL. I was going to scare you, but they stopped me.

NOAH. Who stopped you?

TZIRL. Whoever was with me.

NOAH. Aha—Hatzkel?

TZIRL. I . . . I don't remember who.

NOAH. Oho, so you don't remember, eh? I think you're a liar.

TZIRL. You're a liar yourself! Just who do you think you are? That's what I think of you! (*She snaps her finger at him, then stamps her foot.*) I hate you . . . and I hate your father, too!

NOAH. And all I wanted was a peaceful stroll to greet the morning. Don't flatter yourself that I came running at daybreak just to see you.

TZIRL. What does it matter to me if you did or didn't. It's no concern of mine. Maybe you came to see my grandfather? Oh yes, I know. You came to play with our goat! (*She mimics him.*) Good morning, goat.

NOAH. If you must know, I came to see your grandfather. I happened to see him from the mill while he was walking in the cemetery.

TZIRL. It's no concern of mine.

NOAH. (*Angry.*) I don't know why I'm wasting my time. I might as well go home to bed.

TZIRL. So go, then! And you might as well know, I despise your father. I love your mother, but I hate your father!

NOAH. And I hate your father! And that's that. (*Noah turns to go.*)

TZIRL. Just look at him! Rrr! Trembling with anger. And that wants to marry me yet! (*Noah stands undecided, with his face turned from her.*) So why don't you go? I thought you said you were going to bed.

NOAH. If I ever hear your father shoot his mouth off that he's going to burn down our mill, I'll take a stone and split his head open. Just once more!

TZIRL. Go get me a pitcher. I have to milk the goat.

NOAH. What? Go into your house? Never! And you tell that Hatzkel that if he ever comes to our mill again, I'll throw him down the stairs.

TZIRL. You think you're so strong, eh? Hatzkel is stronger than two of you.

NOAH. You're dreaming. He isn't half as strong as . . .

TZIRL. He told me how a big wagonload of lumber fell over in the woods, and he lifted it right back again all by himself.

NOAH. Ha! That's his story. He's always bragging.

TZIRL. And come to think of it, he's much better looking than you.

NOAH. Now I've heard everything. Better looking! With that button of a pug nose, and . . .

TZIRL. Anyway, I like him better than you.

NOAH. So why don't you marry him then!

TZIRL. I thought you were going to get me a pitcher.

NOAH. Suppose you get Hatzkel to fetch it for you. Catch me running errands for you. Get Hatzkel, that . . . that . . .

TZIRL. When your father builds a mill for you to have for your own, then maybe I'll marry you.

NOAH. What happened suddenly to the great Hatzkel? What's so great about him?

TZIRL. You just have to look at him, and then look at you. There's no comparison.

NOAH. He's nothing but a big-mouthed braggart. I don't know why I came here. It wasn't to see you. I don't know where you got the idea I ever loved you. You're always prowling around here in the cemetery. Your goat grazes on the grass that grows on the graves, then you drink her milk. You better watch out or an evil spirit will get into you with the milk. Do you think when you put on airs and pretend you're good it impresses me? Not a bit of it. Then when you start playing your cute little tricks, I can't stand you!

TZIRL. What do you mean about the goat and evil spirits?

NOAH. Just what I said. This morning your grandfather put the goat out to graze among the graves. I saw it. When an evil spirit enters into you, people will be afraid of you, they'll run away from you. Then, do you know what they'll have to do to you? They'll grab you and put you in a barrel that they'll nail down tight and roll it down a big hill. It'll bounce and then crash open. Then you'll fall out and the evil spirit will fly away. (*He laughs.*)

TZIRL. Stop! Keep quiet or I'll pour a pail of water over you! I know, you're just trying to scare me. If you don't like our living in a cemetery, then your father ought to see that we could buy a place and put up our own mill.

NOAH. So-o-o, papa should help your father open a mill so we should lose our bread and butter. Brilliant!

TZIRL. You and your father! You're both alike!

NOAH. And you're the same as your father!

TZIRL. I wish you'd go away, just leave, and don't ever come back!

NOAH. Whoever said I came to see you!

TZIRL. Oh . . . go away! (*Noah is torn. He reluctantly turns to go.*) (*Tzirl speaks tenderly.*) Noah, come here.

NOAH. What now? What do you want?

TZIRL. Come here, a little closer to me. Someone would think you're afraid of me.

NOAH. Let them think what they like. Maybe I am and maybe I'm not.

TZIRL. Come closer. I'm really glad you came. (*Pause.*) Tell me it's a lie.

NOAH. What's a lie?

TZIRL. What you said about the evil spirit, that it will enter into me just because I live in the cemetery, and the goat . . .

NOAH. (*Interrupting.*) Who knows, who can tell . . .

TZIRL. If I told you I hate Hatzkel, would that make you happy?

NOAH. Love him or don't. It doesn't mean a thing to me. You're always teasing me, playing a game of cat and mouse. I don't like to be teased.

TZIRL. (*Angry.*) Only you are allowed to play games. You were lying to me about the evil spirit. Go away! And you needn't ever come back again. Some way to love me by frightening me out of my wits! (*She picks up a stick and chases the goat away.*)

NOAH. What have you got against the goat? What did the goat do?

TZIRL. I don't care to listen to you anymore. Why do you stand there? Just leave me alone; go home.

NOAH. You can't chase me like the goat. I'm not going.

TZIRL. (*Exploding.*) I hate you! (*She covers her face with her hands and runs into the house. Noah stands irresolute, looks after her, then jumps over the fence and leaves. Tzirl comes out of the house as though indifferent toward Noah. Becoming aware that he is no longer there, she anxiously rushes to the fence and calls after him.*)

Noah! Noah! (*Receiving no response, she becomes tearful.*)

(*Dobe enters, sees Tzirl and approaches her.*)

DOBE. My Yentele is almost as tall as you.

TZIRL. (*Angry.*) Your Yentele . . . your Yentele is dead.

DOBE. (*Dazed.*) Dead?

TZIRL. Yes, dead. My father buried her with his own hands.

DOBE. Buried?

TZIRL. So she'll never grow up to be as big as me.

DOBE. Never?

TZIRL. Look. What's that over there?

DOBE. My child.

TZIRL. No. It's our goat. And your children are over there, too, among those graves.

DOBE. There? My children are there?

TZIRL. That's right. Now you go there. Your children are waiting there.

DOBE. All of them? Ah yes, my children. (*She goes off.*)

TZIRL. (*Distraught. Calls toward the house.*) Mama! Mama!

KREINE. (*Coming out of the house.*) What is it? What do you want?

TZIRL. When are we going to move away from this . . . from the cemetery?

KREINE. What a question! What's gotten into you?

TZIRL. Tell me . . . I want to know.

KREINE. Better keep your mind on what you have to do. Have you milked the goat yet?

TZIRL. No, and I won't milk her any more.

KREINE. What happened all of a sudden? What's got into you? (*Kreine collects some logs from a stack near the fence.*)

TZIRL. Why does papa say he's going to set fire to Haim Hersh's mill?

KREINE. What are you talking about? Don't you dare say such a thing!

TZIRL. That's what papa said.

KREINE. It's that Noah. Just let me lay my hands on him. He'll never dare show his face around here.

TZIRL. (*Starting to weep.*) Don't worry. He'll never come here again.

KREINE. And I thought it was going to be a beautiful morning. Bah! Go bring me the pitcher. (*Tzirl exits into the house. Kreine is puzzled and stands in a quandary. She throws down the logs.*) Tzirl! Come here, I want to talk to you. Come here!

TZIRL. (*Returns from the house.*) What do you want now?

KREINE. What's going on? Did anything happen today? (*Tzirl remains silent. Kreine feels her forehead.*) What's wrong with you? Don't you feel well, God forbid?

TZIRL. I don't know.

KREINE. (*Puffs at Tzirl three times and then spits—a custom to exorcise the evil eye.*) No harm come to you, please God. I think you have a little fever. Let's go into the house. We'll say a prayer to chase off the evil one. (*Kreine leads Tzirl into the house. From the distance is heard Dobe's song.*)

CURTAIN

ACT II

Later that morning. The interior of Haim Hersh's house. The room is a kitchen and living room all-in-one, dominated by a large, typical stove. Through a small window can be seen a rolling meadow. The rhythmic clang of the adjacent mill is heard intermittently. Haim Hersh's wife, Kreisel, is busily tidying the house. The outside door is pushed open by their twelve-year-old daughter, Hayeh, who is followed by Haim Hersh; he is carrying a pail of water.

HAYEH. Here, let me take it, papa. I can carry it.

HAIM HERSH. Let go of it. Before you know it, you'll hurt yourself.

HAYEH. It's not heavy. I can lift it.

HAIM HERSH. Let go of it, I say. (*He turns to Kreisel.*) You have no better idea than to send her to the well all by herself! That's all we need, that she should fall into the well!

KREISEL. Who sent her? I just told her to bring you the pail so you should draw the water. (*Kreisel scolds Hayeh.*) You'll get it from me if I ever catch you crawling near the well all by yourself!

HAIM HERSH. I came just in time. If you saw her, you'd faint from fright. There she was, her whole body hanging over the edge of the well.

HAYEH. What's all the fuss about. It's not the first time I've gone to the well.

KREISEL. Nobody asked you to go. Don't be so smart! Do you know how deep the well is? I get dizzy when I look down into it.

HAYEH. I don't get dizzy. I look down into it and I see my face like in a mirror. I throw down a pebble, then my face ripples away in the waves, it disappears; then, gradually the water is still again and there is my face whole again.

HAIM HERSH. Just listen to your daughter! What a way to talk. I can just picture what happiness she'll bring to you!

KREISEL. What do you want from her? She's only a child . . .

HAYEH. I'm not a child. Twelve years old is not a child. You think because I'm only a girl I'll break like a glass. All the other kids are already going around barefoot. But me? Oh no, I'm some sort of precious infant; I have to drag around in shoes. I won't wear them. It's too hot already. (*Hayeh sits on the floor and starts pulling off her shoes.*)

KREISEL. What do you think you're doing?

HAIM HERSH. Some bliss we can expect from your daughter, bah!

KREISEL. The way you talk, someone would think I'm the one who spoils her! (*The clanging of the mill becomes louder.*)

HAIM HERSH. From all sides I get it. The mill . . . I can't leave it for a minute! (*He hurries out.*)

KREISEL. (*Turning to Hayeh.*) Just you wait! Don't you let me catch you going alone again to the well! It's lucky for you I didn't say any more about it in front of your father. He'd tear you to pieces if he knew.

HAYEH. I don't care. I'm not a fraidy-cat. I'm twelve years old.

KREISEL. I'm warning you. "Fraidy-cat" indeed! If anything happens to you,

I'll get the blame. That's all I need!

HAYEH. Don't worry. Nothing will happen to me.

KREISEL. Don't be so smart! You think I haven't seen you crawling under the sails at the mill while they turn? You could make one little wrong move and phfft—I'm afraid to say it—and one poof of the sail, and it's all over with you!

HAYEH. When did I go near the sails? I'm not that stupid.

KREISEL. What is it your business to go to the well by yourself?

HAYEH. (*Derisively.*) Who's going to snatch me?

KREISEL. What wicked whim draws you to the cemetery? A cemetery, no less, God forbid . . .

HAYEH. I'm not scared.

KREISEL. But the dead people there . . .

HAYEH. Note lives there, doesn't he?

KREISEL. Of course he does. Note has to live there.

HAYEH. And what about Tzirl?

KREISEL. She too. She's his daughter, so it's her home.

HAYEH. So why isn't she afraid?

KREISEL. Come here, let me braid your hair. The way you run around, people will think you're a little witch. (*They sit. Kreisel combs Hayeh's hair.*)

HAYEH. What's a witch, mama?.

KREISEL. A witch? I mustn't say it, God forgive me.

HAYEH. But why do they live there? Aren't they afraid?

KREISEL. It has to be that way. Dead people have to be buried.

HAYEH. Do they ever come up again?

KREISEL. No, never.

HAYEH. So what's there to be afraid of? Why should I be afraid if they never . . .

KREISEL. Such questions! Enough already!

HAYEH. How about Note? Isn't he afraid they'll do him some mischief?

KREISEL. I said that's enough! Now keep quiet! (*Silence for a moment while Kreisel combs.*)

HAYEH. It's funny. There's Tzirl living all the time in the cemetery . . . and nothing ever happened to her.

KREISEL. How many times must I tell you? Tzirl is Note's daughter. She's Note's daughter and it's all right for her to live there.

HAYEH. How about Noah? Why is he always going over there?

KREISEL. Oh, Noah, may God bless him! What about him? What has he got to do with all your fancies?

HAYEH. I saw him. He was going to the cemetery.

KREISEL. Really? Now, that's all we need!

HAYEH. It's to see Tzirl.

KREISEL. Hold your tongue, you silly goose!

HAYEH. Honest. That's why he goes, to see Tzirl.

KREISEL. I hope your father doesn't hear about it. That's all we need!

HAYEH. But papa did see him.

KREISEL. Ridiculous. Papa didn't see him. If he did, he'd let him have it, all right. He'd give him something to remember forever!

HAYEH. Why shouldn't Papa let him go there to see Tzirl?

KREISEL. Because they're planning to take every morsel of food out of our mouths.

HAYEH. Why should they want to do that?

KREISEL. (*Agitated, rises away from Hayeh.*) Leave me alone. Stop your pestering me.

HAYEH. I only asked . . . (*She finds a pair of scissors, with which she starts to cut figures out of paper. Haim Hersh enters.*)

HAIM HERSH. Where's that son of yours? Where's Noah?

KREISEL. I thought he was in the mill.

HAIM HERSH. Isn't he sleeping?

HAYEH. He's in the cemetery.

KREISEL. (*Slaps Hayeh's hands.*) Who asked you to butt in?

HAIM HERSH. I might have known. To my troubles there's no end. So-o-o-o, you let your son . . .

KREISEL. Why blame me?

HAIM HERSH. Who else? To whom should I talk? You know all about

it and you let him go there! Only I know nothing. You tell me nothing!

KREISEL. What can I tell you?

HAIM HERSH. All you have to do is tell me, then leave the rest to me. I'll fix him. I'll let him have it.

KREISEL. You should bite your tongue first, you old fool!

HAIM HERSH. Just wait and see. He's gone there for the last time!

KREISEL. If the boy wants to go there, you won't be able to stop him.

HAIM HERSH. You'll see, all right. I said he won't go there again!

KREISEL. Shah, shah! You don't have to shout. Just see how you're frightening the child.

HAIM HERSH. For whom am I slaving my days and nights away! Every nerve in my body is worn out in work. So what happens? You connive for my own son to visit my enemies.

KREISEL. Me? Since when did I send him?

HAIM HERSH. You know he's planning to set our mill on fire? Oh, don't think I don't know it. Why, he's even hired some rascals to help him.

KREISEL. How can you believe such ridiculous stories?

HAIM HERSH. Just watch—they'll even steal our horse.

KREISEL. Nonsense. No one will steal him.

HAIM HERSH. (*After fuming about, pounces on Hayeh.*) You—(*He angrily snatches the scissors from her.*) You imp! You're nothing but a spoiled brat! You've been going to the cemetery too . . .

HAYEH. (*Crying.*) I never did! It's not true!

KREISEL. Leave the poor child alone. What do you want from her? Like a bull, he rushes in and starts bellowing. Do you know what you're hollering about?

HAIM HERSH. I know all right! He swears his head will lie low in the dust if he doesn't put up his own windmill, right here under my own nose.

KREISEL. Take it easy. He's not putting up a windmill so fast.

HAIM HERSH. That's how much you know! He's already bought a piece of land right up against ours.

KREISEL. (*Shocked.*) Real enemies!

HAIM HERSH. So now you know. Now you've really got something to worry about. I know what I'm talking about. They won't be satisfied till they drive us out like beggars.

KREISEL. And she . . . she has the gall to come here! Just wait, next time I'll scald her with hot water.

HAIM HERSH. Suddenly you're waking up. Where were you till now? But I'll show them. They can't get away with it. They think they'll build a mill, huh! The minute they bring lumber to start, there'll be blood flowing.

KREISEL. Are you sure they really bought a place?

HAIM HERSH. (*Glares at her.*) Where's that son of yours? (*He turns on Hayeh.*) Where's Noah? Tell me!

HAYEH. I don't know.

HAIM HERSH. Tell me the truth, Kreisel. Has our Noah been over there to see his daughter? (*Silence.*) So answer me! Yes or no!

KREISEL. What's got into you today? Did you fall out of the wrong side of the bed this morning?

HAIM HERSH. So don't answer me. I know what I'll do. I'll fix him —with my enemies he'll go? I'll whip him to an inch of his life, then out of this house he goes! (*He looks for the whip.*)

KREISEL. (*Becoming frantic.*) You must be out of your mind! Are you crazy? What are you doing? (*She turns to Hayeh.*) Don't let him go! He's a madman. (*Sound of the mill becomes much louder.*)

HAIM HERSH. I don't know how human flesh and blood can put up with it. My own wife and children are against me! Thanks to them I'll become a miserable beggar. (*He listens to the sound of the mill as he stands irresolute.*) It's lucky for him that I have to go to the mill. (*He rushes out.*)

HAYEH. (*Looking out of the window.*) He's gone into the mill.

KREISEL. (*Slaps Hayeh.*) Who asked you to open your mouth? Who asked you to tell him Noah has been going there? Answer me.

HAYEH. Why are you picking on me? I wish I could go, too. They never did me any harm. Tzirl is nice, and she asked me to come over.

KREISEL. You listen to your father, do you hear me! They've become mean, nasty people. They want to destroy us. I forbid you ever to go there again! Never! and Noah won't go there either. Just wait, I'll tell him all right, he should remember! (*Noah enters.*) Aha, so it's you. Good morning, my son. Where have you been?

NOAH. Just out for a walk. Trying to clear my head from sleep.

KREISEL. (*Offering him a glass of tea.*) Have something to eat and then go to bed.

NOAH. It's early. There's a long day ahead.

KREISEL. Papa is all worked up. He's very angry.

NOAH. Angry with whom?

KREISEL. He's very upset because Note wants to take the last piece of bread from our mouths.

NOAH. Is that supposed to be my fault?

KREISEL. I didn't say it's your fault. Hayeh says you were over there this morning.

NOAH. How does she know?

HAYEH. I saw you.

NOAH. So what about it? What if I do go there? One thing doesn't have to do with another, does it?

KREISEL. You're asking me? I agree that Tzirl doesn't take after her father.

NOAH. (*Rattled.*) What's Tzirl got to do with all this?

KREISEL. I've said all I'm going to say. (*Haim Hersh enters.*)

HAIM HERSH. Aha, so here you are, my loving son, my breadwinner! A lot of pleasure and happiness I get from you!

NOAH. What's the complaint now? I worked all night in the mill, didn't I?

HAIM HERSH. (*Sarcastically.*) So I'm

a very lucky man, huh? Bah, don't do me any favors.

NOAH. I'm not interested in favors. What do you mean, favors? Do you want me to take a job with some strangers?

HAIM HERSH. Who said anything about strangers? You're all set. You'll go into partnership with the gravedigger and together you'll put up a mill. About us—your father Haim Hersh and your mother, Kreisel—you won't have to worry about us—you'll bury us. Then you'll marry the gravedigger's—oh, excuse me, your partner's —daughter. So you're all set.

NOAH. What a thing to say! You don't really believe . . .

HAIM HERSH. So-o-o-o, maybe you'll tell me to shut up?

NOAH. Mama, what's going on? What does he want from me?

HAIM HERSH. Go ahead, Mama, tell him what we want from him.

KREISEL. How do I know what you want from the poor boy.

HAIM HERSH. He's yours, not mine. You can have him.

KREISEL. Your son . . . my son . . . He was all night working hard, the poor boy. What do you want from him?

NOAH. I've been listening to you, I heard every word—but I don't know what you're talking about.

HAIM HERSH. (*Threatening Noah*) You'll understand this . . . (*He raises his fist to him. Kreisel rushes between them.*)

KREISEL. Have you gone out of your mind? He's crazy . . .

NOAH. (*To Kreisel.*) Let him alone. So he'll hit me. (*Noah lowers his head before his father.*) Go ahead, hit me, if that's what you want. Go ahead, don't worry—I won't hit you back. (*Haim Hersh hesitates. He turns to leave, then suddenly he turns to Noah.*)

HAIM HERSH. Tell me the truth—did you go to the cemetery?

NOAH. Yes, I went there.

KREISEL. You don't have to answer him, my son.

NOAH. I'm not afraid to tell him the truth. Yes, I went there yesterday, I went there today, and I will go there again tomorrow.

HAIM HERSH. I'll cut off your legs.

NOAH. I'll go anyway.

HAIM HERSH. That daughter of his has turned your head upside down. (*Noah remains silent. Haim Hersh deliberately sits down close to Noah.*) Now look. See, I'm not angry. I'm not upset. Now let me talk to you calmly.

KREISEL. Don't listen to him, my son. Nothing good can come from all this. Good God, what do they want from me? Can't I have one day of peace in my life.

HAIM HERSH. (*To Noah.*) Don't worry. Just sit quietly and listen. See, I'm calm, not angry. Now tell me in simple friendship, with common sense—who is your father? Your mother? Who are you, after all? Think —then tell me this: Who is Note, the gravedigger, who is his daughter, and who is her mother?

NOAH. Why? What have I got to do with them?

HAIM HERSH. Aha, I see. You have nothing to do with them, yes? Swear it!

NOAH. I have nothing to do with them.

HAIM HERSH. And the daughter? (*Noah is silent.*) Go on, have you lost your tongue? So-o-o-o, why don't you answer me? It's a very simple question . . .

KREISEL. (*Mimicking Haim Hersh.*) The daughter . . their daughter. That's none of your business.

HAIM HERSH. (*Ignoring her.*) You expect me to welcome as a member of my family that . . . that gravedigger! (*Noah is silent.*) You know he bought a place right near our mill, don't you? You know he's digging a grave there for all of us?

NOAH. He hasn't bought it yet.

KREISEL. (*To Haim Hersh.*) You've got to admit that. It's true.

HAIM HERSH. So you'll marry his daughter. Then people will say, "Look, Haim Hersh and Note, they're in-laws." Tpooh, such fine in-laws all my enemies should have.

NOAH. He's not going to build a mill.

HAIM HERSH. You think you know so much. Well, I know something, too. He has already made a bargain for an old mill in the next village and he's going to bring it right here.

NOAH. How do you know?

KREISEL. (*Unable to hold back her tears.*) It's the truth, my son. We're doomed. They're the ones who are ruining us.

HAIM HERSH. So there you have it, my son. Nothing will satisfy them until they destroy your father. (*Turning to Kreisel.*) And he tries to tell me he doesn't know a thing about it! (*Sarcastically.*) No one told him, and he knows from nothing! Or maybe Note and my dear son have already made a partnership deal . . . (*Haim Hersh closes in on Noah.*) So that's why you go there. Don't tell me, I know all right. (*Noah is dazed.*) Tell me, my fine son, when are they bringing the first load of lumber here? Why are you looking at me like that? As if you don't know what I'm talking about.

NOAH. I don't know . . . you've got me all mixed up. I'm going right over there. I'll make Note tell me the truth. (*Noah rises to leave.*)

HAIM HERSH. No you don't! You're staying right here. I'll handle this in my own way.

NOAH. How can it be true? It's impossible. I know he's not building a mill.

HAIM HERSH. (*Sarcastically.*) Aha, I see. You know.

NOAH. He told me himself. They don't want to live in the cemetery any more, so he's building a house.

KREISEL. (*In tears.*) They're lying to you. They're just trying to fool you.

NOAH. That's why I want to go and ask them, straight out.

HAIM HERSH. What's there to ask, when it's all settled? You'll listen to me! You're not to set your foot in their house again, ever! Do you hear that?

NOAH. All night long I slave away, and this is what I get! A fine good morning!

HAIM HERSH. Don't do me any favors. From now on I'll take care of the mill at night myself. That's all I need, to depend on my children.

HAYEH. How about me? Can I go to the mill?

KREISEL. Keep quiet. Who asked you to butt in? Watch out or your father will use the whip on you.

HAIM HERSH. It serves me right. I'm being repaid. If I had really used the whip on this son of mine . . . every day . . . I wouldn't be shamed now before the world. (*He snatches the scissors from Hayeh and slaps her hand.*)

NOAH. You can whip me all you like —it's not too late. Do you think it'll make me change for the better? After all, I'm your son. Do you expect me to be better than you? (*Haim Hersh stands uncertain, then resolutely starts to remove his belt.*) What do you want from my life? What kind of shame did I bring you? All you can think of is the whip! I'm almost twenty years old . . .

KREISEL. He's right. For other people, a son is a jewel in the family. But you don't know what it means to have such a treasure.

NOAH. I'm not asking to be treated like a treasure here, but I don't want to be treated like a stray dog either. Why should I bring you trouble and misery? If I had only known that Note intended to build another mill here, I would never have set foot in his house. I don't give a fig for him. Wait till he tries to bring his lumber . . . You know what I'll do? I'll pour pitch all over it and then set it on fire!

HAIM HERSH. Suppose he doesn't build another mill here, what about his daughter? Is she going to be my daughter-in-law? Answer me that! (*Note's wife, Kreine, suddenly enters.*)

KREINE. Good morning!

KREISEL. (*Most friendly, as if there were no problems between the families.*) Good morning, and bless you. What a welcome guest at such a good moment!

KREINE. (*Becoming aware of the tension in the household.*) Ah, what a beautiful morning! And busy, busy, busy. I mean the mill; it should always be busy the way it worked away all night long.

KREISEL. (*To her husband.*) Aren't the mills grinding empty now? Shouldn't they . . . (*Noah moves to leave.*)

HAIM HERSH. (*Bitterly.*) Don't trouble yourself, I'm going myself. (*Haim exits.*)

KREINE. (*To Kreisel.*) Oh, Kreisel dear, I am so upset. My child isn't feeling well.

KREISEL. She shouldn't know from harm. What is it?

KREINE. She woke up this morning shining like the sun. Now, all of a sudden, she has a fever.

KREISEL. God forbid. We must keep her from the evil eye.

KREINE. (*To Noah, with a smile.*) Who knows what's wrong with her. Maybe you know something, Noah? Did you say something to her? A father isn't like a mother . . . a father doesn't always think of his child . . .

KREISEL. (*Nodding her head.*) Just my words. It's the truth.

KREINE. Did she say something to you, Noah? Did she say she didn't feel well?

NOAH. Why . . . er . . . to me . . .?

KREINE. (*Crosses to window and looks out.*) Will Haim Hersh come back? I'm afraid. You can hear my heart thumping like a hammer.

KREISEL. Rest easy, Kreine dear. Don't worry about him.

KREINE. You know . . . I have nothing to do with what's happening . . . it's not my fault. My heart is in agony for my child. God forbid that anything should happen to her . . . then my life would really be all over and finished. (*She looks to Noah again; he doesn't respond. She turns to Hayeh.*) Come over to our house for a little while. Your visit will cheer up Tzirl.

KREISEL. Why should God torture us like this? Can I tell you what's on my heart? When did we ever quarrel? Why need we quarrel now? What should I say to you . . . my heart aches to have a bad word pass my lips to you. It would have been better if you had not come over here. My morning has already been black and bitter enough. What can we do to bring peace between us again? Ach, maybe it's no use any more, maybe it's too late.

KREINE. Maybe I should really go now. I don't want that you and I should ever quarrel. My heart is only filled with worry for my child.

KREISEL. What happened all of a sudden? What's wrong with her?

KREINE. I hope nothing is wrong with her, thank God. She is one precious eye in my head. Maybe you can come over to our house, Kreisel. I'd ask Noah, but I'm afraid . . . Do you think he knows something . . .?

KREISEL. (*To Noah.*) Did you and Tzirl have an argument . . .? (*Noah says nothing.*)

KREINE. Kreisel, dear, please come over to us for a while, I beg you. Maybe you can talk over things with my Note. I can't talk to him . . . he just won't listen to me.
(*Kreine weeps.*) Why does life torture us so? If only my daughter could get some joy . . . life could be bright for all of us then. Oh God, why must we always suffer so?

KREISEL. (*Infected by the weeping, becomes lachrymose.*) Your Note won't be satisfied till he has ruined us.

KREINE. What should I do with my Note? When I talk to him it's like talking to the wall. He won't even listen to me. I want nothing special from life, no miracles. But living in that cemetery . . . what a woebegotten life! Why can't we live like other people. I'm not thinking of myself—it's my poor daughter, for Tzirl's sake . . .

KREISEL. I'll try to come over to see
you tonight. Right now isn't easy. If
Haim Hersh should see me . . .
things are hard enough as they are.
I don't want to make them worse.
(*Nodding toward Noah.*) Ach, he's
had his bellyfull from my husband today.
KREINE. God should spare us from any
evil from all this. (*Note, a spade in
hand, appears in the doorway.*)
NOTE. Aha! I thought you'd be sneak-
ing over here!
KREINE. (*Resigned and woeful.*) I'm
leaving right now.
KREISEL. (*To Note.*) Come in. Come
right in. Why should you stand at
the door?
NOTE. I have my own house.
KREINE. God stay with you, Note!
NOTE. Never mind. God is with me,
and I don't want you ever to come
here.
KREISEL. God forbid that we should be
enemies. Believe me, I have no bitterness in my heart against you. So
you could just as well come in already.
KREINE. I only came over here to ask
Kreisel to pray with me to keep the
evil eye away from our daughter.
KREISEL. Of course I'll come. Depend on
me.
NOTE. We don't need you and we
don't want you.
KREINE. Such a stubborn ox! Have some
pity . . .
NOTE. I don't want your help. Keep
your prayers. My daughter will be
well without you and your . . . (*To
Kreine.*) You have no business coming here! (*Haim Hersh appears at the
door. He stops and glares in amaze-
ment at Note.*)
KREINE. (*Fearfully starts to leave, tug-
ging at Note's sleeve.*) Come, let's go
home. (*She succeeds in pulling away
from the confrontation.*)
HAIM HERSH. (*Spits after them.*) Tpoo-
ey! The devil take them! What did
he want here? And with his spade.
Ye-e-s-s, with his spade. He's a little
too early for that . . . ! (*Note, hearing him, tries to force his way back

to fight Haim Hersh, but Kreine re-
strains him and pulls him away.*)
CURTAIN

ACT III

*An early summer evening. Inside
Note's house. Although neither Haim
Hersh's house nor Note's reflects any
wealth, Note's is more meager, but
with an extra feminine touch. In size
and arrangement they are practically
alike. When the curtain rises Noah appears at the open rear window. Noah
looks in and calls.*

NOAH. Tzirl . . . Tzirl . . . Where
are you, Tzirl? If you're hiding, you
might as well know, this is the last
time I'm coming here. So . . . re-
member . . . the very last time!
TZIRL. (*Appearing at door at the left.*)
Go away. I'm warning you, Papa will
be here any minute.
NOAH. I just want you to know I'm
not coming to see you again. This is
the last time.
TZIRL. You sound like it's my fault.
NOAH. Whose fault is it then?
TZIRL. Papa will be here any minute,
I'm telling you. I'm afraid . . .
NOAH. I'm not afraid, of your father
or anyone. I'm going to wait till that
Hatzkel of yours shows up.
TZIRL. Honest, please believe me, I de-
spise him. It's not my fault if he
comes here. It's because of him . . .
he talked papa into the idea of putting up another mill—that's how he
figures to get us to quarrel.
NOAH. Exactly. That's why I'll wait for
him.
TZIRL. Please . . . I beg of you
. . . don't start anything. Please go
home.
NOAH. I want to see how you get
along with your darling Hatzkel.
TZIRL. I'll warn him that you're hiding
under the window.
NOAH. And what do you think I'll do?
I'll crack his head open for him!
TZIRL. So go ahead. See if I care. It
doesn't concern me.

NOAH. I'm coming in. (*He starts to climb through the window.*)

TZIRL. Oh no! Don't . . . keep out! Papa will kill you!

NOAH. (*Jumps in.*) Now I'm ready for him. Let your father come. Let my father come, too. I'm not leaving till I'm ready.

TZIRL. (*Frantic.*) Noah, my darling, please, I beg you, go home. You're dearer to me than my life . . . please, my love, go away, or I'll die of fright! (*She clings to him and kisses him.*) You're crying! Noah, darling, please don't cry . . . (*Sound of approaching voices. Noah leaps out of the rear window. Tzirl remains seated, frightened. Hatzkel enters.*)

HATZKEL. Good evening, Tzirl.

TZIRL. Good evening.

HATZKEL. Alone? (*She doesn't reply.*) You're so quiet. (*Tzirl turns away from him.*) You don't want to talk to me? So! So don't! Why should you be angry with me? Just because I want to help your father? He shouldn't have to slave away at gravedigging for the rest of his life? And how about you? You like to live in a cemetery?

TZIRL. Don't do me any favors. I didn't ask you . . .

HATZKEL. I've got a surprise. Wait till you see what's going to happen soon . . .

TZIRL. What?

HATZKEL. What are you worried about? Absolutely nothing to be worried about. Tonight, maybe any minute, the lumber will arrive. The wagons are on the way.

TZIRL. No, it can't be true. You're lying.

HATZKEL. Ask your father. He hasn't a cent to his name, so I put up all the money. If he runs out of money before the mill is finished, I'll lend him some more.

TZIRL. I'm not interested.

HATZKEL. Wait till you see the house I'll build for us, too.

TZIRL. For whom?

HATZKEL. For whom else? For Tzirl and Hatzkel, of course!

TZIRL. I'll never live to see that day.

HATZKEL. Don't worry. You'll manage to survive.

TZIRL. What do you want here? If you want to see my father, he's in the cemetery. Why don't you go there to see him? (*Kreine enters.*)

HATZKEL. Good evening, Kreine.

KREINE. Such a surprise. A guest.

HATZKEL. Have you seen any sign of the wagons yet?

KREINE. So the lumber is really coming today?

HATZKEL. Really today! It's on the way right now. Do you know, I had to go to ten villages to find enough wagons.

KREINE. We heard that Haim Hersh has a gang of hooligans to keep the lumber from being unloaded.

HATZKEL. Ho ho . . . we'll see about that! I'll match him hooligan for hooligan with some extra. Do you think we're going to just stand there like dummies?

KREINE. I don't know how we'll ever repay you!

HATZKEL. I'll figure out a way to repay myself, so don't worry. Only make sure that Tzirl is nice to me. When I talk to her it's like talking to the wall . . . she simply won't answer.

KREINE. I don't know why she should treat you like that. What has she got against you?

HATZKEL. Maybe she likes playing games . . . teasing me . . . (*Tzirl exits into the other room.*) She's angry with me. When I told her the lumber will be here soon . . . I don't even remember what or how she answered me. Where's Note?

KREINE. I expect him right away. (*The sounds of a horse and buggy riding off are heard from outside. Hatzkel rushes to the window alongside the door.*)

HATZKEL. Someone's run off with my horse and buggy! Whoa! Whoa! (*Hatzkel runs out the front door. His whoas are heard from a distance. Kreine looks out the window. Tzirl slips back in through the front door.*)

KREINE. Where were you? I thought I saw you go into the other room . . .

TZIRL. I don't want him hanging around here.

KREINE. Someone ran away with his horse and buggy.

TZIRL. Me. I did it! I chased his horse and buggy away.

KREINE. What imp of the devil has gotten into you?

TZIRL. I don't want him hanging around here.

KREINE. He's a good soul, my child. He's simply trying to help your papa not to be condemned to being a gravedigger for the rest of his life . . .

TZIRL. I don't want anything to do with him! He says I'm his bride. The nerve of that loudmouth! I loathe him! I won't listen to such idiotic nonsense!

KREINE. He's such an outstanding man.

TZIRL. I don't want any part of him.

KREINE. But your father promised you to him.

TZIRL. (*Shouting.*) He wouldn't dare . . . ! Have I nothing to say about it? If all of you would just leave me alone . . . !

KREINE. Don't holler . . . you don't have to scream like that! (*Hatzkel returns.*)

HATZKEL. Imagine the nerve! Someone unhitched my horse and drove him off. What miserable thieves . . . (*He suddenly turns to Tzirl and eyes her with suspicion.*) I don't suppose you know anything about it? Aha, yes, you . . . you did it!

TZIRL. Yes! I did it! What about it?

HATZKEL. And I was worried about . . .

KREINE. Don't pay any attention to her.

TZIRL. (*Viciously.*) It was I. I untied your horse. I don't want your horse and buggy in front of our house.

HATZKEL. If you think you're going to pick a fight with me, forget it. I just won't talk to you.

KREINE. (*To Tzirl.*) What's wrong with you today? (*Tzirl runs out into the other room.*)

HATZKEL. She must have climbed out through the window. She may try it again (*He nervously looks through the window.*)

KREINE. I don't understand it. God know's what's gotten into her today. She's never behaved like this before.

HATZKEL. I think I know who's at the bottom of it.

KREINE. Why he butts in I'll never know.

HATZKEL. Don't you worry. I'll fix him yet. (*Tzirl reenters and overhears.*)

TZIRL. Whom are you going to fix?

KREINE. My child, if your papa ever finds out what's been going on here, God forbid, I don't know what would happen! If he heard you talk like that and . . .

TZIRL. Don't worry about me. I'm not afraid of anyone. Clear out of the blue, all of a sudden, he's so good to us. But it won't work! Do you hear me? I'm not going to be pushed around like a child any more.

HATZKEL. One might think I'm really in love with your daughter! What do you think, Kreine? (*A very weary Note enters.*)

NOTE. Good evening. Ach, what a day! I'm worn out, for the devil knows what!

HATZKEL. Guess what! The wagons will be arriving any time now.

NOTE. All of them? All at once?

HATZKEL. Even the millstones are coming today. Just imagine, it's taking two teams of oxen to drag just one stone.

NOTE. I've got to hand it to you. Amazing, getting it all together so quickly! (*He has cheered up. Turns to Kreine.*) This calls for a celebration. What have you got for a toast, my wife? Bring it out. (*Turns to Tzirl.*) Hey you, Tzirl, what's wrong with you? We should all be happy . . .

KREINE. (*Busily placing whiskey, honey cake, and glasses on the table.*) She doesn't feel well today. She's got a headache.

NOTE. Wait till you taste this whiskey, Hatzkel. (*He fills two shot glasses and hands one to Hatzkel.*) Here's to your health and long life. May God spare us and see to it that before long I won't have to make a living out of the cemetery any more!

KREINE. It's time already . . .

HATZKEL. Your good health, Reb Note. God should keep you, and your new mill should grind out pieces of gold! The mill is a bargain. (*He drinks. Apparently it's too strong for him, for he coughs and sputters.*) Oh, is that strong stuff!

NOTE. Here, have something to eat with it. This is home-made honey cake.

KREINE. Just taste it. You'll lick your fingers.

NOTE. Aren't you joining us, Tzirl? Have something.

TZIRL. I don't want anything.

HATZKEL. That one is angry with me.

NOTE. Don't give it a thought. She'll get over it. Bring in some goat cheese, Kreine.

KREINE. Go, Tzirl, and fetch the cheese from the store room.

TZIRL. I won't.

NOTE. What's this all about? Something new?

KREINE. You silly girl! Who told you it's dangerous to drink the milk from our goat?

NOTE. What's going on? Since when . . . ?

KREINE. She won't drink the milk from our goat because it grazes in the cemetery.

NOTE. What kind of foolishness is this. I've lived right here in the cemetery most of my life and I've yet to find someone creeping out of his grave. (*He laughs as he drinks again.*) What goes into the ground you can kiss goodbye forever. What ideas you get, my daughter. You grew up in the cemetery, and all of a sudden you're afraid of the dead! Ha! Ha!

KREINE. You shouldn't say such things! You could put the evil eye on all of us. You never can tell . . .

NOTE. Keep quiet with your foolish old wives' tales. (*Raises his glass.*) Gezundheit, Hatzkel! As God is my witness, we should live to see it, the first flour in my mill I'll grind for my own bread! God, only provide the wind to turn the sails. (*Todros enters, carrying a shovel.*)

TODROS. Good evening.

KREINE. Why do you always drag your shovel into the house?

TODROS. Who knows who might steal it.

HATZKEL. You're just in time, Reb Todros. Come, drink a toast with us.

TODROS. Why not? A toast can harm no one. Oh, what a lovely night it is. Note, you should get them to fix the fence. What good does it do to fix it one little piece at a time. I can't understand how a town can be so stingy. (*He picks up a glass filled with whiskey.*) Ah well, good health to us all! If we live, God grant us . . . Note, why don't you talk to them about the fence?

NOTE. The devil take the fence! Good health, everyone! We won't be troubled with the dead any more.

KREINE. Who knows? How do we know things will be better . . .

NOTE. Leave it to me, of course they'll be better. Good health! (*Kreisel and Haim Hersh enter.*)

KREINE. Well, look . . . guests!

TODROS. Before everybody gets into an argument, Haim Hersh, give me a pinch of snuff. (*Haim Hersh gives some snuff to Todros.*)

KREISEL. Believe me, we didn't come here to argue. If anything, we've come to try to settle things without a quarrel.

NOTE. Well, Haim Hersh, what's the good word? Here, why not help yourself to a drink of schnapps?

HAIM HERSH. I . . . I . . . let me put it this way: you're making a mistake. You won't get away with it.

NOTE. Nonsense. I know what I'm doing. So . . . that's why you favored me with a visit?

HAIM HERSH. Yes. I had to come to warn you.

NOTE. Save your breath. I do things my way, and no one tells me what to do. If I'm fed up with being a gravedigger, if I want to throw up this miserable life, God Himself won't stop me.

KREISEL. Ach, one mustn't tempt fate. God should only help you.

HAIM HERSH. Your business with God is your own affair. But if you think you can dig a grave under my livelihood, after I've worked like a slave all my life to build it up, working day and night like a horse till I almost dropped from exhaustion—I want you to know—I won't let you do it!

NOTE. Suit yourself. You say you won't . . . so, keep thinking that.

HATZKEL. Nobody has the right to butt into anyone else's affairs.

HAIM HERSH. So who asked you to butt in? No one asked advice from an empty charlatan like you!

TODROS. That's what I say. Who ever heard of giving up a safe and sure livelihood and going into a partnership with the winds. (*Noah appears at door.*)

KREINE. There's something in what he says.

NOTE. (*Sarcastically.*) Brilliant! They know all the answers. What do they know . . .

KREISEL. You should know how much strength it cost me to make him come here.

NOTE. So out with it! What the devil do you want from me?

HAIM HERSH. Not a thing . . . nothing!

NOTE. So if it's nothing, then . . . it's nothing!

KREINE. Please, we're not animals. At least, let's sit down and talk things over.

NOTE. What's there to talk about? What am I taking away from him? Since when does he own the wind?

HAIM HERSH. It's my bread and butter. How can you take away another man's bread and butter?

HATZKEL. Don't listen to that nonsense, Reb Note. I know what I'm doing, and I put a fortune of money in it.

NOAH. What's the use? He won't listen to reason until that one is made to get out of here.

HATZKEL. Are you talking about me?

NOAH. You can go to hell!

NOTE. You can go there yourself, you . . . you . . . !

HAIM HERSH (*To Kreisel.*) I don't know

why I let you drag me here! If they want to fight we'll do it outside on the road.

KREINE. You talk like a child, Haim Hersh. And you too, Noah, what a way for you to talk! And don't just stand there like that. Come in already. We won't bite you.

HAIM HERSH. He knows what he's talking about.

NOAH. (*Indicating Hatzkel.*) When he leaves the house, then I'll come in.

NOTE. For all I care, you can go to the devil! So don't come in—we didn't send for you anyway!

KREINE. Woe is me . . . he's drunk! (*To Note.*) You'll send me to an early grave yet. What do you want from my life? Can't you talk things over like decent people? What evil spirit has inflamed your heads so all you do is fight and fight?

TODROS. Don't be a stubborn ox, Haim Hersh. Give him a stool, Kreine, so he'll sit down. Aha, that's it . . . (*Haim Hersh sits.*) And what about you, you rascal? Get away from that door and stop stirring up trouble. Come in and we'll talk things over quietly, not like wild animals.

NOTE. What is there to talk about, papa?

HAIM HERSH. And I have nothing to talk about either.

NOAH. What are we wasting our breath for? Let's go home. We know what we have to do!

TODROS. Hold your tongue, you young puppy! Your elders will handle this. (*Todros turns to Haim Hersh.*) Don't be a stubborn fool, Haim Hersh. So he's had a little too much schnapps. But a least you're sober . . .

NOTE. Papa, I'm warning you . . . don't mix in where you don't belong.

TODROS. So, I shouldn't mix in. I'll keep quiet, but we'll see . . .

KREISEL. Don't be upset, Reb Todros. Please, I beg of you, someone has to bring them to their senses.

NOAH. (*Again indicating Hatzkel.*) When he leaves we'll get down to cases.

KREISEL. You've got a fixation about

him. Is he bothering you?

NOAH. Yes, he is! He's a troublemaker.

KREISEL. Then go home. We'll manage without you.

KREINE. (*Forcing Haim Hersh into a chair.*) Well, now, someone start talking some sense.

NOTE. Don't look at me. I have nothing to say.

KREINE. (*Despairing.*) What has happened to us? Suddenly we're enemies. For twenty years we live together, we're peaceful and happy together. Now, phuft, it's all over, we've become enemies.

NOTE. Maybe God willed it that way.

TODROS. Sensible people should talk things over in a decent way.

KREINE. And you, Noah. You're no help just standing there like a piece of wood in the doorway.

NOAH. I'm all right where I am—right here.

NOTE. If it's destined that we should be enemies, then we'll be enemies. That's the way it is. And let me tell you something, you only moved here. But me, I belong, I was born right here in the cemetery.

HAIM HERSH. Your work is much easier than mine.

NOTE. Good. So there you have it. I'll gladly change places with you!

HAIM HERSH. I'm not asking the likes of you to do me any favors! I don't have to come to anyone for anything. I work hard, I strain to the last ounce of my strength just to eke out a measly living. Don't think for all my work and struggling I'm going to let anyone take away my living! (*Haim Hersh excitedly bangs his fist on the table.*) I'm warning you, I won't let anyone destroy me by taking the bread right out of my mouth!

KREISEL. Don't be so excited. Why can't we talk calmly, like sensible people?

NOTE. And I say I'm not taking away anyone's livelihood. You don't think I work like a horse? What kind of life is this in a cemetery, day in and day out looking at corpses! With a grown child, enough is enough. We're going to get out of here and no one is going to stop us!

HAIM HERSH. No one is stopping you from getting out. You can buy yourself another place instead of taking away my trade that has taken me a lifetime to build. And I'm not going to let you destroy it!

KREISEL. You've got to admit he's right. After all . . .

TODROS. Ah, if only your father were still alive, how different things would be.

NOAH. What good are all these old stories? It's Hatzkel's fault. If he hadn't butted in they never would have had any ideas about becoming millers.

HATZKEL. That's what you think. It's all settled, anyway. And don't forget, there's other people's money in it too. So don't be a fool, Note. Just don't listen to them, that's all.

HAIM HERSH. (*Rising.*) So that's the way it is, eh? I see no reason to stay here. It's all empty talk.

KREINE. You've got the wrong idea. God provides enough for all.

KREISEL. You mean He provides enough trouble for all. My dear Kreine, you can't begin to imagine what trouble and woe we're bringing down on our heads. Eternal hate will be our reward . . . not even on Yom Kippur will we be able to atone for it. (*To Note.*) What can I do to beg you to think, think of the . . .

NOTE. I've thought enough already.

HAIM HERSH. Then it's settled. It's useless to talk any more.

NOAH. Let's go home, papa. Come, Mama, you too. When they need us, they'll know where to find us.

NOTE. That'll be the day, when I ever come to you! You'll have a long wait. (*Haim Hersh starts to leave. Kreine blocks his way.*)

KREINE. May I be struck dead if I let you go.

TODROS. I've got a solution. We can all build the mill together and be partners.

NOTE. God gave me hands; they're all the partners I need.

HAIM HERSH. Let them build. (*He

*forces his way out the door and is
followed by Noah.*)

KREISEL. Who put this curse on our
heads! Dear God, how can you make
us suffer so! (*Kreisel leaves.*)

KREINE. (*Trying to stop her, calls after
her.*) Kreisel, not yet. Come back,
Kreisel!

NOTE. They can go to the devil. Good
riddance.

KREINE. Better you should bite your
tongue.

HATZKEL. That's all we have to do is
listen to them! Who do they think
they are, if they think they can
scarc us! He thinks he's such a big
man already. He "won't allow it!"
The nerve of him. As if we're asking him! The wagons should be coming soon. I'll go see.

KREINE. You'd better watch out. Make
sure no one tries to beat you up.

HATZKEL. (*As he exits.*) Ho, ho, that'll
be the day! I'm not afraid of them.

KREINE. You better take stock, Note.
I hope you realize what you're doing.
I don't see what's so terrible with
our life here.

NOTE. I'm fed up with being a gravedigger. It's enough!

KREINE. But to take away a man's
bread from his mouth . . .

NOTE. That's all talk. You yourself said
there's enough for everyone.

KREINE. This Hatzkel, feh, he's not my
type at all. I don't like him.

NOTE. It makes no difference whether
you like him or not. Once we get
on our feet, I'll pay him back what
he laid out for us and he won't
have anything to say in our affairs.

KREINE. He has different ideas. He
wants to be paid back in more
than just money.

NOTE. So what's wrong with that?
Where have you got a better match
for your daughter?

KREINE. I don't want to go looking for
trouble. It's easier to prevent a fire
before it starts. (*From outside come
the noise and confusion of the arriving wagons.*)

A VOICE. (*Heard from outside.*) Hatzkel!
Hatzkel!

NOTE. They're here! The wagons are
here!

KREINE. I pray God they didn't bring
trouble with them.

NOTE. Foolish woman. That's all you
think of. (*While Note and Kreine
are looking out the window, Tzirl
steals out of the house.*)

HATZKEL. (*Appearing at the door.*) Reb
Note, what are you waiting for? The
wagons are here. Come on, just wait
till you see them! Come Reb Todros.
Where do you want them to pile the
lumber?

NOTE. On my new property, of course.
The world can turn topsy turvy for
all I care—I'm not afraid of them!
On my new property.

KREINE. But what if they start something, God forbid!

HATZKEL. Don't worry. My men are all
ready for anything. They'll unload,
and just let anyone try to stop them.
If they have to fight, they're ready
for it. I promised them plenty of
schnapps. Don't you worry about a
thing. Leave it to Hatzkel.

KREINE. Did you see what Haim Hersh
looked like when he left? He looked
like a wild animal. (*Frightened, she
looks around quickly.*) Oh my God,
where is the child? Tzirl . . . where
are you?

NOTE. She was right here a minute
ago. (*Todros exits.*)

A VOICE. (*Outside, closer.*) Hatzkel!
Hatzkel!

NOTE. They're here! I've waited a long
time! Wait, Hatzkel, I'll go show
them where to unload.

KREINE. (*Having looked in the other
room.*) Dear God, where is that girl?

NOTE. What are you so worried about?
So she went out, so what?

HATZKEL. I'll go ahead and show them
the way . . . (*Hatzkel exits.*)

KREINE. (*Sits in despair, tearful.*) Why
did we ever start this terrible business? The devil take it! It will only
bring us misfortune . . . We've come
between the two children . . . they
love each other.

NOTE. What? What are you talking
about?

KREINE. You heard me, all right.

NOTE. With such a . . . a nothing! And that's supposed to ruin my life? That barefoot one dares to interfere in my affairs! I'll beat it out of her head, I will!

KREINE. She's not a child any more.

NOTE. (*Rushing to the other room.*) Where is she? I'll beat her within an inch of her life! It's lucky for her I can't find her. Wait till I lay my hands on her! (*Shouting heard from outside.*)

KREINE. What's happening? Oh, my God! They're starting to fight already! (*Note runs out the door. Kreine runs to look out the window.*) What's happening . . . ? (*She screams.*) Tzirl, Tzirl my darling, where are you? (*Todros enters.*)

TODROS. What a ruffian . . . that Noah!

KREINE. What's going on? Where is Tzirl? Did you see her?

TODROS. The devil only knows . . . what a rascal! You should have seen the way he whacked him with a chunk of wood!

KREINE. Who got hit? Talk already! Who was it?

TODROS. Noah, of course. Did he land a couple on Hatzkel . . . you should have seen it! (*Tzirl runs in; she is terrified.*)

TZIRL Mama . . . !

KREINE. Thank God you're here! Where were you? Just look at you, you're shaking with fright!

TZIRL I'm scared . . .

NOTE. (*Running in.*) So here she is, my fine young lady. You'll get it from me yet. What business do you have running around out there . . . (*He raises his hand to hit her. Kreine runs between them.*)

KREINE. Don't you dare lay a hand on her, you crazy fool. God help you if you dare touch her! (*The noise outdoors rises to a tumult. Note grabs the shovel and hastens to the door.*) Don't take the shovel! Leave it here. Stop him . . . don't let him take the shovel . . . ! (*Note runs out the door. Todros is excitedly looking out the window. Kreine tugs at him.*)

KREINE. Papa! Go stop him! Don't let him fight. Stay here, Tzirl! Why does God afflict us! I'll go myself. Oh God, what's to become of us? (*The tumult grows much louder. Hatzkel runs in.*)

HATZKEL. Where does Note keep his axe? I'll split his head open! (*Hatzkel searches around for the axe.*)

KREINE. Have you all gone crazy? An axe, no less! What do you think you'll do with the axe? Come, papa! We must stop them! (*Hatzkel runs out empty-handed. The frantic Kreine is at the window.*) Oh my God! Look how they're fighting. Look, look . . . they're starting to throw rocks. See how they're flying . . . like apples from a tree in a storm. Oh God . . . they're going to kill one another! (*Kreisel runs in.*)

KREISEL. What are you waiting here for, Kreine? Come, we must stop them! If we don't tear them apart, they'll kill each other, God forbid! There are at least fifty of them at each other's throat! That Hatzkel made them drunk, and they've gone mad! I don't care what happens about the mill. I don't care if they build a new mill . . . let them . . . (*Noah is heard at the window.*)

NOAH. Mama, what are you doing in there with them? Come out of there right away!

KREINE. Noah, please come in. No good will come from what's going on out there. Come in!

KREISEL. Come in, my son!

TZIRL. Please, Noah, come on in!

KREINE. (*To Tzirl.*) Hurry, go call your papa.

KREISEL. He's not there . . . he ran away. Let's go out, dear Kreine, and we'll drag them in by force. Please come, God will bless you.

KREINE. You're right. I'm coming.

KREISEL. Tzirl, you come with us, too. Your father will listen to your tears. If not, I won't be able to live through it. (*A great tumult is heard.*)

KREINE. Oh my God! Let's go quickly. If we don't stop them, God knows . . . Tzirl, you'd better stay here in the house. (*Kreine and Kreisel run quickly out. Tzirl, alone and terrified, clings to the window as she watches in horror. Dobe appears at the doorway.*)

DOBE. All that noise, that yelling and screaming out there on the road. They're waking my children. (*The clamor grows louder and more intense.*) My little ones! My children! They'll be killed by the stones!

TZIRL. (*Edging away from Dobe.*) Please, go away. You frighten me.

DOBE. What do they want from my children? They need their sleep. They'll keep me and the children awake all night.

TZIRL. (*In a panic.*) Get out . . . get out of here!

DOBE. Listen . . . the children are crying. They're all awake now . . . listen . . .

TZIRL. (*Screaming.*) Mama! Mama! Come into the house!

DOBE. Oh . . . my children . . . they're alone . . . they're calling me. (*A renewed crash of noise outside. Dobe runs out. A crying and wailing Kreine forces Note into the house.*)

KREINE. Madman! Enough already! You might as well make an end to my life. I won't live through this. Dig a grave for me and my daughter and finish us off once and for all!

NOTE. I know what I'm doing, and I'll do what I want!

KREINE. I don't care what you'll do, but you're staying right here in the house! (*Note tries to evade her and push through the door.*) I'll kill myself, I'm warning you! Tzirl, come help me . . . don't let him go! (*Todros enters.*)

TODROS. Who would have thought it possible? I never saw such a scrap. Who started such a thing? Putting up a bunch of ruffians to tear at each other like bands of wild animals! If Hatzkel put them up to it . . . who ever heard of such an outrage . . .

KREINE. Papa, don't let your son go out there again.

NOTE. Don't worry about me. Who asked you to quarrel about me! This

is my home, and I do what I want in it! (*To Tzirl.*) And you . . . you . . . and you hang around with that son of his . . . I'll break every bone in your body! Did you put him up to wallop Hatzkel with a chunk of wood?

TZIRL. I don't hang around with anyone.

TODROS. To tell you the truth, I like the boy.

NOTE. He and his father can both go to the devil. They should burn in hell!

TODROS. What a way to talk, Note. You're committing a sin.

NOTE. I'll worry about that, so don't you. As for you, you spoiled brat, how dare you block your father! I'll fix you good and proper! What did you have the nerve to say to Hatzkel?

TZIRL. So? What did I say to him?

NOTE. That's what I want to know. All of a sudden she's crying. I'll give you something to cry about! You little pipsqueak, you dare to . . .

TODROS. Let up, already. Leave her be. She doesn't know what it's all about. To tell the truth, I'm not exactly crazy about that Hatzkel myself. He's too smart for his own good. As for that Noah, I sort of take to him. He's a smart customer, that one.

NOTE. You don't know a thing about anything.

TODROS. I know what I know. If you thought about it, you'd see I'm right.

KREINE. Hatzkel isn't getting your daughter so soon, either, if I know anything about it.

NOTE. Everybody knows everything. So what do you expect me to do about it—sit down and cry?

TZIRL. He's nothing but a big-mouth liar.

NOTE. When I ask you, you'll tell me.

TZIRL. The big shot boasted to me how he was going to make you such a rich man.

NOTE. I said no one is asking you. I'll take care of my own affairs.

KREINE. Isn't it possible that we can still wash our hands of the whole affair? Let him build his own mill. Let him run his own life and we'll run ours.

NOTE. It's a long way from that. That Haim Hersh thinks he can run the whole world, eh? He says he won't allow it, the nerve of him! I lived here long before he got here. After years of working myself to the bone, he comes along and has the gall to dictate to me. Well, you know what he can do. (*Sudden renewed shouting outdoors. Hatzkel, breathlessly frightened, comes running in and then locks the door behind him. A crash as a stone thrown against the door is heard.*)

KREINE. What now, God help us?

NOTE. What happened? Who's out there?

HATZKEL. Stay away! Just wait, I'll fix him yet!

TODROS. I'll bet it's Noah.

HATZKEL. I got away just in time. I couldn't believe it. If I hadn't gotten into the house just then, I'd be all finished . . . he would have cracked open my skull.

NOTE. That settles it. Wait right here. I was beginning to think maybe I should give up the idea . . . but now . . . they can tear me to bits, I won't give in to them!

HATZKEL. They think they can run the whole world!

NOTE. We'll see about that. We'll show them! (*A stone crashes through the window pane. Everyone huddles away from the window's path.*)

KREINE. In God's name, who's throwing the stones . . . ?

NOTE. Who? I'll catch him, don't worry. I'll bury him alive!

TODROS. Watch out! Keep away from the window or you'll be hit by a stone.

NOTE. (*Picking up the stone and looking at it.*) That's quite a chunk of stone. That settles it. We can forget about ever having peace between us. (*A second stone flies through the window. They all stand fearfully looking at the window.*)

CURTAIN

ACT IV

An evening in autumn. Inside Haim Hersh's house. When the curtain rises, Kreisel is seated near the stove, where she is plucking down from feathers. Hayeh is trying to help her.

KREISEL. Put them down. I didn't ask you to help me. You'll spoil the feathers.

HAYEH. I won't. I know how.

KREISEL. Talk to her and talk to the wall—it's the same thing.

HAYEH. See, I know how. (*She shows Kreisel.*) What's wrong with that?

KREISEL. Watch it. Look how you broke the quill. Broken quills cling to the down, then they stick you in the head when you are sleeping. Put it down and hurry to call your papa to come in for supper. Go already. Everything will get cold till you stir.

HAYEH. Please—just let me pluck these ten more feathers. (*She stands fidgeting as she plucks.*) There, only five more left, then I'll go.

KREISEL. (*With a threatening voice.*) This is the last time I'll tell you.

HAYEH. There . . . only two more . . . only one more . . . all finished. Now I'm going. (*Hayeh goes to the door, opens it, and recoils when she sees a figure outside. Frightened, she cries out and runs back to her mother.*) Mama!

KREISEL. What? What happened?

HAYEH. Someone . . . there . . . outside the door!

KREISEL. Who? What are you talking about?

HAYEH. I don't know. Maybe it's that crazy Dobe. I was so frightened! (*Kreisel cautiously goes to the door and peers out.*)

KREISEL. Who's there?

HAYEH. Look there, Mama, behind the door.

KREISEL. Goodness! It's Tzirl. Bless you, my dear girl. What are you doing there, all alone? Don't stand there, come on in. (*Hayeh runs to the door.*)

HAYEH. Tzirl! Come in, Tzirl! (*Kreisel leads the pale and frightened Tzirl into the house.*)

KREISEL. Good God, what happened? What are you doing here, my child?

TZIRL. I hope papa didn't see me run over here. I don't know what will happen if . . .

KREISEL. Don't be afraid. Nothing will happen to you while you're with me, dear child. Tell me, what happened?

TZIRL. (*Tearfully.*) Why must we be enemies? All of a sudden it happened.

KREISEL. (*With a sigh of reluctant resignation.*) God only knows. If I only knew what to do . . . believe me, if I ever wished you harm, it should fall on my head. Every good I want for you. Why have you run out of your house at night?

TZIRL. My father hit me, so I ran away.

KREISEL. Oh my God! How could he do such a thing to such a gentle child.

TZIRL. And that Hatzkel . . . right this minute he's sitting in our house. I hate him. That's why I ran away.

KREISEL. Do you think you did the right thing, my precious? Just think what will happen when your father finds out you're here. That's all we need, God forbid!

HAYEH. How about supper? Shall I call papa in?

KREISEL. (*To Hayeh.*) Wait a minute. I'm afraid papa . . . will . . .

TZIRL. (*Desperately.*) No one can force me from here . . . they can't drag me from here no matter what happens.

KREISEL. Have you spoken with Noah?

TZIRL. No. Suddenly he's my enemy too.

KREISEL. You don't know what you're saying. Why should Noah be against you, of all people?

TZIRL. He never sees me anymore. What can I expect when all of you have become enemies. Where shall I go? What can I do?

KREISEL. So that's why you came here? Ach, you dear, foolish one. Yet, maybe that's how God wants it to be. I have nothing against you two dear children, God forbid I should. It's the men. The two fathers won't stop till they destroy one another. I cry, I scream, I threaten, I plead—nothing helps. What more can I do?

TZIRL. My mother cried, too. She begged. He simply won't listen.

KREISEL. And for what? Neither one of the mills grinds enough for a living.

TZIRL. And Hatzkel hounds my father for money. Where will my father get the money for him?

KREISEL. Tell me, did they need all this?

TZIRL. (*Seeking Kreisel's arms for comfort.*) What's going to be now? Where will it end?

KREISEL. What can I tell you? But I think you'll have to do what your father tells you.

TZIRL. Where is Noah? Is he hiding from me? Why shouldn't I see him?

KREISEL. Noah does what his father tells him.

TZIRL. I'll go to him and beg him . . .

KREISEL. Go to whom?

TZIRL. I'll get down on my knees to your husband. He must try to make peace. It's useless to ask my father. As soon as I try to tell him, he hits me. I'm ashamed to tell you what he does to me.

KREISEL. Hush! Don't think about it!

HAYEH. Let me tell you, if anyone tried to hit me . . . you know what I'll do . . .

KREISEL. Quiet there, you! Who's asking you for an opinion? Better go call your father. Tell him someone's here to see him. Get Noah to come, too. (*Hayeh exits.*)

TZIRL. (*Embracing Kreisel.*) Take me to you. Please, have pity on me. I'm afraid of my father. I need Noah. I can't live without him.

KREISEL. Did you tell Noah? Does he know this?

TZIRL N-n-no. I can't. He's too proud —and so am I. He sticks up for his father, and I . . . please, let me go outside. I'll wait there so that when your husband comes . . . let me wait outside.

KREISEL. I'm more afraid of your father. What will happen if he finds out you're here? He'll do something terrible. He'll smash things. Maybe you should listen to me—go home, my darling child.

TZIRL. (*Frantic.*) No-no! My God, where can I go? What should I do? I'll run away far into the world. I'll run back to the cemetery, that's what I'll do! I'll bury myself alive in an empty grave.

KREISEL. Calm down. I mean you no harm. Look how you're trembling. Don't be so frightened. (*Kreisel kisses and tries to soothe her.*) Don't be so disheartened. It's not the end of the world. Things can still be fixed. (*A distraught Kreine enters.*)

KREINE. Oh, so this is where she is. To my troubles there's no end.

KREISEL. We are not strangers in this house. What evil you think I wish you should fall on me. Innocent children shouldn't know that their parents hold knives at each others' throats.

KREINE. (*To Tzirl.*) Go home! You must go, I'm telling you!

KREISEL. Don't force her against her will. She came here because she knows we are not her enemies. May God will what I wish for you falls on my own head.

KREINE. What do you want from me?

KREISEL. What do you mean? Dearest Kreine, may God destroy me if what lies on my heart doesn't come out of my mouth.

KREINE. (*To Tzirl.*) Tzirl, jewel of my life, please come home with me. Your father will tear the house to pieces.

TZIRL. I'm miserable there. I won't. I'll run to the ends of the world, first.

KREINE. How can you say such things? Why should you be miserable in your own home? Everything I do is for your sake. I don't close my eyes at night watching over you. Without you, what is my life worth?

TZIRL. I'll die before I marry Hatzkel!

KREINE. Did you ever hear anything like that! What are you talking about? So that's why you ran away from your home. So why did you have to run here, of all places? Dear God, why must you continually punish me like this?

TZIRL. If this house doesn't satisfy you, I'll go far away, I'll lose myself among strangers. One thing you can be sure—I'm not taking a step home so long as he is in our house.

KREINE. He's not there, you goose. He left a long time ago.

TZIRL. I don't believe it. I know he's still there. I don't care, do what you will. I have my own heart and my heart knows what it needs. Do what you want with me, mama. You can beat me day and night, cut me into bits—I won't!

KREINE. You've gone out of your mind, that's the truth! Who taught you to say such things?

TZIRL. Nobody. I don't have to be taught to follow what my heart tells me. I won't come home till papa promises he won't force Hatzkel on me. (*Haim Hersh comes in. Hayeh follows him.*)

KREINE. (*Weeping.*) Oh God, dear father in heaven, isn't it enough? What more do you want from my life? (*Haim Hersh, bewildered and suspicious, looks about, then silently sits.*)

KREISEL. Well, so say something. You come in and sit like a block of wood.

HAIM HERSH. (*Sarcastically.*) What's there to say? I'm so overwhelmed with honored guests all of a sudden. I know—maybe there's something the matter with the new mill. Maybe you want me to come over to fix it? I noticed it stands idle . . .

KREINE. You shouldn't say such things, Haim Hersh.

HAIM HERSH. An end to all this empty talk! Let me have something to eat, Kreisel. I've got to hurry back to work. I can't depend on the boy to handle it all by himself.

KREISEL. Patience, please, we can use it. They took the trouble to come here by themselves. Maybe you should listen to what they have to say.

HAIM HERSH. Now, all of a sudden, they have "something to say." What's the use of talking now? What was destined to happen—happened. You women may be lonesome for one another. But me—I'm not lonesome for that Note. Oh yes, old Todros still comes over to scrounge a pinch of snuff—or maybe he comes over here to spy on us, how things are going on in my mill—who knows, and I don't want to know.

KREINE. Be careful what you say, Haim Hersh. God hears everything.

HAIM HERSH. If you came here to smell out what's going on, you might as well know everything, I'm not afraid of anyone. God has been good, the Almighty still takes care of us. Work I have plenty; my health I have, too . . . (*He turns to Kreisel.*) So where is my supper? How long must I wait?

KREINE. A heart like a stone.

KREISEL. You shouldn't talk that way in front of the children.

HAIM HERSH. I'm not afraid if the whole world hears me. The children should also know the facts of life—and the fact is that Haim Hersh and Note are enemies to each other. And let the children know that Note tried to take the bread from right out of my mouth. God knows how a father, for a miserable handful of money, can sell his only daughter. Don't tell me what to say, I know what I know. (*To Tzirl.*) I know the whole story. Your father wants to sell you to that lout, that tramp . . . oh, I know all right! (*To Kreine.*) As for you, you can report to your precious Note that nobody takes my bread away from me!

KREINE. (*Stands indecisive, then suddenly:*) Tpuy on you and your bread! (*Kreine runs out. Tzirl, who has been frozen by the exchange, starts to leave.*)

HAIM HERSH. Just a moment—wait. You can take a message to your father from me.

KREISEL. Don't torture the child, Haim Hersh. Please I beg you. (*Kreisel enfolds Tzirl, kisses her, and leads her out of the house.*) Don't worry, be calm, dear child. No one will harm you. Go home. Don't listen to my husband.

HAIM HERSH. If you know what's good for you and that family of yours, you'll tell your father from me that the sooner he goes back to his cemetery and digs his graves the better off he'll be. If he wants, I'll take the mill off his hands. I'll pay him so he won't lose. Money I have enough. (*He chortles as if visualizing his victory.*)

KREISEL. Haim Hersh, stop tormenting us. Stop it, I'm warning you. You won't be satisfied till you drive me to kill myself.

HAIM HERSH. (*Calling out to the two women who are now out of doors*) Tell your father he's got a surprise or two coming. His present troubles are only the beginning. (*Kreisel returns.*)

KREISEL. Be quiet already. Let up for a change.

HAIM HERSH. She can go to the devil. Who sent for her? What does she want? (*Kreisel hands him a bowl of food.*)

KREISEL. Eat and be quiet. Am I condemned to listen to your shouting all the time? Let up already.

HAIM HERSH. (*Pushes away the food.*) Don't do me any favors. Who can eat when I'm torn from all sides? Why did she come here? Answer me!

KREISEL. Nothing

HAIM HERSH. They sent her for something. I could tell. Why were tears coming from her eyes?

KREISEL. You think you're any better than Note? The way you talked to her, the things you said . . . only a man with a black heart can talk like that!

HAIM HERSH. (*With sarcasm.*) Oh, I see. Maybe you want I should send my son over there to help them, eh? Their mill isn't working, it stands idle. There's something wrong over there . . . I can tell.

KREISEL. So you're satisfied. Now you can leave me in peace.

HAYEH. (*At the window.*) Tzirl just went into the mill.

HAIM HERSH. (*Jumping up.*) What is she doing there? I'll throw her out!

KREISEL. (*Blocking his way.*) Don't! Stay here! Leave her alone!

HAIM HERSH. Let me go! I'm warning you not to stand in my way!

KREISEL. Take a knife and cut out my heart, why don't you? I can't bear any more. I'll leave this house and you'll never see me again. No matter where, I'll run away from you and all my troubles.

HAIM HERSH. (*He tries to open the door, but she presses against it with all her force.*) Let me go, I say! Will you . . .

KREISEL. You'll have to kill me first! You won't go!

HAIM HERSH. You're out of your mind. Just look at you . . . you're like a crazy one.

KREISEL. (*Breaking into tears.*) I'll die before I let you go! You won't . . .

HAIM HERSH. (*Backing away from her and the door. He speaks ironically.*) I've suddenly become an important person. Look how everyone joins up against me. Me!

KREISEL. For once understand. The children love one another. One can't live without the other.

HAIM HERSH. So now it's love! I'll give him love—I'll throw him out like a mad dog.

KREISEL. That's why she was crying. I thought her heart would break. That idiot father of hers wants to give her to Hatzkel.

HAIM HERSH. All of a sudden you're a matchmaker for your son. She'll never marry Noah!

KREISEL. I say she will.

HAIM HERSH. And I say she won't! My head will lie trampled in the dust before that happens!

KREISEL. Nobody will ask you.

HAIM HERSH. That's what you think. Me they have to ask. And it will only be possible if first I'm buried deep in the ground. Hayeh, go tell Noah to stop the mill and come here in the house. We'll see, all right!

KREISEL. Don't go, my child.

HAIM HERSH. (*He starts to remove his belt as if to threaten Hayeh.*) Did you hear me! Go! (*Hayeh runs out.*)

KREISEL. You won't be satisfied till you bury me. What do you want from my life? Why do you torture me?

HAIM HERSH. Just wait till he comes. I'll break every bone in his body. I'll settle things once and for all. Even if it means his life or mine. (*He interrupts his strutting to bang his fist on the table.*) That's all—his life or mine!

KREISEL. You're a madman!

HAIM HERSH. With such a wife and such children—is it a wonder if I go crazy.

KREISEL. Eat. Go eat up.

HAIM HERSH. Eat, she tells me.

KREISEL. Tell me, how can you blame the child if her father is such a scoundrel? When she was here, in this very room, the poor child cried so . . . I thought my heart would break.

HAIM HERSH. There's one way to settle it. I'll take care of them, all right! (*He looks out of the window.*) That's right. He's stopped the mill. Now I'll handle things.

KREISEL. The big talker will take care of everything, eh? Well, we'll see. You're sapping my last drop of blood, you with your . . . (*Noah is heard talking just outside the door.*)

HAIM HERSH. Who's with him? Whom is he talking to? (*Noah appears at the door with Tzirl. He is holding her hand.*)

NOAH. Come, don't be afraid.

HAIM HERSH. Who's that with you?

KREISEL. Tzirl, come in, my child. Don't be afraid of anything. I won't let him harm you, God forbid. (*Tzirl enters and remains near the door.*)

HAIM HERSH. Come over here, my son.

NOAH. What do you want?

HAIM HERSH. So you stopped the mill,

eh? Certain people could get the idea that we're not working because, God forbid, we have no more meal to grind. (*To Tzirl.*) You can report to your father that when hunger plays its pretty little tunes to him, we'll still have enough for our Sabbath table.

NOAH. Why did you want me to stop the mill?

HAIM HERSH. Because you and I are finished. You're not my miller any more—and you're not my son any more, either.

NOAH. If that's the way you want it, that's the way it can be.

HAIM HERSH. Pack up and get out. Don't ever set foot in this house again.

NOAH. That's all right with me. We'll see how you get along without me.

HAIM HERSH. (*Indicating Tzirl.*) What are you to her?

NOAH. To her? Nothing. Not a thing.

HAIM HERSH. Nothing, eh? So what is she doing here? (*Noah stands mute.*) So answer already. I've asked you a question.

NOAH. (*Suddenly.*) I don't want you to shame her when she comes here.

HAIM HERSH. Aha. So, I see how things are. That's that. But why should I shame her? Come here, Tzirl, don't be frightened.

KREISEL. Don't you dare say one cross word to her! God help you if you dare . . .

HAIM HERSH. Come away from the door, Tzirl. Come here. (*Tzirl approaches Haim Hersh.*) You can see how my own son is my enemy. When I ask him something, he doesn't answer.

TZIRL. What harm did I ever do you? Maybe my father did you harm, but it isn't my fault.

HAIM HERSH. True, you have a point there. But, what I have against you . . .

TZIRL. If you only knew how many times I cried and begged my father not to do it.

HAIM HERSH. And, as we can see, he didn't listen to you. But tell me,

who sent you here to turn my son's head? Tell me that!

KREISEL. Haim Hersh, I warned you. What are you trying to do?

TZIRL. None of this is my fault. I even dared to go against my father and mother because of it . . . tell me, what else can I do . . . ?

HAIM HERSH. As far as I'm concerned, you can both go to the devil.

NOAH. Cursing me won't help. It's time you learned I can take care of my own affairs.

HAIM HERSH. (*Derisively.*) You and this bride of yours can get out of here. Go to her precious father— but don't ever dare set foot in this house again. I wouldn't be surprised if you've got the wedding date all set and arranged . . .

KREISEL. Do you really know what you're talking about, Haim Hersh? If God could only be in your heart. Don't listen, Noah, go start up the mill. Enough wasting time here with empty talk.

HAIM HERSH. (*Shouting.*) Don't you dare! It's not necessary—I can still handle it by myself. Do you hear? All by myself! (*Dobe enters and stands near the door.*)

KREISEL. Here's another pest to plague us! Who sent for her? What is it, Dobe? What do you want? Are you hungry?

DOBE. Please, no yelling and hollering . . . My children will cry . . .

HAIM HERSH. Tpfui! That's all we need now . . .

DOBE. I can't open the graves.

HAIM HERSH. (*Calming down and trying to be reasonable.*) She's probably hungry. Give her something to eat. She certainly picked a fine time to come!

DOBE. They're closed in and I can't open their graves. They'll die of hunger.

KREISEL. Who cursed this poor woman? What a mess. As if we don't have enough troubles without her!

HAIM HERSH. What does she want from us? She's everywhere at the wrong time. We can't run away and hide from her. Kreisel, find out what she wants and get it over with. (*Todros, sprinkled all over with flour, enters. Dobe, fearful of him, quietly goes out.*) Another one now. I can see I won't have any peace here today.

TODROS. Good evening . . . who was that who ran out? Dobe? (*Haim Hersh glares at Todros.*) I said good evening . . .

KREISEL. Good evening.

TODROS. Before anything else, Haim Hersh, . . . oh, I can see by your face that an argument is coming . . . first give me a pinch of snuff.

HAIM HERSH. (*Handing Todros his snuffbox.*) Well, what's on your mind?

TODROS. (*In a sing-song voice as he dusts off some of the flour.*) Relax, take it easy. We have plenty of time. What's the hurry?

KREISEL. It's a blessing from God that you came here.

TODROS. For a pinch of tobac, that's why I came. I found myself without any, and you know how it is . . . (*Turns to Tzirl good-humoredly.*) You'd better hurry home, you naughty girl. Your father really gave it to you, didn't he?

KREISEL. That's a fine son you brought up!

TODROS. Let's not have any arguing and yelling, please. I'm here because I believe we should all have peace between us. And believe me, if we don't straighten matters out, who knows where it will all end. No matter what happened, it happened. Now we must make peace.

HAIM HERSH. You're wasting your breath. It's impossible.

TODROS. What's there to fight about? In time there must be peace, so why not now? (*Turns to Tzirl.*) And you, my pretty one, off you go. Go home. There's no reason for you to stay here.

TZIRL. I will not go home.

TODROS. And just look at you, Noah. Is this a way to come into a house? Can't you clean yourself up a little? Now, Haim Hersh, sit down. We've got some things to talk over.

HAIM HERSH. I've got nothing to talk over with you.

TODROS. Just listen to him. One would think I forced myself into his life. Don't worry, soon I'll be ending up in the cemetery anyway.

HAIM HERSH. Of what use is all this talk?

TODROS. Just look how he stands all puffed up. Come on, sit down, here, with me. But first, give me another pinch of snuff so my mind will be clear.

KREISEL. Hayeh, go bring the snuff-box to Reb Todros. (*Hayeh exits to other room.*)

TODROS. What's it all for, I ask? After all, how short is a man's life. So, while I, while all of us are alive, why shouldn't we enjoy peace? I try talking to my son . . . it's no use. He won't listen either. You and he are both stubborn animals. The best thing all around is to make peace, once and for all. (*Hayeh returns from the other room and hands Todros a snuffbox, then Hayeh goes to sit beside Tzirl.*) Ah, Hayele, God will bless you for bringing me the snuff. I'll just take a little for tomorrow. (*Todros starts to fill his pouch. To the others' consternation, he practically empties the snuffbox as he overfills his pouch.*) Yes . . . peace . . . there must be peace, that's all there is to it, I say.

HAIM HERSH. And I say this is all wasted talk.

TODROS. Remember, Haim Hersh, when you were only a little boy?

HAIM HERSH. What about it?

TODROS. Just try to remember. There we were, Note's father and your father—Simcha David, may he be blessed with a place in Paradise—living together with Todros much differently than now. Where would you possibly be now if it weren't for me? We didn't know nights from days, we simply worked and helped each other. And I helped your father till he finished building this house. My horse I gave him to haul the timber, and with my own hands I brought the straw and thatched this very roof. And where is your father now? In his grave where I myself buried him. And what has all this come to? No, Haim Hersh, you and my son simply mustn't fight with one another.

KREISEL. (*Moved to tears.*) God be with you, Reb Todros. But it was your Note who started this by trying to ruin us. One would think he had to, God forbid, because he had no bread for his family. What evil spirit drove him to fight with us? (*Haim Hersh drags Hayeh away from Tzirl, then turns to Todros.*)

HAIM HERSH. So it happened, and that's that.

TODROS. Not so fast. People have to meet each other half way. There's no reason, really, to fight. Noah, please run over and tell Note to come here right away.

NOAH. What's the use? He won't come.

TODROS. Then you go, Tzirl my precious. Tell your father I'm waiting for him here.

HAIM HERSH. I won't let him in here!

TODROS. Did I ask you something? It's enough that I want him, you rascal! Since when are you the Mr. Know-it-all? Have some respect and don't tell me what to do. The nerve of you to talk to me like that. Remember, I was the one who laid your father and mother to rest in the grave of Israel—and now you dare raise your voice to me!

HAIM HERSH. I grant you that what you say is true . . . every word. But tell me this—where were you with your talk when he built the mill?

TODROS. You yourself said it's done, "it's already happened." The main thing is there must be peace. Whoever heard of such a thing—nobody stirs to go over to bring Note here. Ah, you Hayeh, run over and tell my daughter-in-law I need her here right away.

KREISEL. She was here just a little while ago.

TODROS. You mean Kreine was here? Well, what do you know?

KREISEL. Yes, she was here. We're both cursed with bad luck.

TODROS. You listen to me for a change, Noah. Behave like a man. Go get Note to come over here. You're so good at breaking windows, you devil. Now do something right for a change. Get going! Bring Note here.

KREISEL. God help us, Reb Todros, but what can he do. They can't stand the sight of each other.

TODROS. That's all talk—child's play. Noah doesn't have a thing to worry about.

HAIM HERSH. Talk, talk, and talk! I'm going to start up the mill.

TODROS. The mill can wait. What kind of stubborn ox are you? If you weren't such an obstinate mule, we'd straighten things out pretty quickly. Take Note, for instance. He has to behave decently—maybe because he still has a father and shows a little respect. But you, you ruffian, just because you have no father to respect, you ride roughshod over everyone. Show some humility!

HAIM HERSH. Why waste time with all this talk? Just empty words. Noah, go start the mill.

KREISEL. Go, my son, see what you can do. Try to get Note to come back here right away. If I live through this I'll live to see the Messiah.

TODROS. Go, go already. All of you, children. Bring Note back with you, and my daughter-in-law, Kreine, too. And if that other one is there—you know who—you can tell him he can sit there till he turns to stone . . . that's right, children . . . go. (*Noah, Tzirl, and Hayeh leave.*)

HAIM HERSH. (*Indicating Todros.*) Look how he's attached himself to me—just like a burr. Tpfui on the whole business.

TODROS. And tpfui on you, too, you big clown, you! When I say there will be peace, there will be peace! Let me tell you something. When your father's house was already finished, there wasn't a sign yet of a stable. His poor horse was tied up under a leaky patch of a roof. And the cow? Right there next to the horse. It was already almost winter and no place to put the livestock under a roof. What do you suppose we did? We were neighbors, weren't we? Your father's cow calved in my stable. And the calf I took into my own house. Yes, and your mother, may she rest in peace, came over every day to do the milking. And you can talk! What happened if in your father's house there wasn't even a stick of wood to heat the stove for the Sabbath . . . ?

HAIM HERSH. Enough already. If you want me to pay you back, just tell me how much I owe you.

TODROS. That'll be the day when I ask you, you barefoot one, you! I'm richer than you are—and soon I'll be beyond needing anything from anyone. I only told you about the past, your past, because you should know that in our time we never quarreled or hurt one another for no reason.

HAIM HERSH. "No reason" he says.

KREISEL. (*To Todros.*) How can you say, "no reason?"

TODROS. What good did it do when I told them not to build the mill? Did they listen to me? I said that from gravedigging Note could make a secure living—it doesn't depend on the wind's blowing. The people in the town still want him to be the grave-digger. Since he gave up the job, the dead have been dancing among the graves . . . to the music of the wind. And what do you suppose the reason is . . . ? (*Todros has worked himself over to the window and he peers out. Haim Hersh throws his hands askew with impatience as if to say "why is he pestering me?"*)

KREISEL. Are they coming yet?

TODROS. The devil only knows. I can't see them.

HAIM HERSH. As if I haven't enough troubles on my shoulders, that girl has to come around here to pester me. Who needs her? Who sent for her?

TODROS. "That girl" is worth more than you and a hundred mills together! She is the one shining joy of my life. If it weren't for her, do you think for one minute I'd come here? For her sake, I want there should be peace. That no-good son of mine, the scoundrel, he whipped her today. Can you believe it? That anyone should lift a finger against such a golden treasure, tsk, tsk.

KREISEL. This big hero of mine, he, too, wanted to whip his son today.

TODROS. How do they come by such ideas? In his whole life, Note can tell you, I never laid a finger on him. Tell the truth, Haim Hersh, did your father ever beat you? Hah, you don't want to answer. But we know the truth. You and that Note behave like wild animals in the wilderness.

HAYEH. (*Entering.*) They won't come.

TODROS. They won't come? Where are the other children?

HAYEH. Noah is on his way home. Tzirl didn't even go in.

TODROS. So who talked with Note?

HAYEH. It was only Noah.

KREISEL. Noah went in . . . inside their house?

HAYEH. Yes. I was outside and looked in through the window.

TODROS. You should have gone in with him. Why didn't you?

HAIM HERSH. (*With visible disappointment.*) What use is all the talk?

TODROS. I never heard of such a thing —that a son should make so bitter his father's old age . . .

KREISEL. Maybe I should go. What do you think, Haim Hersh? (*Haim Hersh shrugs his shoulders in silence.*)

TODROS. I think you've got a good idea there. It would be better if you went, Kreisel. (*Tzirl bursts into the house and throws herself into old Todros' arms.*)

TZIRL. Grandpa! Grandpa! Help me! He's running after me. He found out I was here.

KREISEL. (*Moving to the door.*) He's coming here?

TODROS. Wait till I get him! I'll let him have it—he'll have nightmares for the rest of his life! (*Noah enters; he is very agitated.*)

KREISEL. So what happened? You went

inside and . . . well . . . ?

NOAH. He started to throw things at me and hit me. He said I . . . (*Note starts banging the window and yelling.*)

NOTE. Come out of there. If you know what's good for you, you'll get out of there at once! Do you hear!

TODROS. Come in, Note. Come on in, you rascal!

KREISEL. Dear God, what could you have against this girl? Come in already.

TODROS. Go out to him, Kreisel. You make him come in. If I go out to him we'll only get into an argument and that will be the finish of my trying to make peace. (*Haim Hersh bolts for the other room.*) Where are you running, Haim Hersh? You must stay here. Come back! We have to settle things right here and now. One way or the other, this is the time! (*Kreisel goes out to Note. Loud arguing between them is heard. Tzirl seeks the protection of the old man's arms.*) My, my, you're trembling, you little goat. Your father has his good side too. He's really not such a terror. Who can blame him for going berserk when he's in such a mess.

TZIRL. Here they come—they're coming in.

TODROS. (*Toward the other room.*) Come on out, Haim Hersh! No sense in hiding yourself. (*Kreine and Kreisel push the reluctant Note in through the door.*)

NOTE. Stop pushing already! It's enough! So-o-o-o, here I am. Now you can finish me, bury me, and make an end!

KREINE. (*To Tzirl.*) My child, what do you want from your mother's life? You want to shorten my years?

NOTE. (*Raising his fist to threaten Tzirl.*) I'm not finished with you yet! I'll teach you to respect your father . . . !

TODROS. We all know already how you earn respect—and maybe love. And that goes for Haim Hersh, too. You're both a couple of . . . I better hold my tongue.

NOTE. You dragged me here, so now what do you want, papa?

TODROS. It's simple. I want there should be peace between you and Haim Hersh.

NOTE. And for that you forced me to come here? What is he—too sick to come to my house? (*Haim Hersh appears in doorway to other room.*)

HAIM HERSH. Who sent for you? Who needs you? Not I, you can be sure. And I don't need this "peace" with you!

KREINE. Believe me, Haim Hersh, we don't wish any evil on you.

HAIM HERSH. (*Belligerent.*) Talk, talk, talk! I'm sick of all this meaningless talk!

TODROS. The longer this mess continues, the less chance there'll be for any understanding or peace.

KREINE. And we'll all be consumed and destroyed, God forbid!

NOTE. If that's how it will be, so let it.

HAIM HERSH. So we'll be destroyed!

KREISEL. Better it should happen to my enemies, please God.

KREINE. I'm not your enemy . . . God knows.

TODROS. So, don't just stand there like a bunch of cocky roosters. We'll sit down like civilized human beings and talk like sensible people. Whatever happened is past and buried. Now is the time to look to the future. If one of you has to buy out the other one, and there's no other solution, then that's the way it will have to be. But no matter what, there must be peace!

NOTE. I'll listen, papa. Let's hear what you want from me.

TODROS. First, sit down.

HAIM HERSH. Go start up the mill, Noah. I'll come soon, too.

TODROS. (*Flares up.*) You stubborn jackass, you. I'll break your bones for you! What are you trying to do to an old man? I swear, you'll drive me to my grave before my time! I won't allow it!

KREISEL. Don't say that. May you have a long and healthy life, Reb Todros.

KREINE. He speaks the truth.

TODROS. Whoever heard of such a thing! As if there isn't enough wind in the world to divide between them. Is the earth so small that you can't . . .

HAIM HERSH. Talk, talk, talk! Enough! Let's get to the point.

TODROS. First we'll have a little schnapps and make a blessing. Bring out the schnapps, Kreisel.

KREISEL. That's a good idea. Of course.

TODROS. And you, Tzirl. Run over to our house and bring a bottle of ours, too.

NOTE. (*Rises.*) I can't see what good all this will do. (*Tzirl beckons to Hayeh and they both quietly leave.*)

TODROS. Maybe you can use some fresh air, Noah. So go out for a little while till we need you. (*To Note.*) Sit down. Don't be a jack-in-the-box. Sit, I tell you! (*Noah goes out of the house.*)

TODROS. (*After Noah leaves, addresses himself to the two men who sit at opposite ends of the table. They stubbornly and proudly are turned away from each other.*) So, here we are. You, my son, pay close attention to what I say. And I expect you, Haim Hersh, to listen carefully. This terrible situation must end. It's enough already. God knows, I'm a stubborn man myself, but there are limits to stubbornness. Because parents, fathers and mothers, are ridiculously stubborn, why must the children suffer? Now, listen to what I'm saying—that other one, that good-for-nothing Hatzkel—may God help him—he made all kinds of promises and dragged you down in the mud. Why? Because he thought that way he'll get Tzirl. But, the truth is, she loves Noah. Be that as it may. And let me tell you something, there's nothing you can do about it when it comes to love. So Hatzkel is maybe rich? God bless him with all his riches. But a gravedigger knows too well how the rich and poor are stretched out together. Heh! Heh!

NOTE. All your talk is getting us no place, papa!

HAIM HERSH. Nothing but talk, talk, talk. Things will happen according to fate.

KREINE. Aren't you concerned about your son?

HAIM HERSH. He's my son and not yours. Let me worry about him.

KREISEL. (*In tears.*) A lot they care about their children! The children are pining away for each other. And their hopes and longings melt away like a burning candle.

TODROS. I'm warning you again, Note, and this goes for you, too, Haim Hersh. You must come to reason. Your stubbornness will ruin all of us.

HAIM HERSH. I refuse to have anything to do with barefoot gravediggers!

TODROS. Shame on you! What a nasty thing to say! You should be ashamed of yourself.

NOTE. So come to the point, papa. What do you want? If I sit another minute the bile will burst in me.

KREINE. Think carefully, Note.

KREISEL. I have no strength left to stand this a minute longer. Haim Hersh, what will be the end? God forbid, it will all go up in flames. That scoundrel will hire some hooligans to set fire to our mill. Then where will we be? (*Tzirl enters with a bottle of whiskey. She is followed by Hayeh. Todros takes the bottle from her and places it on the table. Kreisel brings glasses and sets them on the table.*)

TODROS. Call in Noah.

KREISEL. (*Goes to the door.*) Noah! Come in, my son.

NOAH. (*Enters.*) What is it? What do you want from me?

KREISEL. Just stay here.

TODROS. Now we're all here. Listen, children, listen to an old man. Pay attention to what I say. If you think I'm talking nonsense, then forget it. After all, you're free to do as you please . . . (*Meanwhile, Todros pours the whiskey into the glasses.*) Here, Note, take it. It's your own schnapps.

Now, we'll say a blessing . . . L'hayem, to life! God be with us and may all go well. So, Haim Hersh, L'hayem! Drink to life. Now we must all get busy and not lose any time. The mills stand idle. They have to be put to work. (*No one drinks. The glasses stand untouched on the table.*) It's a sin to waste good schnapps. So, I'll drink by myself. Well, let's take the mill we built— the new one—in that one we'll put the couple, Noah and Tzirl. And that's the way it will have to be. (*No one speaks. They all, silently, steal furtive looks at one another.*)

NOTE. Impossible! Never!

HAIM HERSH. Forget it, as likely as yesterday.

KREINE. God forbid I should have anything against your son, Haim Hersh. God grant him a long and happy life, he's such a fine boy.

KREISEL. It was like a knife in my heart when I saw Tzirl bitterly crying her eyes out, the dear soul.

TODROS. (*To Tzirl and Noah.*) You children love one another. Don't you think it's time you told your fathers about it? They're entitled to know, too. The children will take over the new mill. As for us, we'll go back to the cemetery. The town wants us, they need us there. As for Hatzkel, we'll work things out to pay him back every penny.

NOAH. I'll work so—I mean—I, all by myself, I'll pay him everything. By myself!

TODROS. There's your solution. That's it!

KREISEL. Take your hand from your heart, Note. Say something.

KREINE. Haim Hersh should speak up first.

TODROS. Whoever heard of parents fighting with their children just for bread and butter? You, Haim Hersh and Kreisel, I know you'll do all you can for them. And I know we'll do our best with all our heart and strength. And there will be peace. What else? Yes. Now, children, tell us that you love each other. (*Silence. All gaze downward in embarrassment. Note bestirs himself, rises, and takes up two glasses of whiskey. He hands one to Haim Hersh.*)

NOTE. Come, Haim Hersh. Enough is enough and the past should be forgotten. Maybe that's how God wants it. (*Haim Hersh takes the glass but remains glumly sitting.*)

TODROS. So, what's it to be? Raise your glass, Haim Hersh.

NOTE. (*Winks at Tzirl as he looks affectionately at her.*) I'm proud of her. That's a wonderful daughter I have . . .

HAIM HERSH. She's no better than my son! And let me tell you a thing or two . . .

TODROS. L'hayem! To life!

ALL TOGETHER. L'hayem! L'hayem!

KREINE . (*They joyfully embrace and*

KREISEL. *kiss each other.*)
          Mazel Tov! Mazel Tov!

HAYEH. (*Bewildered, but entering into the spirit of the moment, dances around and shouts.*) Mazel Tov! Mazel Tov!

THE END

HIRSH LEKERT

by

H. Leivick
(Leivick Halper, 1888-1962)

Poets in the Yiddish theatre saw the particular tragic drama of the Jew as an incomprehensible universal affliction. One tragic poet distilled out of the anguished ferment of his own life the deeply stirring travail of all mankind. H. Leivick's monumental contribution to Yiddish literature was inextricably interwoven with his life and times. He spoke for all whose raw wounds poured their blood out on the Siberian snow under the bestial flailing by the Czar's brutes. In *Hirsh Lekert,* Leivick not only immortalized the "passion" of a folk martyr, but also showed the indomitable spirit of his people that helped spark the blaze that consumed the terrible autocracy. Hirsh Lekert helped bring about the downfall of the frightful evil that had enslaved millions for centuries.

In his plays, Leivick broke away from the shopworn formulas of the popular Yiddish playwrights. The grief and suffering of all mankind, not only that of his own people, found expression in his writings which, he explained, in addition to their artistic considerations, carried the "obligation of an ethical mission of universal import . . . ingrained in the national character of the Jew." As a young man he was not content merely to brood about injustice in his life, isolated from conflict as a student of religion. His childhood suffering and deprivation, no different from others within his ghetto community, made him identify with the woebegotten. He joined the Bund and became a political activist. This led to his arrest in 1906 and his being sentenced to four years' hard labor in a Moscow prison. Then he was exiled for life to the bitter, icy loneliness of a prison camp in Siberia, from where he escaped and arrived in New York in 1913.

In his more than a dozen social dramas, Leivick's proletarian ideology is omnipresent. In his poem "A Song About Myself," he tells of the brutally flogged bodies he had seen, drenching the snow with blood. Thus, Hirsh Lekert's anguished, woeful cry is the poet's own memory of "the blood he saw flowing from bodies whipped in prisons." He wrote:

And if I ever remained a writer,
You have but this truth to blame:
That in the blood of each flogged fighter
Lies, too, my flagellated fame.
                              (*reprinted, A. A. Roback*)

Thus, influenced by his own experiences, he plumbed the depths of human suffering. His symbols were part of his life: the theatrical device of Gorki in the character of Luka, who is the mysterious stranger in *The Lower Depths,* and much like Ansky's *Meshulakh* in *Der Dybbuk,* may be considered to serve as a Greek chorus to relate man to an impenetrable religious mystique; but in Leivick's plays the symbols are human beings who point out man's universal plight, be the character the driven old or young Beggar in *The Golem* or the tortured soul of Isaac in *Hirsh Lekert.* His lyricism was fired by emotions that were haunted by the "twitching bodies under the knout,"* for he felt the "pain borne in silence . . . sufferings in life . . . the terrors of death." He actually saw the brutality and suffered as a political prisoner. The cries of the unfortunate under torture, the blood flowing from the naked bodies as they were scourged, became the ink with which he wrote *Hirsh Lekert* and *The Miracle of the Warsaw Ghetto.* His guiding muse was the "loneliness of the exiles in their aimless wanderings on the snow covered tundras."* The allusions to the pathos of human agony he saw and suffered were echoes of the "clang of prisoners' chains and the sighs of the dying revolutionaries in the huts."†

Leivick's awareness of the inequities in the social order, his dedication to socialist-inspired revolution, his dreams and strivings for the brotherhood of man did not blind him to the false idealism of the Russian redeemers in the Revolution who were power hungry, or to the fickleness of the masses, for he faced these problems in his drama *Geduleah Comedye.* That he was a Jewish nationalist is strongly evident in his enthusiastic admiration for the Palestinian and Israeli pioneers, whom he celebrated in his songs to them. He was much bemused by religiosity, as is revealed in *The Golem,* especially that part of the philosophy of orthodoxy which prescribed submission to persecution—*ess iss beshehrt* (it is fated). Yet such fatalism was not acceptable to Leivick, for in his *Miracle of the Warsaw Ghetto* his baffled hero, insulated from reality under the wrappings of his prayer shawl, finally realizes that he must fight, not only for his own survival, but for the survival of his people. The religious canons of the orthodox that obliged them to avoid a confrontation with evil are considerations Hannah Arendt failed to comprehend in her slurs against the Jews.

Leivick's commitment to the Bund, apparently, was in no small way inspired by the martyrdom of the epic hero Hirsh Lekert. The poet did not whine about or wallow in his own misery, but wrote of all humanity. The doomed Lekert's bafflement, frustration, and inarticulateness in the face of evil when he acted in protest against the bestial treatment of the demonstrating Bundists, and the futile efforts by the rueful Isaac to reconcile Jewish humanism with evil reality are dispelled by the ominous cries of the workers outside the prison walls. Unlike his other poems, especially *The Golem,* wherein the brilliantly evocative symbols, allegory, and vision elevate the audience to a kinship with all humanity, *Hirsh Lekert* was written in starkly realistic dramatic terms quickened by passion rather than by metaphor. Leivick's characters cry out for him in his eternal theme against tyranny, against suffering, against injustice, and for the strug-

---

* Meyer Waxman, *A History of Jewish Literature* (New York: Bloch Publishing Co., 1947), 4: 1029–31; A. A. Roback, *The Story of Yiddish Literature* (New York: Yiddish Scientific Institute, 1940), p. 289.
† *Ibid.*

gle toward the creation of a decent world.

The drama *Hirsh Lekert* is based upon a historically true occurrence. It takes place in Vilna in 1902. Vilna was looked upon as the "Jerusalem of Lithuania," the confluence of four cultures: Lithuanian, White Russian, Polish, and Russian—all of them with the small common denominator of Jewish culture. It was the seat of the Vilna *Gaon,* the most revered personality in orthodox Jewry. Some of the greatest Polish poets were born there (some reputed to have been of Jewish descent), as were Polish sculptors, musicians, writers, and scholars. In 1915, in the culturally highly sophisticated Vilna Jewish community, the world-famous Vilna Troupe was formed. The reputable and indispensable Jewish Scientific Institute (Yivo) had its home in Vilna. Vilna was the center of the radical labor movement in the time of Czar Nicholas II, and the Bund was the organization of the Jewish workers.

The full name of the Bund was *Algemeiner Yiddisher Arbeiterbund in Lita, Polen, un Russlan,* and it evolved out of the Jewish Social Democratic Party, founded in Vilna in 1897, which was the culminating organization of Jewish Socialists in pre-World War I Russia. It played a crucial role in carrying Jewish life under the Czar to a crisis. Due to the harsh repression by the authorities, socialistic ideology became part of the revolutionary current. The socialist movement among Jews, effectively started by the enlightened during the 1870s, had a setback in the early 1880s in the wake of the assassination of Alexander II; then it had a resurgence later that decade, grew in activity and in numbers the next decade, and culminated in the formation of the Bund in Vilna in 1897. With the rise of industries in cities such as Vilna, with the attendant exploitation of the workers, the intellectuals found in the workers a potent force toward social change. Thus, abstract theories of political strivings gave way and became absorbed by the economic and social forces from below.

Understandably for Leivick, he has Hirsh, the Bundist, refer to the "workers" rather than to the "Jewish workers." Actually, the early days of the Bund witnessed much agitation for national autonomy for the Jews in a liberated Russia. Voting this idea down, the Bund emphasized its prime objective to be a fight for improvement of conditions for Jewish workers and to further the cause of Socialism among the Jews. The Bund became a constituent part of the Russian Social Democratic Party at its first Congress in 1898, but it retained autonomy in strictly Jewish matters. All connected with the party believed in the need to overthrow the tyranny of absolutism in order to free Russia and, with it, the Jews from the vicious autocracy. Half of the Bund's 3,000 members in 1900 lived in Vilna, a quarter of whom were women, and they worked in textile, leather, tobacco, and match factories. Jewish workers had conducted strikes in Bialystock and Vilna in 1891, in Vilna in 1892, in Warsaw in 1893, and in Bialystock, Vilna, and Minsk in 1895. They organized for strike funds and increasingly concentrated on demonstrations in observance of May Day. The Convention of 1900 in Kovno concentrated on demonstrations against the government. This led to arrests and deportations to Siberia. In the play, Isaac is all too aware of the inevitability of violence and the toll it took of the Jewish workers; his humanistic doubts were rooted in a sincere religious ethic.

Zubutov, mentioned in the play, was the chief of the Moscow division of the secret police. He attempted to split the Bund, in 1901, by organizing a non-political Jewish workers' party: *Yiddishe Unabhengige Arbeiterpartie.* With a third of the Bund members who joined, it lasted until 1903.

Hirsh Lekert (1879–1902), a young Jewish shoemaker, was active in the Bund. He was born and raised in orthodoxy in Vilna. In the aftermath of riots instigated by government provocateurs during the May Day demonstrations in

1902, the governor of the Vilna province ordered the merciless flogging of twenty-six demonstrators, of whom twenty were Jews. The central committee of the Bund published a manifesto calling for revenge. Because the Bund was officially opposed to terrorist tactics, an independent group of workers within the Bund organized for action. Floggings had a demoralizing and humiliating effect upon the Jewish workers. Hirsh Lekert resolved upon an act simply to defend Jewish honor; he was one among many who were determined to act.

Hirsh Lekert's shot merely wounded the governor, but he was condemned to death by a military court and hanged on June 10, 1902. For many years the anniversary of his death was observed by the Jewish workers' movement. On the twentieth anniversary of his death, a memorial to him was erected in Minsk; it no longer exists. Although Lenin dissociated himself from Lekert's act, other prominent leaders in the workers' movement supported it. The inspiration he provided for others grew in momentum; a case can be made to support the theory that his martyrdom rallied workers and helped bring about the 1905 Revolution. Hirsh Lekert has been immortalized in popular songs as well as in at least two plays, one by Kushnirov in 1929, and this one by H. Leivick.

Despite the Bund's declaration against terrorism after Hirsh Lekert's attempt on the life of the governor of Vilna, the government intensified its repressive measures against the Bund. The Kishinev pogrom of 1903 swelled the ranks of the bund (ca. 25,000 to 30,000) with Jews determined to defend themselves against similar outrages. In 1904–1905, the Bund's 40,000 members split away from the Russian Social Democratic Party because Martov, Lenin, and Trotsky denied them autonomy and identification as the only Jewish Socialist Party. It remained independent until 1906. After the 1905 Revolution, the new order permitted the Bund to come out into the open. It was then able to print daily and weekly organs in Yiddish and Russian. With the return of a reactionary regime, 1908–1910, Bund members were arrested, many emigrated overseas, and the result was a decimation of its intellectuals. From 1910 to World War I, the workingmen became more active in the Bund and it had a greater influence upon the Jewish community. Its 1910 Convention used Yiddish as its language currency and endorsed Yiddish as the national language of the Jews; Yiddish was to be used in Jewish schools. After the 1917 Revolution, the Bund grew significantly and many of its members were elected to political office. But it soon splintered into various groups and many of its members joined the Communist Party. In Russia, from the October Revolution to 1920, the Bund gradually declined, but devotees continued its work in successive foreign capitals—Berlin, Geneva, and Paris. The Soviet government suppressed the Bund in 1920. After surmounting problems in Poland, the Bund became a strong cultural and political force there until World War II.

HIRSH LEKERT

by

H. Leivick

A Dramatic Poem in Six Scenes
Translated from the Yiddish by David S. Lifson

CAST OF CHARACTERS

HIRSH LEKERT, a young shoemaker
HIS WIFE
HIS MOTHER
HIS UNCLE
REB ZELIG, an elderly Talmudist
MENDEL, his son, a water-carrier
ISAAK, leader of the Bund Committee
USISHKIN, a member of the the Bund Committee
RUCHEL a member of the Bund Committee
RAISEL, a member of the Bund Committee
YOSHKE BOYGER, a Bundist
FAYVEL SHLUGER, a Bundist
RACHMIELKE, a Bundist
WOLFKE, a Bundist
TANTE, owner of a tearoom
VON WAHL, Governor of Vilna
BLIND MAN
HIS GUIDE
THE SILENT ONE
    Various Jewish Workers. Jewish Citizens. a Rabbi, Prison Guards
The action takes place in Vilna, May 1, 1902, and a few days later.

Scene 1 Hirsh Lekert's home in the Jewish quarter of Vilna. The morning of May 1, 1902.
Scene 2 Ruchel and Isaak's room later that day.
Scene 3 A street adjacent to the synagogue. Sundown of the same day.
Scene 4 A working-class tearoom. Evening, two days later.
Scene 5 Hirsh Lekert's home. Ten o'clock, a few nights later.
Scene 6 The death cell in the Vilna Prison. Middle of the night a few days later.

SCENE 1

The Jewish quarter of Vilna, May 1, 1902. The basement dwelling of Hirsh Lekert. To the upper right is a door leading to the one room, a small chamber where Reb Zelig Miches lives and spends most of his time in prayer and Talmudic study. He shares the hovel with his son, Mendel the water-carrier. Down right (in front of Reb Zelig's chamber) is the kitchen, dominated by an oven. The main room is poorly furnished: there are two beds and an empty table that is flanked by a pair of long benches.

It is early morning. On the lighted oven, a pot of potatoes is cooking. Hirsh Lekert's wife and mother are straightening out the room, cleaning and attending to the cooking. The mother is sick and moves with difficulty; around her head is wound a wet cloth. The wife, around 21 years old, is pregnant; she is pathetically tired, with a face that reflects suffering beyond her years. The women are haphazardly dressed, each with a kerchief on her head.

Visiting them is Hirsh Lekert's uncle, a well-meaning, pragmatic Jewish shoemaker. He stands at the door between the kitchen and the main room. He carries his prayer shawl and phylacteries under one arm; in the other hand he holds several boots.

Through the window to Reb Zelig's room comes the sing-song drone of the scholar.

UNCLE. Ach, that is some nephew to have, your Hirshke. A guest now all the way from Ekaterinoslav and he still hasn't found time to find out a word about his uncle or aunt.

MOTHER. You can talk! Better you should ask if we have had a chance to see him. He only arrived yesterday. And like you see, he hasn't even warmed the edge of a chair.

UNCLE. (*To the wife.*) Well—and what do you say about it? (*She remains silent.*)

MOTHER. (*Sarcastic.*) Maybe strangers come cheaper to him. You would think strangers have cried their eyes out more than I have or his wife. (*The Mother weeps.*)

WIFE. (*Pleading.*) Mother . . .

UNCLE. It's time you got used to all this. After all, Hirshke is not an ordinary person. He is a revolutionist.

MOTHER. Please, stop with your jokes.

UNCLE. But there you have it—it's not a joke. I really mean it. That's all you think it is—a joke and that's really the truth. He is a person who suffered a year in prison, then he was under parole for another year. With them he is a notorious person. He came here alone, by himself?

MOTHER. Escaped.

UNCLE. (*With wonder.*) From right under their eyes? Ach, this is some Hirshke!

WIFE. And what's happening here in Vilna, you probably know?

UNCLE. What a question! I know fear, fright! Governor Von Wahl—he is the most brutal of all! He beats, he tortures. For the Jews he's worse than Haman. And the men won't take it any more. With them it's coming to a head—the first of May.

WIFE. Exactly for the first of May he had to show up! (*She weeps.*)

UNCLE. Don't cry . . .

WIFE. They will arrest him again.

UNCLE. He should know that he has to be careful now. He will soon become a father . . . (*Wife guiltily moves into the kitchen.*) It's a blessed thing for a Jewish wife to be a mother. Nothing to be ashamed of. (*There is now the Wife's sobbing and Reb Zelig's chant.*)

MOTHER. God pity her. She's such a good child.

UNCLE. (*He edges to the door of Reb Zelig's chamber, and speaks as if to himself.*) A Jew sits and studies, and the whole world is lost to him. How different from the rest of us—we're always busy, busy, busy. (*To the Mother.*) Where is Mendel, his "learned" son?

MOTHER. Where should he be? Some one has to work. He's out with his pails of water.

UNCLE. That's how it goes. The father is such a studious man, and the son—a water-carrier and a simpleton, a moron. (*He pauses to savor Reb Zelig's chant.*) Ah, this is some melody—a pleasure, sweet as sugar. (*Raisel enters. She wears a fringed black blouse. She remains briefly in the kitchen with the Wife, and then enters the main room.*)

RAISEL. Good morning.

MOTHER. A good year to you, good year.

RAISEL. Well, how do you like your "guest?"

MOTHER. Thanks, daughter.

(*To the Uncle.*) This is Raisel. (*Raisel returns to the kitchen.*) She is the daughter of Abraham the harnessmaker. She fainted away for my Hirshke, worshiped the ground he walked on. And he—no! and always no. He wouldn't have her. And she, a good earner—a dressmaker. Well, now they are again comrades.

UNCLE. Also with "them," I suppose.

MOTHER. Well, what else, of course. But she's a good child. Always, every week, she used to come to ask what do we hear from Hirshke—always with love and so politely, to make our hearts feel easier. And some times she'd come with a bit of money to help out. Even now she probably loves Hirshke. (*Raisel comes back into the room, pulling the Wife by the hand along with her.*)

RAISEL. Enough crying already. Enough, dear. (*To the Mother.*) And how does he look, your "visitor?" Terrible?

WIFE. No, not that terrible. But in some ways strange.

MOTHER. He's become the silent one. Strange. You've never seen anything like it!

UNCLE. It's not so strange and not so terrible. Let him only again take a shoemaker's last in his hands, a hammer—(*To Raisel, with sarcasm.*) Will you really go today to the holiday procession of your "Torah?"

RAISEL. What do you mean?

UNCLE. I mean, er . . . how do they call it among you? Yes, with the Red Flag.

RAISEL. (*Laughs*) Yes, we're going.

UNCLE. Make Hirshke sit home today. Tell him, Raisel!

RAISEL. This I can't tell him.

UNCLE. Ach, is this a bunch! (*The Mother drags herself painfully to the bed and sits with difficulty on its edge where she moans quietly. Raisel conforts her.*)

RAISEL. Lie down, grandma.

MOTHER. How can I? (*Mendel, carrying two tubs of water yoked over his shoulders, enters. He is around 30 years old, with an overgrown, reddish beard, dressed in tatters, almost barefoot. His face is distorted by a constant grin that hides a compassionate person.*)

MENDEL. Hirshke? Is he here?

UNCLE. What is it, my brilliant sage?

WIFE. Don't bother him, uncle.

UNCLE. Are you finished with carrying the water all over, Mendel?

MENDEL. Through carrying—a cholera on all his sides!

UNCLE. Whom are you cursing?

MENDEL. Shepen. He thinks because he's rich . . . Seven pails of water I carried for him, and—and only a ten kopek piece. He should drop dead!

UNCLE. (*Mimics Mendel.*) "He should drop dead."

MENDEL. (*With sudden anger, to the Uncle.*) You only know to make fun! No! I'm not afraid any more of Vilna. And I won't keep quiet. I won't take it lying down!

UNCLE. (*Moving back, away from Mendel's outburst.*) Watch out—watch out! Just look how excited he got!

MENDEL. (*Suddenly calm.*) Is he well, Hirshke?

MOTHER. Yes, Mendel.

MENDEL. (*Joyfully laughing.*) Good! That's my comrade all right! (*To uncle.*) We went together to the same school. (*Reb Zelig appears on the threshold of his chamber. He is a thin old man, tall, with a white beard. He does not greet anyone, but stands at his door and angrily looks out.*)

ZELIG. Come in here! (*Mendel quickly obeys and goes past Zelig into the chamber. He is followed by the old man who slams the door shut. Soon his melodic chant will start again*)

UNCLE. That's some father for you—a bandit!

MOTHER. The old one is devoted to him. He looks after him, prepares his food, and even makes his bed, just like a mother.

RAISEL. What a drudgery for a person— a water-carrier! (*The Mother rises and crosses into the kitchen. Raisel follows her.*) What is it? Anything wrong? What's the matter?

MOTHER. In her condition, it's hard for her. Sit, why don't you sit down? (*The Mother speaks as if to herself.*) Not even a whole piece of underwear on her body. Not one real dress. (*Reb Zelig's voice continues. Hirsh Lekert enters. He is of medium height, with a black moustache, broad shoulders, firm steps; his face is emaciated but shows a straightforward, stubborn, earthy, and sincere* person. *His smile is youthful. Hirsh sees Raisel through the kitchen door and goes into the kitchen. Raisel embraces and kisses him.*)

UNCLE. (*Runs after Hirsh.*) So here you are, my fine fellow. How is my handsome nephew? (*Uncle embraces Hirsh, kisses him, and pulls him into the main room.*) We waited so long for you. (*The others follow the Uncle and Hirsh.*) Let me look at you. Such talk, all over, about you. Ach, the things they are saying!

HIRSH. What things?

UNCLE. That you don't dance anymore, that you don't jump anymore, that you even don't talk anymore.

HIRSH. And how is my aunt?

UNCLE. Thank God, she's well. (*Hirsh turns to his mother who has sat down on the bed again, with her head supported by the cushion.*)

HIRSH. What is it, mama?

MOTHER. It's my head, may it never happen to you.

HIRSH. (*To his wife.*) And what's wrong with you? You are so pale. (*He puts his hands on her shoulders and looks attentively at her. She is enlivened by his touch.*)

WIFE. It's nothing, Hirshke.

HIRSH. You've been crying again.

WIFE. No, oh no!

HIRSH. (*Cupping her face in his hands, pats her cheeks.*) You cry too much. (*His wife suddenly hides her face on his shoulder and sobs.*) Ah, this is not the way. This is not good.

WIFE. Please, I'm sorry. Excuse me.

HIRSH. Have you eaten already?

WIFE. We were waiting for you.

HIRSH. But why? (*He is suddenly uncomfortable, feeling that everyone's eyes are upon him. Raisel has retired to a corner, but has not taken her eyes off him. He turns to her.*) Nu, Raisel?

RAISEL. Nu, Lekert?

HIRSH. Why all of a sudden "Lekert" and not Hirshke?

RAISEL. I really don't know myself. You now seem to be someone else.

HIRSH. I can't forever remain happy-go-lucky Hirshke, Hirshke the young.

RAISEL. Aren't you sorry for this year in prison?

HIRSH. No—oh no!

RAISEL. I envy your every minute there. Were you there together with Comrades?

HIRSH. For a short while, at first. Then in a single cell.

RAISEL. All alone?

HIRSH. Yes, except for those few days around eight months ago when they let my wife come to visit me for two days.* But solitary is not so terrible. Our kind needs it, to think over one's life.

RAISEL. Nu, so did you think it over?

HIRSH. (*Diffidently.*) Yes, I tried to learn, you know, to read and write.

UNCLE. (*From the kitchen.*) Ach, is this a Hirshke! He knows already to read and write.

HIRSH. Uncle! (*To Raisel.*) And how about you? I hear you, too, are now really in the Movement.

RAISEL. (*Proudly.*) Yes!

HIRSH. But me you never let convince you? You were, for some reason, angry at me.

RAISEL. (*Joyously.*) Why remind me, Hirshke? It is not necessary. (*Enraptured.*) I am so envious of you. So envious . . . (*Quietly to him only.*) Are you coming today?

HIRSH. (*Aside to Raisel.*) How can you doubt it? Of course!

RAISEL. It's time I went. We'll see each other later.

HIRSH. I want to talk with you. There's lots to talk about. I hear things aren't exactly a holiday here.

RAISEL. Not now. (*Then to all.*) Have a good day. (*Raisel leaves.*)

UNCLE. (*Approaches Hirsh and taps him on the shoulder.*) Listen, my good friend. Your apron you have. So take it and put it on. You'll sit at the bench in my house, you'll take the needle, you'll take the cobbler's thread, and we, both of us, just like that, we'll hammer away.

---

* Allusion to the wife's visit is not in the original. I interpolated this visit to provide for the wife's pregnancy, not otherwise indicated by Leivick.

HIRSH. No. I will go to a boot factory.

UNCLE. Why to a factory? In my house, there at your very own work bench, it'll be a wonderful feeling . . .

HIRSH. I'll go to a factory.

UNCLE. You won't be mistreated by me.

HIRSH. No. I'll go to a factory—there —with fellow workers.

UNCLE. (*Lost.*) Ach, what a Hirshke! (*He starts to gather his things quickly.*) Ah, well, be well all of you . . . (*Uncle starts to leave, hesitates, then puts his arms on Hirsh's shoulders, looks into his eyes, and begs him.*) Listen sometimes to your uncle. I beg you to do as I ask this once—don't go to the demonstration today.

HIRSH. (*Noncommittal.*) Uncle . . .

UNCLE. Ach, dear God in heaven . . . (*Uncle, disappointed, leaves. Wife seats herself on bed at the Mother's feet. Zelig's chant is heard.*)

HIRSH. If all I'm going to have is mourning and weeping over me, I might as well get out and ride back where I came from.

MOTHER. (*Rising.*) Nu, what do you expect us to do, my son? We are lonely.

HIRSH. And what should I do? Tell me! You must understand—that's what I am—a revolutionist.

WIFE. Not everyone just creeps into the fire.

HIRSH. At each step there is a fire. What do you mean I creep? I go— I must.

WIFE. You can't be changed anymore. We can't convince you otherwise. But why can't you be careful? They will send you to Siberia.

MOTHER. Do you have to sacrifice your life? (*Hirsh remains silent.*) Why are you silent?

HIRSH. (*Agitated.*) It is hard for me to talk when you cry. So, what can I do? You must understand, I am now a revolutionist—with my whole heart, mama . . .

MOTHER. And you will make the whole world over, Hirshke?

HIRSH. You will see, mama. In a few years from now, the whole world will be free. First Russia, then the whole world will follow. You'll see, there'll be no more poverty—the rich people with all people will be equal. And no one will ever hurt any one else. You will see, mama, only a few more years, no more. Let us only get rid of the Tzar.

MOTHER. (*Frightened.*) Hush! Oh woe is me. Please talk quietly.

HIRSH. Don't worry, mama. Nobody hears.

MOTHER. Wiser heads than yours couldn't change anything.

HIRSH. Because till now the working people kept quiet. But now—-they are rising . . .

MOTHER. (*Directly to him.*) Have you forgotten that a child is coming? Why did you ever have her come to Ekaterinaslav, eh?

WIFE. My heart is collapsing.

HIRSH. What's the matter with you? I'm not dying yet.

WIFE. I am afraid. Look how I'm trembling in fear.

MOTHER. (*Seizes his hand. She, too, is trembling.*) Hirshke! (*Both women wail.*) (*Shuddering.*)

HIRSH. What's all this? Mourning over me already? (*Zelig's voice provides the obligato. Enter Yoshke Boyer, Fayvel Shlosser, Rachmilke Balagule, all robust young men, fighters, Hirsh Lekert's former comrades, members of the "Bund," activists.*)

RACHMILKE. Good morning. (*The new-comers stand near the door as the greeting is repeated among all present. The men sense the heavy atmosphere in the room.*)

WIFE. A good year.

HIRSH. Why are you all cluttering the door? Come in?

MOTHER. (*Throws herself into the bed again.*) Who's here? Who are they?

HIRSH. My comrades, mama.

RACHMILKE. Enjoy your new guest.

MOTHER. Just don't take him away from us.

WIFE. Please, sit down.

FAYVEL. (*Aside to Hirsh.*) Things don't look too good here. Maybe we had better go.

HIRSH. Sh, sh. Sit a while.

YOSHKE. I like to have a good talk.

HIRSH. Nu, that suits me.

FAYVEL. Tell us more about the prison, about Ekaterinaslav.

HIRSH. Not now. Maybe later. Right now I want to know what's doing here in Vilna, with our local Bund.

YOSHKE. What could we tell you? To put it mildly, it's not good. As a matter of fact, it's bad. Von Wahl makes it intolerable.

FAYVEL. He keeps on arresting right and left, no one is safe. As for the movement—it's really in a bad way. Our best men are jailed, and those that are left—

RACHMILKE. They won't let us raise a hand. What are we supposed to do? Mumble a prayer?

YOSHKE. Let me tell you, no matter how you look at it, it stinks. (*In a hushed voice to Hirsh.*) Even the committee itself is afraid, to put it mildly.

RACHMILKE. (*Exasperated.*) You mustn't go here, this one you mustn't touch, that one you must spare! Bah! You remember how we used to do it in the old days? How we used to fix those policemen or gendarmes all right, or smash the glass windows of a jailhouse, or land a few on a strike breaker or his "cute" boss. Ah, yes. it was a pleasure the way you used to toss one so that smoke would come out. And now—better don't ask. The only thing to do is to take your hands and soak them in a barrel of nice words . . . bring out a bottle, Hirshke—to hell with that damn Von Wahl!

FAYVEL. What do you mean "a bottle" all of a sudden? That's a nice how-do-you-do! How can our front line battalion be drunk on the First of May.

YOSHKE. When your heart is sad and depressed . . . (*Zelig's voice is now more pronounced.*)

RACHMILKE. What the . . . what's that?

HIRSH. That's Reb Zelig at his studies.

YOSHKE. Our front line battalion is as good as dead, to put it mildly.

FAYVEL. Von Wahl has saturated all of Vilna with soldiers, with bayonets, Cossacks with ammunition—and we, today we will even be unarmed, without weapons.

HIRSH. What do you mean? Explain it.

FAYVEL. That is the decision of the organization. Our own chairman of the committee insisted on that point.

HIRSH. (*Outraged.*) Isaak?

FAYVEL. He was the most stubborn and we couldn't convince him otherwise. Even Usishkin couldn't get him to budge. Usishkin wanted us all to be armed.

YOSHKE. Lately, Isaak is afraid of a fly speck on the wall.

FAYVEL. And when we tell him something, he has only one answer: "I don't want any blood."

HIRSH. But what does the rest of the committee say?

FAYVEL. The whole committee wants today's demonstration to be peaceful. Nu, good! nu, good! Even Usishkin went along and agreed. But the point is, will Von Wahl be peaceful?

YOSHKE. (*Sarcastically.*) Oh yes, he's a man of peace—with two wagon-loads of rods he had hauled in from the woods. They're all prepared and ready in the prison yards—ready for our behinds, to put it mildly.

FAYVEL. Whips, sabers, rifles—these are not enough for that monster. He also has to punish us on our naked bodies.

HIRSH. It's an affliction of the devil only knows what evil spirit!

RACHMILKE. I won't take it lying down! I'm going to show them!

FAYVEL. (*Derisively.*) Again you're making a stand—again you're going to show them?

RACHMILKE. You'll see! I'll make it, alright! Bah, these intelligentzia, I'll show them all right. That committee will have to listen to me or I'll break their bones, I will.

FAYVEL. Stop screaming. Since when does screaming help?

YOSHKE. Von Wahl is out to kill today.

There'll be murder, to put it mildly.

RACHMILKE. I don't intend to go to the demonstration without my revolver . . .

FAYVEL. (*Cautioning him.*) Keep quiet! (*To Hirsh.*) And since Ruchel has been together with Isaak, she's become as big a coward as he. What a pair!

HIRSH. Ruchel . . . with Isaak?

FAYVEL. You didn't know it?

HIRSH. (*Very disturbed, paces back and forth around the room.*) Who would expect such a thing in Vilna. And here I was afraid I wouldn't catch up with the advances our Vilna Bund had made—who knew how far you had gone ahead . . .

FAYVEL. Vain thoughts! Let me tell you something worse—our Bund has been cursed with a catrastophe—the plague of Minsk Zubotovshina.

HIRSH. What does that mean? I don't understand . . .

FAYVEL. You haven't heard about Zubutov yet, but you will. He's the wolf of Minsk, a colonel in the gendarmerie, in sheep's clothing. He poses as a friend of the workers, organizes them into so-called unions under the protection of our "merciful" tzar. But in reality, his intentions are something else: to fool them into crawling into his trap, that we should make peace under his bloody domination. There you have it—a new darkness and slavery, and then what? They'll probably throw us a little larger crumb of bread.

HIRSH. How can they be fooled like that?

FAYVEL. You'd think that even Isaak . . .

HIRSH. (*Contemptuously.*) Isaak . . . ? (*Mendel emerges, with his yoke of tubs, from Zelig's chamber.*)

MENDEL. (*Sees Hirsh and rushes to him with great joy.*) Hirshke!

HIRSH. (*Momentarily bewildered, embraces Mendel.*) How are you, Mendel?

MENDEL. (*Grabs Hirsh's hand.*) Good, Hirshke. Let me kiss you! (*Mendel kisses Hirsh.*)

HIRSH. Still on the job carrying water, I see, ha?

MENDEL. What else? Sure.

HIRSH. And how is your papa?

MENDEL. You can hear for yourself—he's studying.

HIRSH. He's still a harsh father?

MENDEL. Yes, he doesn't change. (*Laughs broadly.*) I know where you were—in prison.

HIRSH. And you are not afraid of me—a dangerous criminal?

MENDEL. No. I like you more because of this. (*The other men laugh.*)

HIRSH. But anyhow—don't tell anybody you saw me. Say nothing about me.

MENDEL. I know—life is not safe. (*Starts leaving, then turns to Hirsh.*) Will you take me along with you to the woods, Hirshke?

HIRSH. The woods? What woods?

MENDEL. To a meeting. (*The others laugh. Mendel turns fiercely on them.*) Why are you laughing? Look, Hirshke is not laughing at me. He was in prison—he knows about life. That's why he doesn't laugh at me.

FAYVEL. He speaks like a man.

MENDEL. (*Stamping his foot.*) I am a man, too. You think I don't know anything—I know! Today there will be a demonstration. The murderer has already sent out two wagon loads of riders, damn his soul! (*Zelig appears at the door to his chamber.*)

ZELIG. Go already. (*Mendel quickly leaves. Zelig stands at his door and surveys all present. Suddenly he goes to Hirsh Lekert and extends his hand.*) Sholem Aleichem, stranger. Welcome

HIRSH. (*Embarrassed, extends his hand and they shake.*) Aleichem Sholem. How are you, Reb Zelig? (*Reb Zelig pulls his hand back and retreats to his door, then turns to face Hirsh.*)

REB ZELIG. How should I be? At least my chamber is not a prison. (*Reb Zelig exits to his room, slams the door, and again loses himself in his chant. The others look at each other in surprise.*)

FAYVEL. There's a queer duck for you.

(*Meanwhile Hirsh's wife has prepared the table, and brought the steaming pot of potatoes, which she pours out upon a plate.*)

HIRSH. I haven't time to eat now. We have to go. (*The men have risen and gathered near the door. The Mother rises.*)

WIFE. But eat a little something first.

HIRSH. (*Crossing to the door*) Don't wait for me. Go ahead and eat.

MOTHER. Hirshele!

HIRSH. I must go. (*Hirsh exits. Mother collapses, Wife sits forlornly at the table, alone, as the steam from the potatoes rises.*)

CURTAIN

SCENE II

Ruchel and Isaak's room. It is simply but tastefully furnished. Isaak, in student attire; Raisel, Wolfke, and Usishkin are engaged in an intense argument with Isaak who stands apart from the others, biting his nails in anger. Ruchel paces about, muttering and directly arguing. Usishkin, a former Talmudic student, dressed in tatters, carries on his shoulders a basket of books for sale. He is a constantly enthusiastic youth, coughs frequently, and is a member of the committee.

USISHKIN. Come, come, Isaak, anger neither becomes you nor helps matters.

ISAAK. It becomes me better than the rags you pull over you and call clothes—and those shallow romances you call books and carry all over—nonsense for servant girls.

RAISEL. What's wrong with servant girls?

RUCHEL. Enough already, for heaven's sake!

USISHKIN. Nonsense you call it. Please tell me why "nonsense," please? (*He pulls some books out of the basket and reads some of the titles.*) "The Lessons of Life," by Lunkiewitch; "The Time of the Grandfathers";

"Die Shtriemel"; "Bontche Schweig" —these aren't just "story" books, brothers. As for myself and my rags . . . let that go for some other time, or maybe never. I hate to talk about myself. Among the poor people, from out of their depths, I find everything—everything. And about myself I can forget. It's the same thing, you know, whether once in the Talmudic Academy or now in the Bund. And you, too, should forget about yourself once in a while. You're so angry that you don't hear what you are saying. Look at me— I'm not angry. Today is the first of May—why should I destroy my holiday spirit?

ISAAK. I have the holiday spirit as much as you have.

WOLFKE. It's already five o'clock and the demonstration will begin at seven. It's time we got started. Let's go.

RAISEL. (*Upset.*) I never expected such talk from comrade Isaak.

RUCHEL. My dear Raisel, let it alone. We've had enough of this.

ISAAK. (*Flaring up anew.*) Not enough!

RAISEL. (*In tears.*) He keeps torturing us like this—all day long.

WOLFKE. He should be strengthening our spirits. Instead . . .

USISHKIN. (*Exasperated, turns to Raisel.*) He's become a real riddle to me. One word doesn't stick to the other, as though he's saying things to spite us.

ISAAK. You know very well it's not in spite. And you all know why I am against today's demonstration.

RAISEL. But it's been decided. The committee called it.

WOLFKE. And we should go joyfully. You have no right to stand against . . .

ISAAK. Rights I have forever.

USISHKIN. No, not forever, not without limit. Comrades Wolfke and Raisel may think—God knows what.

ISAAK. I want them to know, especially them, the best of all the masses. I want them to think, to understand, to appreciate.

RAISEL. Here we are, loaded down with packs of proclamations that Usishkin himself entrusted us with so we would distribute them tonight at the demonstration. Why do you lay stones on our hearts?

ISAAK. Because the stones are already here, whether you like it or not. The stones are here.

USISHKIN. We know all that. We know all about the taste of Von Wahl, the Cossacks, prison, Siberia. That's why, and because . . .

WOLFKE. We are ready.

ISAAK. I'm telling you Vilna will have a blood bath today.

USISHKIN. Vilna has already been bathed in blood.

ISAAK. A demonstration is not everything.

USISHKIN. Nothing ever stopped us. We were never afraid of rifles or prisons. I listen to your talk, Isaak, and I wonder . . . never have I heard words like yours in the Bund.

RAISEL. My God—Oh my God!

USISHKIN. Do I have to tell you how Von Wahl has us caught in a vise —how he'll choke us? Our best people are condemned, in the prisons. The masses have become resigned— disappointed and disorganized. They don't know whom to believe any more. Any spy, informer, or a Zubutovnik can come in and win over all these souls from us. Meanwhile the whole Jewish population is being uprooted, torn apart by persecution, and everybody asks, "Why do we keep silent?"

ISAAK. So . . . let them ask.

USISHKIN. And everybody is thinking: it's all over, the Bund is dead. And how about our efforts to create brotherhood? Is that dead, too? The brotherhood between the Polish and Lithuanian workers? That's why today is important—to warn Von Wahl and to show him our unity is alive!

ISAAK. The Polish and Lithuanian workers will stay away.

WOLFKE. What do you mean? They will come!

RAISEL. (*To Isaak.*) You're the only one who makes obstacles!

ISAAK. They will not come. And the fact that we live, Von Wahl knows that too well. For whom, then, did he prepare his militia and their rods?

USISHKIN. Do you want me to tell you what's on my mind?

ISAAK. Go ahead, tell me.

USISHKIN. For the sake of our comradeship I'll keep quiet. (*In despair he bolts for the door.*)

RUCHEL. (*Intercepting him and blocking his way.*) I beg you . . .

USISHKIN. (*Deeply agitated.*) You talk to me about patience, about restraint. How do you know when to be patient and when to be in a hurry? When it is the right time to lead the masses in a demonstration and when a demonstration is impossible to achieve anything? And when one should be afraid of a wild animal of a governor and when one should show no fear?

ISAAK. I listen to myself, and then I know when and what.

USISHKIN. To yourself? Who are you that the destiny of everyone should depend on your moods? Tell me straight out: You are afraid, today, because of blood. And what will be tomorrow, and after tomorrow? Will blood tomorrow suddenly become water? Or maybe you can tell me clearly that you have another way, another plan maybe? (*Isaak remains silent.*) So answer! (*There is a strained silence.*) What's the purpose of all this talk? A decision by our organization is holy—and the decision of the masses is still holier. Our workers don't theorize. They are always ready, come what may!

RAISEL. We stayed awake, working all night, sewing the flags, Ruchel and I. What didn't we stitch into those flags! Everything—waiting for this day when we'll unfurl the flags and they will fly over our heads. Nu, the day is here, and Wolfke, our flag bearer, stands without any spirit, and we, too, stand with him . . . just stand and weep as though our flags were already lying dead. (*She cries and seeks comfort in Ruchel's arms.*)

RUCHEL. We've had enough arguing. Usishkin, don't go away. We'll make tea. You want something to eat, too, no?

USISHKIN. No. I'm not staying.

RUCHEL. Just look at you. Don't tell me you're not hungry. And look how you're coughing.

USISHKIN. Not important . . . just listen to your logic. To spill blood on the First of May—oh no! That's out! But to hunger—to cough, that we're allowed on the First of May like any other day. (*He laughs ironically.*)

RUCHEL. Nu, Usishkin?

WOLFKE. I don't see why all these arguments. We must go to the demonstration, be part of it and that's all there is to it. We have to carry the flag, hold it high and strong, and that's all there is to it!

USISHKIN. (*Slaps Wolfke on the shoulders with enthusiasm.*) You're right—that's it! Yes—let's go! (*He leads the way out as Raisel and Wolfke leave with him. Isaak throws himself face downward onto the divan.*)

RUCHEL. What's the matter with you?

ISAAK. Oh, just leave me alone.

RUCHEL. I tried not to butt in, but . . .

ISAAK. I think I'm going crazy today . . .

RUCHEL. (*Trying to comfort him.*) Isaak . . .

ISAAK. I've never been so full of doubts, I'm being tortured by them . . .

RUCHEL. So tell me. You know you can tell me everything. Why?

ISAAK. I'm losing my reason, going out of my mind.

RUCHEL. What happened all of a sudden to make you so unsure, to question our . . .

ISAAK. Not all of a sudden. I've been tormented by these doubts for a long time, just eating away inside of me. I kept quiet and didn't tell you because I thought it will pass.

RUCHEL. You're just over-tired. You've been under a terrible strain, and not enough sleep. No wonder . . .

ISAAK. No, it's not that at all. Something else. (*His whole body is convulsed in a shiver.*) It's about tonight—this very night . . .

RUCHEL. Look how you're shivering . . .

ISAAK. Everything inside me has turned over—topsy-turvy. I realize it's not proper, it's not honest to keep up the spirit of others while alone, in my heart, I hear these doubts— oh Ruchel, it's frightening—terrible.

RUCHEL. It is that—really terrible.

ISAAK. We're the leaders, hah? Who gave us the right?

RUCHEL. It's a good thing we also have other leaders who don't torment themselves and eat their hearts out like you do. Take Usishkin . . .

ISAAK. There must be, somewhere, a different truth.

RUCHEL. But first, there must be a healthy mood.

ISAAK. (*Beside himself with resentment.*) And I am, as far as you're concerned, I'm sick. And you—you're so sure that the demonstration must take place?

RUCHEL. (*In tears.*) Either we have it today, or we don't need it—ever. (*A knock on the door. Ruchel quickly composes herself and opens the door to Hirsh Lekert; he enters. Ruchel is overwhelmed by surprise, then rushes joyfully to him with outstretched arms.*) Hirsh Lekert! What a guest! Isaak, look who's here!

ISAAK. (*Rises and warmly shakes hands with Hirsh.*) Ah . . . ! (*Hirsh, overcome, half ashamed and fearful, stands at the door.*)

RUCHEL. Lekert, dear, why stand at the door? Come in, such a beloved guest. (*She is flustered with excitement, but joyfully leads him into the room. Hirsh is uncomfortable and edges his way back toward the door.*)

ISAAK. What goes on? Where are you going? You're not leaving already?

HIRSH. (*Awkwardly.*) I'll come some other time.

RUCHEL. Why—you just came . . . ?

HIRSH. (*Sits.*) Well . . . er . . . ach, let it be.

RUCHEL. There is so much we want to hear from you—so much. Isaak, just look how much he changed. Imagine! He sits down and keeps his mouth shut.

HIRSH. (*After a heavy pause, stands up.*) I did not come here to be your guest, for a social visit.

RUCHEL. What are you talking about?

HIRSH. I want to know if it's true?

RUCHEL. What?

HIRSH. That you don't want the revolution?

RUCHEL. What are you talking about?

HIRSH. (*Speaking with more force.*) I came to tell you that I don't like it . . .

RUCHEL. What are you talking about?

HIRSH. You see, I know. I know everything.

RUCHEL. What do you know?

HIRSH. There are many things I don't like, but the main thing, that our action detail will not be armed today, that I don't like at all. (*Isaak bursts out laughing.*)

HIRSH. (*Inflamed.*) What are you laughing about?

ISAAK. When did you arrive in Vilna?

HIRSH. What's the difference? And what if it was only yesterday?

ISAAK. (*Also aroused, angry.*) And who sent you to give us advice?

HIRSH. I come on my own, uninvited.

ISAAK. So. That's a nice how-do-you-do, believe me. What do you say, Ruchel? Each member of the masses will come here to dictate to us.

HIRSH. Each one may come. and speak the truth.

ISAAK. What truth?

HIRSH. What one? There is only one truth!

ISAAK. I can't believe it. It's like I'm living in a dream world.

HIRSH. The action detail must be armed today! The only way to fight the Tzarist regime is with arms!

ISAAK. Don't use such a tone with me. Who do you think you are? Whom do you represent?

HIRSH. The masses.

ISAAK. That's just great. Ruchel, please, you listen to him . . . (*Isaak rushes out. Hirsh tries to follow him, but Ruchel intercepts him.*)

RUCHEL. Please, I want you to stay here—just for a few minutes.

HIRSH. There's no time, I must get to the demonstration.

RUCHEL. There is yet enough time. If you like, we'll go together.

HIRSH. (*Stands near door and gazes at her.*) Somehow today all of us have tears in our eyes.

RUCHEL. How does it happen that a person who has not been seen for two years comes in with such greetings?

HIRSH. I did not come as a guest.

RUCHEL. (*Leading him by the hand.*) Come, dear Lekert, that's not the way. Suppose, just let's imagine, that you came here just to visit me alone. (*She leads him to a chair; he sits.*) You escaped from Ekaterinoslav?

HIRSH. (*Reluctantly.*) What difference does that make?

RUCHEL. Not even once did you write us, not one word.

HIRSH. I don't know how to write. You know that.

RUCHEL. But in prison they teach it. You could have learned.

HIRSH. What's the purpose of all this? What difference does it make?

RUCHEL. We'll be able to do it now, yes? You'll become a member of our circle—you'll learn.

HIRSH. No.

RUCHEL. Why? (*Hirsh remains silent.*) At least, give me a smile. You look so glum. I remember your cheerful smile, the way you used to smile at me. And say straight out, "I like you, Ruchel—" or, don't you love me anymore?

HIRSH. And let's suppose I do. Now our kind are not supposed to give in to such things.

RUCHEL. What things?

HIRSH. Oh, making love and such involvements. Our people must have clear heads. So, to you I won't come. No!

RUCHEL. This is what they taught you in prison, eh?

HIRSH. Yes.

RUCHEL. (*Flirting, taunting.*) And you didn't long for me?

HIRSH. (*Uncomfortable, mutters.*) Longed for you . . . didn't long for you . . . what difference does it make? (*Scowling and impatient, rises.*) I can see that the revolution is furthest from your thoughts.

RUCHEL. What do you mean?

HIRSH. You are in no hurry, I can see, to get on with the revolution.

RUCHEL. And the revolution depends on us?

HIRSH. If not us, then on whom?

RUCHEL. Patience, my dear. We must wait.

HIRSH. Isaak, you, and the others— just like turtles you creep along. But the working people can't wait.

RUCHEL. You are wonderful, like a big baby. But you don't have to be so angry.

HIRSH. I am not angry.

RUCHEL. That's good.

HIRSH. To tell the truth, I really did want to see you. But our people, we must not weaken, sighing and mooning. When one lives in a basement, one knows his place—in the ground.

RUCHEL. I don't understand.

HIRSH. When one has a wife, a wife that looks at you with pain in her eyes, and a mother who cries over her cursed life—then what? So, to you I won't come any more. We are not equals.

RUCHEL. But—I love you as a wonderful comrade . . .

HIRSH. No! A brother must know to clench his fist like this—and then smite himself on the head. (*Hirsh demonstrates as he clenches his fist and bangs the side of his head with it.*)

RUCHEL. Please, tell me, how did you find things at home? Did they change much; what's new there? Are you getting along well with your wife? Tell me, please.

HIRSH. What can I tell you? What means this "getting along well?" She is a good person. And she suffers. We live in a basement—the garden of Eden it's not. What are you driving at? Do you mean, do I hate my wife?

RUCHEL. No, I don't mean that.

HIRSH. Soon she will give birth to a child—there, in the basement. And I will be—who knows?

RUCHEL. Where should you be?

HIRSH. (*Bursting forth, almost incoherently.*) Yes, oh yes! What can one say, what can one think? They suffer such pains—all on account of me. And the whole world suffers. Our whole world lies down at the heel in the basement. And what am I— a special piece of fine leather for the upper part of the boot? No, it's not that, comrade Ruchel, not that at all.

RUCHEL. Go on—speak!

HIRSH. Take a piece of raw boot leather—first it has to be washed and then well stretched. And a person? The same thing. And if a person sat in prison, what of it? A political prisoner is already something special, ha? And what does it mean, and of what use am I, ha? One must be pure, one must redeem himself.

RUCHEL. You are a good, pure person.

HIRSH. No, I know better than that. I was a crude, vicious ruffian all my life. I had time to think things over in prison. In that way, prison was good for me. Now I know that —that—you understand . . . What was I? A fighter . . . a brawler . . . free with my hands. With my hat tipped on a side, I gallivanted all over. And now—what? Again to become a brawler, a hooligan, ha? Run after an injured pig, and nothing more? Punch, hit, swagger, and show off my big muscles? No, no!

Now I know that with our whole life, we must with our entire soul, with our heads we must give up everything—yes—no holding back! We must lay it on the line, that's what should be done. Let's know that this is in earnest, it's not child's play—let's not say it's only a little dance, because . . . if not . . . what the sense . . . why must people be condemned to a basement? You understand? Yes—let them give it back—everything—everything—

RUCHEL. (*Puts her hands around his neck and gazes into his eyes.*) Hirsh —Hirsh Lekert . . .

HIRSH. You understand? You're lying on your cot in prison at night, and all of a sudden you hear a voice— forgiven! (*From outside violent beating of drums is heard.*) Here comes Von Wahl to greet us!

RUCHEL. (*Embraces him with fear.*) What will happen today?

HIRSH. (*Holding her off.*) You are afraid? And I go forward with joy to meet him! (*Hirsh exits.*)

CURTAIN

SCENE III

(*Evening, the sun has just set. The synagogue yard. No people are seen to be going to the evening prayers. An occasional Jew hurries by and disappears into a doorway. A Blind Man and his guide stand on the synagogue steps.*)

BLIND MAN. Where are all the Jews today? Curse them all.

GUIDE. You know where.

BLIND MAN. What if I know! Not even the miserable poor are to be seen.

GUIDE. Not a one.

BLIND MAN. Here we are, with the First of May—that's all we need! Socialists, curse them. Are all the stores really closed? (*Pause.*) When will it start?

GUIDE. Soon, I suppose.

BLIND MAN. But the evening prayers —why don't they come to the prayers?

GUIDE. They tremble in fear to go out into the streets—full of cossacks.

BLIND ONE. Damn them! That's what they do—they scare all the Jews from coming to the evening prayers. I didn't even make forty kopecks today. In the middle of the week they arrange strikes! Damn all of them! With red flags, against the Tzar, no less, and they yell curses in their language. They have their own language, damn them all—did you ever see a red flag?

GUIDE. How would I ever . . . ?

BLIND MAN. So, there's going to be a big fight maybe?

GUIDE. He'll give it to them, all right, that governor. They'll get a real bath.

BLIND MAN. Damn him too!

GUIDE. (*Alarmed.*) Sh . . . sh . . .

BLIND MAN. What do I care for any of them? So if there is a Tzar it doesn't bother me . . . but the evening prayers . . . the evening prayers . . .

GUIDE. He prepared two wagon loads of rods for them. They'll get a real taste of them, and in the proper parts . . . (*Hirsh, Raisel, and Fayvel enter. Hirsh has overheard the Guide.*)

HIRSH. Better you should bite your stupid tongue.

BLIND MAN. What rotten luck now? Who is there?

FAYVEL. (*Contemptuously.*) Idiots!

HIRSH. (*To Guide.*) Where did you hear this?

GUIDE. People talk, so we hear. What do we know?

HIRSH. Do you know how to read?

GUIDE. So I know how to read—so what?

HIRSH. (*Thrusting a proclamation upon the guide.*) Here, read this. After you read it you'll know whom you have to curse.

BLIND MAN. What is he giving you, ha? Don't take it!

GUIDE. (*Holding leaflet. He starts to*

shake in fear.) Oy—take it, take it back. I'm afraid—they'll put me in chains.

RAISEL. Leave them alone; let them go.

GUIDE. (*Grabs the Blind Man.*) Let's go, Moyshe. If we're found with them we'll be sent to Siberia.

BLIND MAN. Oh, my affliction—and now this woe—woe is me! (*Blind Man and Guide quickly and fearfully exit. A few Jews hurry by in the background, as though pursued by demons, and disappear in various doorways.*)

FAYVEL. Look. Just look how they steal by, how afraid they are.

RAISEL. Why worry about them? They-'re going to the synagogue. So, let them go. Here, Hirshke, I have this package for you. (*She hands him a pack of leaflets, which he takes.*)

HIRSH. Good, good.

RAISEL. We'll spread it like beautiful snow over the theater later. For the time being, hide it somewhere.

FAYVEL. How about your revolver? Have you got it?

HIRSH. Yes.

RAISEL. You intend to disobey the decision of our organization?

FAYVEL. We won't shoot, so don't worry. But we can't tell what will happen. Besides, we must guard our flag bearer.

RAISEL. It doesn't seem right, Hirshke.

HIRSH. That's right. But the decision is a terrible one.

RAISEL. At least be careful. We will meet here later. (*Raisel exits. More Jews hurry by and into the synagogue for the evening prayer. Most appear to be fortified by their faith, and, therefore, have more self-assurance.*

Mendel suddenly appears with his tubs swinging on his yoke as he starts crossing the courtyard. He sees Hirsh Lekert and rushes to him with outstretched arms and a beaming smile.)

MENDEL. Take me with you, Hirshke! I want to go to the demonstration!

HIRSH. Why, you're not afraid!

MENDEL. Mendel is not afraid.

HIRSH. Here, you know how to read. See for yourself. (*Hirsh hands Mendel a leaflet.*)

MENDEL. (*Eagerly.*) Sure! Oho, thank you, Hirshke.

HIRSH. Hide it.

MENDEL. I know, I know. (*He hides leaflet in his bosom.*) They'll never find it on me. I am not afraid of anyone in Vilna.

HIRSH. How about our spreading a few leaflets around the synagogue yard, eh?

FAYVEL. We are not allowed to do that. Those were not our instructions—we weren't asked to do it.

HIRSH. Then only a few leaflets. (*Hirsh passes a few leaflets to the passing Jews, who become terrified— some flee, some of the more substantial oppose and threaten Hirsh and Fayvel. Others who have the leaflets thrust upon them furtively look at them and quickly discard them, and two of them take the leaflets and hasten away. Mendel observes it all and reacts with joy. Some of the Jews express their outrage.*)

FIRST JEW. They'll bring calamity on their own people—self destructive Jews!

SECOND JEW. The streets are not enough for them? Here they have to come?

FIRST JEW. Don't you dare touch these—it's forbidden!

THIRD JEW. It's not so terrible. It wouldn't hurt just to look into—just to see what's written there.

FIRST JEW. (*To Fayvel.*) On account of you, we Jews suffer.

FAYVEL. Nu, so run to the governor, grovel and flatter him, that hangman. Tpfui!

SECOND JEW. Vilna is being destroyed!

THIRD JEW. (*To the other two Jews.*) Just for curiosity's sake, take a look at this leaflet. What language! I tell you it's burning fire!

FIRST JEW. Feh, it's not legal. Here we'll stamp it out! (*He throws the leaflet to the ground and rubs it out with his feet.*)

HIRSH. (*Livid.*) Don't! Stop that!

FIRST JEW. So, maybe you want to make a fight here?

HIRSH. But you are already starting to fight—

SECOND JEW. We have this small corner for ourselves, the sanctuary of a synagogue yard only—and you have to take this away from us . . .

THIRD JEW. It's not right, we're Jews after all—it's not right to talk this way. It's words, just read it here— bloody words. (*Zelig enters.*)

ZELIG. Evening prayers, everybody!

A JEW. We have no minion—there aren't enough Jews at the synagogue.

ZELIG. What do you mean—not enough! One Jew is enough. (*He sees Hirsh and shrieks at him.*) You come even here?

FAYVEL. (*To Hirsh.*) Let's get out of here—who needs this?

HIRSH. (*To Zelig.*) Why are you yelling?

ZELIG. Who then should yell? They, the rich ones? (*He points to the other synagogue-going Jews.*)

FIRST JEW. Feh, Reb Zelig.

ZELIG. Woe to the sinners, and twice woe to the persecutors!

FIRST JEW. The scholar and the eccentric—the sacred and profane.

ZELIG. The rich one and the scabs.

FIRST JEW. Tpfui. (*He runs into the synagogue, with his fellow worshipers laughing as they follow him.*)

FAYVEL. I told you, let's get out of here. (*Fayvel and Hirsh exit.*)

ZELIG. (*To Mendel.*) What are you doing here?

MENDEL. You see—I'm carrying water, papa.

ZELIG. Home—go home.

MENDEL. I want to stay here.

ZELIG. I said go home!

MENDEL. Today, I don't obey you.

ZELIG. What?

MENDEL. I want to see them wave the red flag.

ZELIG. What kind of a flag?

MENDEL. And I must guard Hirshke.

ZELIG. *You* guard *him*?

MENDEL. I like him.

ZELIG. (*Pained and helpless.*) FO-O-O-O-L!

(*Zelig exits into the synagogue.*)

MENDEL. I'm coming. (*He enthusiastically exits in direction of Hirsh. The scene now takes on a holiday mood: workers arrive, dressed for the First of May. Some men carry canes, women are in varicolored blouses with red dominating. Youth predominates. Although most arrive from one side and leave in the direction of Hirsh and Fayvel, some remain and cluster in circles. Leaders urge them to move on. One of the leaders is Usishkin, with his basket load of books on his shoulders. He urges lingerers to move. Yoshke and Rachmilke and Raisel, accompanied by a few girls come in. Wolfke arrives, with a furled flag under his coat. There is much movement, with Usishkin ubiquitously stirring various groups as he appears and disappears while he gives orders. Local Jews and those in front of the synagogue briefly look on in wonder, then hastily run indoors and lock their doors. A Demonstrator reads to others.*)

A DEMONSTRATOR. "Never has the Tzarist regime shown its viciousness, its bestiality and torture so openly. Never before have we, the Jewish workers, been forced to endure the most terrible tortures from the bloody Tzarist jackals, never before have they thrown masses of us into prison, sent us to Siberia when we only tried to correct our miserable conditions . . . "

USISHKIN. (*Running to the Speaker.*) Comrades, don't gather in groups. Keep moving. Go to the German Street—comrades, everybody to the German Street . . . (*He succeeds in getting them to move on, all except the color guard.*) Are all of us here of the action detail?

RACHMILKE. We are all here. What else?

YOSHKE. Who has an ax?

USISHKIN. It will arrive in time. (*A man saunters by. Usishkin speaks to him.*) Go to the German Street. No noise, no demonstrations yet. Wait till we unfurl the flag. And don't listen to ridiculous rumors. Keep up your spirit—keep up your courage! (*The passerby and Usishkin leave. The scene becomes a section of the city. Many people are marching. There is much movement, much color, great excitement. Out of the din, some voices are distinguished.*)

FIRST. They say the Polish workers are not coming.

SECOND. Neither are the Lithuanians.

THIRD. That gives the hangman a good excuse—only Jews.

FOURTH. They will slaughter us today.

FIFTH. So what? Tpfui—anyone who is afraid can go home!

SIXTH. Yes, we'll let him know, that hangman—only Jews, yes Jews, always first!

SEVENTH. And we are proud to be the first!

EIGHTH. Who are those people over there? They look suspicious. They're spies!

NINTH. The less said, the better. Let's remain calm. Remember—discipline! (*Hirsh and Fayvel come into view. They are excited, carried away with enthusiasm.*)

FAYVEL. It's wonderful, wonderful I tell you!

HIRSH. Look at the streaming hordes —ach—they make the streets dance in the holiday—ach—our Jewish workers . . . !

RAISEL. I feel like dancing—what a beautiful evening, look. (*She pulls Hirsh over to Wolfe.*) Get to know each other better, Hirshke, Wolfke.

HIRSH. (*Shaking Wolfke's hand.*) Ah, you are the lucky one today—you are our flag bearer—

WOLFKE. Yes.

YOSHKE. We envy him, all of us.

WOLFKE. I am myself envious.

RACHMILKE. We will guard him well, you may be sure. We will surround him like a bridegroom under the wedding canopy.

WOLFKE. And our bride is the flag. (*Hirsh seeks out Fayvel, who lurks at the periphery of the group.*)

HIRSH. What's wrong? All of a sudden you seem so gloomy?

FAYVEL. The Poles have betrayed us.

OTHERS. (*Echoing realization that they are alone.*) Betrayed? Yes, really betrayed.

FAYVEL. Without them, what do we amount to? We are too few.

HIRSH. (*Sharply.*) Few? One fighter is enough! (*Isaak and Ruchel arrive. Ruchel seeks out Hirsh, but he turns away. Ruchel clings to Raisel.*)

ISAAK. I hope all of you have obeyed the decision about arms.

RACHMILKE. If we only had a chance to get at a policemen or a spy . . .

ISAAK. This is no time for any arguments.

YOSHKE. (*Derisively.*) That's great. Von Wahl with his rifles, with his whips, with—

ISAAK. You heard me. I want an answer. Who of you has arms?

YOSIIKE. I

RACHMILKE. And I.

ISAAK. Hand them over. (*Both men surrender their revolvers, but stand baffled and angry. Isaak hides the weapons in his pockets.*) Von Wahl and his whole army are waiting for only one shot from our side—and then, a blood bath over all of Vilna—everybody will suffer, both the innocent and the guilty.

HIRSH. A blood bath will take place anyway.

ISAAK. Do you have arms with you, too?

FAYVEL. You can trust us.

ISAAK. I don't want any arguments.

VOICES. We mustn't destroy our discipline.

RUCHEL. (*Pleading.*) Hirsh Lekert!

WOLFKE. Why isn't comrade Usishkin afraid!

ISAAK. I want to know who else has arms?

HIRSH. It seems that there's some kind of law that always it must be only our blood that flows. (*He hands Isaak his revolver.*) Fayvel, hand it over. (*Fayvel surrenders his revolver to Isaak.*)

RUCHEL. (*To Isaak.*) How will you manage with all these guns?

ISAAK. Better that one man, myself, be arrested than many.

HIRSH. I am giving you my gun, but you should know, anger boils inside me.

ISAAK. I don't want to listen to such talk.

HIRSH. It seems that I will always oppose you.

ISAAK. But I will not fight with you.

USISHKIN. (*Comes running.*) Quick, the masses are getting out of control—

ISAAK. (*Loudly.*) They must be controlled, made to stay calm. We must have discipline, caution. No one should waste himself.

USISHKIN. I'll tell you when to unfurl the flag. Let's go. (*All but Usishkin hurry off. Two suspicious-looking strangers enter and we hear them at the edge of the demonstration.*)

FIRST. There will be no demonstration! No stand will be made! Everybody go home! Peace with the government!

SECOND. The workers will be allowed to start official unions!

FIRST. We don't need the Bund!

SECOND. The leaders on the committee sit safely at home while they send the workers out to spill their blood!

USISHKIN. Spies! Zubutovniks! Catch them! (*The two have run off, with Usishkin in pursuit. There are outcries from afar.*)

VOICES. Down with Nicholas the second! Down! Down! (*The vacant synagogue yard. Mendel appears. He listens to the distant shouting as he stands in the middle of the courtyard. The Blind Man and his Guide hurry by.*)

GUIDE. Don't stand there. It's dangerous. Run—run!

BLIND MAN. To whom are you talking?

GUIDE. It's Mendel. He stands there like a statue. (*Outcries come nearer. Shrieking mingled with whistles blowing, clatter of horses' hooves, confusion.*)

BLIND ONE. Woe! Woe is me! (*Blind Man and Guide run off. Mendel, carrying his tubs, hurries to the side from which the noise is coming. The screams become louder yet. Mendel stands in anguish with hands outstretched toward the noise. Bruised, beaten, disheveled demonstrators retreat, running backwards through the synagogue courtyard. The stream of them carries Mendel with them, his tubs lost and scattered. A few leaders try to rally the masses, to stem the retreat—without success. Conflicting voices rise above the din.)*

Don't run!

We're afraid!

Stand up and fight back!

Swords, sabers!

Victory to the Bund!

Death!

We've lost. All is lost!

Up with life!

Down with the murderers! *(The panic explodes into a maelstrom. Mendel, running, returns. He raves inarticulately. Isaak appears—he is wobbly, tattered, staring in horror.)*

MENDEL. Where—where is Hirshke?

ISAAK. Everything lost . . . killed . . .

MENDEL. *(Lamenting.)* Hirshke's blood is spilling?

ISAAK. *(In a daze.)* It's spilling, spilling . . .

MENDEL. You lie! He's not killed.

ISAAK. *(Suddenly aware.)* What do you want?

MENDEL. Hirshke? They can't kill him!

ISAAK. Which Hirshke?

MENDEL. He is a giant, he's our . . . *(A great outcry. Isaak puts his hand to his forehead—he sways, is about to swoon. Usishkin comes running. He grabs Isaak.)*

USISHKIN. Isaak!

ISAAK. I've no right to be alive.

USISHKIN. *(Wild with anger and despair.)* Shut up!

ISAAK. The blood is on my head.

USISHKIN. You've gone out of your mind! You're crazy—

ISAAK. Yes.

USISHKIN. Then don't stand in our way—do you hear? Don't stand in our way anymore! *(Usishkin pushes him aside and stands alone with outstretched arms against the new wave of the retreating masses. Among the crowds are Hirsh Lekert and Raisel, who vainly try to turn the tide. They are thrust aside, manhandled and beaten. Hirsh is beaten up and bloody.)*

MENDEL. Hirshke! Hirshke!

USISHKIN. *(Continuing to try to turn back the retreat.)* Back! Back! Our comrades are fighting for our flag. Look, they're holding, they're standing firm, they're not yielding while you're running away. Don't leave us alone!

RAISEL. Save the flag. Help us!

VOICES. Out of the way!

HIRSH. I will stand in the way! You'll only run away over my body! Brothers, Bundists, please, we beg you—

VOICES. Away—Who are you?

HIRSH. One of you— *(The jam becomes more confused. Hirsh, Raisel, and Usishkin frantically try to rally the retreating mob. Hirsh sees Mendel.)*

Mendel—help us! Don't let them run. Stop!

MENDEL. *(Running among the retreating people.)* Don't run! You're running away—and Hirshke should die? Stop! Go back! *(The congestion is intense. Many are fighting their way through. They break through the obstacle of the stalwarts. Raisel and Mendel are dragged along by the mass. Hirsh Lekert succeeds in holding his ground, but he is trampled and remains lying on the ground. As the confusion subsides, he is alone. Fayvel enters; he is supporting a battered Wolfke. Both are in a bad way.)*

WOLFKE. Let go . . . I can't . . . *(He disentangles from Fayvel and falls to the ground.)*

FAVEL. We can't stay here. Let's get out of here.

(Fayvel reaches for and takes Wolfke's hand.)

WOLFKE. *(Reacts in pain.)* No! Don't touch my hand—they broke it. *(He moans.)*

The flag—I couldn't save it. (*He sees Hirsh.*)

Hirshke—

HIRSH. (*Comes to, rises.*) Don't yell—

WOLFKE. We lost the flag.

HIRSH. (*Jumping into action.*) Let's get everyone together. Let's stop the running away—

FAYVEL. There's no one left any more . . .

WOLFKE. They ran away—they left us all alone.

HIRSH. Then we must fight alone.

WOLFKE. Maybe it would be better if they arrested us with the others.

HIRSH. Don't worry—they'll arrest us all right. So let them arrest us. What must be will be.

FAYVEL. Oy, will we pay them back . . .

WOLFKE. Pay or not, our flag wasn't saved.

HIRSH. Yet, ourselves we saved.

WOLFKE. Shame—oh what shame— (*Wolfke hobbles off, broken and in despair.*)

HIRSH. Fayvel, listen to me. One has to offer up his whole life—

FAYVEL. How? What does it mean?

HIRSH. Exactly what I say, that's what I mean. As for the flag, I won't weep over it. Another one can be sewed. (*Fayvel wearily, silently looks at Hirsh, shakes his head and leaves. Hirsh stands against a wall like a statue. From another direction Mendel enters. He gathers up his tubs, yokes them on to himself when he sees Hirsh, to whom he joyfully runs.*)

MENDEL. Hirshke, how are you?

HIRSH. Quiet, not so loud.

MENDEL. Where is the flag? Did you bring it?

HIRSH. It's not here. The flag is not here.

MENDEL. I want to see the red flag.

HIRSH. (*Pointing to his bloody head.*) Here, look! See the red flag.

MENDEL. Blood . . .

HIRSH. Yes, this is our red flag.

MENDEL. I will run and get water. I'll wash off the blood.

HIRSH. Don't bother. Let it go . . .

MENDEL. (*Wiping at Hirsh's wounds with an edge of his cloak.*) Next time I see you, I'll have full tubs.

HIRSH. Thank you—dear brother of mine.

MENDEL. (*Still at trying to stop the flow of blood.*) Oy, I'm going to scream—

HIRSH. Sh, Mendel, we must be quiet.

MENDEL. But look how the blood is flowing from your head—I'm going to scream. I can't help it, I must. (*Mendel holds his own head and runs about while screaming.*) Jews, Hirshke's blood is flowing— Jews! Jews!

CURTAIN

SCENE IV

Evening, two days later. A lower class tea room, which Bundists frequent. The owner is a warm-hearted old woman whom everyone calls "Tante," which means Aunt, as one of their own. Usishkin sits asleep, his head on his arms that rest on a table. He is pathetically spiritless. The front door suddenly resounds with a great banging upon it. The door is flung open and Hirsh Lekert rushes in. Tante holds his shoulders as she tries to calm him.

TANTE. Hirshke, Hirshke, what's the matter with you?

HIRSH. (*Irrational, as though drunk.*) Let me in, Tante, let me in.

TANTE. So come in, I'm letting you. Don't scream and holler.

HIRSH. Let go of me—I can't stand being held down. They held on to me, stood guard over me for two days and nights, watching over me like jailors over a prisoner.

TANTE. Who? Where?

HIRSH. Both of them—my mother and my wife, taking turns standing at the door and keeping it locked so I couldn't get out of the house. Two days, Tante, two days and nights.

TANTE. I smell whiskey on your breath. Are you drunk?

HIRSH. No, Tante, I'm not drunk, I swear to you. Look at me. See, I'm standing straight. One bottle, Tante, one small bottle—I'm being choked. I'm going out of my mind, Tante—I can't bear it—

TANTE. What happened to you, Hirsh? What's the matter?

HIRSH. The lashes, Tante. That hangman, Von Wahl! Oh, how many of our comrades were beaten? Tell me, how many?

TANTE. Sh. . . sh . . . control yourself— (*Hirsh roams the room and heads for the door.*) What are you doing? Where are you going?

HIRSH. It's a fire that's burning inside me. I want to go out—into the streets and scream—Brothers! Comrades! Why are you silent?

TANTE. Sh . . . careful. Who knows who can hear you.

HIRSH. (*Suddenly collapsing as if in defeat, whispers hoarsely.*) What shall I do, Tante? The Bund isn't dead, is it? Look at him, he's sleeping now, our comrade Usishkin— (*Hirsh staggers quickly toward Usishkin and tries to arouse him.*) Comrade—

TANTE. (*Dragging Hirsh away.*) Don't trouble him. He's worn out and sick.

HIRSH. (*Roaming the room.*) We are despised and chased—we are punished and persecuted.

TANTE. Sit down. Here—I'll give you some tea—

HIRSH. (*Suddenly raving.*) Don't let them in, Tante. They ran after me. With lamentations upon my head. They're coming, Tante—are they coming?

TANTE. Nobody is coming.

HIRSH. Lock the door. I don't want to look at them. I hate them—hate them! Yes, they're my mother, my wife—but—but—what can I do? What should I do, hah? Picture it— they were guarding the door—I could just bust—they wouldn't let me out. I waited my chance, then I smashed a window and ran out—get me another bottle, Tante, please get me one. Von Wahl is choking me. He will choke everybody—I want some schnapps.

TANTE. Hirshke—you're a Bundist. You mustn't drink—Bundists don't drink —it would be a shame on you.

HIRSH. Yes, Tante, excuse me. But— but I can't stand it. Look how comrade Usishkin sleeps like after a calamity. And our flag—such a weak thing. And our hands are empty, while the hangman stands safe and satisfied with his job. Alas, so many beaten bodies—and all of Vilna washed in blood. Yet, Vilna is quiet. Revenge, Tante, revenge—!

TANTE. Sh—quiet.

HIRSH. T'hell with it; I'll smash all the panes in the windows, yes, even here. Why do we sit here and sleep? (*Hirsh rushes over to Usishkin and bangs on the table. Usishkin rouses himself.*)

TANTE. Are you crazy or something?

USISHKIN. What's happening?

HIRSH. (*Suddenly cowed and ashamed at the spectacle of poor Usishkin.*) Please, excuse me.

USISHKIN. Are you drunk?

HIRSH. No, Comrade, no. Sleep, sleep. (*Suddenly changes and starts to sing.*) We are shot at, we are being hanged . . . Sing with me, Comrade, you, too, Tante.

USISHKIN. You reek from whiskey. I don't like that.

HIRSH. I won't drink anymore—I swear to you. Sing with me. I was depressed—it was my grief—so I drank a little. Shall we despair? Sing with me. Come, dance with me. We'll dance a hopke on the head of Von Wahl. Why are you looking at me like that? Are you angry with me?

USISHKIN. (*Rises and places his hands on Hirsh's shoulders.*) No, I am not angry with you, brother. You are wonderful.

HIRSH. (*With renewed hope, with joy.*) Bless you, stay well. When many of our brothers are killed, comrade, and when only one remains, the last one, and this last one gives his life away—are we supposed to cry over it, ha?

TANTE. (*Brings him tea.*) Here. Drink,

Hirshkele.

HIRSH. (*Eagerly but seriously.*) Give me a revolver, comrade.

USISHKIN. What do you want it for?

HIRSH. (*Brushing aside a direct answer.*) I must have a revolver, I must— (*A group of workers enter with a few girls. They sit around the table and greet each other.*)

FIRST. Tea, Tante.

TANTE. Soon, soon. (*She goes out.*)

SECOND. Look who's here—it's comrade Usishkin.

THIRD. We thought you were arrested.

USISHKIN. So far, not yet, as you can see.

FIRST. Watch out for spies—they're everywhere, damn them!

SECOND. You'd better be extra careful. They're looking for you.

USISHKIN. I might as well face it. They'll probably find me. (*Tante brings tea to the newcomers.*)

FIRST. (*Pointing to Hirsh.*) A new face. Who is he?

TANTE. Our own, one of us. What's new, children?

FIRST. Terrible news.

SECOND. The number of the lashed comes to thirty.

THIRD. And Von Wahl sat right there counting the lashes.

FIRST. The whole prison yard is covered with Jewish blood.

A GIRL. (*Weeping.*) Stop it!

HIRSH. (*He has overheard. He jumps up, and with passion.*) Thirty?

TANTE. Hirshke, control yourself.

HIRSH. And nobody gave it back to them?

FIRST. (*Throwing up his hands helplessly.*) So many soldiers around, everywhere—

HIRSH. But thirty of us! (*Hirsh pounds his head with his fists.*) Thirty, thirty! (*Wolfke, with a bandaged head, comes in. He sits at Hirsh's table. Hirsh subsides.*)

USISHKIN. Oh, here is Wolfke. (*He embraces Wolfke.*) Oh, how are you?

SEVERAL. How is your hand?

WOLFKE. (*Contemptuously.*) It won't kill me.

USISHKIN. (*Pats Wolfke on shoulder.*) Dear comrade, don't be in such a black mood. We must not despair. It does not suit you, nor anybody else. Bundowitzes must not lose their spirit. (*He hails Tante.*) How about a glass of tea, Tante?

TANTE. Right away—with pleasure.

WOLFKE. When the flag is entrusted to you, you must stand by it until your last breath, and you mustn't give it up. And I failed, I gave it up. And you, all of us are cowards! They should throw us out from the Bund!

HIRSH. Let us sing our oath, let us swear again—

WOLFKE. Like scared mice we ran from the demonstration. And in the prison, two sections packed with those arrested. Why didn't they do something—break windows at least—but something in protest? Were they trembling for their skins? A revolutionist is not the boss over his own body!

HIRSH. You are right, it's true. We are swine—no good! (*He rises and stands in the middle of the room and speaks with a choked voice.*) Instead of sitting here—why are we sitting here? A Jewish revolutionary must—(*Rachmilke and Yoshke enter.*)

RACHMILKE. (*Indicating Hirsh.*) Look, here he is.

YOSHKE. We looked all over for you.

RACHMILKE. We went to your house— wow, what a wailing there!

YOSHKE. Noise and more noise. Such a weeping of the women.

RACHMILKE. Did you break the window?

HIRSH. What else could I do?

RACHMILKE. Your wife is looking for you now. She'll be here soon.

HIRSH. She shouldn't be let in, Tante. If she is, something terrible will happen—it will be awful!

RACHMILKE. Look at him. He's trembling. He's afraid.

HIRSH. (*Flaring at Rachmilke.*) Keep quiet!

RACHMILKE. Shame on you!

HIRSH. Hirsh Lekert is not afraid of

anybody. It's just . . . It's only that I have pity on her—pity. And you, keep your mouth shut!

USISHKIN. Why are you so excited?

HIRSH. (*Trembling again.*) Tell me this; you're an educated man, a scholar. Can a man put up with all their crying, their lamentation over him as if he is already dead? That whole basement of mine weeps, all four walls are weeping—Here, look, like this the women sit, they wring their hands, their mouths distorted, their eyes swollen, and they lament: "Hirshke, you are killing us without a knife—" Damn it! Give me a knife and I will really go killing. I am being eaten alive inside by the disgrace of the lashings. And the torment of the smile of the hangman hits me with all its force right in my face. Vilna is a scab—and we are all scabs. And I lie on the bed and can't sleep. So I start singing our oath. Then the wail of the women gets louder. Should I choke with what's in me, hah? (*He sits, beaten. Then he jumps up again.*) But I must sing the oath—the holy oath of the Bund. Why are all of you silent? Sing along with me! Revolutionists must sing. Or aren't we allowed that either?

TANTE. Allowed—but not too loud. I will keep watch. (*She goes to the door.*)

HIRSH. Comrade Usishkin, sing along with me. (*Hirsh starts alone, but soon Usishkin, then Yoshke, and finally Rachmilke join in.*)

Brothers and sisters of toil and poverty
All who are scattered and dispersed—
Together, together—our flag is ready
She flutters in anger, from blood she is red—
To the oath, to the oath—to life and to death.

Ah, that's marvelous. Now everybody! All of you! (*Wolfke soon joins in, as do the others. Some sing quietly, with apparent pain of memory, some with repressed ecstasy as though reliving their past dedication. Hirsh is carried away with the enthusiasm of religious fervor.*)

The sky and earth will listen to us,
Brightest of stars our witness will be,
To our oath of blood, our oath of tears—
We swear, we swear!

USISHKIN. (*Overcome with emotion, embraces Hirsh.*) You're a wonderful person, as sure as I'm alive. As long as we have such as you, what are we afraid of? So, they have tortured us; they will torture us again. Our blood is still red, and the tyrant is still thirsty for it. But revenge will come—

HIRSH. Yes, yes! I mean—yes, that's right—revenge. (*Suddenly there are loud voices behind the outside door. One is the voice of Hirsh Lekert's wife. Hirsh fears her and becomes frantic.*) Don't let her in here, keep her out— (*Tante and Hirsh's Wife enter.*)

TANTE. (*Laughing apologetically.*) Nu, here she is, Hirshke.

HIRSH. (*Uncertain and impatient.*) What are you doing here?

WIFE. (*Embarrassed and frightened.*) Come home—Hirshke.

HIRSH. (*Slumps into a chair and buries his face in his hands.*) Ach!

WIFE. (*Follows him and reaches for his hand.*) Come home with me.

HIRSH. (*Jumps away from her.*) No— I won't go.

WIFE. Bandit, rogue! Smasher of windows— (*Raisel and Ruchel come in.*)

HIRSH. Well, what else could I do to get out? Please forgive me.

WIFE. Come home. (*She turns to Raisel.*)
Raisele, Raisele, please help me.

HIRSH. Don't make a fool of yourself.

WIFE. You'll be arrested. I want you to come home.

HIRSH. I can't go home right now—

RAISEL. (*To wife.*) Nu, my dear. It's no use. He will come home later.

WIFE. He will not come. I know. He hates the house. (*She falls, weeping, to her knees.*)

USISHKIN. (*Moved.*) Don't cry, my dear woman. Please don't cry. You'd be better off if you went home.

WIFE. I never did this—I don't run after him. I leave him alone. But today—I can't stand it anymore. How can a man give up everything, everybody . . . ?

HIRSH. I don't sacrifice anybody but myself—only myself. Nu, come, let's make an end to this. (*He leads her by the hand to the door. Once at the door, he pulls back with an outcry.*) Go away! Leave me alone! (*He pushes her through the door and closes it behind her. He then sinks into a chair at a table. Silence.*)

RACHMILKE. Tpfui!

RUCHEL. Was Isaak here?

USISHKIN. What, you haven't seen him?

RUCHEL. You mean he wasn't here? He's lost. (*A silent figure enters and stands at the door. His ghost-like face makes all the others uneasy.*)

USISHKIN. You are looking for someone?

SILENT ONE. (*Trembling.*) No one.

USISHKIN. Don't just stand there near the door.

SILENT ONE. Let me stand.

USISHKIN. Are you one of our own?

SILENT ONE. Yes.

USISHKIN. Are you sick? You're shaking so. Here, sit down at a table.

SILENT ONE. No . . . no . . . (*Pause.*) (*Isaak enters. He appears to be a shadow of himself, tired and bitter.*)

RUCHEL. (*Joyful, yet alarmed.*) Isaak!

USISHKIN. Look, look! He's alive. Where were you?

ISAAK. What difference does it make where I was?

USISHKIN. We were looking for you, for two days already.

ISAAK. (*As he sits.*) You didn't have to do that. (*He sits with his head in his hands. He seems demoralized.*)

RUCHEL. (*Attempting to comfort Isaak.*) Isaak . . .

ISAAK. You will all fall on me—oh, I know . . . but—

RUCHEL. What do you want to do?

ISAAK. I'm telling all of you—openly, I'm not keeping back anything. I . . . I simply can't go on any more.

USISHKIN. Isaak!

ISAAK. Now I know, it's all very clear to me. I have no more doubts. Now I must say what I must—the whole truth.

USISHKIN. What truth?

ISAAK. The truth as I see it.

WOLFKE. You don't make sense. Talk clearly. (*All of them are focused on Isaak.*)

ISAAK. My trial is my verdict. There doesn't seem to be any difference who plays with people's lives and bodies. Yet, nobody has the right over that —nobody. Neither the wicked man nor the just man. The way of blood and of death is not the truthful way. There is another way.

FAYVIL. Which way?

ISAAK. The way of patience.

FAYVIL. Muddled words.

ISAAK. Why muddled? I am telling you clearly. We have to change our tactics in our struggle with the government.

FAYVEL. Zubatovchinik!

ISAAK. Zubatov is a tzarist gendarme. But when there comes an honest one—

FAYVEL. Treason!

A VOICE. What good is name-calling?

ANOTHER VOICE. Let's listen to what Isaak has to say.

A VOICE. There's some truth in what he says.

WOLFKE. He's out of his mind. Ruchel, what is he talking about?

USISHKIN. (*Amazed, grabs Isaak by the arm.*) Isaak, what are you saying? (*Turns to the others and screams.*) Comrades, he talks of despair!

ISAAK. No, not of despair.

FAYVEL. He has betrayed the Bund, betrayed the revolution. (*Fayvel runs over to Hirsh Lekert, who sits with both hands supporting his head.*) Hirsh, do you hear what's going on here? Do you hear? (*Hirsh looks up in shock, stares silently at Isaak.*) He was my teacher, he was the one to stir me, inspire me. And when there was a call to action—he became frightened. Who was the one to send me to protect our arrested brothers? Because I have strong hands, who sent me to murder spies and strike-breakers—not you? And now you want to wipe clean those delicate hands of yours and call it quits? And all of the blood you'll leave to me—to poor Fayvel?

ISAAK. (*To Fayvel.*) Judge me.

FAYVEL. Like you give a revolver to somebody and say—shoot me.

ISAAK. (*Hands a revolver to Fayvel.*) Here, shoot.

RUCHEL. (*Grabs the revolver.*) You're out of your mind!

ISAAK. (*Sighing.*) You, too, are against me. I know.

RUCHEL. Now is not the time to talk about what's between me and you. It's a question of the movement, the revolution. (*She is shaking; she runs to Isaak and embraces him.*) Say it's not the truth. Say it was only a passing moment of despair. We're all human.

ISAAK. (*In Ruchel's embrace.*) I can't say that.

RUCHEL. (*Devastated, retreats to a chair.*) I love you. I say this openly so everyone can hear. And before everybody, I get down on my knees and beg you—take back your words.

ISAAK. You, yourself, said that it is no longer a question of you and me.

RUCHEL. Exactly—forget about you and me. Think of what is important—not of even one comrade, but all of us. This is no time for despair.

ISAAK. I have thought it through. I am determined.

RUCHEL. (*Rises and speaks as though she were the voice of Judgment.*) Take back the words you have spoken. Deny them.

ISAAK. And if not? (*Isaak irresolutely walks toward the door. Others rise as if to leave. Hirsh Lekert springs up and blocks Isaak's path.*)

HIRSH. You cannot leave here now. I say you won't leave!

VOICES. What's he doing? What does he mean?

HIRSH. You'll stay here, I say. Right here. If necessary, I'll keep you by force. Take a good look at me. I'm Hirshke the whistler, Hirshke the tough guy, Hirshke the good-for-nothing, the scoundrel. I listen to you and I hear the boiling inside you. (*Hirsh taps his own chest.*) Here, just listen to it, here, right here. (*Hirsh stretches out his hand.*)

ISAAK. Let me go. I want to leave—right now.

HIRSH. (*Hirsh turns upon Isaak with murder in his eyes.*)

Should I curse you? Should I hit you, beat you? Or should I raise my hands against our comrades? or should I just fall to cursing? Ai, ai, ai—to whom? To our representative, maybe? (*Hirsh turns to Usishkin.*) I don't understand any of this. What does he want? I hear him talking about something, about blood. He says something like "Judge me," then "Sentence me." Whose blood? Tell me whose? (*Points to Isaak.*)

His blood, or the blood of our own who were lashed? (*Thus far the Silent One has remained quietly away from the others, at his position near the door, as though a stranger apart from them. Suddenly, as if inwardly torn apart, he screams.*)

SILENT ONE. Silence! (*Silent One falls, beaten and prostrate, like a log of wood upon the floor. Others rush to him.*)

USISHKIN. What's wrong with you? (*They crowd about and come near to the Silent One.*)

SILENT ONE. Don't come near me! (*All freeze and look upon him.*)

USISHKIN. Who are you?

SILENT ONE. The thirtieth one to be beaten. (*He sways as if to fall again.*)

A WOMAN. Let's put him to bed, comrades. (*The Woman, Usishkin, Rachmilke, and Yoshke, with others, tenderly, compassionately attend to him and help him out. From behind the walls, from the other room, we hear his painful moaning.*)

HIRSH. (*To Isaak, with new-found confidence.*)

Now you can go. All of you can go. The one who now gives orders is he who was whipped. Whatever he tells me to do, I will obey. I know now what must be done. Now I know what to do.

SCENE V

Late at night, perhaps 10:00 o'clock. The Mother is really sick, reclining in her cot, Hirsh's Wife sits near her. Ruchel and Raisel impatiently walk around the room, intermittently looking through the window. They try to cover up their worries in order to hide them from the Wife and Mother. A small candle flickers.

RAISEL. Well, how do you feel, grandma?

MOTHER. (*With her face to the wall.*) Nothing helps, it doesn't get better, my little one.

WIFE. Try to sleep.

MOTHER. I'm trying. God knows I'm trying. (*The Mother stirs impatiently as though to rise.*)

RUCHEL. Lie down until the guests arrive.

MOTHER. What guests?

WIFE. Some people are coming. They want to see Hirshke.

RAISEL. Yes, grandma. Hirshke is expecting them.

RUCHEL. And when they come, we'll spend the time together.

RAISEL. To celebrate Hirshke's return from Ekaterinoslav.

MOTHER. But it's so late.

RAISEL. For a celebration with a party, it's never too late, grandma.

MOTHER. (*Rises and looks around.*) But where is Hirshke himself?

WIFE. He comes and he goes. One minute he's here, then like the wind he's gone. All the time, he comes and goes. He just left.

MOTHER. (*Pats her daughter-in-law.*) You look tired, my darling. You don't look like you're ready to dance at a celebration. (*Wife sits with her head sunk low.*)

RAISEL. We will help you welcome the guests. (*Mother again lies down.*)

WIFE. Sleep, mama. (*To Raisel.*) We should prepare something for the guests. There's nothing in the house—we have nothing.

RUCHEL. Leave it to them. They'll provide everything.

WIFE. Some tea at least, I should prepare it. Some sugar . . . (*She bends over her mother-in-law.*) I think she's asleep. I'll come back soon. (*Wife prepares to leave.*)

RAISEL. Have you any money at all?

WIFE. I will borrow some. (*Wife exits.*)

RUCHEL. (*Quickly to Raisel after the Wife leaves.*) I'll run over to the center and see what's happening.

RAISEL. It's still too early.

RUCHEL. But this uncertainty is driving me out of my mind. I can't just sit here.

RAISEL. And you think it's easy for me to "just sit here?" (*She bends over the old Mother.*)
She's sleeping. Yes.

RUCHEL. What a pity. They're such a pair of poor creatures.

RAISEL. Don't talk about it. (*Pause.*) I hope our luck holds out so that we're not made a couple of liars. Maybe we'll really be able to celebrate.

RUCHEL. What do you think? Do you think we'll be lucky?

RAISEL. We must! So many of our comrades are helping him. Even that cadaver, Usishkin. Did you see him, Usishkin?

RUCHEL. (*Coming to Raisel, embracing her, and burying her head in Raisel's shoulder.*) And Isaak? What happened to him? Where is he?

RAISEL. Don't weep, my dear sister.

RUCHEL. I will go to the center.

RAISEL. Hirshke, himself, will soon be here. He promised. The less he marches around the center the better. It's still early.

RUCHEL. I haven't the patience to sit here. (*Ruchel exits. Raisel is apprehensive each time a new noise is heard. Isaak enters. He is in tatters, unshaven—a wreck of a man.*)

RAISEL. (*Frightened.*) Isaak—is it really you? Where have you been?

ISAAK. What difference does it make

where I've been. This is Hirsh Lekert's house, isn't it?

RAISEL. Yes, this is it.

ISAAK. Why are you staring at me like that?

RAISEL. You look terrible. Where have you been? Were you hiding in the woods?

ISAAK. Maybe. What difference does it make? Does Ruchel, too, want to know where I was?

RAISEL.* Didn't you run into her? She left a few moments ago.

ISAAK. It's so dark outside. Maybe if I run after her . . .

RAISEL. She definitely doesn't want to see you today.

ISAAK. But I want to see her.

RAISEL. Not today.

ISAAK. Can I see Hirsh Lekert?

RAISEL. Not today, either.

ISAAK. May I, at least, sit down a little? (*He does not wait for an answer and sits.*)

RAISEL. (*Looking at him with fear as she wrings her hands.*) Just look at you. You're a sight.

ISAAK. Who's that lying down over there?

RAISEL. Hirsh Lekert's mother. She's sick . . . (*Hirsh Lekert enters, but, surprised and fearful at seeing Isaak, remains at the door.*)

ISAAK. (*To Hirsh.*) You will excuse me.

HIRSH. I am busy today.

ISAAK. I want to wait for Ruchel.

HIRSH. No, not today.

ISAAK. I won't hinder you. I won't be in the way.

HIRSH. (*Approaches Isaak.*) What did you do with yourself? You've made yourself look like a walking corpse.

ISAAK. And when you die, you think it will be different?

HIRSH. (*To Raisel, with despair.*) Raisel, what does he want? Who sent for him?

ISAAK. I came to warn you. I came to hold back your hand—even from Von Wahl.

HIRSH. (*Outraged.*) How do you know?

ISAAK. It's no secret.

HIRSH. You've become a stranger to us. You have no right to interfere.

ISAAK. I know, I have no right, I know all right. I came not to interfere, not to give you advice, but to tell you what I foresee; I see far, far ahead.

HIRSH. I know what you see—I know you already. You have only one mission, to cut off somebody else's feet from under him, to freeze one's soul. You can only see the spirit of gloom and darkness.

ISAAK. Yes, I see her. And I also see the fires that burn within her. Fire heaped on fire, and death heaped on death. I'm telling you I see destruction on the way, destruction of MAN!

HIRSH. Why did you come here? To tell me that?

ISAAK. I'll tell you again. All will be mired in blood, all will rot in decay, and the black mold will keep rotting, putrefying everyone's blood, whether it be yours, Von Wahl's, or mine. One blood for all, one stench, and one color. And it will be corrupted green and gall from all of us.

HIRSH. You cover your filthy words by quoting Scriptures.

ISAAK. You've even turned Ruchel's head.

HIRSH. You sound like you're completely crazy. Who sent for you? Get out and stay out!

ISAAK. So where shall I go? Oh, you're so foolish, Hirsh Lekert. You are my folks' people, and such simple children . . . You are not pulling along cripples, nor are you torn apart by my grief—yet you are forever with God—eternally. And when you do go to shoot Von Wahl, and after that if you succeed in getting away with it, you will run away, escape. But I, suppose I shoot Isaak, myself, I will not escape, I cannot run away. I must see Ruchel. Please help me.

HIRSH. (*With finality.*) She is not here.

---

* I have taken liberties with the text at this point in order to make plausible the fact that Ruchel and Isaak did not encounter each other when she left the house.

ISAAK. Then I'll come back again. Later. (*Isaak grabs Hirsh's hand.*) Remember what I told you, remember my words. And if you will not listen to me, I'm telling you your hand should not succeed! (*Isaak leaves.*)

HIRSH. (*He embraces the deathly frightened Raisel.*) He's out of his mind. Tell me, Raisele, my comrade, my friend—why did he curse me? I'm going to revenge all the tortured souls. What does he have against me? He succeeded in disturbing my right hand. (*Hirsh sits forlorn.*)

RAISEL. (*Kisses him.*) Hirshke, don't be frightened. Your hand will aim straight and true. (*Firmly, with determination.*) Get up. I'm commanding you.

HIRSH. Raisele, what a wonderful soul you are. Please don't forget me. Ach, where is everyone?

RAISEL. Here they come. (*Ruchel and his Wife enter. Hirsh signals Raisel to leave with Ruchel.*)

HIRSH. Wait outside for me. (*Raisel and Ruchel exit.*)

WIFE. Just look, how they both disappeared.

HIRSH. It doesn't matter. They'll both be back soon. We'll have a gay time, dear wife, and we'll all dance. (*He embraces her and presses her to him with affection.*)

WIFE. (*Surprised and happy.*) What is with you, Hirshke?

HIRSH. Why? Don't you want me to embrace you?

WIFE. But it's been such a long time since you did. You leave me alone for days and nights on end, and in my condition now . . .

HIRSH. Well, you must please forgive me for those days and nights. Ah, my loyal wife, so good, so honest . . .

WIFE. (*With tears as she happily clasps him.*) Hirshke, my love. You're so wonderful today, that I'm crying for joy—

HIRSH. It's only that I'm always so mixed up—and so worried. But you know, don't you, that I'm not entirely a bad husband? You know I mean well . . . (*He kisses her.*)

WIFE. But I'm not angry at you, my love. You think I don't know where you go every night? I know, Hirshke, you go to meetings, I know. You are now a different—a special person. And everybody likes you, believes in you. This gives me pleasure, I'm really proud of you. But, just the same, the heart suffers and trembles.

HIRSH. And here, all the time I believed you hated my comrades.

WIFE. No, oh no. You are making a big mistake. But, all the same, I am a very lonely person, Hirshke.

HIRSH. (*With a warm, tender embrace.*) You are a perfect one, dear one, and so good.

WIFE. I have a happy piece of news for you, my darling. I wanted to tell it to you this morning, but I felt embarrassed.

HIRSH. What is it?

WIFE. Since this morning, yet—today I'll tell you. Ah, I've been today, the whole day, so happy. Ah, Hirshke, I know it will be a boy— (*He shudders.*) What is it, Hirshke? Look how you're shivering!

HIRSH. (*His legs buckle, he staggers and slumps into a chair.*) It's nothing. Don't be scared. Something happened, I don't know what, and I felt suddenly faint. (*He rises.*) Enough. No more. (*Hirsh kisses his wife, tears himself away from her, runs over to his mother, who is asleep on the bed, and falls to his knees and buries his face close to hers. He then jumps up and runs to the door.*)

WIFE. Where to?

HIRSH. Good night, my darling. (*He quickly runs out.*)

WIFE. (*Yelling.*) Where did he go? (*She runs out the door and soon returns. She stands bewildered. She grabs her head and screams at her mother-in-law.*) Where did he go?

MOTHER. (*Crawling out of her covers, shivers.*) Who? What?

WIFE. Hirshke!

MOTHER. On my enemies' heads, such

dreams. Who was it that crept over my face? And almost made holes out of my eyes?

WIFE. My heart is being torn apart—I am scared.

MOTHER. (*Puts her feet down. Raises her arms akimbo then lets them fall helplessly to her lap.*) Ach, my dear daughter, my dearest one. (*Ruchel and Raisel enter with exuberance. They try to erase fear in the Mother and Wife.*)

WIFE. (*To Ruchel and Raisel.*) Tell me the truth. Where did he go?

RAISEL. He went to get the guest.

MOTHER. Again with the guest business? What kind of guests in the middle of the night?

RAISEL. A comradely celebration, grandma. We will make tea and we'll all dance.

MOTHER. Can't we put it off till tomorrow? I don't feel well, I must stay in bed.

RUCHEL. Tomorrow the guest will be gone, grandma. And today he *is* here. He is attending the circus. And when the circus is over, he will come out. That's when Hirshke will meet him and bring him.

MOTHER. What kind of circus? What are you talking about?

WIFE. But why didn't he tell me that?

RAISEL. He asked me to tell you that.

MOTHER. The house is such a mess. It's not been cleaned. (*She gets up from bed.*)

RUCHEL. You must stay in bed.

MOTHER. It's not me to lie around when guests come. (*To Ruchel and Raisel.*) And why do both of you look so confused, ha?

RUCHEL. Oh no, we're fine—never better. (*Ruchel and Raisel embrace one another and appear very happy. Zelig enters from the outside and walks toward his chamber. He stops near his door.*)

ZELIG. A good week.

MOTHER. Good year, a good year.

ZELIG. (*Indicating Ruchel and Raisel.*) Why all the merriment?

MOTHER. It's Saturday night, Reb Zelig. Young people act foolishly.

ZELIG. Have you ever seen such things! Ugh—females! It is my house.

RUCHEL. Who's taking your house away?

ZELIG. Who's taking? So take, take. But meanwhile, it's still my house. So they come to my house to make merry! Looseness—what?

RAISEL. We're in your neighbor's house, not in yours.

ZELIG. Wait, I'll get another neighbor.

WIFE. Don't be in such a huff. Excuse us.

ZELIG. I will be in a huff if I wish. What do I have here—noise—celebrations? What is the celebration, ha? Too many legs are stamping around here. Good-for-nothings, wastrels—

WIFE. Who?

ZELIG. Too many are walking, running, jostling. Yesterday, before yesterday. Gangs. Vilna is crying, Vilna is lamenting. And gangs brawl, shout, sing—libertines! And yours too. I know, a jailbird—

WIFE. Not for robbery, God forbid.

ZELIG. I wish it would be for robbery, I wish. (*He turns away from the others.*) So Vilna is lamenting, it's tormented —so who cares? And what is in Vilna today? Jews who scream with big mouths. They should scream their heads off! And if you lament, toward whom is such lamenting aimed? On the rebels, they cry—or on the maliciousness of the wicked man—But maybe on the whipped behinds, ha? (*He slams his door as he exits into his chamber. The others have been sobered, are depressingly silent. Soon the melancholy, mad, pinched voice of Zelig is heard chanting his prayers! Suddenly, from outside tremendous outcries are heard. Running feet, clattering of horses, whistling, shouting, and shooting.*)

WIFE. (*Screaming.*) Where is Hirshke? (*Wife, followed by Ruchel and Raisel, runs outside; the mother hobbles after them. Zelig runs out of his chamber.*)

ZELIG. (*Screaming.*) What's going on? (*Mendel rushes in, with his tubs askew on his shoulders, shouting joyfully.*)

MENDEL. He's got him! He got him!

ZELIG. Mendel, what is it?

MENDEL. (*Dancing with excitement.*) He caught him. Hirshke did it—

ZELIG. Whom?

MENDEL. He fixed him—but good, that hangman . . . !

CURTAIN

SCENE VI

Late at night. The death cell in the Vilna Prison. Hirsh Lekert, with heavy iron chains on his legs, sits on the floor with his shoulders back against the door. With a piece of coal he draws figures on the floor and walls, appearing like a little boy with a toy.

GUARD. (*Through the grates in the door.*) What are you doing in there? (*Hirsh Lekert ignores him.*) Stand up in there, you crackpot. (*Guard bangs his keys against the door.*)

HIRSH. Leave me alone—

GUARD. If I come in you'll . . .

2ND GUARD. Don't talk so much. Open the door and let him have it.

HIRSH. Away—let me be. (*A knocking and scraping at the door, the rattling of the key in the lock. The door starts to swing open as Hirsh scrambles away from it. The Guard enters, in his hand an oversized key, on his belt a revolver.*)

GUARD. Did you hear what I said to you?

HIRSH. (*Laconically.*) I'm not deaf.

GUARD. I'll take you down into the dungeon.

HIRSH. So—take.

GUARD. (*Spits.*) Take—how can I take you? There's no time left.

HIRSH. Surely not yet—It's the last hour . . .

GUARD. The last hour, you simpleton. Why are you smearing up the floor with the coal?

HIRSH. I'm not smearing. I'm drawing a picture.

GUARD. What kind of picture?

HIRSH. Can't you see.

GUARD. (*The Guard peers closely, then recoils.*) Gallows?

HIRSH. Yes. I drew a picture of my gallows. That's how it will look, early in the morning before daybreak.

GUARD. With his own hands? Who does things like that?

HIRSH. Get me another piece of coal. How about it—?

GUARD. You're either a child or a devil —which—tell me—tpfui on you— (*He spits toward Hirsh. Second Guard enters.*) Just look at him. He draws pictures of gallows.

2ND GUARD. (*To Hirsh*) How do you know how a gallows looks? Did you ever see one?

HIRSH. No. Did you?

GUARD. Yea, I saw.

HIRSH. So, is my picture correct?

GUARD. Exactly. Right on the nose. You're such an odd one!

2ND GUARD. You needed this, you idiot, hah? To creep right into the flames —to shoot the governor?

HIRSH. I was taking revenge for my brothers.

2ND GUARD. The fact is, you missed him.

HIRSH. I did hit him.

2ND GUARD. (*Mocking.*) You're some shot. His excellency, the governor, is very much alive.

HIRSH. No—he's not alive!

2ND GUARD. Ach, you devil, believe us when we tell you—he's alive.

HIRSH. So let Von Wahl live—I don't care, but the governor is dead.

2ND GUARD. Do you know what you're talking about? No matter what, you're going to die. Aren't you sorry?

HIRSH. It's really a beautiful world I'm leaving. So, I'm really sorry. (*From outside, voices are heard.*)

VOICES. Long live Hirsh Lekert! (*Both Guards run out as they tightly close the door. Clanging of doors, rattling of keys, much running is heard to the obligato of the Guards' warning of Silence! Silence! Hirsh slumps onto his cot. He goes through the gamut of emotions, sits and wrings his hands, then rises and starts to draw a life-size scaffold and victim, when the Guards again enter.*)

GUARD. Stop already with your pictures. Your people are coming to say goodbye to you. (*The Guard steps outside and ushers in Hirsh's Uncle, Mother, Wife, and Mendel. Hirsh stands with his back to the wall in a futile attempt to hide his macabre drawing. The visitors remain awkwardly standing near the door. Hirsh, intent on hiding the drawing, remains immobile. The tableau is broken when the women frantically, hysterically, run to embrace him as they utter heart-rending cries.*)

HIRSH. Why must you cry?

UNCLE. (*To the women.*) Didn't we agree to something?

WIFE. (*To Hirsh.*) You left me—for what?

MOTHER. My son . . .

HIRSH. Cry—then finish it and stop. (*Hirsh embraces his Uncle.*) You at least are my own, a shoemaker.

MENDEL. (*Appears at door.*) Look, Hirshke, I'm not crying.

HIRSH. Come here, Mendel.

MENDEL. (*Approaches Hirsh and grabs his hand. Mendel's face radiates a fiery adulation of Hirsh.*) Hirshkele?

HIRSH. (*Embraces Mendel.*) Don't let anyone cry after me.

MENDEL. I will make sure.

HIRSH. I die for a holy cause—for the workers' cause. (*Hirsh embraces his Wife.*) You are good and dear, yet I've caused you so much pain. You must not hold any bitterness against me.

WIFE. Oh, oh, now everything is lost. (*The Wife cannot control herself, her legs buckle and she is about to collapse, but the Uncle and Mendel hold her up.*)

HIRSH. (*Quickly and with determination.*) Don't! No weeping! (*Under Hirsh's gaze, the others control themselves.*)

UNCLE. (*Pointing to the drawing.*) Why did you sketch that?

HIRSH. The end. It's like it's all over already. Already, after the gallows. So everything is fine with me now. All of you can now be calm and at peace, and everything will now go more quickly.

MOTHER. My son, sign the paper they want, so you can be pardoned.

HIRSH. (*Stretching out his trembling, imploring hands.*) Mama! (*He turns to Mendel.*) You tell me, do you want me to crawl to them, to beg?

MENDEL. Hirshkele, don't beg.

HIRSH. Thank you, brother of mine. Because of this, let me kiss you. (*Hirsh embraces and kisses Mendel.*)

MENDEL. I know what you mean. I know—the workers will take over the whole world, and all people will again be brothers.

HIRSH. Yes, Mendel, yes! All people, all!

MENDEL. I will meet you, yet, in the streets, Hirshkele. You will know me. You will find me with my tubs on my shoulders.

HIRSH. I will recognize you right away.

MENDEL. Let me kiss you again. (*They embrace and kiss. Mendel steps backward from Hirsh. He stands upright with flashing eyes.*) Don't be afraid, Hirshke, when you go out from here at daybreak. Pretend that you, too, are a water carrier, that you are going out with two full tubs on your shoulders. You hear, Hirshke?

HIRSH. I hear.

MENDEL. You were at the well and filled the tubs full to the brim. That's why you must go firmly, calmly, and not upset them too much so you won't spill a single drop—just like a good water carrier.

HIRSH. Ah, my dear brother. (*Hirsh suddenly breaks down. Mendel catches him.*)

MENDEL. Hirshke, you are crying. Don't cry! Even at my father's they sing with joy.

HIRSH. (*Recovers and stands resolutely.*) You're right. Really, why should

I cry when I know so many brothers remain on this world, so many comrades. And I? Who am I? So, the truth, why should I lament. I would only like to ask that I should be a little bit remembered. And you, dear wife, when you give birth to a son—

GUARD. Finished! (*The women fall frantically, hysterically upon Hirsh. Mendel tears them away.*)

MENDEL. No weeping, no tears! (*Mendel leads them to the door, away from Hirsh. Each backs out the door in order to get a last look at Hirsh. Hirsh stands calmly with his head held high and looks upon them with a radiant smile. Mendel, as though transported in religious ecstasy, is the last to leave. When the door closes, the cries of the women's lament are heard but are quickly stifled. Hirsh stands transfixed and does not notice the Rabbi's entrance.*)

RABBI. In these last moments of life—

HIRSH. Ha? What?

RABBI. —each soul must confess.

HIRSH. Ah, if you only could have listened to what Mendel said.

RABBI. What Mendel?

HIRSH. My comrade since childhood. If I would ask that dear soul, that good Mendel to put down his neck for me, he would immediately do it. And you—no, not you. So why have you come here? (*Pause.*) Confession? I deny nothing. My heart is clean, very pure. As for death, to be afraid of death is definitely not dignified. No, that's not for me.

RABBI. But, in the meanwhile, you did spill blood and almost committed murder.

HIRSH. (*Trembles.*) Blood? Did you say the same thing, too, about Von Wahl when he spilled the blood of my brothers? (*Rabbi remains silent.*) Will you, then, tell him that today? That he spilled blood! Will you tell him that? (*Rabbi is silent.*)

HIRSH. (*Assertively.*) Will you? Will you tell him? (*Hirsh pushes the Rabbi to the door. The Rabbi yields and allows himself, with steps backward,* bewildered, to be forced through the door. Hirsh shudders and sinks to the cot. He hides his face in his hands. The key in the door is turning to lock the door when a command is heard.*)

VOICE. Hold, attention! (*The door opens again. The Guard, in a panic, enters.*)

GUARD. (*To Hirsh.*) Attention! Stand up, you! (*Von Wahl, with his staff and prison overseer enters. Hirsh raises his head, but remains seated.*) Stand up! (*Hirsh remains seated. Two guards hurl themselves at him.*)

VON WAHL. (*Ordering the guards back.*) Let him sit. (*He approaches Hirsh and studies him.*) Still so young. How old are you?

HIRSH. Old enough. As old as I need to be.

VON WAHL. That's right. Still, too young to be so certain.

HIRSH. Yet, more certain than young.

VON WAHL. I can revoke the death sentence if—

HIRSH. I am not begging you for forgiveness.

VON WAHL. Then tell me why your face is so pale? I can hear your teeth chattering.

HIRSH. So they will chatter a while and then stop.

VON WAHL. That's so. A simple shoemaker, I'm told. (*Hirsh turns his face away from Von Wahl.*) And you really, truly, wanted to kill me?

HIRSH. That my bullet did not strike you, that I regret. But, now it does not bother me; it is better this way. Von Wahl will always be the murderer, not I. And even if I did not succeed, my comrade will succeed.

VON WAHL. Who is he?

HIRSH. (*Hirsh rises and stands proudly.*) My comrade is the whole world. (*From outside are heard cries.*)

VOICES. Long live Hirsh Lekert!

VON WAHL. (*To one of his staff.*) Silence them! Drown them out with the beating of drums. (*Orderly exits. Much clanging of keys and locks.*) Is the gallows ready on the military field?

PRISON OVERSEER. Everything is ready, your excellency.

VON WAHL. And right next to the gallows, the grave?

PRISON OVERSEER. Also ready, sir.

VON WAHL. All the soldiers are to march over the grave. I want no memory, no sign of him to be found. Beat the drums. Take him, this shoemaker.

(*Guards try to grab Hirsh Lekert in order to lead him.*)

HIRSH. (*Thrusting the guards from him.*)

I'll go alone. (*The procession starts. The drums and bugles drown out all outcries from other cells and from the outside. The curtain falls as the drums continue. The curtain rises. The noise of the drums has given way to the hum of a sewing machine. The scene is a tailor's work room. Ruchel and Raisel sit near the machine and sew.*)

RUCHEL. (*Singing to the tune of a folk melody.*)

When Hirshke went out of the house
He said good night, good night.
When Hirshke approached the circus,
A little while, some time he spent—

RAISEL. (*Taking up the song.*)

Then the tyrants, our Hirshke they took.
And in the horror that followed
One comrade said to another,
We lost our bravest brother.

RUCHEL.

Four o'clock in the morning
They brought Hirshke to the military field.
And Hirshke said for the last time,
My dear brothers, a very good night—

RAISEL.

Brothers of mine, I am being hanged.
No longer may I do a thing.
Ah, brothers, don't forget me,
But make them account, the tyrannical regime,
For all our woes.

THE END

YANKEL BOYLA

by

Leon Kobrin

(1872-1946)

At the beginning of the Gordin era, remembered as the "first golden epoch" of the Yiddish theatre (ca. 1892–1902), a dynamic young Jewish writer, who had been inspired by the giants among his contemporary Russian writers, arrived in New York in 1892, abandoned his adolescent efforts at writing in Russian, and started an important and successful writing career with translations from the Russian for Yiddish-language journals. Leon Kobrin had left a life of penury in "der heim," Vitebsk, where he was born in 1872, for a new life that started with bitter years of hard work, long hours, and suffering in New York as a cigarmaker, shirtmaker, and baker. Reference is made to "der heim" to underscore Kobrin's past, for his plays were rooted in that traditional milieu that had enriched the writings of those immortals among the Yiddish writers. The powerful impact of ghetto life in the tenements provided him with themes for insight-filled dramas that reveal a world of considerable historical and social significance. His inspiration was found in the lives of Jewish workingmen with their family problems of reconciling Old-World folkways with the daily urgencies of adjusting to the ways of the New World.

Perhaps not so poetic, metaphoric, or literary as the works of Hirshbein and Pinski, Leon Kobrin's plays were powerfully dramatic and ideal for the stage. He was very much aware of the school of naturalism of Zola, Flaubert, Norris, Crane, and Dreiser, so that he immersed himself in realism and wrote with a dramatic intensity that brought the fateful, compelling tragedy of a Thomas Hardy-like situation to the Yiddish stage. Yet more than a malevolent fate compelled his heroes to an inevitable doom, for they were caught between the irreconcilable forces of loyalty-demanding tradition and native, human passions. Thus, in truth, Kobrin's works, as Hippolyte Taine had suggested for great folk literature, were wrung out of his race, his milieu, and his moment.

Like his popular fellow playwright Z. Libin, Kobrin was among the first to write on American-Jewish subjects, particularly of life in the tenements, of the tug-of-war between generations, between immigrant parents and their mod-

101

ern, American children. The generations' cleavage was colored by the mystique of shtetl life and lore that hearkened back to the past. After publication of his translations from the Russian in 1893, he succeeded in having critical essays and his first original story published in 1894. His writings and publications gained in volume and momentum, and in 1898 his first book, *Yankel Boyla and Other Tales,* received high critical acclaim and he was hailed as another Gorki. In collaboration with Jacob Gordin, his first play, *Minna,* was written and produced in 1899. That same year, his second play, *East Side Ghetto,* starred the famous Bertha Kalish. From then on to his death, Kobrin wrote many plays about the Jews, whose traditions were confronted and challenged by new values. A high point in his career as playwright was his dramatization of Israel Zangwill's *The Children of the Ghetto.* In addition to his many plays, Kobrin wrote novels that were first serialized in the Yiddish dailies; translated from the world classics of Shakespeare, Gorki, Chekhov, de Maupassant, Turgenev, and Tolstoy into Yiddish; wrote his autobiography that is an invaluable picture of Yiddish theatre and literature in America; and published his collected works.

When, in 1912, he encountered interference by his producer with the content of his famous play *Children of Nature* (also known as *Yankel Boyla* or *Dorf's Yung*), he successfully produced the play independently. Concurrently he organized the Jewish Playwrights' Association "to make the dramatist independent—to make it possible for him to express himself freely as he feels, and not as the manager expects him to." All of his works had high professional polish: plots were well organized, characters were conceived and developed with extraordinary insight and verisimilitude, and themes were so diversified that they demonstrated Kobrin's wide range of interest, creativity, and originality. All this was executed in bold, dramatic terms with strong emotional currents that did not shy away from erotic sensuality counterpointed by lyric, idyllic moments. The uninhibited passion of his writing never sank to bathos. Kobrin helped the Yiddish theatre and its dramatic literature to come of age, to rise above its tawdry operettas, vulgar melodramas, derivative problem plays, and spurious historical and Biblical vehicles for transient stars. His plays are unmistakably expressions of the Jewish folk, both in *der heim* and in their stimulating and volatile life in the tenements, where their immigrant psychology, according to Isaac Goldberg, directed the homesickness for the old country to a yearning upon themselves and formed a strong nationalistic feeling.

The universal problem of intermarriage has been a recurrent and popular theme in world literature and has had a sufficiency of exposure in the Yiddish theatre. A decade before the premiere in New York of Korbin's *Yankel Boyla,** Romania's great playwright, Ronetti Roman, had written the Romanian language drama *Manasse,* which received critical praise as possibly Romania's greatest play. The play, about the intermarriage of a Jew and a Gentile girl, caused anti-Semitic riots by students in Jassi; the play was forced to close. It was a different story in New York's Yiddish theatre, no longer proscribed by a Czar's ukase, no longer self-censored for fear of anti-Semitic hoodlums; a theatre supported by waves of immigrants seeking freedom, dignity, and culture among their own. In addition to the theme of tragic, illicit love, Kobrin forthrightly and courageously presented the destructive, insurmountable obstacle of ignorant superstition encountered by young lovers, who are thereby doomed.

The play is about Yankel, a village boy, who is torn between his love for a Gentile girl and his vow to his dying father not to marry outside his faith. Obliged to marry a girl in his faith whom he does not love, while his real love

---

* The spelling of *Boyla* varies in different texts, i.e., Boila, Boyle, Boyleh, Boile, with full voice given to the final syllable. This text uses Boyla.

is carrying his unborn child, the bridegroom hangs himself on his wedding day. The drama unfolds with intellectual honesty, for the hero is shown without unusual attributes for a village youth with limited worldliness, while the Gentiles are sympathetically, possibly more virtuously portrayed than the superstition-bound Jews, with the exception of the village's venal priest. The ignorance of Jews in small villages, isolated from modern intellectual currents, traps them in a world that dooms them to tragedy much like the slothful, grim world of Tolstoy's *Power of Darkness*. Realism is also well served in *Yankel Boyla* in its portrayal of the rough, earthy Russian village life with a brutally penetrating view of the Jew at society's lowest level. The curse of superstition that terrorized Yankel demonstrates how it can repress universal human emotions, atrophy the soul, and lead to inevitable tragedy. The play is part of that folk literature that pointed the way to emancipation for the masses from the dark pit of enslavement in which they were shackled by blind religious devotion with its irrationality. The theme is focused on a village swain whose personal tragedy started when he could not escape the ghettoes of mind and spirit.

YANKEL BOYLA

English Version by David S. Lifson

by

Leon Kobrin

CAST OF CHARACTERS

JOSHUA, an Innkeeper
FRUME, his wife
YANKEL BOYLA, their only son
NACHUM NOVOSELSKER, Joshua's brother
CHAYKE, his daughter
HIRSH BAER, a fisherman
ZALMAN ZIRELE'S, a young fisherman
CHATZE TREINES, a fisherman
PROKOP, an old peasant
NATASHA, his granddaughter
ITZE PASTERNAK, boss of the fishermen
                    Peasants, Village Musicians, etc.

The play takes place in a village adjoining a large fishery in the province of Mogilov, near the Dnieper River.

ACT I
  Scene 1

        A fishermen's workroom attached to the home of Prokop; it is on the shore of a lake. Late in a spring morning.

  Scene 2

        Later that day. A room in Joshua's house, which is adjacent to his tavern.

ACT II

The yard outside the fishermen's workroom.
Early morning, mid-summer day.

ACT III

The fishermen's workroom.
Morning, early autumn.

ACT IV

A few days later. A room in Joshua's house.

ACT I

SCENE 1

Before the curtain rises, a Russian folk song is heard. Then the curtain rises on the fishermen's work room that is dominated by a large table. Near it is a Russian stove with its couch. Along the back wall is a large window through which the lake is seen, and through which the sun streams. Enter Chatze Treines, a skinny, middle-aged Jew, with a sleepy-looking face adorned by a ragged, yellowish beard, dressed in a heavy canvas shirt that covers the traditional, orthodox undergarment, and young—say around 23 years old —Zalman Zireles, a robust, lusty youth with a weatherbeaten face, who is dressed in a black vest, wide boots with long uppers, together with other peasant-fishermen, sit on the earthen floor while they repair a large net with long wooden needles and heavy thread. All, except Chatze, are singing the Russian folk song.

ZALMAN. (*When the singing has stopped.*) Ach! When Yankele Boyla sings that song, that's really something to hear. That's when the shikses would lie down for him. As true as I'm a Jew, I envy him!

CHATZE. As true as you are a Jew? Gevald! You are a Jew, Yankele Boyla is a Jew, old Hirsh Baer is a Jew . . . (*Disgustedly.*) If such as you are Jews, then God help us! And can you be counted in a minion for holy prayer, such Jews? You're as much Jews as Ivan or old Prokop. I mean, really!

ZALMAN. Aha, he's already starting in on us with his screwball logic, mixing up one thing with another, this philosophe! Just knock it off! Tell me, why, in the middle of nothing, you come in as if from another world and begin to mix up one thing with another? Stick to your job, fix the net, and stop bothering me, you— you philosophe! Hirsh Baer will be here any minute and the net is still not fixed. And the boats aren't ready yet, either. He'll give us all holy hell.

CHATZE. My heart aches for you, Zalman. I knew your father well. He was a real Jew. While you are an— er—er, no better than a goy I mean, really!

ZALMAN. (*Mockingly.*) I, too, mean "really," Reb Chatze. If I am not so religious, then I will be whipped. So why does it bother you?

CHATZE. All right, be spiteful, Zalman. But He, the Almighty, He sees, He hears, and He writes it down. How did the wise man always say: *Locher Tzadik Levrochoh,* the sinful person lives till that time when he must stretch out his legs, and then? Ah then . . . gevald! (*Chatze lowers his head with a sigh as he bends to his work.*)

ZALMAN. Quiet. Here comes Nachum Novoselsker. Let him hear your babbling nonsense. (*Nachum Novoselsker enters. He is shortsighted, has a wide brush of black beard, wears cotton trousers, and an open caftan with one gray sleeve and the other yellow. His naked chest is visible. On his head he wears a cap with half a visor.*)

NACHUM. God help us! What a heat, little ones! (*He scratches under his arms.*) It's so hot and humid. That's

what we can expect, a hot July, just
wait and see.

ZALMAN. So, you're sweating, Reb
Nachum, eh? How does our philosophe here say it, "I mean, really!" I
have an idea how you won't sweat.
Lie down in your heavy winter caftan and pants along with us in the
ice house, on the ice between the
fish. Then you won't sweat. It'll be
all right; after all, you're some fish
too.

NACHUM. So you're laughing at the
way I'm dressed, eh Zalman? What
then should I wear? Maybe I should
put on my sabbath clothes, what?
That would be a bitter sin if I have
to go to town and don't have anything to wear.

CHATZE. (*Rising.*) A good day to you,
Reb Nachum.

NACHUM. (*Squinting his shortsighted
eyes.*) Eh, eh, you'll excuse me. Is
that you, Reb Chatze? What do you
say to that—I didn't even notice you.
See for yourself—a shortsighted
horse and half blind. So how are you
old boy?

CHATZE. Eh, Reb Nachum, we exist,
we work, we make—sins we make.
Good God, be careful today, be careful of sin tomorrow. When you've become a fisherman in a village far
from your synagogue, far from your
fellow Jews, it is hard to keep from
sinning. You never pray together,
and the sanctification of a hymn you
never hear. Not even an Amen is
said. Ah, Reb Nachum, to make a
living—gevald! Since I've been a
fisherman these past six months, I'm
no longer a real Jew. I'm not joking
when I say that without an act
of faith to hold on to, what is a Jew?
Where? Here? Tpfui! Good God,
without a good deed, it's like a body
without a soul. I mean, really!

NACHUM. (*Sighs.*) Ah, how true, Reb
Chatze. You're right, it's exactly so.
If you'll excuse me, a Jew without a
good deed is, for example, like a
horse without its harness, or like my
mare without the whip. You, at least,
Reb Chatze, have plenty of good

deeds to your credit from before: A
man from the big city, if you'll excuse me, who went to the synagogue
regularly, squeezed in a prayer now
and then, or was called up before
the congregation to read from the
sacred scroll, and sometimes even
dipped himself in a real Jewish ritual bath, and good deeds like that . . .
but when you take such a good-for-
nothing like me, you should excuse
me, who have lived all my life in a
little village, yes, since my childhood
on . . . ech, you should excuse me, it's
disgusting. Ah, they will tear our flesh
in the hereafter, and we can't complain! Oh, will they whip us!

ZALMAN. Reb Nachum, when you go
into the hereafter, you should wear
your cotton caftan and those pants of
yours. Then, when they whip you,
they'll whip right into the cloth . . .
you won't feel a thing.

NACHUM. Nu, Nu, Zalmanke, the devil take you! Don't sneer at Jewishness. You aren't Yankele yet. You're
a big city boy, and your father probably didn't hold back giving you
a beating once in a while, either, so
you should be a pious Jew. As for
Yankele, he's a special case when he
goes away from our Jewish ways. As
an only son, he was spared being
whipped by his father. So he grew
up like a wild one. You should excuse
me, he doesn't know, for example, a
single word of Hebrew. Oh, to bring
up good Jewish children, they should
be pious Jews, they must know the
whip. Why, do you think, they make
straps with long strands like noodles,
or whips, or birch rods? Because, you
should understand, my Zalmanke,
Jewish fathers should have with what
to discipline Jewish children. If you
want, for example, that a horse
should behave properly, he must be
beaten. And if you want, for example,
that Jewish children should be genuine, pious Jews, the lash must teach
them, aha, you should excuse me, and
don't say a word!

ZALMAN. Here, in this world we must
be beaten and in the hereafter we

will be beaten. (*He has nodded to Chatze and then Nachum.*) Oy, oy—it's some pleasure to be a Jew!
(*Zalman sings.*)
Shasshinka, mashinka dzenka parashinka, oy liuliu, oy liuliu . . .

CHATZE. You hear that, Reb Nachum? Sashink and mashinka. But what else could he have learned to sing from these fishermen, maybe something from the heart? Oy, Reb Nachum, what a bitter life this is! How it tears our Jews away from Jewishness—I mean, really!

NACHUM. You're right, Reb Chatze. What a life! Where have you ever seen so many Jewish fishermen who work like these lowdown uncircumcized? There was a time when Hirsh Baer was the only Jewish fisherman in the village, and now . . . (*From the outside yard Hirsh Baer's commanding voice is heard.*)

HIRSH BAER. (*Off.*) Chatze, Zalman. The wolves should devour you.

ZALMAN. Hirsh Baer is yelling. He's mad already. (*Yells out his response to Hirsh Baer.*) Reb Hirsh Baer, we're almost ready. (*Turns to Chatze.*)
Reb Chatze, you'd better tell off this loudmouth; he shouldn't yell at us like that, that old sinner . . .

CHATZE. (*Quickly applying himself to working on the net.*) He has every right to yell. Here he is in charge of the fishermen. He is supposed to give an account of us to the boss. (*Enter Hirsh Baer, with a patriarchal, long, white beard, wearing a wide cloak and a black leather apron, large work gloves, and wide, yellow boots. He is lame in one leg.*)

HIRSH BAER. Why aren't the boats ready? I expect the boss to come back from town any minute, and . . .

ZALMAN. We'll finish the net right away, then we'll take care of the boats. Look, Reb Hirsh Baer, here on the right edge we found a big hole . . .

HIRSH BAER. How big?

ZALMAN. (*Laughs.*) As big as Chatze's head, at least.

HIRSH BAER. As long as it's not bigger than Chatze's head, there's no danger. It should just not be as big as your stupid mouth, you silly ass, you, your heart should only stop for a minute. (*Hirsh Baer removes the cloak and then starts removing innumerable sacks that are wrapped around his middle.*)

ZALMAN. (*Surprised at the sight.*) Wh—wha—what are all these sacks, Reb Hirsh Baer?

HIRSH BAER. (*Chuckling.*) These sacks? They're a sure sign that God does not abandon such a pious man as me. Actually, I don't really need them. (*Starts to laugh as he tells his story.*) Oh, that dumb peasant head! Just listen to this story. I was riding past Ivan, the elder churchwarden's place, with a load of fish for the ice house. He stops me with a greeting—ah, a good health, Hirsh Baer, good health. Carrying fish? Fish, Reb Ivan. So, he reminds me that yesterday I had asked him to lend me an axe. If I want, he tells me, I can go into his storehouse and pick out an axe. Well, right away, I knew that Reb Ivan wants to be left alone with the fish. So I think to myself, Good, Reb Ivan. You can stay here alone with my fish, while I will be alone in your storeroom. Then we will see who will whistle at whom. *Trasze twoyej materi!* Know your own mother! To come to the point, I go into the storeroom and turn around to watch Reb Ivan. There he was, crawling around on all fours among the fish, like a good swine, you should excuse me, and he pulls some fish out of the pile and hides them in his bosom. Meanwhile, I see in the storeroom a fortune of sacks. Quickly I take off my cloak and start to wrap sack upon sack around me. To hell with the fish Reb Ivan stole from me. Amen. I put on my cloak again, took a good pinch of tobacco, picked up the axe and "haida," went out to Reb Ivan. He's standing there near my wagon, with both hands across his bosom, you know, covering the fish so that I won't notice the bulge. But I start to tickle him under his armpits, kitzle, kitzle. He shakes and giggles so much that the fish slip out from his bosom. That Reb Ivan really thought he had put one over on me—ha, ha, ha . . . (*All but Chatze laugh.*)

CHATZE. And I heard that the Rabbi from Chelm said in a sermon that he who steals a horse or as little as a needle, whether from a gentile or a Jew, it makes no difference, it's one and the same thing, he's a thief just the same. Feh! I mean, really!

HIRSH BAER. How do you do, the wise scholar from Chelm speaks again. What do you say, do you want a pinch of the tobacco, Chatze? You and your stupid Chelm donkey, you. So I have stolen from him, eh? I only made an exchange with him. When I wasn't looking he took fish from me, and when he wasn't looking I took some sacks from him. (*The clanging of a gong interrupts him.*) The boss is back from town! Nu, wise man of Chelm, Zalman, Archip, Stephen, step lively—out with the net and attend to the boats. (*The men stretch the net, then expertly and quickly fold it and carry it out.*)

ZALMAN. Hurry up, Reb Chatze. Come on! The boss!

CHATZE. (*Helping with the net.*) You should be so afraid of God as you fear the boss. (*All but Hirsh Baer and Nachum go out. The men are heard taking up a folk song quietly, outdoors.*)

NACHUM. Reb Hirsh Baer, I hope you have not forgotten, for example, that I once asked you to hire Yankel for a fisherman.

HIRSH BAER. (*Sarcastically.*) If you will put up a quart of schnapps, we'll hire him. That's all we're missing among our fishermen, a smart alec character like Yankele.

NACHUM. Only a quart? I'll give you a whole barrel of the best spirits if you'll only make him become a some-

body. You must try to understand, Reb Hirsh Baer, what my miserable situation is. For example, Yankel is my Chaykele's intended groom— ach, it's a disgusting situation, don't ask.

HIRSH BAER. The match is really on between Yankel and your Chayke?

NACHUM. (*Tragically.*) What then, Reb Hirsh Baer? *Tkias Kaf,* it's all settled, you should excuse me! Who would have expected that Yankele would grow up to be such a gypsy, for example? Just her luck that it happened to my Chaykele. She had just been born, only one week old, and Yankele was a little puppy, two years old,—and my brother Joshua says to me at that lucky occasion, "Nachum, my dearest and closest, you have a newborn daughter, Chaykele, and I have my young puppy, Yankele. Let them be bride and groom . . ."

HIRSH BAER. (*Impatiently interrupting.*) I know, I know. You came to an agreement that the puppy should take the newborn, but the puppy grew up to be a wild animal. Now you're saying he's no good for your Chaykele. I know all that, so why do you keep telling me the same old story and bothering my head with it?

NACHUM. It hurts so much, Reb Hirsh Baer, you should excuse me! For example, take me, I'm not such a great scholar, yet I can recite a chapter of Thilim from the good book—but Yankele?

HIRSH BAER. How is Joshua?

NACHUM. He's barely alive. He actually sent for me today. He says he wants that the nuptials should take place with Chaykele right away, today! Ach, if my brother Joshua were only in good health, I would tear away the agreement from him by force if necessary, even with a fight. But like this? Go and fight with a sick man! He can die, for example, and then what? There would be no peace at all on account of him. Ach, it's depressing, you should excuse me. (*A noise off.*)

HIRSH BAER. Quiet, let it be. The boss is coming. And you, don't talk so much either, you donkey. Go get Yankele and send him over here. Let him, by himself, ask the boss.

NACHUM. Will you also throw in a good word?

HIRSH BAER. Yes, yes already. Anything as long as you won't bother me.

NACHUM. You'll get a real surprise from me; you won't be sorry. (*Enter Itze Pasternack. He is around forty years old, good looking, with broad shoulders and a black beard, and dressed like a sophisticated man of the city. Zalman, carrying a valise, follows him.*)

ITZE. Hello, Reb Hirsh Baer. Oh, it's really hot! (*Wipes his forehead.*)

HIRSH BAER. Sholem Aleichem. Greetings. (*To Zalman.*) Zalman, tell Natasha about the samovar.

ZALMAN. (*Yelling toward the main house.*) Natasha! Natasha!

NATASHA. (*From the main house.*) Yoo ho, ho-ho.

ZALMAN. Bring the samovar. (*Natasha enters, her long, blonde hair braided, and wearing a red shawl. She has beads around her throat, and is dressed in a short, colorful skirt and large shoes without shoelaces on her naked feet. She shuffles in with a steaming samovar.*)

NATASHA. Here's the samovar. Stop hollering, Zalman. You'll have plenty of time to gulp down the tea. (*She places the samovar on the table, then rubs her nose in her sleeve.**)

ZALMAN. And where are the glasses?

NATASHA. I'll bring them, I'll bring them right away. (*She shuffles out.*)

ZALMAN. (*Attempting to ingratiate himself with Itze.*) It's really hot, boss, eh?

ITZE. Oh boy, what a heat!

ZALMAN. Make yourself comfortable. Here, take off your cloak. (*Zalman assists Itze in removing his cloak and puts it aside.*) You can say it again, it's really hot! You're soaking with sweat, ha? Here, let me help you take off your boots. (*Itze sits while Zalman pulls off the boots, then Zalman sticks his nose into a boot.*) Wow! What a stink. It's murder! (*Zalman throws the boots under the table and hands Itze a pair of slippers.*) Do you want some tea, boss? I'll give it to you. (*Natasha enters with glasses.*)

HIRSH BAER. Just look at the way he bows himself before the boss, and his mouth doesn't stop chattering. Zalman, if there's anything I despise, it's when someone grovels like a dog. No matter how you suck up to him, he won't have you as a son-in-law, you stupid ass! Here, Natasha, pour the tea.

NATASHA. Here, I'm pouring, I'm pouring, Hirsh Baer. What queer people. It's terribly hot, so they steam themselves with boiling tea. (*She pours.*) Here, steam yourselves good. Here, take . . . (*She wipes her sweating forehead with her sleeve. All but Natasha seat themselves at the table.*)

ITZE. Natasha, call in Chatzele to have some tea.

NATASHA. Who? Chatzele? Oh, Chatze. Yes, Chatzele. (*She looks at Itze and scratches her back.*) Did you bring it?

ITZE. Bring what?

NATASHA. The present.

ITZE. Oh, I forgot it again. Well, Natasha, no fooling, next time I promise I won't forget again. I'll bring you a gold ring next time, God willing.

NATASHA. Ha, it's not right to fool people, not nice.

ITZE. This shikse is a smart girl . . .

HIRSH BAER. (*Rises from the table and approaches Natasha, offering her his snuff box.*) Here, I have a present for you. Take a pinch of snuff. Here, take it . . . (*He thrusts the open box under her nose.*)

NATASHA. (*She jumps away and starts to sneeze.*) Are you crazy? Damn! Your hands should wither, Reb Hirsh

---

* One would surmise that, by means of this piece of stage business, Kobrin attempted to establish how uncouth Natasha was.

Baer. (*She sneezes and laughs. The others join in the laughter.*)

CHATZE. (*Enters, wipes his hands on the sleeves of his shirt, and sits at the table.*)

Natasha, peel us some potatoes. (*Natasha turns to go but is detained by Itze.*)

ITZE. Natasha, wait—Here, have something sweet. (*Itze hands her a few pieces of sugar.*)

NATASHA. Ah, thanks. (*She places one piece of the sugar in her mouth, the rest she hides in her bosom. Suddenly there is heard from outside the sound of a nightingale. Natasha stands still and joyfully smiles.*) Do you hear? That's Yankele. He can imitate all the birds, that rascal! (*Natasha runs out to the house. Yankel appears at the window of the yard facing the lake. He enters the fishermen's room. He is wearing a black jacket, a red, flowered kerchief around his neck, and long boots that are smeared with pitch.*)

YANKEL*. (*In a basso voice.*) Good morning.

HIRSH BAER. Look who's here, a stranger! How is the scholar, Boyla? and look how dressed up you are. Are you an aristocrat, a count maybe, Yankele? Look, with a bandana around his neck, the boots polished with pitch. What kind of a holiday are you celebrating today, Yankele?

ZALMAN. He's going to visit his bride, a lame old mare, isn't that right, Yankele?

YANKEL. Listen you, Zalman, don't be such a smart aleck. Just keep quiet! (*Yankel sits astride a chair. Natasha enters with potatoes cradled in her skirt. Upon seeing Yankel, she nods happily to him, and wipes her nose with her fists. He winks at her. She contentedly sits in a corner and starts to peel the potatoes.*)

YANKEL. (*Turns to Itze.*) Boss, I heard that you were here, so I came . . .

HIRSH BAER. Thank you for your trouble, Yankel.

YANKEL. Allow me, Reb Hirsh Baer, allow me. I have a favor to ask from you, Boss . . . (*He scratches his head.*) I mean Mr. Boss. I have decided this is no way to live, just going around doing nothing. So I told my father that I'm going to see the boss and tell him I want to become a fisherman, so what the hell!

HIRSH BAER. Ach, a plague on this Boyla. Did you ever hear the like? *He wants to do the boss a favor!*

ITZE. (*With a smile.*) I know what he means. He's trying to say he has a request to make of me, not a favor.

YANKEL. (*Enthusiastically rising from his chair.*) That's it, Mr. Boss, that's it, a request . . . By God, that's it. Do me, Mr. Boss, the request—or a favor or what else. (*All except Chatze laugh. Natasha looks around and then also laughs, covering her mouth with a hand that holds a potato.*)

CHATZE. (*With pained expression.*) That also claims to be a Jew! Gevald!

HIRSH BAER. (*Chanting as if reading a prayer.*) Oh, is this Yankele a Talmudic scholar! Is he a genius? So, Yankele, the great Talmudist, we will take you on as a fisherman when you can conduct the benediction of the carp.

CHATZE. You're all some bunch of Talmudists! You ought to be ashamed . . .

ZALMAN. Reb Hirsh Baer, let Yankel recite the parts of the female anatomy—*Isichu Mekimon.*

YANKEL. (*Angry.*) You, Zalman, I told you before you'd better keep quiet. Don't you stumble and mumble. I can say it better than you: Izeheyu maka . . . maka . . . (*He cannot pronounce the Hebrew phrase, becomes angrier and spits.*) Tpfui! The wolves should tear you to pieces, Zalman! (*He scowls at Zalman and sits, while all the others laugh. Suddenly the sharp caw of a crow is heard. Yankel jumps up in fright.*) A crow! The wolves should grab her!

HIRSH BAER. Just look how scared he is

---

* In the original, Yankel's speech is indicated as very thick and accompanied by a stutter.

of a crow. Would you think a healthy specimen like him would be scared that somebody would come and grab him? After his little three-year-old sister died two years ago, he was so afraid of the dark that he didn't go out of the house at night for a whole year. But now, he's no longer afraid of live girls, but they have to be much older than three years. (*He affectionately pokes Yankel, who laughs.*) Ach, you rascal, the devil take you. Now he's laughing. You like that, eh?

YANKEL. I'm not afraid. I'm afraid of nobody. But, a crow is a pagan bird, and when she caws, it's an evil sign, it means there's going to be bad times—tpfui!

ITZE. So, Yankele, it seems you want to be a fisherman? Are you sure you'll work hard and not loaf on the job?

YANKEL. Who? Me loaf? (*He sticks out his chest and thumps it.*) Mr. Boss, may I drop dead if I loaf. I should die if I'm lazy, Mr. Boss . . . (*He involuntarily makes a gesture as though to cross himself.*)

CHATZE. (*With great alarm.*) Oy, look! He wants to cross himself!

YANKEL. (*Bewildered.*) Tpfui! (*Drops his arm.*) I'm not crossing myself. I'm as good a Jew as Chatze, as Hirsh Baer, or as you, Mr. Boss. I did not cross myself. It's only a stupid joke of mine . . . (*He bangs on his head.*) *Vat Zoraza,* what a lousy disease!

ITZE. Zalman, give Yankele a pair of fisherman's boots. Well, Yankele, you start your month tomorrow.

ZALMAN. (*Rises, crosses to a corner from which he brings out a pair of fisherman's boots.*) Here, Yankele. You better pull your part of the net or Hirsh Baer will pull out your guts.

YANKEL. I'm not worried, so don't you. (*He handles the boots with enthusiasm and dances around with them.*) Aha! I'm a fisherman! I am a fisherman!

HIRSH BAER. Satisfied now, Yankele? So, dance. Give us a dance and show the boss how talented you are.

YANKEL. (*Serious.*) No, no. Some other time. (*He approaches Itze.*) Spasibo, Bal A Boss—thank you, Mr. Boss. (*He presses Itze's hand, and half bows to him.*)

HIRSH BAER. So, it will have to be another time, my brilliant scholar. (*Turns to the others.*) Chatze, Zalman, out with the boats! Boss, are you going with us?

ITZE. Yes, yes . . . (*All rise and leave for the door, Zalman being the last one; as he passes Natasha, he stealthily tickles her. The others claimed a potato from her as they left. Yankel has observed Zalman's gambit and glares at Natasha. When all the others have finally left, Yankel, with his boots slung over his shoulder, approaches her and excitedly grabs her to him.*)

YANKEL. Listen, you!

NATASHA. (*Still giggling.*) What?

YANKEL. Natasha, I heard that Zalmanke and you are hanging around together. If that's true, Natasha, watch out for your sack of bones!

NATASHA. What do you mean, me and Zalmanke? What are you talking about, Yankele? I love only you, Yankele, and that's all. Zalmanke is a no-good fool, and as far as I'm concerned he can go burn!

YANKEL. (*Embraces her passionately.*) Do you mean it, Natasha? Tell me the truth. Go on, say it! Ah, Natasha, I'm so mixed up . . . I love you so much, Natasha, ah how I love you, you witch! (*His embrace becomes more intense.*)

NATASHA. (*Squeals.*) Yankel, don't squeeze so hard. You'll squeeze out my soul!

YANKEL. (*Releases her.*) How much do you love me, Natasha? How much, ha?

NATASHA. I love you very much, Yankel, my eagle. I should die on this spot if I don't love you. (*Puts her arms around him.*) Yankel, my wild beloved eagle!

YANKEL. (*Laughs in an assumed basso tone.*) Ho, ho, ho! (*Tenderly caresses *her head.*) You're my beautiful one. Ah, what a lovely imp you are, may the wolves devour you.

NATASHA. You're fooling me, Yankel. You don't love me. You already have a bride. Your Uncle Nachum's Chayke . . .

YANKEL. Chayke? Tpfui! She is my bride? Ha, ha, ha! Natasha, I should drop dead like a dog if she is my bride! I hate her, Natasha. Chayke is an ape, not a girl, a twenty-year plague on her!

NATASHA. (*Holding him tighter.*) Yankel, your bride should be a beauty, the prettiest girl in the village. You know, the kind of girl the village boys' eyes fall out from staring at her, that's the kind of girl. You are the best dancer, the best singer in the whole village. And you're so healthy and strong, my singing bird, just like a young oak tree. By God, Chayke is not worthy of you. What kind of a girl is she? She can't even dance, she can't sing, and she never goes to any of the fairs . . . (*She suddenly stops.*) Oh, here she is! (*Chayke appears at the door. She wears her father's boots, a short dress, and a cotton cloak. She is thin, with a tired and worn-out face; her head is covered with feathers. She comes in abruptly. Seeing Yankel with Natasha, she stops, out of breath, and wrings her hands.*)

CHAYKE. (*Frightened.*) Yankele! I'm looking all over for you—it's your papa. He's dying—and you're standing here with this . . . this shikse . . . Oh, Boyla!

YANKEL. What are you babbling about? What do you mean he's dying? You should die, you fool, you ape you!

CHAYKE. Oh, Yankel, I shouldn't live till tomorrow if I'm lying. I tell you, he is dying. Hurry, run home. You'd do better to say a chapter of the Psalms when your father lies dying than make love to a shikse!

YANKEL. Are you really telling me the truth, Chayke? Is he dying? Look, Chayke, if my father is not dying and

you're fooling me, I'll break your neck. Remember! (*He threatens Chayke with his fists.*)

CHAYKE. He is dying, I'm telling you! We all knew he was dying. Your dog, Barbos, was barking all night. Run home right away. I'm going to call the fishermen so they can go say the prayer for the dying. (*Chayke quickly leaves.*)

YANKEL. Natasha, my father is dying. I think she told the truth. Barbos really did bark. I heard him myself. I'm going home. (*He speaks to her tenderly and with grief.*) And I was hoping to go with you to the woods, my darling Natasha. I'm sorry.

NATASHA. Go, darling Yankel. (*She kisses him.*) I'll come later to your father's inn. (*He leaves as the curtain falls.*)

CURTAIN

ACT I

SCENE 2

A room in Joshua's house, which is adjacent to his tavern. The room has smoke-covered walls. Near the door is a bed with the very sick Joshua on it. Frume, his wife, wearing a white wig, stands weeping at the head of the bed. Nachum stands in a corner silently praying with a book of Psalms in his hands. From the adjoining tavern room is heard the singing of the peasant patrons as they drink.

JOSHUA. (*Groaning.*) Oh, oh, those peasant goyem! Frume, beg them not to yell so much. Gevald, Frume, where are the Jewish men? I'm dying. Where is Yankele? At least I should pray the *Vidu* like a Jew! (*Taps his heart rhythmically in prayer.*) *Chutusi, Evisu, Psheti, Lefunechu,* Oh God, dear Father, all my life I have lived among the goyem . . . I'm a blind man, an ignorant fool. Your Jewishness I have not observed. Don't punish me too harshly, dear God. Woe is me, where are our Jews? Nachum, my own, where are you?

FRUME. (*To Nachum.*) Nachum, Joshua is calling you.

NACHUM. (*Approaching the bed, speaking with compassion.*) You're calling me, Joshua, my dear brother?

JOSHUA. I want to pray the *Vidu*, but I don't know it by heart. Maybe you know it, Nachum, my own?

NACHUM. (*Scratching his armpit.*) I? How should I know it? For example, what trouble I have to stumble through the Psalm book, you should excuse me. O brother, my dear one, we are both some scholars of the Talmud. We'll both get our share of beatings with an iron rod in the other world—ach, don't ask!

JOSHUA. (*Clutching Nachum and trembling with fright.*) Oh, oh, will they punish us there . . . they will roast, burn . . . fry in hot frying pans . . . boiled in barrels of fat. I'm so frightened. I'm not a good Jew. Oh, save me, don't let me die! I'm afraid to come before God . . . and my boy, my Yankele, will he be able to say *Kadish*, the prayer for his dead father like a good Jew? Oh, oh . . . (*He falls back on his pillow with a forlorn sigh, and resumes the rhythmic tapping on his heart.*) Chutusi Eyvusi, Psheti, Lefunechu . . . (*From outside the roar of a bull.*)

YANKEL. (*Loudly, from outside.*) Tschoch, tschoch, tschoch! Ho! Ho! Grab him. Stop the noise!

FRUME. Yankele is here now. (*Joshua mutters. The singing stops.*)

YANKEL. (*Enters, with the boots hanging from a shoulder and speaking over his shoulder.*) The bull broke away. Run after the stupid animal!

FRUME. Sh, sh, shah . . . (*Yankel looks at her, then he stares at his sick father, throws the fisherman boots to a corner, and approaches the bed.*)

YANKEL. What's wrong, Papa?

JOSHUA. Dressed like a highwayman. (*Yankel looks around, frightened.*)

FRUME. (*Weeping.*) Yankele, look, your papa is dying. How will we live?

YANKEL. (*Falls close to the bed.*) Papa, my dear Papa—you musn't die, you won't die . . .

JOSHUA. You, Yankele? Just look, look at the end . . . oh, will they whip with iron rods! At least say the prayer for the dead for me like a true Jewish son? Woe is me!

YANKEL. (*Crying and stuttering.*) Papa, I'm t-t-telling you, you will not die. I'm t-t-telling you! I should drop dead if you will die!

JOSHUA. Oh, woe is me! I'm t-t-telling you! A Jew talks like that . . . my only son. Oh, he will not be able to say the prayer for the dead . . . "I'm t-t-telling you." Save me . . . It's so awful to die . . .

NACHUM. Yankele, take me for instance. Can't you talk like me? What is so hard to talk like a Jew?

FRUME. Yankele, my son, talk to him like a real Jew. Say: Papa, you will not die, God will have pity . . .

YANKEL. (*Bewildered and stuttering more intensely.*) W-w-what do you w-w-want? I d-d-don't speak like a Jew?

JOSHUA. Oy, woe! Let him better keep quiet. Nachum, my own dear one, where is Chaykele? The contract . . . have mercy . . .

NACHUM. The contract? (*Scratches himself under the armpits, with a wry face, then suddenly, with sobs, implores his sick brother.*) Joshua, my dear heart, release me from the agreement, have mercy. Am I not a Jew, too? Don't you think I, too, would like that my Chaykele's husband should be a real Jew, for example? Release me from the agreement, and don't complain.

JOSHUA. No, no! Have mercy on me. At least let me know he'll fall into Jewish hands.

FRUME. Nachum, he is your only brother. He's dying. Don't drain out his last drop of blood from him! Woe is me!

NACHUM. Nu, nu, what can I do? So let the agreement stand. Maybe it's fate, destined that way, for example.

YANKEL. (*Agitated.*) Papa, w-w-what are you saying? Chayke my bride? What do I want with Chayke? Chayke? I don't love her. (*He scratches his head, laughs, and then spits.*) Ha, ha, ha—Chayke my bride! Tpfui!

FRUME. Yankele, my own son, what's wrong with Chayke? You will marry her like all good Jews do . . .

YANKEL. I'm to marry Chayke? Oho! Mama, she can drop dead for all I care. I will not marry Chayke, and that's that!

NACHUM. Yankele, to marry Chaykele don't suit you? Maybe she's not good enough for you? What a calamity.

JOSHUA. If you will not agree to marry Chayke, the grave will spit me out . . I'll never rest in peace . . .

FRUME. Yankele, look, your father is dying! He will never forgive you . . .

NACHUM. Yankele, your father will strangle you. This is not a joke, for example!

YANKEL. (*Stares at Nachum incredulously.*) My father will strangle me? Me? Me? (*He points at his dying father and laughs.*) Ha, ha, ha—he's going to strangle me?

JOSHUA. (*Feverishly raising himself from his pillow.*) Yes, yes! I will come to you from my grave and strangle you—you—you goy, from my grave you gentile, you goy . . . ! (*He falls back exhausted upon his pillow.*)

YANKEL. (*Frightened.*) Papa, oh, dear papa!

JOSHUA. Yankele, be a Jew—a true Jew. If not, I will have no peace in my grave . . . (*Yankel is thoroughly frightened.*)

NACHUM. (*Whispering ominously into Yankel's ear.*) You hear? This is no joke, for example. He will come back and strangle you, then don't complain. (*Yankel, frantic and bewildered, confused and frightened, is in a panic.*)

FRUME. (*Approaches Yankel and caresses his head.*) Yankele, do this favor for your father . . . After all, what's wrong with Chayke?

YANKEL. (*Trembling.*) You're all devils! What do you want from me? (*He cries pitifully as he wanders about the room, wiping his tears on his sleeve. From the tavern loud singing of the peasants rises.*)

JOSHUA. Oh woe! Don't let them sing! Yet among goyem to die . . . ach, Almighty God, where are my Jews?

FRUME. (*Runs to the door and yells out.*) Please, friends, have pity and be quiet. My husband can't stand the noise! (*Quiet again.*) (*Hirsh Baer, Chayke, and Chatze enter. Yankel wipes his eyes with his sleeve and glares venomously at Chayke.*)

CHAYKE. (*To Nachum.*) Papa, papa! Why is Yankel so angry? (*Yankel snarls at her.*) Papa—look! He looks at me just like a wolf!

NACHUM. Chayke, just keep quiet! It's not your worry how he looks at you, for example. I have a whip for you, so don't complain! (*Chayke quickly edges away from Nachum in fear, and stands near Yankel as she stares at him.*)

FRUME. (*Approaches Yankel.*) See, Yankele. So what's wrong with Chaykele? Come over here, Chaykele. (*Chayke approaches Frume, who affectionately pats her on the cheek.*) See, Yankele, a really good girl, may no evil come to her.

YANKEL. The wolves should devour her! (*He walks away as he wipes his eyes with his sleeve.*)

CHAYKE. (*Following him.*) Now you're crying? Aha, you plague, I told you that your papa is dying! (*She also starts to weep.*) But don't cry, Yankele, God will . . .

YANKEL. Leave me alone, you horror! (*He flees from her and goes out the door.*)

CHAYKE. He can't stand me, that devil! (*She weeps afresh as she wipes her eyes with her fists. Frume approaches to comfort her.*)

HIRSH BAER. (*Goes to the dying Joshua.*) Joshua, what kind of foolish tricks are you up to? Get up and laugh at death! Who ever heard of such a thing? To die? What for? What's your hurry? You have plenty of time for that nonsense!

CHATZE. Reb Hirsh Baer, better you should tell him to say the *Vidu*. Just look—so, this is the same end for all of us, I mean, really! (*He sways and intones the* Thillum) Ashri Tmimi Derech Hahalochim Bsiris D' . . . (*Nachum prays after him.*)

HIRSH BAER. I know it, Chatze. That's how it goes—we catch the fish and the devil catches us!

JOSHUA. (*Gasping.*) The agreement . . . Nachum, the agreement . . .

NACHUM. Where is Yankele?

CHAYKE. I'll go call him. (*Chayke runs out.*)

FRUME. (*Calling.*) Yankele! (*Frume also runs out, after Chayke.*)

JOSHUA. Reb Hirsh Baer . . . (*Hirsh Baer approaches Joshua.*) I want to make sure my Yankele will fall into Jewish hands. Have pity on me, make sure that the contract is carried out. (*Enter Yankel, Frume, and Chayke.*)

FRUME. (*Wailing to Yankel.*) Yankele, after he dies he'll never give us peace or rest. My son, agree to the contract!

YANKEL. (*Groaning.*) Oh, what do you want from me? I'm going out of my mind! (*With a sudden scream.*) Oh, let it be! All right, let it be! (*Turns to Chayke and snarls at her.*) You miserable monkey, the wolves should tear you to pieces and devour you! (*Chayke is petrified with fright.*)

HIRSH BAER. (*Holding a kerchief aloft.*) Yankele, come over here. (*Yankel goes to Hirsh Baer.*) Chayke, you too, over here. (*Chayke goes to the other side of Hirsh Baer.*) Now, each of you hold an end of this kerchief . . .

NACHUM. And what's supposed to happen now, Reb Hirsh, if you'll excuse me?

HIRSH BAER. I shouldn't know from trouble how I don't know. Chatze, you're the scholar and Talmudist, what do we do to arrange matters?

CHATZE. (*He has been sitting near the bed.*) My dear Jews, woe is me, you don't know what to say on such an occasion? (*He rises and crosses to Hirsh Baer.*) Reb Nachum, what will you give the bridegroom as dowry?

NACHUM. Money, for example, not a broken penny! I'll give him a cow, not the speckled one, you should excuse me, but the black one. Yes, and two heifers, for example, and the old mare . . . and . . . what else? (*Scratches his head.*) Oh yes, and Chayke, you should excuse me, and don't complain.

CHAYKE. Papa! But papa! Didn't you promise that you would also give fifty rubles?

NACHUM. Stupid! Keep quiet, where is my whip? (*Chayke retreats from Nachum in fear.*)

CHATZE. And what will you give, Reb Joshua, to balance the dowry?

JOSHUA. (*Moaning.*) Everything—everything I possess.

CHATZE. (*Enthusiastic.*) My dear Jews, be witness to the agreement of the contract. And from today on, Chayke and Yankel are plighted bride and groom before God and before all people. (*All exchange "Mazel Tov" greetings. Frume, weeping, kisses Chayke and Yankel.*)

JOSHUA. Yankele! (*Depressed and crestfallen, Yankel goes to his father.*) Now I am content, Yankele. (*Joshua holds Yankel's hand and groans.*) Be a good Jew, Yankele. Ach, how they will flog us with iron rods—I am so frightened—(*Yankel shudders.*) Reb Chatze—Vidu . . .

CHATZE. (*With a melancholy voice.*) Dear Jews, Reb Joshua wants to say his confession. Start, Reb Joshua: *Ashmosi Begodosi Lefonechu* . . . (*The sick man quietly repeats after Chatz, while the others stand mournfully with lowered heads. Frume sobs and Yankel is choking with rage.*

Nachum leans his forehead against the head of the dying man's bed, as he rhythmically pounds his heart as each word is chanted. Chayke weeps into her sleeve. Natasha enters and edges to Hirsh Baer.)

NATASHA. *(Whispers to Hirsh Baer.)* How is Reb Joshua?

HIRSH BAER. Sh, sh, sh . . . He's dying.

NATASHA. Look, Yankele is crying . . . my God!

HIRSH BAER. He's just been engaged to Chayke, and now he's crying for his father.

NATASHA. *(Bewildered.)* Engaged? To Chayke? *(She holds her head in a state of shock.)*

CHATZE. *(Suddenly stops his prayers and looks at Joshua.)* Reb Joshua! *(He shakes Joshua.)* Reb Joshua! *(With tears in his voice.)* Boruch dayan, ehmess! . . .

FRUME. *(Raises her voice in lament.)* Joshua! Almighty God, woe is me! *(She rips off her wig and tears her hair as she gives vent to frightful screams.)*

YANKEL. *(As he falls upon his father's body and raves.)* Papa!

OTHERS. *(They pray with lowered heads.)* Boruch dayan, ehmess! Blessed be the true judge! *(Natasha stands transfixed as she crosses herself in a daze.)*

CURTAIN

ACT II

Two months later. The yard outside the fishermen's room. A path leads to the lake. It is early in a bright morning, with the sun sparkling on the lake and the crowing of roosters and chirping of birds filling the air. Natasha stands over a samovar and fans at its low flame with the upper leg of a boot. Prokop, an old Russian peasant and Natasha's grandfather, dressed in a linen shirt and sandals, no covering on his head of gray hair, is planing on a table near the window.

PROKOP. That's right. Today is the fair in our village, ha Natasha? *(Natasha, occupied with her own thoughts, does not hear him.)* Natasha! Did you suddenly become deaf? I'm talking to you!

NATASHA. *(Coming back to reality.)* What is it, grandpa? Did you ask me something?

PROKOP. Tu, tu, I asked you something. Ech, there's something that's not just right with you today, my girl. What's on your mind? What can a silly girl like you be thinking?

NATASHA. Oh, I think plenty, grandpa. For instance, why are people people? Why aren't they birds? Can't you see, grandpa, how freely the birds sing in God's world and they're not at all afraid of people? Ah! *(Interrupts herself with a long sigh.)*

PROKOP. Oho, so that's what you're thinking, Natasha. *(Laughs good naturedly.)* When a person is a person, it proves he does not have to be a bird . . . and, God be blessed, it is good like that, that a man is not a bird . . . Ach Natasha, if a man would be a pagan bird, he'd be a worse pagan than a hawk, worse than an eagle. God's birds would then not sing so happily if man were up there among them in the air. Tu, tu.

NATASHA. *(Looking out toward the lake.)* The fishermen aren't in sight yet. It's so late for them . . .

PROKOP. They'll be here soon enough. Are you going to buy anything at the fair today?

NATASHA. Zalman promised to buy me a present at the fair, and Yankel too . . .

PROKOP. Good. That's good, Natasha. Tu, tu. You could take presents from them. After all, you wait on them and serve them. They practically live in our house. Now listen to me, Natasha, and remember that Yankel and that Zalman are young oxen while you are a young heifer. Take the presents they give you, but pay them back only with a kind word, a thank you. You know how strict I am about certain things. Tu, tu!

NATASHA. (*Angry, slams the boot against the samovar.*) Grandpa! What kind of nonsense are you talking about today?

PROKOP. Better that your old grandpa *talk* nonsense than you, my dear little chick, *do* foolish things . . .

NATASHA. (*Annoyed.*) I don't need any gifts! How greedy do you think I am? What are you talking about, grandpa? (*She takes a kerchief from her bosom, opens it, and takes out a coin, which she holds up to show him.*) Here, take this money that the boss gave me yesterday—only don't talk like that, grandpa! (*Natasha runs into the house.*)

PROKOP. (*Yells after her.*) Natasha! (*Stands looking after her and shakes his head.*) Tu, tu, what's the matter with her today? (*Lights his pipe.*) She's angry? Why? For good advice? No . . . tu, tu.

(*He lifts the board he had planed up to his shoulder, and calls out to Natasha.*)

I'm going out to the field. (*He goes out. From the house, Natasha is heard singing a sentimental folk song. She soon comes out singing, both her hands behind her neck, sinks to the ground. Her song becomes most tearful, then she hides her face in her lap and stops her song as she silently sobs while her body shudders. Meanwhile the birds chirp happily. From the direction of the lake comes the song of the returning fishermen.*)

NATASHA. (*Jumps up.*) Yankel! (*She rushes to the samovar and blows out the flame. Her whole being is filled with happiness and love. She hurls herself foreward and waves both hands in the direction of the fishermen.*) Yoo hoo, Yankel! Yoo hoo! (*Yankel enters, wearing leather apron and leather gloves, and runs to her. Natasha eludes him and runs around the yard as she joyfully laughs. He catches her.*) Yankel, let me— with your wet gloves!

YANKEL. (*Laughing, throws away his gloves and embraces her with his red hands.*) Now, is this better? Or may-be like this? (*His arms are now around her waist.*) Oh, you little imp, the wolves should devour you, you witch! (*She laughs. Hirsh Baer, Chatze, and Zalman enter. Hirsh Baer chuckles, Zalman is angry, and Chatze shakes his head disapprovingly.*)

HIRSH BAER. (*With good nature.*) Ha, ha, Natasha, on an empty stomach you are already taking on a bull calf . . . ach, youth! (*He removes his apron and caftan and hangs them on the door.*)

ZALMAN. (*Angry.*) The samovar isn't even ready yet. It's Boyla's fault. He doesn't let her prepare the samovar, a plague on his bones. (*Natasha carries the samovar indoors.*)

YANKEL. Zalman, I warned you not to bark like a dog. When I get hold of your bones, you'll whine like a dog.

ZALMAN. Don't threaten me. I, too, can break your snout! (*Zalman exits into the house.*)

YANKEL. The wolves should devour him! (*Yankel and Chatze remove their aprons.*)

CHATZE. Oh, woe is me. And when it comes to praying—that's forgotten. Yankele, it's already two months that your father, may he rest in peace, died. Why don't you say Kadish for him? Soon it will be the sabbath, and almost just before the prayers, you're playing around with a shikse! Oh Yankele, don't you remember his words on his death bed? "Be a true Jew—oh will you be flogged with iron rods." And he is being whipped there, Yankele, oh how he is being beaten, the poor thing! And you—he will not forgive you either, Yankele. Beware! With the dead you don't fool around. I mean, really! (*He hangs his apron on the door.*)

YANKEL. (*Sobered and frightened.*) Why won't my father forgive me? Who says I don't say Kadish? I say it on the Sabbath when there's a minion. Yet he talks! Why are you threatening me, Reb Chatze? Why won't my father forgive me? Ech, the devil take you! Where is my prayer book—I'm going to pray! (*Yankel exits into house.*)

HIRSH BAER. (*Sits at the table and pulls out of one boot a flask of schnapps, and from the other a small glass. As he talks he fills the glass from the flask.*) It seems that Yankel is more afraid of his father buried in the ground than he is of us on top of the ground—ach, the devil . . . (*He drinks in one gulp.*) You there, you philosphe—can you get such good alcohol in the cemetery?

CHATZE. (*Sighs.*) They'll hand you such alcohol there that it will take your breath away . . . with iron rods. Feh, Reb Hirsh Baer you of all people, a Jewish elder! It is now before fearful days . . . It will be signed and sealed . . . The least you could do is drink after the prayers.

HIRSH BAER. You know, you're right, Chatze. But I like to pray with exaltation and rapture, which I can only achieve when I take a drink before —not after! (*Yankel is at the open window with prayer book in hand; he is praying.*) You see? Only Yankel can pray with such exaltation. Each word rolls delightfully out of his mouth, it could open your foolish brain!

YANKEL. (*Praying at the window—stuttering and stumbling through the words*) "*Vehulom puschim esh pihem bekadusha ubatora . . .*"

CHATZE. (*Holding his hands to his ears.*) Oh, woe! He is ruining the prayers! "*Bakudasha,*" he's chopping wood! Yankel, *Bedudihu,* woe is me! *Ubhovtora,* gevald! (*Zalman comes out of the house.*)

YANKEL. (*Praying.*) *Umbrukim umshapkim*—don't worry, Reb Chatze. I'm saying it the way it is in the book. (*He disappears from the window.*)

CHATZE. Well, well, what can I do? And I must keep quiet! At least, I'll go pray. What a bunch of Jews! (*Chatze exits into house.*)

ZALMAN. Reb Hirsh Baer. Give me a drink from your flask.

HIRSH BAER. Did you say your prayers yet?

ZALMAN. Not yet.

HIRSH BAER. Then I'll give you a disease, not schnapps. A Jew should not drink before his prayers . . . says Chatze . . .

ZALMAN. Reb Hirsh Baer, just a wee bit. (*He rubs his stomach.*) I've got an awful feeling right here. Something or other didn't agree with me.

HIRSH BAER. You'll find castor oil in the house. According to Chatze, a good Jew can take some of that before the prayers. (*Rises.*) Come, my Talmudic friend, we'll go pray. (*They exit into the house. The sounds of a wagon and Nachum's voice, "whoa, whoa." Nachum and Chayke come in from the road. Nachum holds a whip, which he waves in the air. Chayke is dressed in new clothes.*)

NACHUM. (*He hears his horse neigh, and looks to the road.*) Tpfui, tpfui, Vasiutka! Look, Chaykele, look at our handsome Vasiutka, like a bird, bless his heart, he wants to fly home. (*Sound of the wagon again.*) A fire in your intestines! (*Nachum runs out toward the wagon. Natasha enters with the samovar, which she places on the table. She does not see Chayke.*)

CHAYKE. Natasha, oh Natasha. Is my Yankel here?

NATASHA. (*Shudders, turns to Chayke and spits.*) Oh, it's you.

CHAYKE. Is my Yankel here?

NATASHA. Your Yankel, ha? Her Yankel! (*Angry, Natasha laughs mockingly.*) What a nerve you have! Your Yankel indeed! Tpfui, you pig! First go to the lake and wash your snout, you disgusting thing . . . her Yankel! Tpfui, you should drop dead!

CHAYKE. (*Wipes her face with both hands.*) What's the matter with my face, Natasha?

NATASHA. Your face, huh? That isn't a face, it's a snout. A disgusting one, that's what you have. (*Natasha angrily wipes the table.*)

CHAYKE. Natasha, why are you cursing like that? Did I do you any harm?

NATASHA. Yankel isn't here. Go, get out! (*Chayke is bewildered.*)
And Yankel said you are a disease and not a girl and that you should drop dead, that's what he said. (*Yankel comes running out of the house.*)

YANKEL. (*Gleeful.*) Natasha! (*He suddenly sees Chayke, stops in his tracks, scratches his head, and mutters.*) The wolves should devour her!

CHAYKE. Yankel, oh Yankel! What does this shikse want from my life?

NATASHA. Your bride, Yankel! Look at her! Ha, ha, ha . . . Take her to the lake and wash her snout for her! Tpfui . . . you should both drop dead if she's your bride! (*Natasha in great anger flees into the house.*)

CHAYKE. What do you say now to that shikse? *She* doesn't approve your marriage to me . . . what can you say to her?

YANKEL. (*Scratching his head.*) You really should wash that snout of yours, it shouldn't look so disgustingly greasy —the way it shines. What are you looking like that for? I hate the way you look.

CHAYKE. (*Innocently.*) How do I look? Boyla, why are you picking on me? You'll soon be saying you hate to see me alive . . .

YANKEL. (*With anger.*) True! It's true! I hate to see you alive—it's true! Who asked you to come here? Why?

CHAYKE. I came with my father for the fair, to help your mother in the inn. You might come, too, to give a hand and help . . .

YANKEL. Good. I'll come. So now go!

CHAYKE. I'll wait here for my father. He had to chase after the horse! Oh Yankele, our Vasiutka is a ball of fire, he flies like the devil!

YANKEL. The wolves should devour your Vasiutka!

CHAYKE. What are you talking about? What have you got against the horse, you Boyla?

YANKEL. Well, you don't want it to happen to Vasiutka? So let them devour you!

CHAYKE. (*Aroused in anger.*) They should devour you for both of us! Boyla you, what have you against the horse, and what have you against me?

YANKEL. Go, go to the inn already. Stop annoying me.

CHAYKE. (*Mimicking him.*) "Go, go to the inn already. Stop annoying me." And this is supposed to be my bridegroom, this Boyla! (*Her voice turns gentle as she shows him her new dress.*) Yankele, oh Yankele, look. See? A new dress.

YANKEL. (*Scratches his head as he looks at her dress.*) Go, go to the inn and stop annoying me . . . so, you're a beauty, a regular doll! Go—go!

CHAYKE. (*Starting to cry.*) Why are you driving me away? What have you got against me? Nothing pleases you . . . why are you tormenting my life? May a disease shrivel your bones! (*Nachum enters, but is looking back toward his horse and wagon. He is carrying his whip, which he hands to Chayke.*)

NACHUM. (*To Chayke without looking toward her.*) Here, hold these, Ah, that eagle—don't let him run off! (*He turns and sees Yankel.*) Ah, Yankele! God be with you, my boy. (*He sees that Chayke weeps.*) What is this? Why is she crying, for example?

CHAYKE. (*Crying bitterly.*) He insulted me, this Boyla . . . he can't stand me . . . he hates me!

NACHUM. Shah, sh—be quiet, stop crying! He doesn't like you, for example? He's right. A bride is not supposed to be liked. A wife you have to like, but not a bride, so don't complain! (*Chayke now cries louder.*) Well, quiet! Where is my whip? (*Chayke, frightened, runs to a side, out of his reach.*) Yankele, why did you insult her?

YANKEL. What kind of insult? I told her I would come to the inn to help out, that's all!

NACHUM. (*To Chayke.*) So what are you crying about, you donkey? May the devil take your father . . .

CHAYKE. I hate him, too. Just for spite I'll hate him. The way he behaves to me, that's the way I'll behave to him . . .

NACHUM. Quiet! Let me have that whip! (*She edges further away from him, holding the whip behind her. Nachum goes to Yankel and places both arms around him.*) Yankele, I want to tell you a secret. I just came from your mother. Guess who visited her last night, for example.

YANKEL. Who?

NACHUM. Your father! (*Yankel jumps away from him in fright.*) Yes, your papa. He came to her, in a dream, you should excuse me. Oh, how awful he looks, Yankele, black as the earth. Your mother said he was in a white shroud, with ashes in his eyes, and he cries and weeps for her and complains to her: Frume, my dear heart, oh do they flog me! Without stopping, without a moment's letup! (*Yankel trembles violently.*) Yankel, he said, is not pious. Make him to be a good Jew, and don't complain . . .

YANKEL. (*Sobbing.*) What are you talking about, Uncle Nachum? Is that what my papa really said? But I do pray . . . from the prayer book, I pray every day . . . and I say Kadish every sabbath. What else am I supposed to do for a father? What else? (*He sits at the table and holds his head in his hands.*) Ach, my God, my God!

NACHUM. Maybe you should say sometime a chapter of the Psalms, for example. What do I know? Maybe he has there more than enough troubles if he has to come to complain to your mother, if you'll excuse me, and don't complain.

CHAYKE. (*Self-righteously.*) It's because he's making love to shikses, that's why Uncle Joshua is being whipped in the other world. (*Triumphantly, she courageously runs over to stand next to her father.*)

YANKEL. (*Stung and bitter.*) You too? I need your big mouth too? You idiot, you, what else do you want from me?

HIRSH BAER. (*Showing himself at the open window.*) Aha, the great Reb Nachum is here with his beautiful harem. What's new, Nachum?

NACHUM. Ah, God be with you, Reb Hirsh Baer. Will you be at the fair today?

HIRSH BAER. If you can promise that I'll get the real thing there, then I'll come.

NACHUM. Come along, Reb Hirsh Baer. It's going to be one bang after another, you should excuse me, and don't complain. How about it, Yankel, are you coming with us?

YANKEL. (*Snaps out of his despair.*) Ha? Oh, I'll come with the fishermen.

NACHUM. Well, Chaykele, get into the wagon. There's no time left! Reb Hirsh Baer, don't forget. (*He retrieves the whip from Chayke and switches it as they leave.*)

CHAYKE. (*As she leaves, she looks to Yankele for some sign. He turns away and ignores her.*) A fire in his intestines! (*Exits after Nachum. The wagon is heard leaving, accompanied by Nachum's whipping up the horse.*)

NATASHA. (*Entering and hurrying to Yankel.*) So-o-o, your great beauty left, huh? (*She taunts him with bitterness in her voice as she confronts him, hands on her hips.*) So that's your bride—ha ha ha! Your bride! (*Laughs scornfully into his face.*)

YANKEL. (*Distressed.*) It's all wrong, Natasha . . .

NATASHA. What's so bad about such a bride? Just wash her ugly snout and she'll be passable—ha, ha, ha . . . !

YANKEL. It's all wrong, Natasha. My father . . .

NATASHA. What has your father to do with it?

YANKEL. I can't pray properly, Natasha, that's what. (*He bangs his hand, for emphasis, on the table.*) Ach, if only I could say the prayers properly. (*He sits disconsolately at the table with his head lowered in misery. From the distant village is heard a harmonica, accompanied by singing.*)

HIRSH BAER. (*Entering from the house. A flask of whiskey protrudes from his pocket.*) Natasha, how about a glass of tea? Hurry up, we have to go and see what's happening at the fair . . .

NATASHA. Right away, Hirsh Baer. (*She signals Yankel with a wink which he does not see. She disgustedly spits.*) Tpfui! My tormentor! (*She exits into the house.*)

HIRSH BAER. So, Yankele, what are you dreaming about?

YANKEL. (*Troubled.*) Ach, Reb Hirsh Baer, it's no good.

HIRSH BAER. What are you talking about? What's no good?

YANKEL. Uncle Nachum says that last night my papa came to my mother . . .

HIRSH BAER. What? Your papa came to your mother last night? Aha, I guess in the other world there's a shortage of women. Oh boy, what a reprobate your father is! Such a sinner! Such a short time and already your papa misses his wife . . .

YANKEL. He was complaining that I'm not a pious Jew . . .

HIRSH BAER. As far as that goes, he's not far from wrong. After all, why shouldn't you learn a chapter of the Mishnah or a page of the Gemorrah, Boyla? Bless your sinful heart . . .

YANKEL. (*Rising.*) My God! I'm going out of my mind! I just don't know what to do . . .

HIRSH BAER. Here, take a pinch of my snuff . . . sit down, you wild one. You get too scared from all kinds of foolishness. Your mother had a dream about your father because she's probably always thinking about him. You know, I often dream about my snuffbox. Do you mean to say that my snuffbox comes to my dreams? What sick nonsense!

YANKEL. Why, isn't it true, Reb Hirsh Baer?

HIRSH BAER. It's as true as your father is now a butcher in the other world. Go, do me a favor and get my snuffbox, I forgot it in the house . . .

YANKEL. (*Scratches his head, much relieved.*)
It's not really true. Why does my papa complain about me? After all, I do pray from the prayer book. Ach, the wolves should devour it. (*He exits into the house, from where his voice is heard.*) Zalman, let Natasha bring the tea! (*A loud outcry from Zalman and Natasha's laughter.*)

ZALMAN. (*Entering from the house.*) Ow! He almost tore my lungs out. Reb Hirsh Baer, he nearly killed me, that Boyla.

HIRSH BAER. A sacrifice for a good Jew . . .

ZALMAN. He's going to convert, that Boyla. Just watch and see.

HIRSH BAER. So, there'll be one less talmudist among the Jews . . .

ZALMAN. Not a chance to get near her. One doesn't dare touch this shikse . . .

HIRSH BAER. So why do you have to touch her? You are a pious young man—but Natasha is not a m'zuzah.

ZALMAN. Oho, Reb Hirsh Baer! Don't you also go looking for your snuffbox in her bosom? That's not bad . . .

HIRSH BAER. At least, I'm looking there for something! What are you looking for—a heartache for yourself? (*Yankel enters from the house with the snuffbox.*)

YANKEL. (*Over his shoulder toward Natasha, who is still indoors.*)
Get dressed like a young lady, Natasha! (*He hands the snuffbox to Hirsh Baer, then turns to Zalman.*) Good, ha? I gave it to you, all right? Want some more? (*He grabs Zalman's arm.*)

ZALMAN. Let go, Yankel, ow . . . honest to God, I like you . . . let go!

HIRSH BAER. Why don't you stop fighting over that shikse—the devil take both of you!

YANKEL. Well, what do you say Zalman, you won't act like a dog, eh? You won't touch her, huh? Now, remember, Zalman! (*He releases Zalman.*)

ZALMAN. (*Slapping Yankel on the shoulder.*) Healthy as a bear . . . if only I had your strength! Let it go, we're good friends. Today at the fair, Yankele, we'll dance, hip hop! (*He grabs Yankel and whirls him around and sings a native song.*) "A great day is coming, red eggs are carried, carried, red eggs are carried . . ."

YANKEL. Now you're a good fellow, Zalman, and I like you like that. (*He calls in to Natasha.*) Natasha, I'll wait for you at the inn. I'll go and get dressed like a gentleman. (*The distant music and singing from the villages grow louder.*) Natasha, they're dancing already! (*He runs off.*)

ZALMAN. Reb Hirsh Baer, will you treat me at the fair today?

HIRSH BAER. (*Laughingly showing his fist.*) I'd like to treat you all right, but I have no strength left. (*Natasha, dressed in a red dress, bedecked with beads and ribbons, runs out of the house.*)

NATASHA. Reb Hirsh Baer, going?

HIRSH BAER. Just look at her! How beautiful you look in your red dress, your ribbons . . . will you dance with me?

NATASHA. Will you buy me a present?

HIRSH BAER. Of course, a good pinch of snuff. Where is my snuffbox? (*He playfully lunges to look for it in her bosom.*)

NATASHA. (*Eludes him and laughs.*) You'll burn yet, Reb Hirsh Baer. (*She runs off.*)

HIRSH BAER. (*Shouts into the house.*) Chatze, stop wasting time. Come, we'll see what's doing at the fair.

CHATZE. (*His voice comes through the window.*) Leyolim yehu udom yera shumim. (*Chatze appears at the window, with prayer shawl over his head. He enthusiastically bounces up and down,*

nodding to Hirsh Baer to indicate he's hurrying and will go along as he quickens his praying.*) Uhmoidu el hames uduber emes bleben . . . Hai!—Hai!—Hai *Veishchum Veiamer.* (*He disappears from the window.*)

HIRSH BAER. (*Takes out his snuffbox.*) Just listen, Zalman. Do you hear how he prays? Ach, damn it, it saddens the heart! (*He takes a pinch of tobacco to his nose.*) I cannot pray like that. I pray from a hassidic prayer book, he from an orthodox book. One prays this way, the other differently. Who knows what the real and true way to pray is? After all, what does a foolish little person know? Maybe the priest, Areseni, is right when he argues with me when we're having a few drinks together. "Grass, Hirsh Baer. Everything is grass. A person is a person as long as he is alive, whether he is a rabbi, a priest, a Turk, or some other devil . . . as long as he's alive, he's a person. When he dies, he's no more than a corpse . . . "

ZALMAN. But—how about in the other world?

HIRSH BAER. In the other world? He doesn't believe in it. He's a heretic, this priest Areseni. He tells the story of the deacon Archip . . . he was a big drunkard. For a shot of schnapps, he'd go to the ends of the earth. When this Archip was dying, the priest Areseni says to him, Brother Archip, I beg you to come to me from the other world as my guest. I will treat you with such a drink . . . ach . . . like you never tasted anything like it in your entire lifetime. And . . . Archip never came! What do we learn from that? Might we say that this Archip has a head like a dumb peasant and forgot all about it? But you ask, how could that be? When he was alive, did he ever forget? What then? Simple— he did not come because he cannot walk, he cannot stand—because he must lie there and rot. Therefore, the priest Areseni must be right—that when you're dead, you're dead—a corpse. (*While Hirsh Baer has been telling his story, Zalman has edged over to him, stolen the whiskey flask from his pocket, and standing behind him, takes a long drink.*)

CHATZE. (*Again appearing at the window.*) Hai, hai, hai. *Abinu shebshumayim chei vekayim! Hai, hai, hai! Eshui eminu zeduku vachesed . . . bebur shemuch hagaduhl . . .* (*Disappears.*)

HIRSH BAER. However, Chatze says that the end of a goy is a corpse, but the end of a Jew is a saint. Who can say what happens in the hereafter? And what difference does it make? What happens to all Israel, let happen to Hirsh Baer. In the meanwhile, we'll go to the tavern and get a taste of the real world of today. (*He rises and puts his hand to his pocket to discover that the flask is missing, then sees it in Zalman's hand.*) Ah, you should have a heart attack, Zalman!

ZALMAN. I'll buy you some more. (*Zalman runs off, with Hirsh Baer in pursuit. The scene darkens to indicate passage of a brief period. As the lights come on, the scene is the same, but empty. Spirited music is heard from the direction of the village. A harmonica and fiddle play a simple country dance tune. Natasha enters, followed by a drunken Zalman, who clutches at her. They are followed by village youths dressed colorfully in holiday attire.*)

ZALMAN. Let's dance right here, Natasha. Play—the wolves should devour those musicians! (*He sings and dances with Natasha. He soon stops.*) Well—that's enough, Natasha! (*He grabs her shoulder.*) Do you want the ring now? (*He throws his hat on the ground.*) Ah, if we're alive, let's really live it up! (*He retrieves his hat.*) Oh, let it go. I spit on everyone! I'll live it up and spend every kopeck I have—so do me something! Natasha, why do you love Yankel? This Boyla, what's so wonderful about him that you love him? There must be something more between the two of you than just flirting, hah? No? A plague I'll give you, not the ring. Let Yankel buy you one! What's going on between you two? Natasha, you devil! (*He grabs her arm. She pushes him away.*)

NATASHA. What do you mean "between us two?" What are you croaking about, you raven? I don't want your ring. Burn in hell with your ring.

ZALMAN. Easy there, you little imp. May your eyes pop out of their sockets! Don't be so mad. Here is your ring. (*He fumbles at his pocket and brings out the ring, which he slides onto her finger. The villagers, peasants, and youths are drinking and dancing. Yankel has entered. He is dressed in holiday attire, with fancy black jacket, highly polished black boots, his cap tilted tipsily on his head, looking very much the dandy. He has been drinking a bit, and dances around some of the couples, whom he teases and with whom he banters. But he has observed Zalman placing the ring on Natasha's finger.*)

YANKEL. The wolves should devour her! So that's it, she takes gifts from that dog. I'll break her bones. (*He rushes over to Zalman, whom he forcefully hurls away from Natasha.*) Get out of here or I'll tear out your guts! (*Yankel pulls Natasha over to himself.*)

ZALMAN. (*At first confused.*) So, you want to fight? Come on, just try it! (*He places his hands defiantly on his hips.*) I'll show you I'm not afraid of you. I'll make ashes out of you . . .

YANKEL. (*Lunging at Zalman.*) Ha? (*Zalman runs away.*)

NATASHA. Yankel, are you drunk?

YANKEL. I don't want you to take any presents from him! And you're not to go out with him—I won't have it! (*He grabs her hand and tears off the ring from her finger.*) I won't have it.

NATASHA. Yankel, my finger! (*He hurls the ring on the ground and stamps on it, then grabs her arm and pulls her to him.*)

YANKEL. I'll buy a ring for you, Natasha, I'll buy you one—the wolves should devour you! (*Chatze comes out of the house. Zalman reappears and calls Chatze to him.*)

ZALMAN. Just look, Reb Chatze. Do you see? He's dancing with a shikse, this so called mourner . . . Just watch and see, he'll convert yet, this Boyla, and he'll marry her yet. You'll see! (*Zalman leaves.*)

YANKEL. (*Overhears Zalman, whose words sober him.*) I'll convert? I? (*He stands confused as he looks about him in fright.*) I'll convert?

CHATZE. Yankel, what do you think you're doing? Don't you have any pity for your father in his grave? Shame! Here you are in mourning and you're dancing. Yankele, no good will come of this. You'll come to a bad end. Remember, your father will not keep quiet, I mean, really. Wait, I'm going to send your mother to you. (*Chatze leaves.*)

YANKEL. (*Mutters in confusion.*) My God! My God! (*Pulls Natasha to him.*)

NATASHA. Why are you pulling me so?

YANKEL. I'm afraid . . . this is terrible. Go away, Natasha, go away!

NATASHA. What are you babbling about, Yankel? Are you drunk?

YANKEL. (*Sits on the ground. Natasha sits down beside him. He mutters to himself, then looks off behind him in fright.*) Natasha! Do you see someone? Look, do you see?

NATASHA. (*Looks around.*) Whom do you see? Ach, you're drunk, Yankel!

YANKEL. (*Mutters.*) Al malich nehman shmay yisrael . . . shmay yisrael—I don't know any more! My God, shmay yisrael . . .

NATASHA. Are you praying, Yankel?

YANKEL. Natasha, go away! (*He painfully blurts out.*) Ah, Natasha, after all I am a Jew—and I have a father —he is being tortured over there, oh, how he frightens me, how scared I am! Natasha, I am out of my mind. I'm not allowed to cross myself like a Christian. And to pray like a Jew I don't know how! My God—*shmay yisrael, shmay yisrael*—(*He covers his face with his hands and trembles violently.*)

NATASHA. (*Tearing his hands away from his face.*) Yankel, my eagle, you're crying? (*He looks unhappily at her.*) Yankel, what's wrong, what's the matter with you? My poor darling. (*She makes the sign of the cross over him.*)

YANKEL. (*Jumps up in agonized fright.*) What are you doing? What are you doing? Don't make the cross over me! (*He remains standing with his eyes popping out as he sobs violently. Natasha also jumps up in fright and stands staring at him as she trembles. Zalman again appears and goes over to the drunken peasants.*)

ZALMAN. (*Stealthily to the peasants.*) Here, fellows. Here are five coins for some refreshments. Drink and enjoy—but for this, you'll break Yankel's bones. (*The peasants laugh and talk conspiratorially among themselves.*)

A PEASANT. (*Walking up to Yankel.*) Hey Yankel! You drank our fiery stuff, eh? Now buy us some of your hot stuff. (*Yankel stares at him like a mummy.*) What are you staring at me for? Come on, buy . . . (*Peasant grabs Yankel by the front of his jacket and shakes him.*) Buy—and if not . . . (*He punches Yankel's chest.*)

NATASHA. (*To peasant.*) Why are you beating Yankel? You—you Ukrainian sot!

YANKEL. (*Wildly raving.*) Beating me? (*Yankel hurls himself at the peasant, wildly striking out at him.*)

THE PEASANT. (*Yelling to the other*

peasants.) Hey boys! On your guard —let's at him. (*The others join the first peasant in an attack upon Yankel. They pummel him and tear his clothes. Yankel fights all of them and gets the upper hand. They flee, with Yankel in wild pursuit.*)

NATASHA. (*Chasing after Yankel in fright.*) Yankel, enough. My God, he's out of his mind.

YANKEL. (*Punching a peasant whom he has caught.*) You dare start up with me. So let's really fight—the wolves should devour you! (*Hirsh Baer, slightly drunk, enters.*)

HIRSH BAER. Hey, what's going on here? (*He throws himself among the fighters and separates them. They stand apart.*) And here I thought you were dancing, and now I see you were really fighting. Why don't you all go fight your mothers! (*Yankel, with torn shirt, looks for his cap.*)

NATASHA. (*Picking up Yankel's cap.*) Are you hurt, Yankel?

YANKEL. (*Proudly.*) Me hurt? Ha!

NATASHA. (*Embracing him passionately.*) You're so strong, my own Yankel. My bear, you wild one, my beautiful eagle—how you mowed them down with your strong hands—ha, ha, ha! (*The surly and beaten peasants "lick their wounds"—one tries to stop the blood from his nose, another holds his ear, another tries to ease the pain in a leg. All mumble and look bitterly at Yankel.*)

ZALMAN. (*To Hirsh Baer.*) Reb Hirsh Baer, did you ever see such strength like this Boyla? I wish I had it . . .

HIRSH BAER. You don't need strength, because if a pig would have horns, he would destroy the world. You go play with your mother. (*He takes out a bottle of whiskey from his bosom.*) Artiem, Ivan, Nicolai, Yankel —here, drink up and make peace. You shouldn't insult Yankele. He may be a wild one, but he's an honest man, without any false nonsense, a good person the way God made him. If you won't put a finger in his mouth, he won't bite it. You don't start up

with a bear—he has sharp claws. Ha, Ha, Ha! Yankel, come over here. (*Yankel and Natasha go to Hirsh Baer.*) Yankel, I really like you. I always liked you. But now that I have poured some schnapps in me, you should excuse me, I like you more than ever. (*He hands Yankel a small glass into which he has poured whiskey.*) Drink up, my boy. (*Yankel holds back—doesn't take it.*) Drink up, bless your heart. (*Yankel drinks.*) Here's another for a chaser. (*Yankel drinks the refill.*) Attaboy! And now, just one more. (*Hirsh Baer holds another glassful out to Yankel, who reaches for it. Hirsh Baer pulls back his hand.*) Oh yeah? A plague on you—this one I drink myself!

YANKEL. (*Swaying and laughing.*) Ha, ha, ha—that's good spirits, Reb Hirsh Baer. First class spirits. The best. And I'm a little drunk—Ha, ha, ha . . .

HIRSH BAER. As for you, Zalmanke, you I'll give a plague, not schnapps. And you fellows, make peace with Yankel and I'll give you some schnapps. (*The peasants who had fought with Yankel crowd around him and boisterously cheer him with cries of "Yankel! Yankel!" They goodnaturedly slap him on the shoulders. Hirsh Baer hands over the bottle of whiskey to the peasants, who pass it around and drink from it.*) And now, let's have some fun . . . my friends— and you Yankel and Natasha! I'd like to see how you dance. Come on, dance a little for me. Ho, ho, I can dance, too, but on one foot . . .

ALL. Come on—dance Yankel! Dance Natasha! (*One peasant starts to play his harmonica, another his fiddle. Yankel and Natasha start to dance; soon most of the others are dancing with them. Chatze appears.*)

CHATZE. Ach, he's really dancing, the bereaved son. That's how he mourns for his dead father! Gevald! (*Yankel overhears him and shudders.*)

HIRSH BAER. Dance, Yankel. Don't pay

attention to him, that Chelm donkey!

ALL. Dance Yankel, dance! (*Yankel recovers and swings into dance again with Natasha. The others dance and become more boisterous.*)

ZALMAN. There comes his mother. (*Nachum comes running in; he is carrying a few bottles of whiskey in both hands.*)

NACHUM. (*From the edge of the crowd.*) Yankel, a plague on your heart. Don't dance with the goyem, and don't complain! (*Nachum runs off.*)

YANKEL. (*Looks at others while he continues his dance.*) Hey—I'm dancing all right! Hey, musicians, let's go—a little livelier. Hey, Natasha, hip, hop! (*Yankel slaps the top of his boots, then jumps into the air and down into a Tartar folk dance as he circles Natasha.*)

ALL. (*Others circle around Yankel as he does a virtuoso dance solo.*) Hai, hai—attaboy, Yankele—(*Chayke comes running in. She sees Frume approaching and yells to her.*)

CHAYKE. Oh, Aunt Frume. He's still dancing with that shikse! (*Turns toward Yankel.*) Yankel, here comes your mother! (*Frume comes running in. Her sleeves are rolled up.*)

FRUME. Yankele, my unfortunate misfit, your poor father will come again to torment me—woe is me! (*Yankel stands stunned.*)

HIRSH BAER. Yankel, don't listen to your mother's nonsense. Come on, dance. (*Yankel again plunges into the dance.*)

FRUME. Yankele, you heretic, why don't you let your father rest in peace in his grave? (*He continues to dance.*)

CHAYKE. Just wait, you, you'll see. My uncle will yet fix these goyem! (*Suddenly Yankel hears his father's voice.*)

VOICE OF DEAD JOSHUA. Yankele, be a Jew! Oh, will you be flogged!

YANKEL. (*Still dancing, but trembling with fear, he shrieks.*) Do you hear? You hear? (*He looks about in fright.*)

HIRSH BAER. Dance! (*Again Yankel hears his father's voice.*)

VOICE OF DEAD JOSHUA. Yankel, return to our Jewish life! (*Yankel runs to his mother.*)

YANKEL. Mama, did you hear him? (*He clings to her in fear.*)

HIRSH BAER. He has, if you'll excuse me, loaded himself with plenty of schnapps. Now he's hearing things in his head. (*Yankel stares toward the open window of the house, where he imagines he sees his dead father clothed in a shroud.*)

VOICE OF DEAD JOSHUA. Yankele, be a good Jew! Oh, will they punish you!

YANKEL. (*Crazed with fright.*) Mama, mama save me! (*Throws himself on his knees as he faces the window.*) Oh, papa—yes, I will be a Jew . . . I will, I will . . . be a Jew. Don't touch me, don't come near me . . . ! (*He throws himself into a crouching position as if to ward off blows from his father's spirit.*)

CURTAIN

ACT III

In the fishermen's room. Hirsh Baer sits on a bench, where he is polishing his boots with grease. Chatze sits at the table as he inserts fringes into his religious vest, which is spread on the table. Zalman is occupied with sewing a button on his jacket. Through the window is seen the gloomy, gray landscape, over which a storm is raging.

CHATZE. (*Carefully straightening the strands of the fringes and intoning.*) Aleph for the sake of a good deed, beth for the sake of a good deed, gimmel for the sake of a good deed . . .

HIRSH BAER. Chatze, you know what I think—you're a big lummox, you should excuse me. You simply don't understand anything. Here you are putting on the ritual fringes on Yankel's religious vest, and you made him into a pious Jew already so that he grunts and belches his prayers almost like you . . . What good does it do you, you Chelmner brain? Don't you understand that the fewer the saintly men to arrive in the other world, the better it will be for you there, you should go thrash your mother?

CHATZE. (*Enthusiastic.*) It's not true, Reb Hirsh Baer. God's mercy is very great—I mean, really. Who would have thought a month ago that Yankel's apostate and gentile heart would so fearfully turn back to Judaism. (*Claps his hands with fervor.*) Oh, God, our dear Father, who else but You could show such miracles! The weakest heart You make strong in your faith . . . a spark of Jewishness You fan ablaze into a flame, into a holy fire . . . oh, dear God! It is time for penance, and Yankele prays with all his heart. Yankele says a chapter of the Psalms . . . and here is his ritual vest. And he himself begged me to sew on kosher fringes. Good heavens, see what great miracles God performs—good heavens, I mean, really! (*Arrests his enthusiasm and returns diligently to his work on the garment, as he starts again to intone.*) Aleph for the sake of a good deed, beth for the sake of a good deed . . .

HIRSH BAER. I mean also—really, Chatze. Every time something is wrong —you blame God. When a healthy man becomes sick, when a sane person goes crazy—whom do you blame? Poor old God!

ZALMAN. You can say all you want that Yankel has returned to being a good Jew—but in the village everybody is saying that he's going to convert and marry Natasha.

HIRSH BAER. Listen, you smart alec Zalmenke—your heart should stop for a while. All this gossip came out of your stupid head. You better watch out; if Yankele gets his hands on you, you might as well say goodbye to that idiot head of yours! The devil take you. (*Zalman laughs. Hirsh Baer looks out the window.*) Ach, the storm has really spread. Well, today we'll have to stay home and rest. Zalmanke, please look what's doing out there with the boats. I hope they didn't tear away from the shore.

ZALMAN. I'll get dressed. (*He puts on his jacket while he looks out the window.*) Ah, those waves have really gone wild on the lake—look, they jump and spring like white sheep. (*He puts on his cap.*) I'm going.

HIRSH BAER. Zalmanke, as long as you're going, ask the storm why it's making such a terrible noise. Maybe it wants a pinch of snuff?

ZALMAN. It wants a good swallow of that real stuff of yours. Hand over your flask, and I'll give it to him . . . (*He laughs.*)

HIRSH BAER. I'll give you a real clout on the head . . . Go! (*Zalman laughs and goes out. Hirsh Baer goes to the window and looks out.*) Oh boy, it's raising hell out there! Autumn is really coming on the world . . . every year at this time, the lake starts a turmoil and throws itself around as if it's having a fit . . . the trees in the forest begin to complain of pains in their sides that stick into them like knives—so they moan and groan, then scream in pain . . . and it helps them as much as cupping helps a corpse. The cold wind is their Angel of Death—he tells them, "Blessed Be The True Judge" . . . ach, and almost like only yesterday it was summer. Our whole life is like this: here we are, we blossom, then we grow, and before we know it, we dry out. (*He sighs as he sniffs a pinch of snuff. Prokop bursts open the door and hurries in from the roaring wind and rain. He quickly closes the door and wipes the rain from his head.*)

PROKOP. That's some storm, I must say! Tu, tu! (*He takes out his pipe and fills it; soon he is smoking it.*) You're not going on the lake today, Hirsh Baer?

HIRSH BAER. No, Prokop.

PROKOP. Tu, Tu. And I have to go again to the woods. I've already brought in two wagonloads of wood, but I have to go a third time—tu, tu! To lose a day's business is a sin, brother. Hirsh Baer, you're a clever person—maybe you can give me some advice. There's something wrong with my Natasha. Some one maybe gave her the evil eye, or maybe she's sick. Whatever the reason is, I don't recognize her as the same Natasha. All she does is sit in our side of the house—she sits and thinks and sighs. What's it all about? Ech, by God, it's beyond me. I just can't make her out. Hirsh Baer, she's the only one I have in God's world. Give me your good advice—what should I do? Should I take her to the priest or should I take her to town to see a doctor? Huh, Hirsh Baer?

HIRSH BAER. Marry her off, Prokop, and that's it. For a girl like Natasha, the best doctor and medicine is a young, healthy peasant.

PROKOP. You're right, Hirsh Baer. It's too true, and I thought of that too. But Natasha won't hear of it . . . the best boys in the village want her, but she says only no and no. Ech, what will I do with her? (*Above the howling wind is heard a wild roaring sound from outside.*)

HIRSH BAER. The wind. (*Again the animal-like raving is heard.*)

PROKOP. No—that's not the wind. That's the shriek of a person, tu, tu. It sounds like someone's being strangled.

HIRSH BAER. (*Suddenly aware.*) Oh my, it's Yankel! He must have had another nightmare! (*Again the shriek.*)

CHATZE. You're right. That's Yankele all right. He's had another awful dream. Woe is me!

PROKOP. Where is Yankel?

HIRSH BAER. He hasn't been feeling well. He didn't know what to do with himself, so he went to lie down on the fresh hay in your barn.

PROKOP. He'd better not do any mischief to the hay and scatter it about. Well, I'd better get going to the woods. Ech, what miserable weather, tu, tu! (*Prokop leaves.*)

HIRSH BAER. What's the matter with Yankel? All of you frightened him so much with your nonsense about dreams and punishment that now he's more afraid of the dead than the living. A plague on all of you! (*Yankel, bewildered and dazed, hay in his hair and on his clothes, sobbing and barely able to stand, is led in by a smiling Zalman. Yankel sees Chatze and staggers to him.*)

YANKEL. (*Moaning.*) Reb Chatze—again! Ah, Reb Chatze—it happened again.

CHATZE. What?

YANKEL. (*Confused and trembling all over, clutches at Chatze.*) It's my father. Again—my father . . . !

ZALMAN. (*Laughing.*) I heard someone screaming near the lake like an ox being slaughtered. So I ran into the barn and there's Yankele, lying in the hay and thrashing about with his arms and legs and raving like a madman—"Don't come near me! Leave me alone!" I had to give him a couple of punches until he snapped out of it . . . ha, ha, ha!

HIRSH BAER. What are you laughing at, you stupid donkey! (*He turns to Yankel.*) Yankel, don't be such an idiot. Stop thinking so much about your father—then you won't dream about him so much. (*Hirsh Baer patiently talks to Yankel as though to a child.*) Don't be a fool, Yankel. Your father is very pleased with you now. You've become a good, pious person, like this Chelmner wants, just like your Uncle Nachum wants—it should happen to them what they made of you. Tpfui—they should go to the devil! (*Turns to Zalman.*)

Well, what are you standing for, you clown. Have you taken care of the boats yet?

ZALMAN. I pulled one of them up on the beach already.

HIRSH BAER. How about the others?

ZALMAN. I'll go right away. (*He mimics Yankel.*) Yeeow! Don't touch me! Oh boy, I let him have a couple of wallops! Ha, ha, ha! (*Zalman runs out.*)

HIRSH BAER. Ach, only on a fallen tree will the sheep jump.

ZALMAN. (*Reenters.*) Reb Hirsh Baer, the priest Areseni wants to see you. He wants some fish and he has some real good alcohol for you. How about some of the real stuff for me?

HIRSH BAER. Areseni the priest? (*He goes out with Zalman.*)

YANKEL. Reb Chatze, what should I do?

CHATZE. First of all, put on your religious vest. (*He helps Yankel to put on the vest.*) Maybe he came to check up on you because you were going around without it. What did he say to you?

YANKEL. He—he—he said . . . he said . . . (*Yankel shudders.*) Be a pious Jew, he said. But why now, Reb Chatze? I have done everything right. I pray regularly, so why now, Reb Chatze? (*He covers his face with his hands and shudders.*)

CHATZE. Maybe it's because of your previous sins, from before. How do I know? Woe is me.

YANKEL. Oh, maybe that's it. Yes—I sinned! Oh, did I sin! (*He mutters to himself.*) Oh, my God—*shmaye yisrael, shmaye yisrael!* Reb Chatze, where is the prayer book?

CHATZE. (*Handing him the holy book.*) Do you want to repeat a chapter of the Psalms? Go ahead, pray Yankele. I'll pray with you. Ach, what a God we have, I mean, really! (*He riffles through the book, selects a page.*) Ah, here it is. Say with me: *Layuvim Shni* . . . chapter

lahmed . . . today it's still Monday . . . (*He sits at one side and chants from memory.*) *Nizmav shiv hanuhkas habys ledovid* . . .

YANKEL. (*With the same chant as Chatze's, in a heartrending, sobbing voice.*) *Mishmov shiv charruhkas habyash lehduvid* . . . *aremike hadohnoy chidalushiny hulay shemahkte huhvay li* . . . Reb Chatze, what, for example, happens to a Jew when he sins with a Christian girl?

CHATZE. (*Praying to himself.*) *Usser lehafsig*—well, er—(*He continues to chant the prayer so that the individual words are not distinguishable.*)

YANKEL. (*Also continuing to pray.*) *Haduhnoy helishoh min shul nofshi hoyshiuner mimordi vayer* . . . So what do you say, Reb Chatze, ha?

CHATZE. Hm, what?

YANKEL. When one sins with a Christian girl . . . what happens, huh?

CHATZE. When one sins with a Christian girl what happens? Woe, I mean really. Much worse than with a Jewish girl! Stoning is not enough for that . . . burning is like nothing, like a bit of spit—I once heard from a holy man from Chelm, a very saintly man who spoke about this very sin. Listen to this, Yankele, it'll do you good. (*Chatze starts to hold forth with fire and brimstone in his voice, with an evangelical fervor in his chant.*) When a Jew has sinned with a shikse in this world, what happens to him when he enters the other world? First he is smeared all over from head to foot with foul pitch, then he is handed over to the angel of hell. (*Yankel becomes more and more overcome by terror.*) Then what does this angel of hell do? He orders that the most beautiful woman, Lilith, be brought to him, may her name be blotted from memory—Lilith, you should know, is not just a woman you can play around with. She is a spitfire—a firebrand whom no Jew should know. A tongue of sulphur and acid, eyes that shoot out lightning, and unbelievably seductive. The sun's face doesn't glow like hers. She is almost as beautiful as our mother Rachel, the prophet Jacob's wife, I mean, really. You can imagine how beautiful she is when you realize she is the tool of the most evil passion, she is related to Ashmedai, the lord of all devils and evil spirits. The point is that Lilith, this wicked one, starts in with the Jew who has sinned with a shikse in this world. She takes a look at him, and lightning strikes him and sets his brain on fire, then she says to him, "Better say your prayers." And a sharp knife cuts through his heart. She is not ashamed of any strange thing, this Lilith, may her name be erased from memory—she makes all kinds of sensuous and debauched gestures: she caresses him here, there, all over until she bewitches him . . . he forgets in what world he is and wants to respond to her, to caress her. And that's the moment. She grabs him, just as he is standing all smeared up with foul pitch, and bang—throws him right into the fiery oven—bang—right into the fire! (*Yankel writhes in agonized fear.*) The fire leaps at him from all sides—he screams for mercy from her. And she, this Lilith, with a crowd of ghosts and imps dances around the fire, laughing at him, taunting him: ha, you sinner, you will sin with a shikse, ha! (*Chatze, with glaring eyes, points both hands at Yankel.*)

YANKEL. (*Grabbing both of Chatze's hands.*) Reb Chatze, Reb Chatze enough, enough! (*Yankel clutches at his own head.*) What should I do? Please, don't scare me like that! I'm going out of my mind. Tell me, what should I do? Reb Chatze, I'm even afraid to die! (*Bewildered.*) Ach, Reb Chatze—ach Reb Chatze, ach!

CHATZE. What is it, Yankel?

YANKEL. I . . . I . . . (*Beats his own breast.*) My God, my God! Shmay yisrael, shmay yisrael. (*He sobs pitifully.*)

HIRSH BAER. (*Enters, carrying a bottle of whiskey.*) God sends water to the fish, fish to the priest Areseni, and me a bottle of real, purified vodka . . . (*He notices Yankel crying.*) Yankel's crying? Ach, but God doesn't send a good wallop to this Chelm donkey. Why are you crying, Yankel? What kind of nonsense did he fill you up with again?

YANKEL. No, Reb Hirsh Baer, Reb Chatze is a decent man, he tells the truth . . . Reb Hirsh Baer, I have sinned—oh, how I sinned . . . What shall I do?

HIRSH BAER. Let yourself be eaten alive by Chatze and he should only choke on you—that's what you should do! You've turned into being a pious Jew, you maniac, what more do you want?

YANKEL. (*In despair.*) B-b-but Lilith— the one with the burning eyes? The one with the lightning? And she throws one into the fire. Yes, right into the fire. And the tar is burning, and it's cutting to pieces, and it's burning, burning. My God—shmaye yisrael!

HIRSH BAER. Lilith? (*He turns on Chatze.*) So—you started already to scare him with Lilith too?

CHATZE. I only told him the sermon of the holy man from Chelm . . . So what's wrong with that? It won't do him any harm, I mean, really!

HIRSH BAER. That Chelm nut made you crazy and now you're making him crazy! (*Yankel seats himself, bows his head and sighs. Nachum, Frume, and Chayke enter.*)

NACHUM. God help us. (*Sighs as he seats himself.*)

HIRSH BAER. Oho, welcome. I see the whole gang is here. What are you sighing about, Nachum? Do you want a pinch of snuff?

NACHUM. Reb Hirsh Baer, it's no good. Joshua again, today, was with me, you should excuse me.

FRUME. And you think he wasn't with me today, huh?

CHAYKE. And to me—Uncle Joshua has come to me now the second night . . . (*Yankel jumps up with a scream, accidently knocks over a pot that smashes to pieces. The others jump up in fright. Yankel frantically looks around.*)

HIRSH BAER. Tpfui on all of you! Oh, you really could make the sanest person crazy with your dreams. God in heaven, how long yet will Joshua be coming to you? How about you going to him for a change? And if you like, you can take with you to him this Chelm scholar also, and let's make an end of this once and for all.

NACHUM. This is not a joke, Reb Hirsh Baer, for example. He heard it too in the other world what they're saying in the village—that Yankel wants to convert . . .

CHAYKE. And marry that shikse . . . Just wait, you'll see, Boyla, he'll make a good accounting of your deeds, your father! (*She weeps into her elbow.*)

FRUME. My Joshua nearly strangled me in bed last night.

YANKEL. (*Practically crawling, with outstretched arms, to his mother.*) Me? Who, me? I will convert? Me? Mama, I should die like a dog. Ah, what do you all want from me? (*With great passion.*) Mama—it's not true, no—not true. May my papa strangle me if it's true . . . my dear mama, I am a pious, a devout Jew . . . (*He sobs pitifully.*) I'm a pious Jew. I say my prayers . . . regularly . . . Reb Chatze, you know how devout I am, tell my mother. Reb Hirsh Baer, you tell her!

CHATZE. I mean, really. Is he pious! Such a blessing on all good Jews.

HIRSH BAER. Leave him alone, you and your dreams, all the bad dreams on your heads. Come here, Yankel! (*He pulls Yankel to him. Yankel clings like a child to his breast.*) Hush, shah, shah, Yankel, don't cry. You are now pious. God sees and He's certainly proud of you. And don't listen to them, they're crazy. Ach, what is this one, Yankel? A big little bird with a brain, a powerful bear with his strength. Annoy the bear and it's woe to all of you, but if you annoy the little bird, then woe to it.

YANKEL. Reb Hirsh Baer, you know the truth . . . you know, so tell my mama. Oh, dear father—you are now like a father to me, so you tell her that when my father comes to her, she should tell him I'm a good, a pious, a devout Jew. I say the Psalms, I say the morning prayer . . . (*He frantically clutches at Hirsh Baer.*) Dear father, Reb Hirsh Baer, you're now my father, Reb Hirsh Baer, have pity and help me . . .

FRUME. What do you want me to tell him, Yankel? As if he doesn't know already that you want to convert and marry Natasha?

YANKEL. What! I marry Natasha? Who, me? With Natasha? Oh, my God, my God! *Shmaye yisrael, shmaye yisrael!* (*He strikes his head upon the wall and weeps helplessly.*)

HIRSH BAER. This is Zalmanke's doing. It's a big lie—a big lie . . . !

CHATZE. This is absolutely a lie—a big lie. Yankel hasn't even looked at another girl, let alone a shikse. I mean, really.

YANKEL. (*Trying to compose himself.*) Him and his stories—Zalmanke's! I'll tear out his miserable guts, I will. Mama, Chayke is my bride— only Chayke! (*He wildly grabs Chayke's hand.*) She is my bride, the wolves should devour her! I'll marry her. Only have pity, don't torture me!

CHAYKE. (*Joyfully.*) Papa, oh papa, do you hear what Yankel is saying? Oh, I believe him . . . Yankel, your father told us a lie . . . a cholera on . . .

FRUME. (*Interrupting.*) Woe is me,

Chaykele. Whom did you curse with a cholera?

CHAYKE. (*Frightened.*) I didn't mean Uncle Joshua. (*She gasps and quickly covers her lips.*)

NACHUM. Where is my whip? (*Chayke springs behind Yankel in fear of her father.*) You stupid cow, you. There in the other world he's suffering for you; you should get a stroke, then don't complain.

FRUME. Reb Hirsh Baer, we went to the Rabbi at Ostrovne and told him the whole story about Yankel. And he told us that even though Yankel is still in mourning, we should get him married as quickly as possible to save him from being converted. So we decided the wedding should be in three weeks from now, the second day of the end of Succoth. Help us, Reb Hirsh Baer, to make sure he marries a Jewish girl! (*She sobs.*)

HIRSH BAER. I don't know what more you want? He said himself he will marry Chayke. So what else do you want?

FRUME. Do you hear, Yankel?

YANKEL. All right! I'll get married.— I'll marry her.

NACHUM. Be sure and see to it, Yankel, that you don't mislead us, for example. A good portion of it I want to take care of before the wedding. We have to arrange with Rabbi Baikel, to be sure he'll approve, and that the groom is really going through with it and that the wedding is sure, so don't complain!

YANKEL. (*Agitated.*) I'll go through with it! I'll marry her—even if the wedding is tomorrow. Only leave me alone! (*He punches his head in despair.*) Give my head a rest—the wolves should devour all of you! (*Zalman enters.*) I'll marry her—only stop tormenting me!

ZALMAN. So-o-o-o, you're getting married, Yankel? With whom?

YANKEL. (*Hurls himself upon Zalman and all his bitterness explodes on him.*) With Natasha, you dog! With Natasha! (*He hurls Zalman to the ground and beats him.*)

ZALMAN. Yankel. Help—police. Yankel, have pity . . . !

YANKEL. (*On top of Zalman and pressing him down with his knees.*) So, I'll convert, huh? I'll convert?

ALL. Yankel, let him go . . . !

HIRSH BAER. (*Assisted by Chatze, he grabs Yankel.*) Leave him alone, Yankel. His soul will be damned without your help. (*He succeeds in pulling Yankel away from Zalman.*)

ZALMAN. (*Staggering to his feet.*) Oy! He nearly killed me!

YANKEL. (*Evading Hirsh Baer's grasp and chasing Zalman.*) I'll convert, huh?

ZALMAN. (*Fleeing.*) He's gone crazy! (*Zalman runs out.*)

YANKEL. (*Yelling after Zalman.*) I'll tear out all of your guts—the wolves should devour all of you!

NACHUM. I don't know what's got into you that you carry on like that. Yankel, stop howling like that. Look, I'm here, and your mother is here, and your bride is here. So have a heart and behave—show some feeling, you should excuse me, and don't complain.

YANKEL. (*Raving.*) I'm not complaining! It's you who are complaining. So I'll marry Chayke. I'm a pious, devout Jew. I say my prayers. I pray every morning. What else do you want from me? Get out! Get out of here! I'll . . . (*He hurls a chair to the ground and it smashes into bits.*) Get out—you're driving me crazy!

HIRSH BAER. Yankel, don't destroy Prokop's house. And the rest of you, please go and be well . . . you heard him . . . he'll marry her . . . so in the meanwhile get the hell out of here!

NACHUM. Well, let's go. Goodbye, and you should excuse me. Come, Frume, Chayke.

CHAYKE. Yankel—be well—goodbye. (*He remains silent.*)

FRUME. Goodbye, my son. How foolish you are to be so angry, so bitter. Do you think we mean you any harm, maybe?

YANKEL. (*Suddenly embraces her and speaks with compassion.*) Mama! Here, here . . . my head is on fire . . . I'm all on fire. Mama, don't be hurt, don't be angry—I didn't want to insult you, I didn't want to hurt you. Tell papa when he comes to you again that I'll marry Chayke . . . Mama, dearest, I'll get married, I'll be pious. Tell papa he should stop tormenting me, he shouldn't frighten me so . . .

FRUME. Yes, yes—I'll tell him. Woe is me, just look at you—you look terrible! Ah, be well, my son . . . (*She exits with Nachum and Chayke.*)

HIRSH BAER. At last, they're gone, thank God. Good riddance. (*Yankel sits at the table—a picture of despair. Hirsh Baer gazes out the window.*) It's clearing up. I think we'll still be able to go out on the lake today. Chatze, I think we ought to check up on the boats. Come on, Chelmner, roll up your sleeves.

CHATZE. How about it, Yankel. Are you coming with us?

HIRSH BAER. Have pity, let him rest a while. Ach, Chelmner, Chelmner! You're Yankel's angel of death, you! So, come already, you foul excrescence of your mother. (*Both leave. Yankel remains seated with a bowed head, deeply engrossed in himself. Natasha enters on tip-toe, looks around carefully.*)

NATASHA. (*Approaches Yankel.*) Yankel. (*He jumps up with a wild outcry, looks at her in fright, and starts to sob. She is also frightened by his outcry.*) What is it—why are you frightened, Yankel? Are you sick? Just look at you, my eagle. (*He slumps down at the table and buries his sobs in his arms.*) Yankel, why are you crying? Why? You, too, feel as bad as I do? (*Puts her arms around him.*) Come, don't weep, Yankel, stop it, please. Let's better talk . . . we are alone . . . It's now four

weeks that you've been avoiding me. Why, Yankel I never did you any harm? Please, look at me . . . (*Embraces him.*) I love you so . . . ah how I love you, my eagle. If you only knew how much I've suffered these weeks . . . Yankel . . . my Yankel . . . (*Holds him tightly.*)

YANKEL. (*Raises his head and moans.*) Ah Natasha, I've suffered too . . . so much. Oh, why aren't you a Jew, Natasha? (*He desperately holds her and looks into her eyes.*) Natasha, you're so beautiful, I love you more than life. Your eyes Natasha, your eyes—Lilith—witchcraft is in your eyes, you're a witch—you're Chatze's Lilith! Oh, Natasha, oh. (*He kisses her wildly and holds her passionately.*)

NATASHA. (*Desperately holding him.*) Yankel, what did Chayke want here? Why have you avoided me these last four weeks? I waited for you in the woods, but you never came. I looked for you even here, but you made out as if you didn't notice me! Why? Ah, I thought I'd go out of my mind.

YANKEL. Ah, keep quiet, you devil, keep quiet! Oh, my Natasha, oh! (*He kisses her with abandon.*)

NATASHA. (*Burying her face in his breast.*) Ivan, the fisherman, told me that you will convert and marry me.

YANKEL. (*Jumps up, pale and frightened.*) Convert? Me? (*Bitterly through his teeth.*) Natasha, Chayke is my bride, Chayke. You are a witch—a devil. Stay away from me. I'm telling you, you're a devil. Get away from me—I'll kill you! Get away, you witch, away . . . !

NATASHA. (*Clinging to him.*) Yankel, you're going to marry Chayke? And what will I do, my only darling? Yankel, I'm going to be a mother.

YANKEL. (*Pushes her away from him.*) You? A mother. You! Witch! Devil!

NATASHA. (*Falls to the ground.*) Kill me! Kill me! If you won't then my grandfather will . . . kill me! (*Beats her breasts.*)

YANKEL. (*Sinks down beside her with lamentation.*) Natasha, oh, oh my Natasha! (*He wildly kisses her as he moans. Suddenly he jumps to his feet.*) What am I doing? My God, what should I do? My God! My God! *Shmaye yisrael! Shmaye yisrael!* (*He gasps for air as he thrashes about to grab hold of some comforting reality; then he runs out of the house.*)

NATASHA. (*Frantically reaches for him, as she rises.*) Yankel! (*She falls back and buries her face in her lap.*) Yankel . . . (*She cries bitterly. Prokop enters, pipe in mouth, and sees Natasha on the ground. He removes the pipe from his mouth and scratches his baffled head.*)

PROKOP. (*Calmly approaches Natasha.*) Natasha! (*She shudders, moans, and lifts her sad head and looks at him with pained eyes that pray for his kindness.*) Tu, tu, you are still sick? Why are you looking at me like a newly plucked chicken, girl? Ha?

NATASHA. (*Quickly crawls to him and embraces his knees.*) Grandpa—oh grandpa—forgive me! I am cursed. I'm lost—lost. Kill me, grandpa—please kill me! I'm a bad woman, a wicked girl! Soon—ah—soon I'm going to be a mother, grandpa. I've sinned! Kill me! I'm to be a mother. (*She crawls to him, embraces and kisses his feet.*) Kill me!

PROKOP. (*Trembles all over.*) Are you crazy, girl? What are you talking about? Natasha, you're making it up! (*Steps away from her, scratches his backside, confused, and gasps for breath.*) Tu, tu, so that's why she's been acting so queer! You devil, you! (*He stands, angry, while she sobs. He goes to her and kicks her with the side of his foot.*) Get up, girl. Stop your damned screeching! Get up and talk sense—who is the man? Ha?

NATASHA. Yankel, grandpa, Yankel!

PROKOP. (*Agitated.*) Yankel? That nonbeliever? That Jew? (*He glares at her venomously. Pause. Talks between his teeth.*) So, what now, girl, so? (*Slowly, deliberately, with threatening fists, he approaches her.*) What shall I do with you now, you slut! (*He stands over her with raised fists.*)

NATASHA. (*On her knees, with bowed head.*) Kill me, grandpa, kill me! I don't want to live anymore!

PROKOP. (*Lowers his fists.*) Tu, tu! Ech, Natasha, ech, you low-down whore, you, what have you got against my old, gray head? Weren't there enough fellows in the village who'd give their lives to get the beautiful Natasha? Why did you have to get involved with a non-Christian? Natasha, what's to become of you now? What honest peasant will now even look at you? Ech, you slut, you harlot, didn't I warn you to be on your guard, ha?

NATASHA. He was my beautiful eagle, dear grandpa. I am guilty . . . my sinful heart is guilty . . . I loved him, I confess my guilt! (*She is on her knees, in supplication with arms outstretched to him.*)

PROKOP. Tu, tu, you are guilty all right! (*He taps his pipe on his hand and blows through it to clear it, then fills it with tobacco.*) Who else should be guilty but you? (*He lights his pipe and smokes. He paces back and forth, and finally confronts her.*) Well, girl, what happens now? If your seducer were a peasant, a Christian, I would drag him by his head to you and make him marry you! But Yankel, the non-Christian! (*He has worked himself up to a frenzy of anger and hurls himself at her.*) You loose slut, if you wanted to be loose, why couldn't you do it with your own kind? I'll kill you I will, you bitch, I'll kill you! (*He raises his fists to her.*)

NATASHA. (*Clinging to his legs.*) Do it, grandpa, do it! I don't want to live!

PROKOP. (*Kicks her away from him.*) Get away from me. I'm not through with you yet! I'll take care of you later! Where is that heretic? When I get through with him, he'll be glad to cross himself. If not, I have my axe, I'll use it on him the way I use it to chop wood in the forest. Where is he? (*He runs out.*)

NATASHA. (*Running and screaming after him.*) Grandpa, no! My God, he will kill Yankel. Grandpa . . . ! (*She runs after him. The lights dim to indicate a brief passage of time. When the lights go up again, Yankel enters. He wears a melancholy expression as he goes to the table, picks up the Book of Psalms, and kisses it. Prokop enters, pipe in mouth, axe over his shoulder, with controlled bitterness and anger. With eyes mirroring his madness, he goes to Yankel.*)

PROKOP. (*Grabs Yankel's arm and swings him around to himself.*) Heretic, come here! (*Yankel turns to him with fear. Prokop holds him firmly and looks him directly in the eye.*) What did you have against my Natasha? Answer me! (*Yankel lowers his head and sobs like a child.*) Answer me, you heretic worm! What did you have against my girl?

YANKEL. (*Helpless.*) My fault, Prokop. It's my fault!

PROKOP. Tu, tu, your fault. Why should Natasha suffer if you're guilty? What should I do with you? Answer me.

YANKEL. I don't know . . .

PROKOP. (*Releasing Yankel.*) You'll have to marry her.

YANKEL. (*Shocked and frightened.*) Ha?

PROKOP. (*Holding the axe as a threat over Yankel.*) You'll go with her to the Priest Areseni and you'll convert!

YANKEL. No! No! I'm a Jew—I'm a Jew!

PROKOP. (*Shaking the axe at Yankel.*) You'll get this axe on your head from me if you don't convert.

YANKEL. (*Bows his head to Prokop.*) Here, hack away, Prokop, hack! I will never convert—I am a Jew! A Jew! A Jew!

NATASHA. (*Appearing at the window—screams.*) Hirsh Baer. Zalman. Chatze. Help! (*She runs into the house and grabs the handle of the upraised axe.*) Grandpa—no! (*Zalman, Hirsh Baer, and Chatze come running in.*)

PROKOP. He's going to convert, by God, or I'll kill him! (*He grabs the axe free from Natasha's grasp and hurls himself toward Yankel again.*) Will you convert, you Jew?

YANKEL. No, no, no! I'm a Jew—a Jew—a Jew. (*Zalman grabs the axe away from Prokop.*)

PROKOP. (*Prokop grabs Yankel by the throat and starts to choke him.*) What did you do to my Natasha, you dog! (*Prokop forces Yankel to the ground as he chokes him. The others spring at Prokop and drag him off as the curtain falls.*)

CURTAIN

ACT IV

In Joshua's tavern, where preparations are being made for the wedding of Yankel and Chayke. Nachum is dressed in his sabbath caftan, with the sleeves rolled up. He runs around in excitement as he busily arranges the tables and benches. Frume helps him, while Chayke, all dressed up like a bride, is polishing a pair of copper candlesticks.

FRUME. We have to hurry. It's so late. People will be coming soon, and I'm walking around like a peasant girl, not dressed yet—woe is me!

CHAYKE. Papa, oh papa, where did Yankel disappear?

NACHUM. Why are you asking today for Yankel? You? Why is Yankel on your mind today? Today is your wedding day, and you mustn't think about your sins, and don't complain.

CHAYKE. (*Polishing the candlesticks.*) Papa, ah, papa, under the wedding bower, God forgives all sins, ha?

NACHUM. Of course. That's why, for example, we have the canopy, in order that God forgives all sins . . .

(*Hirsh Baer enters.*)

CHAYKE. Papa, tell me papa, will God also forgive Yankel his sins, ha?

HIRSH BAER. Yankel's sins? The priest Areseni forgave him for ten rubles . . . ech, I swear, if that priest Areseni had not straightened out this Natasha business, who knows where Yankel would be now . . . maybe in paradise! And you, Chaykele, you'd have to look for another sucker! Ah, how you are radiant today, Chaykele, a real beauty, an offering for a prince!

FRUME. What are you talking about? It is really a miracle of miracles. What would we have done if the priest Areseni had been stubborn, God forbid, and wouldn't take any money and insisted that Yankel convert? This way Yankel really remains in the Jewish fold, thank God . . . his father's faith helped Yankel this time . . .

HIRSH BAER. Oi, dear children all of you, children, children, even so, my heart aches for Prokop and Natasha. True, they are gentiles, but . . . ech, I swear. Prokop was so decent, so wise—and what is he now? There he sits and drinks—everything he had, his whole household, is gone for drink. And Natasha, poor thing, is getting ready to go to her aunt in Novoselsk where she'll give birth. It's bitter and pitiful, as I live. Even if they are gentiles, they also weep with tears. And when Natasha moans, it tears one's heart out and one sighs with her. (*He takes a pinch of snuff.*)

NACHUM. Ah, if you'll excuse me, Reb Hirsh Baer, you really are a heretic, honestly. Chatze is right. What were we supposed to do? Let Yankel marry her?

HIRSH BAER. That is another question . . . From both sides it is forbidden, Nachum . . . That's what it comes to—he's damned if he does, and he's damned if he doesn't . . . He gets it from all sides, I swear!

NACHUM. So, don't complain, if you'll excuse me!

CHAYKE. Papa, oh papa—will I cry today at the wedding, so God should forgive Yankel his sin . . . oh, did Yankel sin—that devil! (*Prokop, drunk, staggers in.*)

PROKOP. 'Rish Baer? Tu, tu, (*Smacks his lips.*) You going t o have a drink with me, ha? Frumke, how about a glass . . . ?

HIRSH BAER. I'm not drinking, Prokop. You'd better go home now. Natasha wants to say goodbye to you before she goes to her aunt in Novoselsk . . .

PROKOP. (*Looking at Hirsh Baer sadly and smacking his lips.*) Natasha? Tu, tu. (*Laughs like a child.*) I have no Natasha . . . ha, ha, ha . . . gone— no more . . . (*He points to the ground.*) She went with the devil down to hell! She's not mine—she belongs to the devil! So much for Natasha. So, Hirsh Baer, are you drinking—yes or no?

HIRSH BAER. Go home, Prokop . . . Man alive, what's going to happen to you and everything you've got?

PROKOP. What I've got? Let it burn. What do I need anything for? Do you think I'll take it all with me to the grave, or what? (*He laughs like a child.*) I don't need anything— nothing. Tu, tu! Drink—that's it— one after the other. Drink and the devil take everything else. (*He dances drunkenly.*) Drink, and forget your troubles. Sing your songs, then die like a dog—Tu, tu, he, he, he . . . ! (*He sings, clapping his hands in time with his song as he leaves.*)

HIRSH BAER. (*Sighs.*) Lost. He's a lost soul. We can say for Prokop a prayer for the dead like *Rabonim Kadish.*

NACHUM. A prayer for the dead for Prokop? What are you talking about, Reb Hirsh Baer? Say, for example, something special, so why, if you'll excuse me?

HIRSH BAER. Ach, I completely forgot. The special prayer, *Rabonim Kadish,* can only be said for such a holy man like you, Reb Nachum, the great saint. Ech, I swear! Here, for your brilliance, take a pinch of snuff.

FRUME. Where is Yankel? Now that Prokop went away, Yankel doesn't have to hide any more. Woe, Reb Hirsh Baer, is Yankel afraid of Prokop! You've no idea. The moment he sees him, no matter how far away, he starts to tremble all over and he hides himself. That axe really scared Yankel.

HIRSH BAER. Maybe he's hiding from Prokop for another reason. Once, I accidentally broke the leg of a little dog. After that, whenever I saw that poor dog limping along, I would turn my head away. How do you think anyone feels when he breaks a person's both legs . . . ?

NACHUM. So, who cares what happened before. Let the devil take it, as long as Yankel has become a man. It's now a week since Joshua has appeared to any of us. It's a good sign. Because we're going ahead with the wedding, he's appeased, at peace.

CHAYKE. Reb Hirsh Baer, ah, Reb Hirsh Baer. Oh, did they make a suit of the best clothes for Yankel! Wait till you see it under the wedding canopy—it's beautiful! And a watch with a chain for him—and here, I have a lovely kerchief for him too! (*She unfurls a white silk kerchief, which she shows to Hirsh Baer.*)

NACHUM. Chaykele, Chaykele, you're not supposed to think of Yankel today—it's sinful, you should excuse me . . . !

CHAYKE. Ah, but he creeps into my thoughts. (*She pounds her head. Yankel, perturbed, enters.*)

YANKEL. Did he leave? (*He sees Hirsh Baer.*) It's you, Reb Hirsh Baer? Ah, it's painful for me—I can't look on . . .

HIRSH BAER. At whom?

YANKEL. At Prokop. Such a pity. Ech, Reb Hirsh Baer, the wolves should devour me—I'm a curse . . .

NACHUM. Yankele, don't curse yourself today! After all, today is your wedding day.

YANKEL. Wedding or no wedding, I'm no damned good, and that's that.

HIRSH BAER. Yankele, don't be a fool. Nicer people than you do things like that—even worse. You're not the first and you won't be the last. Chase it out of your head. Ah, here is your bride, Chaykele. You have to think of her only.

NACHUM. (*Interrupting.*) And don't complain!

YANKEL. (*Pulls Hirsh Baer to one side and whispers to him.*) Reb Hirsh Baer, Chaykele is a disease, I can't stand the sight of her . . . she is my bride, that's what my father wants—but the wolves should devour her! Reb Hirsh Baer, it's no good—it's all wrong!

HIRSH BAER. Calm down. Take it easy, my boy. Chayke, where is Yankel's silk kerchief?

CHAYKE. (*Puts the silk kerchief around Yankel's throat.*) Oh, how beautiful. Wear it in good health, Yankele. Show Reb Hirsh Baer your watch and chain . . .

YANKEL. Why did you throw this kerchief on me? (*He tears it off his throat.*) You'd do better to put a rope around my neck and choke me! (*Pulls a watch and chain out of his pocket and thrusts it at her.*) Take this back, too—here, take it!

HIRSH BAER. (*Holding Yankel back.*) Yankel, wear the bride's presents. Don't shame her, you fool. If you gave her a gift she'd gladly wear it. Frume, where are Yankel's new clothes? Let him put them on . . .

FRUME. They're in the next room. My hands are soiled . . .

CHAYKE. I'll get them for Yankele right away . . . (*Chayke exits.*)

YANKEL. (*Pacing about, then quietly*

stands before Hirsh Baer.) Reb Hirsh Baer, I heard she's going away today to her aunt in Novoselsk. Is this true?

HIRSH BAER. Who?

YANKEL. Her; you know, Natasha. (*He sighs.*)

HIRSH BAER. Don't think about her. Forget her . . .

YANKEL. I have five rubles. I want to give them to her . . .

CHAYKE. (*Entering.*) See, Reb Hirsh Baer. Look how beautiful it is. Made from the best cloth, may he wear it in good health. (*Noise of wagon bells and arrival of horse and wagon.*)

NACHUM. Ah, that's Chatze with the canopy from the town. Frume, get a move on! People from town are arriving!

FRUME. Oh, woe is me. The tables aren't set yet. Chaykele, take the guests into the other room.

CHAYKE. (*Shoving the clothes at Yankel.*) I'm going. Here, Yankel, get dressed, you plague! After all, you're the groom. Why are you just standing there like a statue? (*She runs out.*)

CHATZE. (*Entering. He is dressed in his sabbath clothes.*) Well, they're here—the canopy, the sexton, the master of ceremonies, the musicians, I mean, really! A Jewish wedding!

NACHUM. Did my horse run well, ha, Reb Chatze? What a horse, for example, ha, Reb Chatze?

CHATZE. A horse is a horse. The ten starving Jews he had no trouble bringing here.

HIRSH BAER. If he was able to pull such a big mess as you, Chatze, he must be some wonderful horse.

CHATZE. Well, let's go to the guests. After all, they're strangers here, but good Jews. We can't neglect them. I mean, really!

FRUME. I've got to get dressed. I'll be right out. (*She exits.*)

NACHUM. Come, Reb Hirsh Baer, meanwhile let's enjoy ourselves. Yankel, get dressed right away, quickly—don't be such a dope—a

misfortune on you! (*Nachum, Hirsh Baer, and Chatze leave.*)

YANKEL. (*Yankel remains standing, looking at the new clothes in his hands, then hurls them in disgust to the ground.*) The wolves should devour you! (*The croaking of a crow is heard from outside. Yankel shudders. Natasha enters; she is carrying a bundle. She is dressed in white, with a kerchief around her head. Her walk is faltering. He sees her and remains struck dumb, unseen by her.*)

NATASHA. Grandpa! Ah, he's not here either. (*She sees Yankel and shudders, turns to leave but he bars her way.*)

YANKEL. Natasha! (*She stands mute.*) You're going to Novoselsk?

NATASHA. Get away from me, you murderer! Away, you bandit! Better if they took me dead to my grave than that I should go as a tramp to my aunt in her town . . . !

YANKEL. (*Going to her, pleading.*) Natasha, forgive me . . .

NATASHA. Away—get away from me, you bandit! I'll tear your eyes out! (*Hurls herself at him—remains standing, broken up and sobbing loudly.*)

YANKEL. (*Beating his breast.*) Yes, yes, Natasha. Do that! Tear out my eyes. Tear out my heart! I am no good— I am everything you say. Natasha, ach Natasha, I'm so miserably unhappy—oh, my God! (*He breaks into bitter sobbing.*)

NATASHA. So, you're miserably unhappy! Ha, ha, ha! With a silk kerchief around your neck like a count! And in the next room the musicians are waiting for you with your bride. You criminal, why did you want to destroy me! I was an honest girl, now I'm lost. I was an orphan in God's world—no father, no mother, only a grandfather I had, a dear, good grandfather—now I've lost him too. He even refused to say goodbye to me. My God, my grandfather cursed me! (*The croaking of a crow is heard from outdoors.*)

Natasha shudders in fright.) Do you hear? Listen, how the evil bird is croaking? She echoes my grandfather's curses. On your head!

YANKEL. (*Fearfully crouching away from the sound of the crow.*) Oh, what should I do? Tell me. I'll do anything to help you. (*Beats his breast.*) Natasha, I want to help you—I'd even die for you, Natasha!

NATASHA. Yankel, eagle mine, you alone can help me. I love you so dearly, my poor darling. Yankel, convert yourself—for me . . .

YANKEL. (*Horrified, he backs away from her.*) No, no, no! Natasha, I am a Jew. Lilith will throw me into the flames! Oh, Natasha, why aren't you Jewish? I'm so miserably unlucky! I love you, but you're not a Jew. I want to save you, but I am a Jew! (*He continues his helpless sobbing.*)

NATASHA. You should drop dead, you criminal, if you won't convert. Your Chayke, when she marries you, she should lose you, lose her father. lose her mother as I did. And if she has a grandfather, he should curse her the same way my grandfather cursed me. You should die, and your Chayke should drop dead. (*The croaking of the crow again.*) Do you hear the crow? The evil bird! You will surely drop dead! (*She goes toward the door.*)

YANKEL. (*He hurries after her. He is bewildered.*) Natasha! (*She hesitates. He takes out the five rubles from his pocket.*) I have five rubles; here, take them! (*He forces them into her hand.*)

NATASHA. Away from me! (*She hurls the gold piece away.*)

YANKEL. (*Takes out his watch and chain.*) Take them, take! My beloved, take everything . . . (*Takes off the kerchief from his neck and hands it to her.*) Here, take this . . . have pity on me . . . (*Prokop staggers in, drunk. He carries a heavy coil of rope.*)

PROKOP. Frumke! Where is Frumke? I brought this rope. I want half a quart of schnapps for it!

YANKEL. (*Falling at Prokop's feet.*) Good old man, Prokop—forgive me! I have sinned against you—oh, how I have sinned. But against my father and against God, I made a greater sin! (*He kisses Prokop's feet as he moans and sobs.*)

PROKOP. (*Oblivious—drunk.*) Frumke, half a quart! (*Yankel rises and hands over his watch to Prokop.*)

YANKEL. Here, take the watch, grandpa, and give me the rope. (*He forces the watch into Prokop's hand and takes the rope.*) Forgive me, Prokop! Forgive me Natasha! (*He exits with the rope.*)

NATASHA. Grandpa, say goodbye to me. Wish me a good journey.

PROKOP. (*Staggers out.*) Frumke, a half a quart only—where is she? (*He goes out.*)

NATASHA. (*Running after him.*) Grandpa, say goodbye to me! (*She suddenly stops in her tracks.*) The rope . . . (*She is confused. Hirsh Baer and Chayke enter.*)

CHAYKE. Where is he? Everyone is asking where is the bridegroom? (*Chatze runs in.*)

CHATZE. Reb Hirsh Baer, woe—Yankel hanged himself! (*He runs out, with Chayke and Hirsh Baer after him. Natasha runs to the door, then backs away with an unearthly shriek. Outside there is a great turmoil, shrieking, and crying. Prokop appears and stands at the door.*)

PROKOP. Frumke, a half a quart . . . !

THE END

RECRUITS

Israel Axenfeld (1787-1866)
and Lipe Reznik (1890-ca.1943)

Plays on the Yiddish stage rarely offered tender moments of love between a young man and a girl—or anyone at any age except between a mother and child. It seems that all scenes between a youth and his beloved in Yiddish drama contained confrontations between them whereby the drama of their meeting was to resolve the urgencies that kept them apart. Neither light, romantic banter nor torrid, sensual love-making fit the customary formula of the Yiddish play, except one in the memory of this playgoer, this Yiddish-theatre *patriott*. That one memorable love scene was in the Artef production of Lipe Reznik's communist-inspired adaptation of Israel Axenfeld's *Der Ehrshter Yiddisher Recrut in Russlan* (*The First Jewish Recruit in Russia*) with the co-title, *Ahzoy Ihz Gehven* (*That's How It Was*). The scene was a warm moment of groping affection, a balcony scene very unlike the confident balcony scenes in *Romeo and Juliet* and *Cyrano*. In this play the consummation of love is thwarted in a story as compelling as that of Héloise and Abelard. But both Axenfeld and Reznik were bemused by the social forces that conspired to destroy the wholesome, natural, human love of a boy and a girl.

Axenfeld was a dedicated *maskil*. Fully to understand the varied interests, dedication, activities, and philosophy of the *maskilim* in the Haskala movement requires an encyclopedic treatment. In an all-too-brief simplification, the Haskala movement is described as an almost evangelical campaign that was inspired by Moses Mendelssohn in Germany around the time of the birth of our own republic. Its objectives included the emancipation of the Jews from their physical and mental ghettos into fulfillment as modern citizens so that they could participate in and benefit from the Enlightenment that was sweeping over Europe. Activists, *maskilim,* who sought to cut the bonds of those traditionally tied to their spiritual, intellectual, and social past by physical propinquity and theocratic demands employed various modernizing concepts, philosophies, and methods. Some employed moral suasion to weaken the fanaticism of the orthodox devout, some sought various forms of apostasy, and some contemptuously propagandized against the reactionary, superstitious charlatans who used their self-serving religiosity to enslave

141

the minds of gullible, uncultured, provincial Jews. Haskala as a movement to eman-
cipate the Jews from their medieval ghettos in order to bring them into the main-
stream of the Enlightenment cannot be simply and rigidly categorized. The
maskilim ranged from mild scoffers to zealously fanatic reformers, from lay edu-
cators to Hebrew poets and scholars.

Israel Axenfeld (b. Nemirov, Russia, 1787; d. Paris, 1866) was a *maskil* who,
as a pioneer in Yiddish literature, wrote with the express intention of discrediting
the ignorant superstitious mountebanks who posed as "holy" men and preyed upon
the ignorant and gullible masses. A Jewish Chaucer was long overdue. History
has judged Axenfeld to have been violently anti-Hassidic. After receiving a traditional education in Jewish orthodoxy, he married while he was quite young,
became a merchant, and soon abandoned that career to become a notary public
in Odessa. During the Napoleonic wars he traveled on behalf of the Russian army
commissary, which enabled him to polish his proficiency in the Russian, Polish,
and German languages in addition to his intimacy with Hebrew and Yiddish. During 1820–1821 he lived in Brody, Galicia, and then practiced law in Odessa from
1824 until he left to join his sons in Paris in 1864.* During all this time he wrote
Yiddish stories, novels, and dramas, which circulated among the Jewish intelligentsia in Russia in manuscript form. Publication of his works was proscribed on
two fronts: because he exposed the venality, rascality, and hypocrisy of some reactionary Hassidic rebbes, none of the few Jewish publishers would take on his
work; and because the authorities considered his work revolutionary, no publisher
in Russia would publish him. Not till he was almost 75 (1861) were any of his
works published: a novel, *Der Sterntichel,* and the drama *Der Ehrshter Yiddisher
Recrutt in Russlan.* They were published in Leipzig.

The author's sharp, devastating ridicule of the Hassidic rebbes found a recep-
tive disciple in the Soviet writer Lipe Reznik (b. 1890 in Makarov, Kiev; d. ca.
1943), when Axenfeld's works were exhumed and published in two volumes by
the Yiddish Section of the Ukrainian Scientific Institute in 1931 and 1938. These
works provided a perceptive, on-the-scene picture of Jewish life during the first
half of the nineteenth century in the Russian Pale, albeit biased by Axenfeld's
virulent antipathy toward certain Hassids. Reznik's early writing was distinguished
by its symbolic verse. During the Hitler period his atavistic preoccupation manifested itself in exciting poems of Jewish nationalism. The details of his death
are obscure, and rumors of his victimization by official purge have not been substantiated Five volumes of his verse, four plays, and many of his children's stories
have been published. The play *Recruits* or *That's How It Was* satirizes and ridicules
Hassidic superstition while it demonstrates, as did Axenfeld's original version, the
sanctimonious hypocrisy of the liberal, upper-class Jews who sold out the workers
in order to protect their own security. Reznik added tender love scenes and compassion for the downfallen.

The hypersensitivity of most Jews, honestly come by through millennia of
persecution, may block possible future productions of this important play. But its
production by the incomparable Artef troupe in New York in 1935 under Benno
Schneider's direction (he was a product of the Habima) was sensationally successful. Despite Axenfeld's bias or anti-clericalism, he was one of the first major
Yiddish writers to provide, together with Ettinger, Gotlober, Lefin, and Levinsohn,
a poignant picture of the life of the Jews in the shtetles early in the nineteenth
century.

---

* Axenfeld's two sons were Auguste Alexander (1825–1876), a professor of internal
pathology at the Sorbonne, and Henri, a painter who frequently exhibited in London
and Paris (dates unknown).

In addition to the daily travail, deprivation, and harassment of the unfran-chized Jews under the Czars, a new plague descended upon them when Czar Nicholas I, perhaps motivated by a benign wish to allow Jews to participate more fully in Russian life, decreed in 1827 in a ukase that Jews were to be recruited into the Russian army. The young Jewish boys (as young as ten years of age) were often kidnapped while at innocent play, bound in ball and chains, and impressed into the Czar's army. They became *Nicholayevske Soldats*—for twenty-five years! Aside from the impact upon an individual family of the tragedy of a son torn from its midst, the Jewish community was bereaved when a youth was lost to Judaism. Axenfeld showed how reactionary, intolerant, bigoted rebbes, in league with rich merchants, connived to have sons of the poor serve in the Russian army in order to spare the sons of the upper classes. Critics of Axenfeld and of his school of anti-Hassidic *maskilim* have not been able to disprove his indictment. Molière's *Tartuffe,* despite its anti-clericalism, is often produced without condemnation by the clergy and the Catholic world. It should be hoped that like toleration will enable this excellent epic of a folk to be produced again and again simply because it is excellent drama and good theatre. To quote Horace, the play entertains and en-lightens. Axenfeld wrote to Gotlober, "[I wrote] for the ordinary Jew who could read no other language. Those who will read these books, while amused, will . . . learn something about morals and etiquette, and indeed all useful sciences too." Expressions such as Axenfeld's suggest the dedication of those in the Haskala movement who made possible the magnificent work of Bialick, Mendele, Peretz, Sholem Aleichem, and others.

Axenfeld's *Recruits* is a faithful portrait of Jewish life in Czarist Russia and of the social forces that dramatically reached their climax in tragedy. The au-thentic shtetl types, with their all-too-human shortcomings as well as virtues are theatrically and felicitously rendered without caricature, while the plot, enriched with realistic detail, is an adumbration of the then-emerging school of naturalism. The original play was not written necessarily as a stage piece, according to its author, but was intended for dramatic readings among interested groups as was then the vogue. Nonetheless, he evidenced a good ear for the regional Yiddish then prevalent in Southern Russia, both in idiom and intonation. Reznik tightened the plot, provided character development and dimensions, and built a powerfully cumulative suspense while emphasizing Axenfeld's thesis.

RECRUITS

or

THAT'S HOW IT WAS

Translated and adapted from the Yiddish
of Axenfeld and Resnick

by

David S. Lifson

CAST OF CHARACTERS

NACHMAN DER GROSSE, a young tailor
FRUMELE, his beloved; daughter of PINCHUS THE REDHEAD. She is 17.
GAVRIEL SHED, the town drunk; a recruit "kidnapper"
CHAIM PLATT, a small-time operator, sometime marriage broker.
TZALYEH, a wheeler-dealer and ward-heeler; father of ROCHEL
REB MOTELE, the Rabbi; an ignorant, provincial fanatic
ROCHEL, TZALYEH's daughter; a vivacious young woman
SHLOIME SPYUCHE, Village Elder, head of the Jewish Council
BRUCHE, his deaf wife.
HIRSH-LEIB, their son; the village idiot
PINCHUS DER ROITER (REDHEAD), FRUMELE's father; wealthy Council Member
VELVEL GELAVYATEH, a hunchbacked fur dealer, busybody, and Council Member
YISROELIK UKRAINER, retainer of AARON KLUGER and an independent lumberman
AARON KLUGER, wealthiest Jew in town; leading Jewish citizen

PERELE, his pretty wife
Their TWO DAUGHTERS, little girls
LIFSHE THE SPINSTER, Tavern Keeper
TUTOR, a young Talmud Scholar
BUTCHER BOY, an apprentice
COBBLER'S APPRENTICE
TWO TAILOR APPRENTICES
POLISH-RUSSIAN PEASANTS
VASSILY, a peasant army deserter
MANAGER (or ECONOM), powerful general manager of Count Nibilitzki's estate
TWO OF HIS BULLIES
AGAFON AGAFONOVITCH, a peasant drunkard
CHANTZE, VELVEL's wife; a matchmaker
FIRST INVALID SOLDIER
SECOND INVALID SOLDIER
DRUMMER BOY
SERVANTS of AARON KLUGER
MACHLE, Nachman's blind mother

The play takes place in the Jewish community of the town of Nibivayleh in the Russian-Polish Pale. The year is 1828, from late winter to autumn.

ACT I

SCENE 1

Early spring. The cold lingers. A street outside the home of the rich Reb Pinchus der Roiter (Redhead).

Nachman, a handsome young tailor, the only child of blind Machle, a widow, walks by with some tailor work on his arm. When he retraces his steps, it becomes apparent that he is loitering, perhaps waiting for someone. He whistles to hide his impatience.

Out of Pinchus's house comes the town drunk, Gavriel Shed. He has a whiskey-reddened face, swollen red eyes, disheveled hair. He is unwashed, dirty, his torn clothes barely covering a starved body, with but skeletal remains of shoes. Under his tattered caftan he holds a bulging bag of money.

Gavriel bumps into Nachman. With a wink and a leer, Gavriel slaps the lump where he is hiding the money.

GAVRIEL. Guess what I've got hidden here. Ah, but you wouldn't know. Stuff like that tailors don't know of. Money! . . . that's right, money. Crazy world, what do tailors know about money, what do they need it for. Nachman, you're such a fine buck, but you're a pauper. Your pockets are empty—you're not weighed down by this stuff. That's why you walk so lightly, like walking on air, crazy world.

NACHMAN. I can't believe it. So much money in your possession and you're still walking around sober? I have a suspicion the money is not yours, eh Gavriel? Either it's Reb Aaron Kluger's or Pinchus the Redhead's. You're only a woodchopper; when would you have so much money for your own? You get only ten groshen for chopping wood, and somebody else enjoys the fire. (*Gavriel changes his taunting tone and tries to ingratiate himself with Nachman.*)

GAVRIEL. Crazy world, I was only joking . . .

NACHMAN. Don't mess around with me. Run along or you'll lose your treasure.

GAVRIEL. You don't think what I said was real? I was only joking. Ah, you're a hot-tempered lad. Come, buy me a drink of whiskey. I haven't earned a groshen all day and I haven't had anything to drink. Be a good boy and buy me a drink. Just one. I'll be your best friend. What do you say, Nachman?

NACHMAN. A friendship in exchange for a drink of whiskey is not worth a fig. With all the rich friends you've got, respectable people and not just a tailor, you can keep your friendship and I'll go my own way. I can manage my own affairs.

GAVRIEL. Crazy world. I beg for one little drink and he gives me a speech.

NACHMAN. I don't believe you are my friend. For a drink, go to the town Council. The elders there will keep you supplied as long as you do their dirty work. Such friends like you I don't need. Run along, I told ·you. Scat! (*Gavriel grumbles and walks slowly away. Nachman turns in the opposite direction. Frumele approaches. She carries a shopping basket filled with her marketing. She is around 17 years old, very beautiful, nicely dressed, good and charming. She is the daughter, the only child, of Pinchus the Redhead. Nachman quickly looks in all directions, takes off his hat as if in greeting to Frumele, and takes out a paper from inside the hat, which he quickly hands her. Frumele hides the paper and disappears into her house. Nachman again looks around, as if to make certain that no one has observed his gambit, then he walks away, whistling. Gavriel is still at the other end of the street. He has an impulse to follow Nachman, but is accosted by Tzalyeh, who enters from behind Gavriel. Tzalyeh is a "wheeler-dealer" who maintains a pragmatic philosophy to meet life's adversities. He tries, as is manifest in his clothes, to maintain a semblance of gentility, which falls short of convincing anyone who knows that Tzalyeh has his price for his loyalty. In a more enlightened community, say a democracy, Tzalyeh would be a ward-heeler.*)

TZALYEH. Gavriel! People say you're a financier and that you're making loads, simply loads of money. On top of it all, you have a compassionate Jewish heart. Give me a donation for Reb Yichiel, the poor cripple, the Baal Shem's grandson, no less. Ah, that blessed Reb Yichiel, Reb Motele said that in his condition, he'll limp when he meets the Messiah. Don't let me keep asking you, Reb Gavriel. Plain is simple; give me a donation. You will earn a blessing.

GAVRIEL. Are you joking? (*Gavriel laughs.*)

TZALYEH. Plain is simple. When do I make jokes in worthy causes?

GAVRIEL. To you, Reb Tzalyeh, I can tell the truth, no? I slave, God knows, I slave. And who takes the profit? Reb Aaron Kluger and Reb Pinchus. Nachman der Grosse was right when he said I was like the woodchopper who chops the wood for someone else to enjoy the fire. And all I get is ten groshen. Nachman, devil take him. If you were a friend, a real nice friend, you would make me an Israeli good-will Ambassador for Reb Motele. Crazy world, maybe I could make out better than exchanging money for rich people when none rubs off on me.

TZALYEH. Nachman der Grosse, you said? What kind of relations, what kind of business do you have with that rotten bum? He's no good, a nothing, a tailor's helper, that's all. Plain is simple. I heard terrible stories about him. He insults respectable people. The Almighty should shield us, what good can a lout like that bring to this town? I heard Reb Pinchus talking about this character, and he was sharp. You said you were talking with him, Gavriel, God forbid? So what do you have to do with a nothing like him? What kind of transactions can you have with such a character? Plain is simple.

GAVRIEL. What are you talking about, Reb Tzalyeh? Crazy world, I would talk to such a peasant? God forbid. I was simply walking on the street and he approached me. I was just coming out from Reb Pinchus's house; crazy world, I was feeling good, you know, happy, so I made a few jokes. Crazy world, what's the harm? (*Tzalyeh stands puzzled, transfixed in thought. Then he pointedly questions Gavriel.*)

TZALYEH. Say, Gavriel, did you see Pinchus's girl, Frumele, when she went into her house? Hah? What? Tell me, did you see her? Say . . . already, plain is simple . . .

GAVRIEL. Why? What's the difference if I saw her or I didn't see her? What am I, on a witness stand in Count Nibelitzky's court?

TZALYEH. Ah, Reb Gavriel, some things are nothing to some people, and a little nothing is a big thing to other people. Plain is simple, yes or no?

GAVRIEL. Crazy world, now I remember I did see something. Yes, I remember. She smiled to Nachman and walked away from him to her house and she was carrying a piece of paper. So, what's a little piece of paper? Why are you asking me, Reb Tzalyeh?

TZALYEH. Good. It's clear to me. Plain is simple. I know everything I need. Yes, all I need is to catch a tattle-tale, then the rest is easy. Yes, I know everything. Plain is simple.

GAVRIEL. Ho, ho. I'm beginning to understand, too. Crazy world, you mean . . . Nachman der Grosse and Reb Pinchus's girl? Yes? So, ho, ho. So I know about it, and that explains more, yet. I saw them last week in Shprintze the Deaf One's store. He was making believe he was looking to buy some binding. And, crazy world, she was there, too. They were talking together, you know, lovey-dovey, and the deaf Shprintze didn't hear.

TZALYEH. So, what did you hear? Out with it, plain is simple.

GAVRIEL. To tell the truth, I didn't hear either. Crazy world, you see, I was in the store across the road. But I know. Tell me, Reb Tzalyeh, do you think we should tell Reb Pinchus about this? After all, he's her father, no?

TZALYEH. You are, how should I say it, one of his cronies. You are very close to him. If anybody should tell him, you are the one. Plain is simple. Who else was here, who else was there? But if you go to tell Reb Pinchus, I will go too. I have a very confidential business to talk over with him, a certain match-making. Oh-h-h-h, have I got a proposal for Reb Pinchus! This will work out just fine.

GAVRIEL. In that case, then I am also entitled to a share in the marriage-broker's fee. Whom can it hurt if Gavriel turns over an honest commission? Crazy world, I'm certainly entitled. (*Chaim Platt enters. A small-time operator, a dynamo of action, a sycophant to Tzalyeh. He has a constant problem keeping his pants from falling, his umbrella from falling as he tries to hitch up his trousers, his hat from falling off as he stoops to retrieve his umbrella.*)

CHAIM. Aha, it's you Reb Tzalyeh. And Reb Gavriel. So tell me, why are you just standing around? What? I have no time, I have so many things to do, just loads and loads. My wife's sister is divorcing her husband, Leib-Behr, today, yes today. Imagine, he started reading foreign languages. Nuh, so how can she live with him? And that Shloime, the fat one, is on his death bed. After all, he's my neighbor. Elik, the school teacher has some gossip about a stolen cow, so they summoned him to Count Nibilitzky's manager to give evidence. Imagine! Meanwhile the children in the school are standing around, or, who knows, walking around, with nothing to do. Pinchus the smuggler stole from Moishe the Little One a blanket from his bed. Imagine! So much is going on, so much to do, I have to run. And I, I have no time for myself, I have to buy so much merchandise, I have so much to do! What, oh yes, you didn't hear about the decree? There is chaos all over the town.

TZALYEH. So talk already! Plain is simple, what decree?

CHAIM. What? The decree from St. Petersburg, of course. God have mercy! I have no time, I must hurry. (*Chaim, in his confusion, tries to blow his nose, stumbles over his umbrella.*)

TZALYEH. Chaim, Chaim! Pick up your umbrella and wait awhile. What kind of decree? Don't run so fast! Wait! A person could go crazy from you. I must tell you something. Wait, it's important, I'm telling you.

CHAIM. Ha, you think I don't know what you want to talk about? Of course I know. But I forget right now. I have so many things to do, so I have no time. Loads of things, interests. Imagine, I'm torn from all sides. (*Chaim again starts to leave. Gavriel, suddenly illuminated, lets out a roar.*)

GAVRIEL. I've got it! I figured it out. Crazy world. That piece of paper that Nachman gave Frumele—it must be a secret letter. Right? Right, Reb Tzalyeh? Chaim doesn't know that we discovered something that is a wonderment. A wonder of wonders, isn't it? When Gavriel sets his mind to it, just watch out for Gavriel. We were just talking about Nachman der Grosse and Reb Pinchus's girl. So what kind of decree from St. Petersburg, Reb Chaim?

CHAIM. I have no time, leave me alone. I have enough problems without that low-down tailor, that needle pusher! He thinks he's such a big

shot in this town and can throw his weight around, that hooligan! That smart alec! Some big shot. His blind mother sells bagels, and his father was worse than he is. Do you know what that bum said? He said that Reb Aaron Kluger, imagine—Reb Aaron Kluger—is nothing more to Count Nibiletzky than a dog, a thieving dog, yet! Lies! Loads of lies he throws around about respectable people. Such a bum, that beggar, that good-for-nothing! Everyone knows that Reb Aaron is the richest man around here. Who can count how much he has? A big store, acres and acres of woods and fields, and businesses—loads of them. And money loaned out on interest, loads of money. Take you, for example, Reb Gavriel, you work for him. How much money is in his money exchange any time, any one time? Definitely loads and loads. And properties, distilleries, breweries, silos —countless loads; freight wagons, small wagons, carriages with horses, and herds of cattle—something scarce. Silver and jewelry—no one can touch him—what a man! *Reb Aaron Kluger,* what a personalty! It's no exaggeration.

TZALYEH. You're right, it's unbelievable. To say such things about Reb Aaron! Simply unbelievable! Tell us, Reb Chaim, what kind of decree, God forbid? (*Nachman appears.*)

CHAIM. You just reminded me, I have no time. It's no exaggeration. That Nachman, imagine, that low-life with Pinchus's girl! Pugh! (*Sarcastically.*) Very nice! I can use such information. It's no exaggeration. What did you say? You don't know? A decree, a plague for all Jews. Recruits! Do you understand? Recruits! Imagine! I have to run. It's no exaggeration, I have loads and loads . . . (*Nachman has heard his name mentioned. He approaches the three; they see him and, with a cry, flee. As they flee, they cry out.*)

CHAIM, GAVRIEL, TZALYEH. Recruits? What kind of recruits? Recruits? (*Nachman looks toward the running three, then exclaims contemptuously.*)

NACHMAN. Slobs!!

Quick Curtain

SCENE 2

Noon, Saturday. At Rabbi Motele's house. The interior shows a large room in which stands a large table, at the head of which sits Reb Motele surrounded by his devout devotees. They are fanatical scholars of the Chassidic cult, poorly dressed in the garb of the medieval ghetto. Alongside the Rabbi is a heavy book of the Cabala.

Rabbi Motele is a doddering, old, unlearned, sanctimonious religious leader of a type numerous among the ignorant, impoverished Jews, who had to settle for this ignorant Rabbi because the more learned remained in the larger cities and centers. Nonetheless, he filled the need for some kind, any kind, of spiritual leader.

His followers gorge themselves as Tzalyeh scurries about from the kitchen to the table with platters of food.

From his young assistant (a boy) Tzalyeh takes several decanters of schnapps, which he distributes around the table over the heads of those seated; Tzalyeh's long sleeves brush against their heads, much to their annoyance. Tzalyeh reaches over the head of one and grabs a piece of fish, which he stuffs into his mouth.

TZALYEH. Plain is simple. I washed myself for the table. It is a good deed to eat the Sabbath meal, especially in the home of such a saint as Reb Motele. It's more so because I'm hungry, simply very hungry. So,

I take a piece of fish and eat. Plain is simple. (*Tzalyeh has been intoning his speech in a typical sing-song lilt. The others smile approvingly.*)

ALL.—Correct.
—Tzalyeh is right.
—Very sensible.

TZALYEH. And what harm can it do to have a little schnapps. You see, whiskey I already drank twice before the fish. Yes? But schnapps! That I will drink and taste at the same time. That's right, no?

MOTELE. Ah, Tzalyeh, Tzalyeh, Tzalyeh. To catch a fish is natural. Some people catch a fish in the river, other people catch the fish on the table. Still, it is accepted as long as you catch. But schnapps you don't catch. Schnapps is delivered.

ALL.—Brilliant!
—So well expressed.
—A very smart answer, ha, ha, ha.
—Not like you, Tzalyeh, with your stale expressions.
—The Rabbi is right.
—Do you hear, schnapps is delivered, not caught.

TZALYEH. But if I can prove that the schnapps, which is on the table in front of you, was sent for and delivered on my command, plain and simple, then I do have the right to drink the schnapps?

ALL.—Oh, scoundrel.
—You found your way out!
—Oh Tzalyeh, Tzalyeh, you rascal!

MOTELE. Tzalyeh, for goodness sake, drink slowly. Schnapps in Hebrew is "Dvosh." See that you don't get drunk. (*Around the table they cluck in wonderment.*)

ALL.—Oh, such wisdom!
—Words from the Holy Scriptures . . .
—Simply holy words!

TZALYEH. Have no fear, Rabbi. I'm simply too far gone, maybe. Simply near the bottom of the bottle. "Dvosh" spelled backwards means "near the end."

ALL.—Oh-ho, Tzalyeh!

—He has good luck today, the rascal.

MOTELE. In my opinion, "Dvosh" spelled backwards means send for more "dvosh."

ALL.—How true!

—Right!

—Definitely so!

—Great!

—Tzalyeh should also contribute his share for the drink.

—He will contribute his "command" instead of money. (*Motele sighs loudly, looks upward with a holy gesture. Speaks as though in a trance. The others quietly sit in awe.*)

MOTELE. Enough of this fooling, enough of these sayings. Let's have a really learned discussion about "dvosh." (*He sighs again.*) Lies and bad deeds are the essential ingredients of sin. It's the work of the devil. Therefore . . . therefore. . . . Do you understand? . . . You can't go to heaven with a . . . just a loaf of bread in your hand. You have to eat and drink heartily. You must struggle against the influence of evil! You must be firm . . . strong! (*He sighs again and rests his head on his fists, which are now upon the book before him. He is perhaps mumbling a prayer. All around him are sighing, mumbling, and looking reverently upward because Motele has spoken such words of wisdom and has found a reason for them not to abstain from food and drink. Motele looks up suddenly as if just awakened and speaks with great urgency.*) Bring us food, immediately! Don't dawdle! Move, Tzalyeh, move! (*Tzalyeh hurries to the women working in the kitchen. He is heard ordering the women about.*)

TZALYEH. All right now! Plain is simple. Hurry up with the food. When the Rabbi says hurry, you have to dish out the chicken soup and the meat, quickly. Ach, I see I'll have to do it myself. (*Tzalyeh appears with a large bowl of soup, which he places on the table. The others start to ladle out their portions. Tzalyeh then brings out a platter of meat.*) Eat, eat, men. Take. I also will take. Don't be bashful. Noodles and roast. Noodles and roast.

MOTELE. Where do you see roast meat? Why, Tzalyeh, are you fooling us?

TZALYEH. Who's fooling anybody? Plain and simple. I said there *is* a roast. I did not say there is a roast *here*. Our neighbor, Reb Pinchus, he has a roast. (*Tzalyeh has filled his plate, but eats from the center platter.*)

ALL.—Why do you eat from the center plate?

—You have already taken your portion, Tzalyeh.

—What are you doing?

TZALYEH. Plain is simple. What I have on my plate, I'll always have—it's mine. But what's on the center plate, that will disappear before I look around.

ALL.—He always has an answer.

—And he's always right.

—He never loses an argument. (*Soon the eating and drinking is over. They quickly say their prayers as they rise and leave the table. Reb Motele exits into a side chamber. Tzalyeh stands guard at the door where he admits supplicants one at a time.*)

TZALYEH. I don't have to say anything. Who argues? Plain is simple— I stand here and simply make money. I'll let you in one at a time. (*To Shloime Spyuche, who is the elected head of the Jewish Council. He is vulgar, a boor, with a stupid look and a thin and feminine voice. His tattered coat was once good, but through its rips can be seen a dirty, blue lining, and the frayed, faded belt fails to hold the garment together so that his dirty white undergarments show.*) You go in first, Reb Shloime. After all, you're simply our Elder. Go in, Reb Shloime. (*Reb Shloime enters the Rabbi's private sanctum. The room has one window. Near the window, Reb Motele is seated on a cushioned chair. In front of him are slips of paper (I.O.U.s) and an opn prayer book. He stares at the notes and sighs. Shloime stands silently looking at Motele for a few moments. He coughs and scratches the back of his head. Motele looks up.)*

SHLOIME. Rabbi, water! I need water for my mills.

MOTELE. What do you want? What can I do for you? Ah, Shloime ben Geitel, tell me, but quick.

SHLOIME. Goodness! It's not a joke, Rabbi! I gave Count Nibilitzki six thousand for those mills. It's not a joke! The little mill, grinds a little . . . the *little* mill; but the big mill stands frozen, the *big* mill! Rabbi, if you won't help me, I'll become a pauper—yes, a pauper I'll become! Before the holidays is the busy season, yes, before the holidays. And because of the frost, the mill is frozen—because of the frost. *(Shloime places some money on the table.)* Please, Rabbi, I beg you, make an end to the frost. *(Motele looks at the money.)*

MOTELE. You're asking me, and I'm asking God. *(Closes his eyes as he makes an invocation.)* Water, water for Reb Shloime. Water. Well, there will have to be water. What good is the frost? Reb Shloime deserves to be prosperous. I will definitely bring to Count Nibilitzki's attention that the mills were frozen for a long time. I won't have it any other way.

SHLOIME. *(Putting down some more money.)* I know if you try, Rabbi, we will have water. Of course, only you can influence that son-of-a-bitch Count. Ah, Rabbi, you've filled my heart with joy. I'll send you a big measure of wheat flour this week, the best wheat flour. Bless me with all your power, Rabbi, bless me. *(Motele blesses Shloime, grunting and groaning for a few moments.)*

MOTELE. "Meh haycheh tayseh." All honest Jews should have pity. "Nu, meh haycheh tayseh!"

SHLOIME. Good day, Rabbi, good day.

MOTELE. A good day, Reb Shloime; go in peace and health. *(As Shloime is near the door, the Rabbi calls him back.)* Reb Shloime! Get the mills in working condition. It is possible that the frost is over and a warm spell is on the way. Do it today. Fix your mills immediately, and go with my blessings. *(Shloime exits in high spirits. He stuffs money in Tzalyeh's hand on his way out. Yisroelik Ukrainer approaches Tzalyeh.)*

YISROELIK. Reb Tzalyeh, please remind the Rabbi about his promise to me.

TZALYEH. Reb Yisroelik, plain is simple. I have to see the Rabbi myself, about my daughter. But since you are such an important man in our town, it is an honor to me to let you go in first. Step right in. *(Yisroelik enters the Rabbi's room. He speaks with arrogance to the Rabbi.)*

YISROELIK. I must move my lumber from my woods so that I can ship it by river to Danzig. If the frost will hold the snow till after Passover, I will be able to take the lumber on sleds to the river. If the snow melts, God forbid, I will be stuck until next year. You must see to it, Rabbi, that it stays cold for at least two more weeks. Then I will be able to deliver thirty thousand rubles worth of lumber. *(Yisroelik lays ten red coins and a piece of paper money on the table and continues.)* Rabbi, you must perform a miracle. *(Motele looks back and forth from Yisroelik to the money. He grunts.)*

MOTELE. It's a pity. Why should good Jews be afflicted with destruction, with damages no less, God forbid? A person can be ruined losing thirty thousand rubles merchandise. To keep such stock a full year is a crime. The Almighty will have pity on us and keep the snow from melting. Because if the snow melts, God forbid, you will have to hire watchmen to guard your lumber from being stolen, and that means expenses on top of losses. I'll have to pray twice as hard. *(He stands contemplating the money.*)

YISROELIK. It's amazing, Rabbi, how a holy saint like you knows so much about business, and how clearly you think in these matters. You're right, it's a real misfortune when the lumber lies rotting in the woods. (*Yisroelik takes out ten more coins and places them alongside the others.*) You know, Rabbi, I depend on you. I'm going into the woods today. Please keep it in mind, Rabbi.

MOTELE. Don't worry, Reb Yisroelik. I have you in mind. Don't worry. Go safely and in good health. You have nothing to worry about any more.

YISROELIK. Then I go with full confidence in you, Rabbi. Please give me your blessing so I can go. I promise to bring you a fine present when I come back from Danzig. All you have to do is to want to, and you can do it, Rabbi. (*Motele places both hands on Yisroelik's head and mutters. He throws back his head and groans.*)

MOTELE. Yisroelik ben Charnak . . . (*Extending his arms over Yisroelik.*) go in peace and good health as soon as you say goodbye to the Rebetzen.

YISROELIK. I know what you mean. If you're telling me to hurry, it must mean I'm going to have a happy and prosperous journey. Keep well, Rabbi. I'll see the Rebetzen, don't worry. (*Motele leads him to the door.*)

MOTELE. Bundle up so that you don't freeze on the way. There's bound to be freezing weather. Go in peace, Reb Yisroelik. (*As Yisroelik passes Tzalyeh, he slips some money to him. On his way toward the kitchen, Yisroelik meets Rochel. Rochel, Tzalyeh's daughter, is a vivacious young woman. Meanwhile Tzalyeh keeps vigil at the Rabbi's door, where he admits more people.*)

ROCHEL. Tell me, Yisroelik, who fooled whom? You fooled the Rabbi or the Rabbi fooled you? If you're going to see the Rebetzen, she's not here. The women told her about a wonderful fortune teller who just came to our town. The Rebetzen went to have her cards read. (*She draws Yisroelik out of earshot of the others.*) Why did you give my father, that fanatical Chassid, money? A curse I would give him, not money. Not even a groshen. He dragged me here and has kept me here for five days now. Now he wants to drag me to Sharifka to spend Passover with my aunt. Won't that be lovely? I might as well go. The whole world is one town. There must be nice fellows there, too. It wasn't so bad last night, was it?

YISROELIK. You crazy or something, you blabbermouth! Stop babbling and tell me what you are doing here. This morning I was in a hurry and forgot to ask you why you come here each day. (*She shrugs.*)

ROCHEL. You think I know? My father should only know so much. He's already found a match for me here. The Council elder's son. Do you know him? People say he's the town fool. It'll be all right. They say it's even better if the husband is a fool. I can depend on the Rabbi to make sure I get married. My father wants the Rabbi to talk to me first. The Rabbi will absolve my sin. (*She laughs.*) When we talk, the Rabbi and I, should I tell him everything? The same way you told him about last night. What is he, a priest? First they married me to a thirteen-year-old boy. We were children. Now they want me to marry the town fool. What am I made of? Clay? (*She turns coquettishly to him.*) What do you think, am I an ugly woman? They'll make me fast. Who wants to fast? If it were up to them I'd have to abstain not only from food. But I know how to handle the Rabbi and my father. (*Yisroelik is impatient to leave.*)

YISROELIK. I'll be passing through Shavrikah, too, during Passover. I hear there are some very pretty girls in Shavrikah . . .

ROCHEL. That's the way you talk! The devil take you.

YISROELIK. There's one special one there. But she's stubborn—"no" really means "no" with her. Maybe you'll teach her not to be so stubborn . . .

ROCHEL. If you weren't in such a hurry, I'd tell you what I'm going to tell the Rabbi. My father thinks that just because the Rabbi says Rochel is pure, he will be able to swear by the Bible that it's so. (*She teases him.*) Nu, Reb Yisroelik, what do you think? Should I tell them about you? (*She laughs.*) Don't worry . . . (*The Rebetzen enters.*) Rebetzen, this man wants to see you. (*Yisroelik goes to Rebetzen, gives her money, they exchange goodbyes, he exits. Rebetzen exits toward kitchen. Motele has a few men around him.*)

MOTELE. Why must a person suffer so. It must be a day only for poor people today . . . I never heard of such a thing. Only poor people! What do they want from me? I'm just an ordinary Jew! They won't let me pray, they won't let me serve the Almighty, they don't even let me pray for the welfare of all the people. Each one wants me to keep just him in mind. Leave, good people, please leave. I have no time for you today. (*All the men leave. While Tzalyeh is ushering them out, Rochel slips into the Rabbi's room without Tzalyeh seeing her. Motele has returned to reading his prayers and is oblivious. Rochel goes to him and starts to cry.*)

ROCHEL. Rabbi, please, Rabbi. What does my father, Reb Tzalyeh, want from me? Do I go anywhere? Do I visit anyone? I don't step a foot out of the house! If he sees me dressing up, just to look presentable, he calls me a wanton butterfly. Right away by him I'm no good. Only you can change him. If you don't, oh Rabbi, they'll have to bury me in an early grave. I can't eat or drink; I don't know day or night. Rabbi, you're a holy man, a good Jew, and you're smarter than any of them. Have pity on me. Why is he driving me to my grave? (*The Rabbi shouts.*)

MOTELE. Tzalyeh! Tzalyeh! Where in this black year are you! Where is that devil! Tzalyeh! (*Rochel hides her mocking laugh. Tzalyeh comes running in.*)

TZALYEH. Here I am. Plain and simple, when the Rabbi calls, I drop everything else. (*He sees Rochel.*) So, you came here by yourself, or did the Rabbi send for you?

MOTELE. Tzalyeh, you devil! What do you want from your daughter? . . . uh . . . (*Looks through his notes.*) . . . uh . . . Rochel bas Esther? (*Rabbi studies the note, then looks at her. Rochel presents a sad, injured look.*) Devil! She's pure. She's a good woman. Don't fight with her, Devil! You hear me! A chaste daughter should be treasured. I tell you she is a pure and honest woman. You mustn't accuse her of anything any more. I won't allow it! (*Tzalyeh, joyfully relieved, raises both hands.*)

TZALYEH. Praised be the Lord. Rabbi, if you tell me she's pure, then plain is simple. Who am I to doubt your word? I won't ever again insult her, God forbid! But Rabbi, how about a marriage? She's a divorcée. Plain is simple, you'll have to see it. Reb Shloime Spyuche, the head of the Council, was here to see you. He has a son—let it be a match, Rabbi. What do you say?

MOTELE. Tzalyeh, Reb Shloime is a rich man. Such a marriage would be a blessing. I'll make him plenty of trouble if he doesn't agree. Ah, such a pious, good man's daughter, such a good woman. So why are you standing there, good woman? Go. Your father won't holler at you any more. You hear, Tzalyeh? No more!

TZALYEH. She wants your blessing, Rabbi. (*To Rochel.*) It's all right. Bend down your head. (*She bends her head to the Rabbi.*)

ROCHEL. Bless me, Rabbi. Some day, if I have money, I will pay you for this. (*Motele blesses her.*)

MOTELE. "Machtayseh, Machtayseh." (*Motele turns to Tzalyeh.*) Tzalyeh, everything will be all right. It's a match. I say so. Yes, I say so and it will be so. (*A commotion outside. Tzalyeh runs to the door. He sees Reb Shloime and a crowd entering. They are all highly agitated.*)

TZALYEH. Rabbi, here he comes. It's Reb Shloime again. All the Elders are with him. All the Nibivayleh Elders, Councilmen, respectable Jews, and God knows who . . . they're here. (*The newcomers crowd into the large room. There are more people outside. Turmoil and shouts from the crowd.*)

CROWD.—The Rabbi should prevent . . .
—Such a decree!
—What a punishment for all Jews!

TZALYEH. Quiet! Quiet, everybody! Here comes the Rabbi. (*Rabbi Motele enters and takes his place at the head of the table.*)

SHLOIME. Rabbi, we need you. For the good of all of us, please guide us. All of us Jews have our lives at stake. You have to save us. You are such a godly man, a saint. Save us! (*Motele has been perusing the Good Book. He looks up.*)

MOTELE. Do I know what the world expects of me? I have no power— but they all come to me. I don't know what they want from me. I'm not a godly man. I'm just a plain man. What do they see in me? Why does the whole world throw its burdens on me? Nu, tell me, what do they want? What is it this time?

SHLOIME. It's this bad decree, Rabbi. It's terrible. The Czar's advisors made him write a ukase announcing that they should take Jewish recruits; Jews they should take! God forbid, they should tear Jewish children away from learning the Torah and earning a living. We just heard that in St. Petersburg they got the ukase ready. Do something, Rabbi. At least *you* have some connection with God, some connection.

MOTELE. Ay, Ay, Ay! It's because of our sins! It's a curse from the Al-

mighty, blessed be He! We have to repent! Such great sins! We are sinners. Ay, ay, ay! (*Motele suddenly becomes silent. He falls forward onto his hands as if he were asleep. Shouts from the crowd.*)

CROWD.—Ay, ay, ay . . .
—Woe to the mothers.
—Rabbi, save us. (*Shouts turn to murmurs, then brief silence.*)
—Shh! Be quiet.
—He is meditating.
—He is talking with God.
—He is "There."
—Shh! Quiet!
—He's in Heaven. (*Rochel works her way to the outside door. On the street are Nachman and his cronies carrying on in laughter and sport. Their noise intrudes upon the indoor seriousness. Tzalyeh rushes to the door and shouts at the noisemakers.*)

TZALYEH. Quiet! You lazy loafers. You good-for-nothing bums. The Rabbi is very busy with the most important mission. Simply very busy. You are disturbing his prayers to the Almighty to save the Jews, plain is simple!

NACHMAN. They say he is in heaven. From such a distance he can't hear us. Let us know when he comes back. Then we'll stop the noise.

TZALYEH. Shut up, you tailor! You buttonhole maker, you! Just wait, you'll be sorry later. Everybody knows what a pious Jew the Rabbi is. He's a saint. Ask anyone. Plain is simple. I'll tell him about you! He'll make dirt out of you, you loafer! (*Tzalyeh returns to the side of the Rabbi. Rochel approaches Nachman.*)

ROCHEL. So, you're the Nachman I heard so much about. Ah, but you're not bad looking at all, Nachman.

NACHMAN. You look pretty good yourself. A pretty tasty morsel, I'd say. Maybe you're the Chassid's daughter, the divorcée, heh? I've heard about you.

ROCHEL. What did you hear?

NACHMAN. You know how people talk, especially about divorcées. Don't be ashamed because of a town full of fools. Nachman's not a fanatical Chassid.

ROCHEL. What is a poor woman to do? At least you don't believe everything you hear. You're a good lad, Nachman. I hear you're a good tailor, too. I have to have a shawl made. Can you sew very fine?

NACHMAN. No one can sew as well as Nachman. Nachman is definitely the finest lad.

ROCHEL. Good, Nachman. I'll send for you to come and take my measurements. You'll make sure it's a good fit.

NACHMAN. You may be sure it'll fit. My measure is filled with pleasure. (*Sudden turmoil among the crowd.*)

CROWD.—The Rabbi! The Rabbi!

—Quiet, everybody . . . (*The Rabbi has aroused himself. Actually, he looks sleepy. The people crowd around him. He moves toward the door in order to address both those indoors and outside.*)

MOTELE. Good people. Fellow Jews. He had to listen. Everything is in the hands of God now. Have no more fear. I don't accept the ukase. It is canceled. *I* don't accept the decree! (*Tumultous rejoicing.*)

CROWD.—We're saved!

—Oh happy day!

—The ukase is canceled!

—Long live the Rabbi!

—Jewish children for recruits? They should live so long!

—We still have someone to defend us!

—God is good! (*The crowd disperses.*)

VELVEL. For example, as the saying goes, Where there is Torah, there is wisdom. The Rabbi didn't want the ukase, so we don't have it. Let us count our blessings. For example, as the saying goes, we can't be pigs. (*Nachman approaches Velvel.*)

NACHMAN. For example, as the say-

ing goes, the Rabbi is baking lice and these ignoramuses are eating it.

VELVEL. What are you saying? For example, do you know? You're no good. Who are you to shoot your mouth off? Do you know who I am, for example?

NACHMAN. You're Velvel, for example. (*Nachman slaps the growth on Velvel's back and taunts.*) Velvel Gelivateh, for example, how would you say? (*Nachman turns to his friends.*) Let's go, fellows! (*They run off as the curtain falls.*)

SCENE 3

A few months later. Noon.

At Lifshe the Spinster's tavern. Wood-paneled walls, grimy with age, rough, worn, wooden floors, wood-beamed ceiling. Benches set into walls. A long, broken, oak table. Small, round windows. All is shabby and slovenly. Candle lanterns suspended from ceiling, supplemented by candle lights in walls. Wall alongside porch has a breakfront with broken, hanging doors, and pots and tankards on inside shelves. Strewn about on the shelves are articles of clothes, boots, prayer books, and so on, left as pledges by Lifshe's penniless customers. Near the door leading to the kitchen is an unmade bed with pillows and a featherbed. Over it are nails used as hooks, upon which hangs a fur-trimmed gown. On a nearby shelf are medicinal herbs; under the shelf is a broad, strong, padlocked chest on which are strewn pelts and odds and ends of male attire. On an opposite shelf are tall glasses, short glasses, shot glasses, and a bunch of keys. On a bar stand bottles of whiskey and jugs of wine. On the wall behind the bar are chalk marks, which are Lifshe's accounts of those who owe her money. From time to time, when her customers ask for drinks and do not pay, Lifshe will chalk up the tab.

The front door is insecurely propped with a stick. It is warped and whimsical in staying open or closed.

Lifshe, the mistress of the inn, is a middle-aged spinster, who wears an old-fashioned hair-piece covered with a yellow bonnet and a kerchief over it. She is pock-marked and has a wart on her cheek, on which sprouts grey hair. She has large teeth, and wears a short skirt tied on with a towel, a scarf around her shoulders, a dress with two large pockets, home-made socks, and crude peasant shoes. A fat, peasant maid, barefoot, ugly, and uncombed, helps Lifshe with the wooden plates that she passes to the customers at appropriate times. In front of bar are a few three-legged stools.

From time to time a few Jews will enter, order and drink some whiskey, eat some bread, and exit.

Seated at one table is a group of Nachman's friends. At another table are Gavriel and a Russian peasant, Agafon Aganovich. At other tables and standing about are Russian peasants. Nachman's friends (apprentices) are drinking, eating, jesting.

APPRENTICES.—Lifshe, more, bring more.
  —More bread.
  —Hurry up, Lifshe!
  —Hey, fellows, Nachman is not here yet.
  —Nachman has his mind on other things.
  —Is it really true?
  —I should say so. I saw them myself, yesterday, near the mill.
  —Well? Is she nice?
  —How do I know? What can you see in the dark?
AGAFON. You're lying, Lifshe! I gave it to you yesterday, you bitch! You're lying. Hand over another quart, you bitch!
LIFSHE. Boys . . . what does this old drunk want from me? He's just pouring the stuff into himself. He's not drinking it . . . just pouring. I'm losing money.
GAVRIEL. So don't give him any. Crazy world. Some people are lucky. She doesn't trust me to drink on credit, but she trusts him!
AGAFON. Lifshe, I told you to give it to me, you bitch. When I tell you something, you listen! Make it a half a quart, then.
LIFSHE. What are you saying, Reb Gavriel? Who wants to start up with him. God forbid, he can make trouble, he can do something . . . anything. (*She agrees with Agafon.*) Agafon Agafonovitch, yes . . . another half quart.
APPRENTICES.—I know her. What a jewel of a girl, a gem. So sweet . . .
  —I think you like her, too.
  —If she looked at you, your mouth would drool, too.
  —So that's why he's always so worked up. It takes a woman . . .
  —Oh boy, is he worked up! It's the end of him.
  —How does he sing it . . .

She's so lovely, she's so sweet.
I'd spend my life at her feet.
She is pretty, she's very nice,
I'd give her my life more than twice.

GAVRIEL. Lifshe, a Jew is begging you for a drop of whiskey. Don't you have God in your heart? Don't you have my pledge? You have my coat.
LIFSHE. Do you know what you're talking about, Reb Gavriel? The coat's value you've drunk twice over. (*She hands him a shot of whiskey.*) Remember! This is the last one . . . No more! (*Nachman enters. He is greeted enthusiastically by the apprentices.*)

APPRENTICES.—You rascal . . .
    —Look who's here.
    —We thought you'd never come.
    —What kept you—as if we don't know!

NACHMAN. Greetings, you bunglers, you drunkards. I can see how you are pining away for me. I can see how you're getting saturated with grief over my absence.

APPRENTICE. What do you expect? We should be fried out, parched, while waiting for you?

TUTOR. In the good Scriptures it says, "Vyashtu"—it means, "They have drunken."

NACHMAN. Look at him. A learned scholar, no less. Watch out you don't "drunken" too much like a sponge or I'll have to squeeze you out.

APPRENTICES.—Let him be, Nachman. His throat was burning.
    —He had to put the fire out.
    —How long did you expect us to wait for you?
    —Ah, Nachman my boy, you really flipped over that girl.
    —They say you're tailoring an apron for her, Nachman.

NACHMAN. You botchers—you bunglers! You're busting out of your skins. You're just jealous.

AN APPRENTICE. When are you getting married, Nachman? (*Chanting like a bodchen.*)

And the Rabbi will pray,
And the bodchen will say:
One thing follows another,
Soon the bride will be a mother.

APPRENTICES—And no more Nachman?
    —No—how sad.
    —No more Nachman.

AN APPRENTICE. (*Chanting like a bodchen.*)

L is a lion,
M is a maiden,

A lion will roar
A maiden will giggle,
And Nachman a cradle will wiggle.

(*Apprentices sing refrain.*)

APPRENTICES.
From the bower to the chamber,
Nachman goes on to the slaughter.
His bride will lead the way,
Poor Nachman thinks it's play—
Poor Nachman's gone away.

NACHMAN. Quiet, you rogues! Don't bury me yet! Nachman's still alive. And, there's plenty work to be done.

APPRENTICES.—Oh boy, work!
    —That's good news.
    —Out with it. Be quick.
    —Tell us.

NACHMAN. (*To butcher apprentice.*) Hey, Butcher boy. Tell them. Don't just sit there. What do you want, an invitation? Tell them about the hides.

BUTCHER BOY. Well, it's about the money from the hides. Ninety kopeks, that's for the hide from a cow. Thirty kopeks from a calf. That's what I had to pay Reb Pinchus.

NACHMAN. Reb Pinchus! That red-headed crook! (*Butcher boy silently hushes Nachman and others as he points toward Gavriel and Agafon.*)

GAVRIEL. Lifshe, since when don't you believe an honest Jew?

BUTCHER BOY. They say that Count Nibilitzki gave his consent.

NACHMAN. Nibilitzki—Pshyakrev! (*An old peasant approaches Nachman.*)

OLD PEASANT. Nachman, if you have God in your heart, be careful. Keep quiet. (*Old peasant points to Agafon.*)

AGAFON. You're a liar, you old bitch. Lifshe, hand over the whiskey.

NACHMAN. Can I believe my eyes! What's going on? A Chassidic Jew and a pious Christian are drinking together—and doing well by themselves?

APPRENTICES.—Watch out. They both have long tongues.
    —If you were smart, you'd make yourself scarce.

—Disappear.

NACHMAN. Where to?

APPRENTICES.—Wherever you find a hole to hide in.

—The Chassid will go hurry to the Council . . .

—And the Christian will go to the Count.

NACHMAN. You meen they're spies? They carry tales?

APPRENTICES.—Where have you been?

—Even before they hear it.

—Watch your words, Nachman.

NACHMAN. So why are we just sitting here? A burial!

APPRENTICES.—A burial?

—He's right—a burial.

—But where will we bury them?

NACHMAN. In the middle of the road, anyplace. Or any corner. As long as they're well out of here.

APPRENTICES.—You're right.

—We're with you, Nachman.

—How will you do it, Nachman?

NACHMAN. Just wait and see. (*Nachman rises and talks to Lifshe.*) Lifshe. Come on, get a move on.

LIFSHE. Here I am, Nachman. What do you want?

NACHMAN. Do you have a strong blanket? But a strong one.

LIFSHE. Of course. For you, Nachman, I always have everything.

NACHMAN. So hand it over. (*Lifshe fetches the blanket. The group of apprentices take the blanket, stealthily approach Gavriel and Agafon. They entice the two and bundle them into the blanket. The group of apprentices dance around with the two being bounced in the blanket as the group uproariously chant Hebrew and Russian prayers over the two drunks. Then they carry them out of the tavern.*)

APPRENTICES. "Stzduke, Tatzil, Mimoves, Tzedek, Liforev, Yahalech, Gospodyyipomiliyu."

GAVRIEL. Ah, Lifshe. An honest Jew you won't believe . . . ah, Lifshe . . .

AGAFON. You're lying, you bitch . . .

BUTCHER BOY. (*To Nachman.*) So what will you do? Tie them up or lock the door to keep them out?

NACHMAN. We don't have to tie them, and there's no need to lock the door.

LIFSHE. Let's have a pitcher of your cheap wine. (*Lifshe produces the pitcher.*) Put it in the middle of the road. Better take two glasses with it. Better be quick . . . (*Lifshe exits with wine and glasses. Apprentices and peasants crowd around door and windows as they look out. Lifshe returns.*) So, Lifshe. What's going on out there?

LIFSHE. They grabbed for it as if they had been a year on the desert.

APPRENTICES.—Look at them grab.

—What a sight.

—One is afraid the other will cheat him.

NACHMAN. Lifshe, when they finish this bottle, give them another. I'll pay.

LIFSHE. Depend on me, Nachman.

TUTOR. You were right, Nachman. They're glued to the spot better than if we had tied them.

NACHMAN. Good. Now, butcher boy, you can talk. (*Nachman's friends gather back at the table.*) But speak to the point. You sputter in spurts like a hatchet on a wooden block. (*Butcher boy has a speech mannerism whereby he starts almost each phrase with "Nu," much to the annoyance of his listeners.*)

BUTCHER BOY. Nu—he imposed a tax. Nu—Reb Pinchus—Nu, that is, Count Nibilitzky gave orders.

NACHMAN. So? And the butchers?

BUTCHER BOY. Nu . . . and the butchers agreed—three groshen on each pound.

APPRENTICES.—Nachman, what's all this about?

—He's babbling. I'm still in the dark.

—It sounds like Greek to me.

—What interest do we

have in the butcher business?

NACHMAN. Do you like meat, you bunglers?

APPRENTICES.—Yes.
—Of course.
—Do I like meat!

NACHMAN. Do you eat meat?

TUTOR. We eat bones, not meat.

NACHMAN. How often do you eat meat?

APPRENTICES.—"Often!" Who eats often?
—Count Nibilitzky, Reb Aaron, Reb Pinchus— they eat often.
—Often—what a joke!

NACHMAN. So, now you won't even be able to afford bones. Pinchus has put a tax on each head of cattle, and so the butchers raised the price of meat.

APPRENTICES.—Damn their hides.
—The bloodsuckers!!
—The devil take their father's father.

NACHMAN. Are we going to let them do it? Are we just going to sit around and curse?

APPRENTICES.—No!
—But what can we do?
—What's the use?

NACHMAN. When the Sabbath is over, tonight, we'll go to the Council.

APPRENTICES.—And then what?
—They're the crooks themselves.

NACHMAN. And then we go to Reb Pinchus.

APPRENTICES.—Save your breath.
—What good can that do?
—And then what?

NACHMAN. And then we'll rip down their signs.

BUTCHER BOY. And we break some bones.

NACHMAN. Good, butcher boy. And we fix up some meat until the tax is repealed. Are you all agreed?

TUTOR. Watch out, Nachman. Count Nibilitzky will call in the soldiers. And the soldiers will butcher us, the way they did last time.

NACHMAN. You're such a wise one!

You've already swallowed your soul in your fright. (*The others taunt the tutor.*)

APPRENTICES.—Why don't you join the ladies' auxiliary in the synagogue?
—They need help on ladies' day in the bathhouse.
—Go grind some horse radish for the Rabbi's wife!

NACHMAN. Listen to me, you botchers. Do we need this smart alec?

APPRENTICES.—What for?
—Throw him out.
—Send him back to the nursery . . .
—Yes, to teach babies.
—Let him join Gavriel Shed.

TUTOR. Remember, you bunglers, when you need someone to write a letter for you, to whom will you go? To Reb Aaron Kluger, maybe?

NACHMAN. Quiet! Let him alone. Let him sit here. He's all right enough. He's just protecting his hide. Are we going?

APPRENTICES. Yes, we're going!

NACHMAN. Fine. Meanwhile, let's have a taste of something. Lifshe, start pouring.

APPRENTICES.—Step on it, Lifshe!
—One more pitcher, Lifshe. (*They drink and sing.*)

NACHMAN.
Listen to me, ladies, and take my advice.
Marry a man who has a trade,
A tailor husband is very nice,
He'll sing a happy tune all day.
He'll give you full share of milk and honey.
No matter what garments he makes
He'll always make some money.

SHOEMAKER APPRENTICE.
A tailor's wife once told me
Sad is my life, as good as dead;
I sit all day and mend and stitch,
Better marry a cobbler instead.

APPRENTICES IN CHORUS.
Oh we have heard and we have seen
A tailor is a charlatan.
Better not to marry him
Let the devil carry him.

BUTCHER BOY.
   A cobbler's wife once told me
   Sad is my life, as good as dead,
   Leather boots I never see,
   Better wed a butcher instead.

APPRENTICES IN CHORUS.
Oh we have heard and we have seen
A cobbler is a charlatan.
Better not to marry him,
Let the devil carry him.

TUTOR.
I am a tutor, a teacher.
Each term I teach a new village,
But I don't get any richer,
No one is willing to pay,
Yet I teach Hebrew and Yiddish
To read, to write, and to pray.

Children won't learn their aleph beth
They prefer their songs and their plays.
When school is over, I'm free as the
   air.
But I've no money, my pockets are
   bare.
All I can do is go home to my wife
The life of a tutor's a terrible life.
So I order a bottle or two,
Now I'm happy, full of cheer
I sing this song just for you,
So L'chaim and have a good year.

(*Noise outside. Some rush to windows
to look out.*)
ALL.—It's his lordship.
   —Not Count Nibilitzki?
   —No, it's his Econom, his Man-
      ager.
   —He's got soldiers with him.
   —They're coming here. (*One of
      the peasants, Vassily, who had
      been sitting in a corner, runs to
      Nachman.*)
VASSILY. Nachman, hide me.
NACHMAN. It's you, Vassily! What are
   you doing here?
VASSILY. Not so loud, quiet. I'll tell you
   later. Hide me—hurry!

NACHMAN. Lifshe. (*Lifshe leads Vassily and Nachman to another room.
   Nachman returns alone. All are
   frightened—quiet. Count Nibilitzki's
   estate manager, called the "Econom,"
   enters with two of his men. The
   serfs bend low to them.*)
MANAGER. Lifshe, bring us something to
   eat and drink. But make it fast. If
   you want Polish gentry for your clien-
   tele, you've got to be quick like quick-
   silver. (*She serves them with the aid
   of her maid. Everyone else is scared
   as he watches and cringes.*)
LIFSHE. Yes, my lord. In a moment,
   my lord.
MANAGER. Serfs, out of my sight. Into
   the corner with you. (*They run.*)
   Jews, to the corner. (*The Jews
   crowd into another corner. All scurry
   away. One peasant, in his confusion,
   drops a stool on the manager's foot.*)
   Ouch—Oaww—you dog's blood,
   pshyakrev! (*Manager beats peasant
   with his crop. Peasant is hysterically
   frightened.*)
PEASANT. Forgive me, my lord . . .
MANAGER. I'll talk to you on the estate.
   After you get twenty-five lashes, I
   may forgive you. You should thank
   the Holy Mother it is only twenty-
   five lashes. (*Turns to his men.*) Give
   him to the men waiting outside. Have
   them take him to the quarters.
PEASANT. My lord, it was an accident.
   Forgive me.
MANAGER. Very well. If I forgive you,
   you will work on Aaron Kluger's
   fields. I promised him I'd send some
   men tomorrow.
PEASANT. My lord, have pity. Tomorrow
   is my day for my plot.
MANAGER. I know. Do you think I'd
   send you to the Jews if you were
   supposed to work for me?
PEASANT. It's my day to work on my
   own field. What will my family eat?
   My crop will rot in the field. Have
   pity, my lord. I didn't mean any
   harm. I'm innocent, my lord.
MANAGER. So-o-o-o, you're innocent!
   And you want Aaron Kluger to call

me a liar? You want a Jew to call me a liar, to call the Count a liar? We have a contract with the Jew to harvest his crop . . . and you dare to say you are innocent! Go complain to Count Nibilitzki; tell him that you are innocent. He will forgive you— ho, ho, ho, ha, ha, ha. It's now his dinner time. Just go to him, he will forgive you! Ha, ha. (*Manager laughs uproariously. Peasant falls to his knees.*)

PEASANT. Bless you, my lord—forgive me. I am to blame. Hit me, beat me, give me twenty-five lashes. I will go to Aaron Kluger's fields. Only have mercy—don't send me to Count Nibilitzki. I kiss your feet, have mercy . . . (*Manager rises, kicks peasant.*)

MANAGER. Miserable animal! Pshyakrev —dog's blood! Take him to the Count. (*The manager's men drag out the hysterical peasant. The manager follows them after he flings a coin to Lifshe.*)

NACHMAN. What does this mean? Why is the muszhik so frightened?

TUTOR. Don't you know? Dinner time is the most dangerous time to be brought before the Count. He has a poor appetite because of some sickness. So he stimulates himself with entertainment.

NACHMAN. This doesn't sound like entertainment.

TUTOR. That's what you think. He has a poor peasant whipped—this whips up his appetite. While the Count eats, they forget to keep count of the lashes, so sometimes a serf is simply whipped to death. And if he doesn't die, believe me, he'd be better off if he did. (*Nachman notices the serfs still cringing in the corner.*)

NACHMAN. Pshyakrev! Straighten yourselves out, uncles.

A PEASANT. (*Crying.*) Have no fear for us, Nachman. Our backs are like rubber now. (*Vassily cautiously returns from his hiding place.*)

VASSILY. Don't look so surprised at seeing me, Nachman. I escaped from

my regiment. Thanks for hiding me, Nachman. (*Vassily turns to weeping old peasant.*) You cry here, old one, and we cry there in the army. Does it make any difference where they whip you to death? But maybe it's better at home than away from home, in the army.

OLD PEASANT. Backs like rubber? Backs more like dogs. Oh, Holy Mother, we have backs like dogs . . .

NACHMAN. And wooden heads, and hands of clay.

VASSILY. What good does it do to scream at us, to insult us, Nachman?

NACHMAN. Because you take it like dumb animals, because you don't speak up, because you keep quiet!

PEASANTS.—What should we do?
　　　　　—What can we do?
　　　　　—Tell us, Nachman . . .

NACHMAN. Even red roosters cry on the roofs of the aristocrats. Not everywhere do people keep quiet. Pshyakrev!

VASSILY. How can you talk like that, Nachman? For such words, for one whisper, even if they suspect you think it, they whip you and drag you into the army. Do you have any idea what it means to be a soldier? You can talk—you're lucky; they don't take Jews to be recruits. Just look— look—(*Vassily pulls up his shirt and exposes his frightfully lacerated back. All present recoil in horror.*)

ALL. Ah-h-h-h-h!

VASSILY. This is what it means to be a soldier. Some of the luckier ones die under the lash. Maybe it's better to starve to death here, or be whipped to death by Count Nibilitzki's muszhiks—that's to be lucky, to be buried by your own family in your own home, your own village. Do you know what it means to be a musketeer? For twenty-five years they scourge your back, they beat you about the head, they torture you with hunger, with cold. Not you, oh no! You're God's chosen children. God, what they do to a soldier, an army recruit for twenty-five years! I ran away. Sooner or later they will capture me. They'll skin me alive, they'll tear me to pieces. You don't know, you can't imagine what it means to be a soldier, what a man becomes in the army . . . (*Outer door opens. Two crippled soldiers enter. One has a stump for an arm. The other soldier is minus a leg, and with a hollow, scarred cheek. Vassily runs in fear to hide, but is frozen at the threshold.*)

FIRST SOLDIER. Where's the Jewish Council?

SECOND SOLDIER. Yeah, the Council.

NACHMAN. What business do you have with the Council?

FIRST SOLDIER. We have an official order, a document from the authorities to the Jewish Council.

SECOND SOLDIER. Yeah. To the Council. (*Nachman motions to the tutor.*)

NACHMAN. Come over here, Tutor. Can you stand up, or do I have to help you? God help you if I must. (*Tutor approaches Nachman, who turns to first invalid soldier.*) Show us the document, buddy.

FIRST SOLDIER. We aren't permitted to show it to anyone except the Jewish Council.

SECOND SOLDIER. Yeah, the Council . . . (*Nachman mimics the second soldier.*)

NACHMAN. "Yeah, the Council, the Council." (*Nachman salutes the soldiers in mock heroic style, then hands them whiskey.*) Here, drink hearty, your highnesses.

BOTH SOLDIERS. Ah-h-h-h-h. (*Soldiers avidly imbibe. Second soldier covers his hollow cheek as he imbibes.*)

NACHMAN. Here. Have another drink. Sit down, rest yourselves. Hey, Lifshe, get these good men something to eat. (*Soldiers prepare to make themselves at home. First soldier starts to take off his coat, finds himself encumbered by his portfolio. He hands it to Nachman.*)

FIRST SOLDIER. Here, hold this, but take good care of it. It contains the orders for the Jewish Council.

SECOND SOLDIER. Yeah, the Council. (*Nachman stealthily extracts a document from the portfolio and slips it to the tutor.*)

NACHMAN. Here, read it. (*While Lifshe and Nachman keep the soldiers occupied with food and drink, the tutor reads the document. Tutor becomes agitated as he reads to himself. Nachman becomes impatient.*) Speak up. What does it say? (*Tutor splutters with fright.*)

TUTOR. "Recruits!" The Jews must provide recruits! The Jews of the village of Nibivayleh must send recruits! (*Tutor flings the document at Nachman and starts running to the door. He trips and falls amid the general pandemonium that follows his announcement.*)

APPRENTICES.—Save yourselves!
    —Recruits!
    —Let's get out of here!
    —Run for your lives! (*All peasants and Jews pile out of the tavern in a wild scramble. A loud turmoil starts out-of-doors. Only Vassily and the two invalid soldiers remain. Vassily looks at the soldiers.*)

VASSILY. Holy Mother, just look at what they do to a man in the army . . .

CURTAIN

ACT II

SCENE 1

In the home of Reb Shloime Spyuche, near the synagogue. It's a new house, straw roof, a real foundation (elevation), unfinished white paint job on the exterior. An open window provides a view of the village. The village Jews are assembled in clusters outside. They mill about, while inside, the house is filled with people. All are gloomy, frightened, expressing moans and groans. At the head of a long table that is covered with a shabby, dirty tablecloth strewn with crumbs, garlic, and cucumber peels, sits Reb Shloime. Next to him is Reb Velvel and Yisroelik. During the commotion Reb Pinchus the Redhead enters and joins the Council Members at the table. The crowd is hurling questions and advice to those at the table. Pushing his way through the commotion, Gavriel Shed comes to the table.

GAVRIEL. Crazy world, even though I am not an official, I called Pinchus the Redhead to this meeting. (*He suddenly spies Pinchus.*) I beg your pardon, friends, I didn't notice that Reb Pinchus is already here. Now folks, you can talk about the "document" that came yesterday. Now that the Council is here, first of all, the Council will tell us what to do. But first, it's crazy, we must send for a drink. Even at a wake, we don't sit without a drink. (*He turns to members of the Council.*) It's crazy, why are you silent? (*Pinchus seats himself with dignity.*)

PINCHUS. The point is, what does the town want? That such a misfortune happened to us Jews . . . the town must decide what to do. This is no joke.

SHLOIME. The Council's opinion is that we don't sign the document. The Council is Council and the town is town. We have no learned sage from whom to ask advice. The man isn't born yet who can accept this misfortune. Why should the Council sign? (*A turmoil arises outdoors, shouting and arguments.*)

CROWD OUTDOORS.—Whoever thought up this misfortune should be torn to pieces.
—The head of the Council should sign.
—Reb Shloime is right.
—Bruche, why don't you say something!
—We are cursed.
—Why are you letting the town be buried? They'll destroy us.
—Bruche, don't let your husband sign . . .
—No, don't let him sign . . . (*Cries all around of "Don't sign." Pinchus rises.*)

PINCHUS. Even though you sent for me, I might as well go home. The mob is cursing and don't know why. But you, the so-called Council, are you so blind that you can't see that it makes no difference whether you do sign or don't sign?

VELVEL. For example, as the saying goes, come in or go out. For example, if the Council's signature is not needed, then the Council would not be asked to sign. For example, I have great respect for you, Reb Pinchus; as the saying goes, a person is like a piece of chalk: if you write, you write up and down. For example, the whole Council is here. You're well liked, that's why we respect you. For example, as the saying goes, a stick doesn't fall without a reason. Not only the Council, but respectable people are here also. For example, they want to be included in the decision. As the saying goes, for example, the children chew what the old ones spit out. And, because the soldiers came from the capital, and brought the proclamation about the recruits, it is really, as the saying goes, for example, blow your nose and wipe your face. For example, you, Reb Pinchus, hold mortgages on everyone in this town . . . (*Velvel continues to talk as Bruche angrily pushes her way toward her husband, Shloime, and flares out at him.*)

BRUCHE. I didn't hear this. What? I'll

bury you ten feet deep if you sign this calamity on the Jews. Do you hear me, Shloime! Your life won't be worth anything. Jews should weep because of you? I have an only son; you expect me to sacrifice him? Don't sign, do you hear me! Do you expect our neighbors to curse me? I will tear you to pieces if you dare lift the pen . . .

SHLOIME. Don't threaten me! Stop with your curses! Of course I won't sign. Under no conditions will I sign. (*Not hearing him because of her deafness.*)

BRUCHE. I never heard of such a thing! What, you insist on signing! (*Rochel, very pregnant, has entered with her husband, Hirsh-Leib.*)

ROCHEL. What's going on, Mom? Here I am.

BRUCHE. Dummy, don't you hear? A calamity has fallen on all the Jews and you don't show any interest . . . (*Mimics Rochel.*) "What's going on, Mom?" If your husband is taken to be a recruit, what will you do? Your baby will be born an orphan. A daughter-in-law is an enemy in my house!

ROCHEL. I couldn't come out. I shouldn't with so many strangers in the streets.

BRUCHE. Just listen to her. She couldn't come out. She's afraid of strangers. (*Turns to Shloime.*) I'll tear your hair out, beard and all. I'll wring your neck. I'll wring you out so that your name will be torn out of you that you'll never have it to sign ever again . . . I'll . . . (*Shloime, disgusted with her deafness, stands and screams at her.*)

SHLOIME. I will *not* sign! Get out of here. Who needs you here. I'm not signing. (*He pushes her away. Bruche, Rochel, and Hirsh-Leib retire from the fray.*)

CROWD. Bruche is right.—Bruche, don't let him sign.—You can't destroy a town.—You mustn't allow it.—If anyone doesn't like it he can get out of town.—You're right, we won't miss him.—Let's get Pinchus's wife. Tziporah will tell him what's what all right. —She'll stop him from signing. (*Velvel leans out the window and addresses the crowd.*)

VELVEL. Bruche, for example, is right. Sure, we won't sign. No. There are only two soldiers. For example, they can't force the whole town. If you refuse, you refuse. As the saying goes, for example, if you don't like it, go pray in your own way. (*He withdraws his head and addresses those inside.*) The town is in good hands, for example, as the saying goes. Yes, for example, the year is not tied to a stick. (*Pinchus rises and speaks loudly to all.*)

PINCHUS. Please, don't take offense, Reb Shloime, Reb Velvel, and fellow Jews. You don't seem to understand what you are hollering about. For heaven's sake, don't act like misguided fools. You don't understand that this bitter plague is not made or unmade by you or me. It's the Czar, bless him; he believes it to be a privilege for Jewish children to become soldiers in his army. That's why he issued this ukase. Your signatures are not needed at all. What the soldiers are asking you to sign is only a receipt—that you received the proclamation. If you don't sign, the plague is still here. You cannot wish it away, you cannot ignore it. Why should you wish trouble upon yourselves? I will show you how wrong you are. Suppose I simply call the soldiers to come here and I'll tell them to leave without our signature. So, what happens? They'll leave. BUT, THE PROCLAMATION IS STILL A LAW. Instead, I suggest we read the document so we'll know what it says. We don't even know what it says and we're arguing. After we read it, we'll know what to do. At least, we won't be punished with a fine and have to pay a lot of money for not responding to the proclamation in time.

CROWD.—It's easy for you, you have only a daughter.—Yes, you'll be able to marry her off sooner.—We can even marry off the younger girls like in the times of the Reductzia.—But what will happen to our boys?—I won't be able to live—my son to be a recruit!—Who can stand by and see any boy become a recruit?—Why are we cursed? (*Universal lamentation, sobs, wails, and curses.*)—Reb Pinchus, you are a saint; your wife is a gem; you are so charitable. We all love and respect you—why do you say we should sign?—No, no, no! Don't sign!—Don't accept the document!—It's a paper of doom.—Throw it back to them.—Under no curcumstances should you sign.—Give it back.

PINCHUS. I haven't got the heart or strength to talk with you. If you're going to be stubborn and listen to the mob, you're going to bring disaster upon yourselves—if you're looking for trouble—I'm warning you. I'm going. My heart is broken when I see Jews behaving like stubborn, stupid mules who won't listen to reason. I'm trying to explain to you as simply as I can.

SHLOIME. We'll send Gavriel Shed to bring the two soldiers here. Then we'll see for certain if the story is the way Pinchus explains it. What do you say, folks, we could try? Speak up, my friends. Reb Velvel, explain to the people outside that we're sending for the two soldiers to find out which way the wind blows. Tell them so they won't be frightened, Reb Velvel. (*Velvel speaks through window.*)

VELVEL. For example, Reb Shloime and all the others are saying we should send for the soldiers. For example, as the saying goes, before a wedding we must argue, for example.

VOICES FROM OUTSIDE.—As long as they don't sign.—We've sent for Tziporah, too. She won't let her Pinchus sign.—No! Don't sign! No! No!

—That's right, when the soldiers come, give them back the paper.

GAVRIEL. Do you think I've got dog's feet or what? Dammit, an official I'm not. A little something to wet my lips, you don't give me. But, all right, I'll go, my friends, and I'll bring the soldiers here. They are at Lifshe's tavern. Who knows how much whiskey they've drunk and charged to the Council. I'll treat myself to a tall shot of vodka and charge it to the Council too. You can bet it'll be a real tall one, my friends. If the soldiers can drink, I'm entitled to a nice drink too. (*Gavriel exits. Everyone is stunned into silence. Velvel breaks the silence.*)

VELVEL. For example, you, Reb Pinchus, you said earlier that we may bring a disaster upon ourselves. For example, what do you mean by that? As the saying goes, a drop of rain doesn't mean a flood. For example, what kind of disaster could it be, for example? As the saying goes, from a swine's tail you can't make a pretty ribbon. For example, from a tangled knot in the hair you can't get a headache. I'm a timid man; Reb Shloime knows me. If you say, for example, that the outcome could be a disaster, as the saying goes, a stick has two ends, for example. Reb Pinchus, tell us what you mean. (*Pinchus speaks loudly so those outside can hear him also.*)

PINCHUS. Listen, folks. I come from a little village. When my father was alive, you should all have long years, and I was still young, I spent all my time in Berdychev among important people. I learned to read and write Russian as well as Yiddish. I heard plenty from people who had seen other countries as well as Moscow and Petersburg. Alas, we poor country Jews know nothing and understand less. I tell you that you don't understand what's going on. We think this is a misfortune. Important people who know say that the Czar is bestowing a privilege on the Jews so that the Jews may have equal citizenship and a voice in the land. Jews should not be like homeless wanderers or foreigners in the land. We don't know what the outcome will be, but regardless, we must not bring the wrath of the Czar upon us, bless his name. The law of our Torah tells us Dina Demalchoosoh Dina, which in plain language says, That which the Czar, bless him, commands must be obeyed, exactly as we must accept good deeds that are mentioned in the Torah. But, you understand, if anyone doesn't want to do a good deed or commits a sin, God will punish him. And the one who does not obey the Czar, in addition to God's punishment, will absolutely be punished immediately. God forbid, if you with your stubbornness will not supply recruits willingly, you will be forced to give them, and in addition, the Jewish community will be forced to pay a huge fine, and still more in addition, our elders may be sent off to Siberia. I know the shock is bitter; I know that until now we Jews have been spared from the requisition for recruits. I know how unbearable it is to send a Jewish child to be a recruit. But you must face it, the doom is here, now. Of what use is your refusal to obey? My heart is broken. I feel the anguish of the mother who must part from her son, or a father and mother who witness their child being taken from them to be a recruit. (*Inside and outside the crowd starts to wail. When a pause in the noise comes, Pinchus speaks again.*) Remember, the situation can become worse. The ukase says that those Jewish elders who refuse to cooperate will also be taken as recruits. You see the added danger you can bring to the community and the danger to our elders? Your foolishness makes you think that the outcome depends on your signature. This is all I have to say. (*Bruche has had a neighbor*

trumpet into her ear what Pinchus said. When she hears the word DANGER *she pushes her way through the crowd to Shloime.*)

BRUCHE. Do you hear that, Shloime? You will certainly suffer if you don't sign. What, you want me to have a husband a recruit? My enemies should live so long. This second you must ask the soldiers to wait—at least till the end of the Sabbath. Then you can sign. Your life won't be worth anything; I'll tear you to bits, I'll finish you, you crazy dog! What are you thinking—you want to throw yourself into the fire? I'll go myself and ask the soldiers to wait, and then you must sign! Do you hear me, you miserable dog? If only a memory of you remained!

SHLOIME. All right then, I'll sign.

BRUCHE. What, you won't sign? Rochel, where are you? Rochel . . . (*Rochel and Hirsh-Leib push their way into the house.*)

ROCHEL. What is it, mommele? Here I am.

BRUCHE. Dummy, don't you hear? We're lost, ruined, and abandoned. They're sending your father-in-law to Siberia and you stand like a dummy. Don't you care? What will happen to us? How could you have such a gypsy's heart not to be here, not to take an interest?

ROCHEL. Your son wouldn't let me. He said if his mother fights, let her fight. Here he is; let him speak for himself.

BRUCHE. Why are you standing like a dolt? You want they should kill your father and kill to death your mother? Don't you feel anything? You're always so smart, answer me.

HIRSH-LEIB. You know, momma, my wife is prettier than you, and she's pregnant, and you're not. I simply needed her outside. So why are you yelling and hollering at her! She's *my* wife and not yours or poppa's.

CROWD.—Don't sign.—Now you see, I told you so.—The devil take the

Council and their fathers' fathers.—The Council has sold us out.—Absolutely. It's their idea, so let them pay the penalty.—Don't sign.—In your fathers' fathers.—They're traitors. (*Nachman and his group of workers rush in.*)

NACHMAN. Yes, sign! Don't sign! The workers don't agree with you.

WORKERS.—That's right. We don't agree.

—We don't want it.

—It's our lives you're gambling with.

NACHMAN. Do you hear, all of you? Do what you like, but don't do the workers any favors.

WORKERS.—We don't want it.

—We won't have it.

—Here's Reb Lazar.

—Speak up, Reb Lazar. You're a boss, they'll listen to you.

—What do you say, Reb Lazar?

PINCHUS. Show some respect. Don't open your loud mouths at the Council. Let Reb Lazar talk. (*Reb Lazar is torn between his friends on the Council and his dependence upon the workers.*)

LAZAR. Let's listen to Nachman. The workers want him to talk. He's got a golden tongue. Belt it out, Nachman.

NACHMAN. Maybe I should quit now, while I'm ahead.

WORKERS.—Enough fooling around.

—Out with it.

NACHMAN. When the Council needs money, from whom does it take? Taxes—from whom?

CROWD AND

WORKERS.—From us.

—From the poor.

—From the workers.

—We pay.

—When don't we?

—We always pay.

NACHMAN. Do you want a little piece of meat? Give up a share to the Council. You want salt? The Council takes its pinch. Before you bite a piece of bread, the Council tears out its hunk. But when there's a calamity, the worker keeps the whole portion . . . of that the Council wants no share.

ISROELIK. What right has he to talk? Why do you let him talk? (*The workers surge toward him with threats, but Isroelik's cronies protect him.*)

NACHMAN. And who gives the last word? The workers are not allowed to butt into Council's business. What are we supposed to be? Oh yes, I know—nothing—less than nothing. Now we know we're really lost. The town must supply a recruit. So-o-o-o, whom will the Council draft to be the recruit? Maybe Reb Aaron Kluger? Reb Pinchusle? Hirsh-Leib, the village idiot? A son of the rich men? We know only too well whom they'll send—the sons of the poor. On the workers' heads—enough! We will not submit to the Council. Forget about us. We've had it. You're no longer our Council—cross off our names.

WORKERS.—He's right.

—Forget us.

—Take our names off your list.

—We no longer belong to the Council.

VELVEL. Idiots. For example, as the saying goes, what will then happen to the Jewish Council? For example . . .

NACHMAN. (*Mimics Velvel.*) "For example, as the saying goes," a stooge is a stooge. We don't want any of you. We don't need your favors.

SHLOIME. You have no shame. Here we are, elderly Jews, respected citizens, city officials for the Jewish community, and you dare insult us! What do you mean, you're "getting out of the Council?" You can't run away from the Jewish community. Forget it. Reb Lazar, why do you allow him to talk? Is that the kind of worker you have in your shop? It's beneath your dignity to listen to him. Whoever heard of such a thing—to get out of the community! You are Jews. What do you mean? You're no longer Jews?

LAZAR. Let him have it, Nachman. Tell him off. I wish I could talk as well as you can. Go to it, Nachman!

NACHMAN. Get out of the community? Why not? Reb Aaron Kluger is a Jew? and Reb Pinchus, ask him, is he a Jew? Does the Council tell them what to do? They don't pay the Council any taxes. They have nothing to do with the Council, and the Council cannot do a thing to them. The Council doesn't holler at them, and yet, we can't do what they do, oh no. We're only workers. Well, let me tell you we won't put up with it any more. What do you say, brother botchers?

WORKERS.—You're right, Nachman.
　　　　—We won't put up with them.
　　　　—Not another minute.
　　　　—Enough is enough.

NACHMAN. In other towns the workers left the Council, and the Council didn't try to stop them. You listen, you Councilmen. We are workers talking. We'll send two men to the government to let them know we're resigning. We'll pay our own taxes; we'll supply our own recruits too, if we have to; but we'll do it for ourselves and not for this Council.

WORKERS.—That's telling them all right.
　　　　—Enough.
　　　　—We're through.

CROWD.
　　(Outside.)—The Council picked a recruit.
　　　　—Tell them, Nachman.
　　　　—They gyp the town.
　　　　—They pocket plenty graft.
　　　　—They steal the Council's money.
　　　　—Thieves, robbers.
　　　　—For their taxes they want to send recruits.

　　　　—The devil take their fathers.
　　　　—What do they care? Do they care for human beings?
　　　　—So what, a poor man is also a human being?
　　　　—Robbers—devil take you all and your fathers.

SHLOIME. Quiet! We must have silence. One at a time.

NACHMAN. You'd better listen to what the workers want. Let us resign without any trouble, and if you won't . . . (Pinchus quietly instructs Chaim Platt.)

PINCHUS. Chaim, run quickly to the courthouse, and to the Count if necessary. Tell them we need a few strong men quickly. They'll know whom to send. Hurry. (Chaim runs out. Pinchus turns to the others.) Enough. Shut him up, that ruffian, that loafer. Get out, you rabble, you botchers, get out of here. I'm sending for the police chief. He'll show you what's what. Just wait, Nachman, you loud-mouth, you'll get yours. You'll be whipped within an inch of your life. You low-down nothing— show some respect. (Pinchus turns to his helpers.) Throw him out! (A few of Pinchus's men crowd in on Nachman.)

NACHMAN. Just you try it, you pious fanatics. Come on, which one is first? Well, speak up, fellows . . .

PINCHUS. You'll be carried out of here. (There is a tussle between Nachman's group and the Council's toughs. A few policemen enter. Sudden quiet—all are frightened.) Quiet, everyone. These men will take care of the mobsters. As for you, Reb Lazar, shame. You're a pious Jew and you fall in with these heathens, these atheists. Do you want the Council to take away your franchise, your license or what?

LAZAR. Who, me? They're nothing to me. Nachman is a clown. I'm not an ignoramus like them. Everyone knows I'm a shamus, an official in the synagogue. Do you think I'd be crazy enough to argue with the Council?

NACHMAN. Just look at him crawl. The tailor is a turncoat. The devil take him. Members of the Council, the workers want your answer.

PINCHUS. (*To the policemen.*) Chase them out! Out with them . . . (*The police push out Nachman and his followers.*) Go—go to the government with your complaints. We'll show you . . .

NACHMAN. Remember! Pinchus, you thief, you swindler, the devil take your father's father . . .

VELVEL. As the saying goes, such no-good tramps. Because of them we have these troubles; how do you say it, one sick animal infects a herd, for example.

SHLOIME. Good people, my friends. Reb Velvel is right. Our town is sick, sick because there is sin in our midst. We must exorcise it even if we have to send for the chief holy Rabbi from Tchernabil.

CROWD.—Sign . . .
—Don't sign . . .

YISROELIK. You know what—how about Reb Aaron Kluger? Let's stop arguing and go to Reb Aaron. He'll know what we should do. Then we can talk with the soldiers. Reb Aaron will know what we should do.

CROWD.—That's right.
—To Reb Aaron.
—He knows. (*Council members rise to leave. Gavriel Shed and the two soldiers stagger in. The soldiers are only slightly drunk; Gavriel is potted.*)

GAVRIEL. It's crazy. Listen, people, the soldiers were just about to leave for the city. But I know their language, all right. So I told them, even if the Council won't sign . . . (*Gavriel has been weaving; he stumbles and almost falls.*) The devil take Lifshe's father. She gave me that drink of whiskey. That Lifshe . . . that old maid . . . the devil take her father's father . . . (*Gavriel passes out.*)

BRUCHE. (*She screams at the prostrate Gavriel.*) You damn drunk. Who told you to tell the soldiers the Council won't sign? Now they'll go back to their headquarters and report, and they'll send my husband to Siberia. Woe, woe . . . why are you all silent? My husband a recruit! Rochel, Rochel . . . (*Bruche goes screaming thru the crowd. Velvel, coming forward, entangles his sleeve in the tablecloth, which he drags along, scattering the debris all over those around the table. He splutters and screams at Gavriel.*)

VELVEL. For example, the devil take you, you drunkard. How does the saying go for example, don't use a stick on a whipped dog. The devil take your father. For example, why did you have to say, for example, that the Council won't sign? As the saying goes, he who hesitates is lost. Such a devil, such a drunkard, for example . . . I'm shaking like a leaf, for example . . . Bruche . . . (*Bruche approaches. Velvel screams in her ear.*) See here, aren't you going to do something, say something, for example . . . (*Bruche and Velvel bear down on Shloime.*)

BRUCHE. Your life won't be worth living. I'll tear you limb from limb, you idiot dog. Tell the soldiers to wait till sundown, after the Sabbath. Tell them I will bring in half a loaf of bread and pickle juice—that will keep them waiting. Tell them. I should only bury you already. Shloime, promise them the Council will take care of them. (*Bruche approaches the two soldiers. The elders crowd around with her as she whispers to the soldiers. Gavriel Shed comes to and tries to stagger to his feet, supporting himself at the table.*)

GAVRIEL. Dammit, who says I'm drunk? Even though I'm not an official, when the Council sent me, I went. Even though it has nothing to do with me. But the honest truth is that Lifshe, the devil take her mother, gave me a sock with her hand . . . but not whiskey. She clouted me on the head. I may be dizzy, but I'm not drunk. (*Gavriel tries to approach the soldiers.*) You were there. You drank the whiskey. Did I even get a smell? (*Shloime and the other elders block Gavriel. They struggle with him and he falls over a stool and shatters it. The soldiers whisper to one another.*)

FIRST SOLDIER. They want us to wait. Let's pretend we must leave in a hurry. Then they'll come across with plenty. (*Bruche is entwined with those around Gavriel. She tries to disentangle herself and becomes hysterical.*)

BRUCHE. My God, I'm going out of my mind. What do you all want from me! Just look, the soldiers want to leave and betray us. They'll send my husband to Siberia! You expect the town to be without a head? Woe to me! I don't have to put up with this. Shloime, resign from the Council. I'm telling you—or I'll tear you to pieces. You've been an elder, a councilman long enough. Let the town get another head man. Why don't you say something? Why are all you people so silent? You expect my husband to be a recruit . . . (*She tears her hair and cries havoc. Shloime starts to whine.*)

SHLOIME. What do you all want from my life? You, too, Velvel, you want to go to Siberia? Lock the doors— block the way—don't let the soldiers leave.

YISROELIK. Take my advice. Let's go to Reb Aaron. But we must hurry. (*The crowd cheers the Council on as they leave for Reb Aaron's. Bruche remains with the soldiers. Bruche rushes to the door to scream at her son and daughter-in-law.*)

BRUCHE. Do you hear? They want to send your father-in-law to Siberia . . . or take him to be a recruit. I have to suffer all this by myself while you hide in your room. Suppose they take your husband to be a recruit, what will you do?

ROCHEL. What do you want from me? Hirsh-Leib said, "If my mother is yelling, let her yell. You stay here with me." Go ask him. (*Hirsh-Leib comes forth.*)

FIRST SOLDIER. Where did they go, the Council?

SECOND SOLDIER. Yeah, the Council.

FIRST SOLDIER. Let's get out of here, away. (*Bruche screams to Hirsh-Leib.*)

BRUCHE. What shall I do? The soldiers are leaving. I'll scream in all the streets—I'll throw myself in the river . . .

HIRSH-LEIB. Why are you so excited about the soldiers? Let them go to hell, good riddance. (*Hirsh-Leib leads the way for the soldiers to the door. Bruche starts to have a fit.*)

BRUCHE. You're as crazy as your father, the dog. Woe is me . . . (*Rochel timidly approaches Hirsh-Leib.*)

ROCHEL. Hirsh-Leib, why are you letting the soldiers go? If your mother begs you not to let them, maybe it's important that they stay. Please, don't let them go.

HIRSH-LEIB. When you scream at me, momma, I don't listen. But when my wife says, "Don't let them go," I listen, and I won't let them go. (*Hirsh-Leib tries to block the door. The soldiers knock him down and leave. Bruche screams. She and Hirsh-Leib chase after the soldiers. Rochel starts to moan in labor pains.*)

ROCHEL. Oi—OI—it's coming. Come back! Hirsh-Leib, Mother-in-law— you're about to become a grandma . . .

CURTAIN

SCENE 2

Reb Aaron Kluger's home, Saturday after mid-day dinner. Well furnished. Roof is shingled, elegant porch, floors scrubbed, furniture slip-covered, large round table, wall clock, mirrors, side tables, wallpapered walls; curtains match slipcovers.

Two very pretty little girls playing, supervised by Nanny, who is bedecked with numerous beads (status symbols). Perele Kluger, the girls' mother, enters. A good-looking young woman, be-diamonded. She approaches and kisses the two girls.

Reb Aaron Kluger enters. The older child runs to greet him. He sits and child sits on his lap. Perele sits with other child.

AARON. Ah, my darling Perele, when I think of our mothers after whom our daughters are named—if only they had lived to share our joy in the children. At least your mother was with us a few years after our wedding, and your father lived to see our eldest daughter born. But my parents didn't live to see . . . I suppose that's fate. It's beyond the limits of our wisdom.

PERELE. It's God's way. If your parents had not died so early, you would not have gone to Warsaw and gotten educated in the ways of the world. You might have remained a village bumpkin, married at fourteen, and I never would have met you. You might have become like Yisroelik or Shloime. I would have married, God forbid, an idiot like Hirsh-Leib like poor Rochel. Ah, let's forget it and count our blessings instead. God should let us live long enough to see happiness come to our children. I hope the town will remain peaceful and be a good place for them to live. But the news about the recruits, everyone in town running around and screaming. Are they going to grab girls to work in the factories? Will they rush to marry off the little girls? What is all this confusion?

AARON. It's all a plain lie. It's because our Jews throughout the land in the little villages are so primitive, so stupid, they can't even read. Any-

one will tell them the most absurd things and they believe it. The most pathetically ignorant of them believe in the Rabbi; they call him the Good Jew—he's neither good nor devoutly Jewish. As a matter of fact, he's probably more ignorant than they are. Yet they listen to him as though each word comes directly from on High. If they could only read Russian, read anything, they'd be able to see in the newspapers that all this is no calamity but really a blessing from the Czar. If the Czar proclaims that a girl less than 18 and a boy less than 20 shouldn't be allowed to marry, shouldn't we thank him for this? When the ukase becomes official it may be 16 and 18, just like in the Torah. But these dumb animals see everything as a calamity. They're like the ignorant Russian muszhiks who think it a calamity when the government insists they build chimneys so they shouldn't smother in their hovels from the smoke. They have to have some sense beaten into them before they allow the government to save their lives, or save them from being blinded or die from gas poisoning. The German peasants reacted the same way when they were told to plant potatoes and alternate their crops. This was to make their lives easier and more productive. But no, they all act like ignorant beasts when wiser heads try to do them a favor. Because our Jews are poor, they marry off their children when they are 13. When the former Polish senate wanted to pass a law to make the marriage age 18 and 20, the dumb boobs, yes, our stupid Jews, quickly started to marry off tiny little children only 8 years old.

PERELE. But when they start to take Jewish boys to be recruits, isn't it a terrible calamity? What a misfortune!

AARON. No. Our Czar, bless him, wants all his subjects to become equal citizen. To live and trade wherever they wish, not the way it has been until now, that in only 15 provinces are the Jews allowed to live and trade. If we want equal rights with the Russians, we must also have equal responsibilities. Because the Jews weren't allowed to offer recruits, the Czar now wants that they should. From this will come the rights to the Jews to live and trade on an equal footing with all Russians. Only after you buy a pew in the synagogue do you have a right to occupy it. It's the same thing. If we supply recruits, we'll have the right to move about freely and trade where we wish.

PERELE. What a bitter pill it is to a mother and father when her child is taken—for twenty-five years! I would die a thousand times, God forbid, if a child of mine were taken. I find no comfort that they take another mother's child. Her woe does not diminish mine. We are both cursed with the worst misfortune in the world. (*Aaron rises, kisses her.*)

AARON. My darling, what a silly notion that a child of ours would be taken if we had a son. As upper-class citizens, we have special privileges from the Czar. He exempts our class from this obligation. This is natural and everyone understands it. (*He is near window.*) I'll have to cut this short. Here comes Yisroelik der Ukrainer. He never comes around on a Sabbath. Look how he is hurrying. There must be trouble. (*Yisroelik enters.*)

YISROELIK. A peaceful Sabbath. I hurried before the crowd gets here. Yes, they're all on their way here. You ought to know why they are coming. They'll be here any minute.

AARON. What happened?

YISROELIK. They sent for me right in the middle of the Sabbath dinner that I should rush to Reb Shloime Spyuche for the Council meeting. It was no use, I just couldn't get out of it. When I got there, not only was the Council in session, but the whole village together with all the poor Jews from the neighboring hamlets were there, hollering and screaming.

You won't believe what went on there when I tell you. A guardian angel must have brought Reb Pinchus there—if he had not got there in time we would really be in trouble. Gavriel Shed, that drunk, stole a third of the money from the alms cup and guzzled a tank of whiskey, and as stinking drunk as he is, they made him the official messenger of the Council. Reb Shloime is in charge; he has no beard, but a behind to sit on he has, and his head —I don't think he knows which end is which. It was a black day for the Jews when he became the head councilor . . . and his wife, that deaf snake . . . she's our first lady! And another Council member is Velvel "for example," with his idiotic sayings that make as much sense as the man in the moon. To join this great cabal, there descended from every back alley and rathole in the village the "big brains." What went on! You would have had plenty to laugh and cry about. Everyone believes that the Ukase demanded that the Council supply a recruit at once. The soldiers who brought the document only asked the Council to sign a receipt—just a receipt. The poor Jews believed that if the Council would not sign then the Ukase would not be in effect. You should have heard the shrieking and howling from inside and outside, from all over the town. Everyone was yelling, "Don't sign! Don't sign!" And the deaf First Lady, Shloime's Bruche, she kept cursing him; under no circumstances was he to sign: "Don't sign, Don't sign!" Even Velvel Gelyevater was screaming like a wild one, "Don't sign; then they won't take a recruit."

AARON. (*Sadly wiping a tear.*) It's a pity, a dreadful pity. Blind. They are so blind, so ignorant. It's a lucky thing this is not a big city. There they would be grabbed away or thrown out.

YISROELIK. Such screaming, wailing, "Don't sign, don't sign!" Then Pinchus the Redhead, God bless him, explained that the ukase is a ukase whether they sign it or not. And if they don't supply recruits, then the Council members would be drafted and maybe even sent to Siberia. Then they really became frightened.

AARON. So what did Reb Pinchus accomplish?

YISROELIK. Did he accomplish something! Did he, just! The dumb cows were frightened out of their wits, and that miserable deaf sow almost went out of her mind. Now she started to scream . . . (*Mimics Bruche.*) "Sign—for God's sake, sign!"

PERELE. You don't mean to say they signed on the Sabbath? It's impossible.

YISROELIK. No, God forbid. But they were all pretty scared by what Pinchus told them. Then they sent Gavriel the drunk to get the soldiers so they could ask them to wait till after sundown, the end of Sabbath. Then the fireworks started. The workers came in and demanded that they be given rights. They started a fight. At that point I got the idea to tell them to come to see you.

AARON. Till they come, I will try to explain something to you. We're living here in comfort, and we have been blessed with a few rubles—it is ours. No one, God forbid, has the right to take it away or the villain will be punished. Now, why is this? Because we have a just land, with police, with a magistrate, a governor, and so on. They protect us from robberies, from all injustices so that no one takes advantage of anyone. And do you know who protects them and us, and everybody? The soldiers. If we didn't have so many soldiers, so many battalions, so many generals, then some barbarians like the French would take away all of us together with our possessions, the police, the magistrates, and the governors. That's why we have to have war, not to let the enemy into our country. Comes the question, who

should go and fight for us? Actually, all of us should fight the enemy. But we don't need so many people. Only a few hundred thousand soldiers are enough to defeat the enemy. That's why it is fated that some should remain at home and some should serve in the army. Each village draws lots, and through the lottery it is decided who shall be a recruit. That's why we must look upon our soldiers as the precious chosen ones who go to fight for all of us. The fathers and mothers must realize that their sons go to war in their place, otherwise everyone would have to go.

YISROELIK. If everyone had your brains, or at least weren't such dumb cows, we'd have no problems. But in our little village, our Jews are simply cows, except they don't give milk. They're not even oxen, otherwise, at least we'd be able to drive them to Warsaw. (*Yisroelik has worked his way to the window and looks out.*) Here comes the whole kit and caboodle of them.

AARON. Go meet them and tell the elders to get rid of the mob. Only the members of the Council and respectable people can come in here. (*Yisroelik meets the elders as they approach the porch. Gavriel tails them, staggers against the porch, and falls.*)

GAVRIEL. The document is really a document . . . (*He sheepishly rises and fades out of the scene. The elders crowd into Aaron's house, kiss the mezuzah on the door jamb, take off their big hats, and keep their heads covered with ritual skull caps. They all greet Aaron with "Good Sabbath," while Velvel loses his hat, bends to retrieve it, and talks as he enters.*)

VELVEL. For example, if I were in charge, as the saying goes, for example, "don't ask the doctor, ask the patient." It is, for example, such a salty matter, that the whole village can't find an answer, so, for example, we all come to you, Reb Aaron, as the saying goes, only the wearer knows where the shoe pinches. For example, it's quite an occasion to come to talk with a great man. As the saying goes, for example, why does the bear dance? Because he doesn't wear an apron, for example. (*Reb Aaron signals the nanny to take out the children. Perele also exits, but remains at a doorway, within hearing.*)

AARON. Sit down, my friends. I know the story already: Reb Yisroelik told me everything, so spare yourselves the trouble. That you first didn't want to sign and then decided to sign is very unimportant. I'll tell my Polish clerk; he'll sign for you. And if you don't sign, it won't mean a thing either way. Let me see the document; I want to see exactly what it says. That's the first thing. Where is it?

SHLOIME. That drunk, Gavriel Shed, has it. We hired him to handle it. For such a job we need someone who knows the ways of the soldiers. The village crier is too old and crippled. Of course Gavriel is a terrible drunk, but when he's sober he's very efficient, and he knows how to handle the soldiers—he talks their language. (*Confidentially to Aaron.*) Also, he will be the recruit kidnapper. A sober man wouldn't want to do it. So let Gavriel be the man. Where is he? He was behind us. Go, Reb Velvel, find him and bring him here right away. (*Velvel exits.*)

PINCHUS. I always thought that my home town of Tityev was an uncivilized jungle. Now I see that this village of Nibivayla is worse. In Tityev at least we had a wise head Rabbi and a stupid shamus—he was even related to me. Here, you don't even have them. The whole countryside is crawling with sages and saints to such an extent that the wise Rabbis have abandoned the countryside. These fanatical, Chassidic charlatans are a disgrace to our people. The

Rabbis actually became afraid of what they were doing, dragging the people deeper and deeper into their fanaticism. They inflame the people and there's no controlling the mobs.

SHLOIME. How do you figure that out? The great Rabbi Yitzhok has had, for a long time, certification to be our head Rabbi. But now and for some time, he won't come here. Because the town has sinned. There is evil somewhere among us. We must tear it out, no matter who it is. Then Rabbi Yitzhok . . .

AARON. (*Angry and outraged.*) That chiseler! That money scrounger, that bloodsucker! I chased him away from here. When my time comes and I come to judgment, you can put it to my credit at least this one good deed that I did for this town. My father-in-law, bless him and may we all live long, had dealings with this saint, your holy Rabbi Yitzhok. His "piety" was to squeeze the last groshen out of a poor man, by force if he had to. He was an absolute robber. My, how much this cost our town. I could think of worthier causes for the money. If we spent the money on more important things, we would have an honest Rabbi and a decent shamus, not a druken lout. Oh, here comes Reb Velvel. I hope he has the document. (*Velvel enters.*)

VELVEL. For example, where did I find him? You guessed it—in the saloon of course, as the saying goes. For example, as the saying goes, money won't spoil a betrothal. For example, Reb Shloime, your wife, Bruche, and your son, Hirsh-Leib, for example, were at Lifshe the Spinster's place with the soldiers. So I told them that Reb Aaron, for example, said they could go home. As the saying goes, if you can't find the gate, jump over the fence. (*Reb Aaron takes the document from Velvel and studies it. Meanwhile, Velvel chatters away.*)

AARON. Look here, it says we have to provide only one recruit, but he must be drafted before the New Year.

He must be a satisfactory specimen, or else he'll be rejected and we'll have to send another. Well, I see that we'll have to plan this carefully. We must be sure to send a satisfactory recruit who won't be rejected. I see that we have some time and we don't have to rush into this. So, please, go home, all of you, and think about this. But be very careful whom you speak to. Let's act confidentially among ourselves.

YISROELIK. What is there to think about, Reb Aaron? The document says that whoever is selected must go.

AARON. We know, we know, Reb Yisroelik. But we have to decide who should go so that we do not harm any of our good kind of people. If it becomes necessary, we can go to the governor and he'll know what to do. Documents can be interpreted in many ways. So why can't it be interpreted the way our elders, the council, the outstanding citizens want it to be interpreted?

ELDERS.—Reb Aaron makes sense.
—We were smart to come here.
—You can depend on Reb Aaron.

AARON. But you must keep all this to yourselves. Under no circumstances are you to let anyone know. (*Perele enters with a maid. They bring in drinks and refreshments, which they bestow on the guests.*)

VELVEL. You are so right. I know, for example, that you appreciate my company because I get along with the best of people, for example, as the saying goes, an ox has a long tongue but he cannot speak, for example.

PERELE. For such distinguished guests, even though under such bitter circumstances, we could at least, how do you say, Reb Velvel, for example, it's always good to make a blessing.

VELVEL. A blessing should be made, especially here among the best people in town. For example, as the saying goes, what the sober man has on his mind, the drunkard has on the tip of his tongue. (*L'Chayems all around. General conversation: "Only at happy occasions," and the like.*)

YISROELIK. Let's drink only at happy occasions. I always enjoy your wise sayings, Reb Velvel. (*Aaron Kluger did not drink.*)

AARON. What we discussed here we must keep to ourselves. Under no circumstances are you to let anyone know what we even think. Think, think carefully who should be the recruit. We'll all get together the day after tomorrow. I'll give this a lot of thought, and then we'll put our heads together. And you, Reb Pinchus, tomorrow, with God's help, please come here around noon. We have something to talk about. (*Hirsh-Leib enters. He's excited, joyful, frantic.*)

HIRSH-LEIB. What did I tell you? Who is Hirsh-Leib? Just guess; I bet you can't guess. (*He confronts Perele.*)

PERELE. The devil take you, Hirsh-Leib. What's all your excitement about?

HIRSH-LEIB. Perele, Perele—you're so wise. Tell me, how many months does it take to give birth? (*Perele winks at Aaron as she humors Hirsh-Leib.*)

PERELE. That depends on the father. If the father is a schlemiel, it could be that even after ten years the wife has no child.

HIRSH-LEIB. Ten years? Well . . .

PERELE. The wife of a *real man* will see to it that they celebrate a circumcision in one year.

HIRSH-LEIB. As long as one year? Well . . .

PERELE. But in the case of a really wise and superior man, his wife gives birth in nine months.

HIRSH-LEIB. Nine months? What about . . . how about . . .

PERELE. But this superman's wife can have a child in seven months.

HIRSH-LEIB. Seven months? And how about four months after they're married?

PERELE. He must be a wise man and a superman above everyone else; there's no one to equal him.

HIRSH-LEIB. (*Overcome with joy and excitement, speechless, he jumps around and with open mouth points at himself* .) Ah—Uh— (*Perele pretends not to understand.*)

PERELE. What are you trying to say, Hirsh-Leib? Speak up . . .

HIRSH-LEIB. That's me—I am that wise man—that superman—no one is equal to me—(*Everyone gasps, exclamations: "He!" "Ridiculous!" "That is a sin!" "The town is now really cursed!"*) How long am I married? That's right—four months!

ALL.—Only four months . . .

—That's right, four months.

—Disgraceful.

—It should happen in a respectable Jewish community!

—This sin brings a curse upon us.

HIRSH-LEIB. Yes . . . my wife Rochel is in labor. The midwife is with her now. I went for her myself.

SHLOIME. It must be a miscarriage . . . it's unheard of . . . (*Others laugh.*) My friends, why are you so gleeful? If it's true, the town has a sin—it is truly cursed. And you lacking in understanding, you laugh. You are no better than the ignorant Polish peasants . . . (*They stop their laughter; they are bewildered.*) Because of her, this calamity has come upon us, this ukase. Woe . . . a Jewish daughter to be a whore! (*All stand petrified as the curtain falls.*)

SCENE 3

The market place, outside Rabbi Motel's house.

People are running and milling about, excited, bewildered.

CROWD.—Did you hear?

—What a misfortune.

—What do you think?

GAVRIEL. It's crazy . . .

CHAIM. It's exaggerated. It can't be.

CROWD.—God's curse.

—Shouldn't we do something?

—Did you hear? There'll be a torrent of blood.

—Where?

—What do you mean "where?" All over the country.

—It's too early to tell.

—Why early?

—Can't you see? The sun sets early.

—At least two hours early.

—Each day it sets earlier.

—It's blood red, just look!

—What do you mean?

—The sky. Can't you see? Just look.

GAVRIEL. It's crazy, the devil take it. I need a drink.

CHAIM. You drunken lout! Blood red. The world is turning over.

CROWD.—What should we do?

—What can we do?

—We all must turn Christian.

—Really! We'll die first.

—That's what the document says, "All must turn Christian." (*A woman passes by; she is singing.*)

—Look at her; she's singing.

—That woman? What's happening to us?

—Her son died this morning.

GAVRIEL. He was only seventeen.

CHAIM. Young and fresh, a wonderful boy . . .

WOMAN. (*As she sings.*) Woe to a mother, to all mothers of sons.

CHAIM. Poor thing. She's gone out of her mind. How awful!

WOMAN. I thank you, my God.

CROWD.—What's that? What is she saying?

—Poor thing, she's out of her mind.

—She's plain crazy.

—How could she . . .

WOMAN. I thank you, God, for your justice, for your mercy.

CROWD.—Just listen to her.

—It's a sin . . .

—Maybe she . . .

WOMAN. (*Dancing and singing.*) Thank You that you took the life of my beloved, my beautiful son.

CROWD.—What is she saying!

—I never heard anything like it.

—What will the Rabbi say?

WOMAN. When I buried him in the cemetery, my heart was joyful. He won't have to be a recruit. His death is a blessing. He was spared from being driven among strangers. All mothers envy me. Why shouldn't I be happy? All mothers are frightened— such pitiful women. Their flesh and blood will slowly perish away. Where will they be buried? No mother will know. I thank Thee, God. I know where my son is buried—in a holy Jewish cemetery. Join me, all you mothers, join me in my joy. My beloved won't become a recruit. He is free. (*A general wailing. Suddenly a new commotion. Noise from off stage.*)

CROWD.—Let her go.

—Take her away, that witch.

—She brought a curse on us.

—She ruined us.

—Beat her.

—Stone her, that whore.

—Chase her out of town.

—Give her proper respect. (*Rochel is dragged in, her hands tied behind her. She is dressed as a bride. Preceding her is a clown, who bangs his cymbals. The mob throws stones and mud at her.*)

—Adultress.

—Bitch.

—Let us see this abomination.

—The town's calamity should only happen to you.

—On your head.

—Witch.

—That it should happen to us, to our town!

—Our sons to be torn away. Better you should be torn to pieces.

—We must save the town.

—Her bastard has gone to the devil.

—Better him than our children.

—Now maybe God will pity us. (*Rochel is dragged to the Rabbi's house. He and the Council Elders come out.*)

GAVRIEL. Quiet, everybody. Wait, quiet! The Rabbi . . .

RABBI. Good people, because of our sins, God punishes. Woe that this should happen among my people! So this is the brazen one, the miserable, shameless adultress.

ROCHEL. Rabbi, please tell them. You yourself said that I am a pious and pure woman.

SHLOIME. Quiet, you bitch. Close your mouth or we'll close it for you, forever.

RABBI. This is the power of evil. This is the way of sin. This is the defiance of the fallen. The Talmud says, "The ways of evil are without shame." If she had more sense, more humility, she would beg God for forgiveness. That this should happen among my people! All Israel must suffer for the sin of one? You guilty one, confess who is your undoer, who is your seducer?

ROCHEL. Please, Rabbi, please recall when you pronounced me pure. Exactly nine months—and from that day I became pregnant. (*Rochel mimics the Rabbi.*) "The Talmud says . . ." from that day, the day you pronounced me pure, I became pregnant.

CROWD.—Shut her up.

—Gag her.

—Hussy, slut.

—Whore.

—Don't let her get away with it.

—Stone her. (*They gag her mouth.*)

RABBI. In the Holy Torah it says, "Thou shalt tear out evil from your midst, and God will remove his curse from all Israel."

CROWD.—Condemn her.

—Stone her.

—Cast her out.

—Like a dog, a bitch.

RABBI. Woe that a Jewish daughter becomes a whore. The holy prophet Ezekial said, "And I will judge you, the judgment of the fallen, and blood will flow."

CROWD.—Judgment.
　　　—For our children's sake.
　　　—Stone her.
RABBI. No, my people. Because of our sins, our Temple was destroyed and the Lord's spirit turned from his people. Therefore the right to stone a sinner, and other judgments have been taken from us. Now, this is the judgment . . . (*He turns to his assistant and whispers to him as he leafs through the Holy Book.*) Look up what it says there . . . (*Then aloud to the populace.*) Our wise men say in the Gemara . . . (*Frantically whispers to his assistant.*) Quickly, where? (*Then to the populace.*) In the various judgments . . . (*Assistant hands him open Book and points to passage. Rabbi reads to the populace.*) "She was brought before the Tribunal on High, and the Arcan took her clothes at her throat to see if they were torn—it made no difference if they were torn. If in shreds, also no matter. But he uncovered her breasts, and undid her hair, then tore off her jewels." (*The Rabbi descends, approaches Rochel, tears dress to uncover her bosom, unbraids her hair, rips off her trinkets, then speaks.*) ". . . and he shall tie her with a rope to a stump, and there shall she stand two days and one night, and all will gaze upon her shame. Then will the Lord remove his curse from us." (*A new commotion.*)
CROWD.—What's going on?
　　　—Stop shoving.
　　　—What did you say?
　　　—It can't be!
　　　—Impossible!
　　　—Is it true? A miracle?
　　　—They're removing the curse? . . .
　　　—Did they change the ukase? No order from the Czar?
　　　—Who did it? The Czar himself?
　　　—Our Rabbi worked a miracle! May he live to 120 years.
CHAIM. What nonsense! Exaggerated! No more recruitment? The Czar him-
self removed it? I don't believe it. He himself changed his mind?
PINCHUS. (*Addresses the crowd.*) My friends. I can't believe it. We have confirmation that the Czar canceled the order. But, we Jews must contain, we must suppress our joy. We must not reveal our good fortune to the Russians or we'll be in great trouble.
CROWD.—Thank the Lord.
　　　—We are saved.
　　　—Our children are ours again. (*Nachman rushes in, climbs onto the porch and addresses the crowd.*)
NACHMAN. Listen, please listen to me. Good people, they're fooling you. You're being cheated . . .
VELVEL. Get down, you damned tailor.
NACHMAN. The Council is fooling you so that no one will hide from being recruited. Don't trust them . . .
PINCHUS. You scoundrel—you loafer— (*Pinchus rages at Nachman as he points to tied Rochel.*) We'll do the same to you. That's what will happen to you. We'll pillory you before we're through with you . . . you . . . you . . .
NACHMAN. My friends, good people, how can you let the Council and that pious, fanatical fraud do this? (*Nachman turns upon the Council and the Rabbi.*) What right do you have to judge her? By what right? (*He turns to his fellow workers.*) What do you say, fellows? Are you going to let them get away with it?
APPRENTICE WORKERS.—No, they can't do it.
　　　—The Council can't judge.
　　　—They have no right.
NACHMAN. Now they invent a story about no more recruits. Let's all of us go to the government headquarters and find out the truth.
PINCHUS. Squealers! You will betray your own kind? Do you intend to be traitors to our community? (*Calling to his helpers.*) Seize him! Grab him quick so he doesn't get away. We'll fix him.

NACHMAN. (*He whistles a signal. The workers rush to his side.*) Come on, you wonderful botchers—let's get them . . . (*The crowd flees as there is a free-for-all between Nachman's fellow-workers and the Council's bullies. Nachman and two apprentices rush to Rochel.*) Untie her, quickly. You two, take her to Lifshe's tavern. She can hide there.

APPRENTICES. You bet. Let's go. (*The two release Rochel and rush her out. Nachman surveys the scene. He espies the frightened Rabbi.*)

NACHMAN. Now, let's tie up this saintly fraud. Hey Tutor, say a prayer over him. (*They tie up the Rabbi in Rochel's place.*) Now, let's go. Don't leave any evidence. (*Nachman and his buddies flee.*)

CURTAIN

ACT III

SCENE 1

At the home of Reb Pinchus. He is alone, speaking to himself as he counts money.

PINCHUS. Seventy-five—100—all I do is pay out—150—they're bloodsuckers—200—250—one would think it's just nothing—300—each one is a leech and has his hand out, grasping and grabbing, grabbing. Orphans—400—widows—poor brides without dowries—450—500—the Society For the Poor—550—You're a big hero and will be blessed with your charity, Reb Pinchus. (*With rising rage.*) Charity, charity, charity. They think money grows on trees. One works hard for each miserable groshen. If they would work themselves, they too would have money. Where was I? 400? Let me see once again—75, 100, 200. It's no small matter to make a match. But he's got to be a decent fellow, not just a nobody. If he's rich,

I'll go . . . who knows. For my darling Frumele, I will go as high as 225 to make sure of a match. Yes, if he's rich I'll go 400, and if he's rich rich, I'll go 450, and if he's a Talmudist, a scholar yet, that's the limit I'll go—500. After all, who am I? Just anyone? Money just doesn't walk in through the door. Ugh, let it be. Tsk, but money is a serious matter. Charity—they come at me from all sides. Let's see, once again. Seventy-five—100—(*Reb Tzalyeh enters.*)

REB TZALYEH. Good evening, Reb Pinchus. (*They exchange greetings.*) I've been planning for the longest time to visit you. After all, I say without envy, mind you, you're such an established person, a rich man who is respected.

PINCHUS. (*Hiding his money.*) So-o-o-o, I'm a rich man, am I? What business is it of yours? Do you have any interest in my money? Did you contribute anything? Maybe you're a partner of mine, already?

TZALYEH. Plain is plain. Now take Reb Motele the Rabbi . . .

PINCHUS. Who needs Reb Motele! What have I to worry about? I'm being torn to pieces; everybody is grabbing at me. Reb Motele, huh; I can do with one blessing less. Charity, charity, charity!

TZALYEH. Shame, Reb Pinchus. Charity is—but plain is plain. Let's forget charity and talk plain. A match for your daughter, God bless her, is plain talk. Have I got a match for your daughter!

PINCHUS. Oh ho. Sit down, Reb Tzalyeh. Now I understand. So, you have a match. Please, sit down.

TZALYEH. In plain talk, bless her, such a daughter! (*Chaim rushes in.*)

CHAIM. I'm entitled to part of the marriage broker's fee. I'm not exaggerating. Tomorrow morning, we should be spared, we'll go make a contract.

PINCHUS. Sit down, Reb Chaim. Tomorrow is yet a long way off. Sit.

TZALYEH. I'm talking plain. Such a

daughter you have, such a house-keeper!

CHAIM. I'm not exaggerating. She is a wonderful housekeeper. But, devil take it, there's one drawback. Why don't you speak up, Tzalyeh? (*Tzalyeh fidgets, scratches his entire torso.*)

TZALYEH. I have to tell you in strictest confidence something that I don't want anyone to know I told you. Plain is plain, it's no small thing, a wedding match.

PINCHUS. If you have a secret, come with me. I have a private room. Come, Reb Tzalyeh, let's go. (*Pinchus and Tzalyeh exit. Chaim remains to snoop about. Pinchus and Tzalyeh soon return. Pinchus walks agitatedly to a door and calls loudly.*)

PINCHUS. Frumele . . . Frumele, come here, I want you. (*Frumele enters.*)

FRUMELE. What is it? Here I am, poppa. (*Chaim sneaks out the door through which Frumele entered.*)

PINCHUS. Tell me, what's going on between you and that young loud-mouth tailor, what's his name—Nachman? (*Frumele gasps.*) Answer me! At once!

FRUMELE. I don't know what you mean, poppa. What are you talking about? You're screaming at me and embarrassing me in front of strangers. This tailor, Nachman, once delivered a vest to me. Well, what of it?

PINCHUS. What letters or notes has he been handing you. Don't trifle. An honest girl must tell the truth. Answer at once!

FRUMELE. I don't know what you're talking about. I don't know about any letters or notes. (*Chaim rushes in waving a piece of paper.*)

CHAIM. Here, this will save your breath. I found this under her pillow. Here it is. A note with rhymes.

FRUMELE. How dare you! By what right do you sneak in to steal my things? Such outrageous nerve; this miserable fool dares to enter my room to steal! (*She snatches the paper away from Chaim.*) You thief, you scoundrel . . .

PINCHUS. Frumele, you must hand over that letter to me, or I will take it with force. And this for you . . . (*He slaps her face.*) You've made me do this. Now hand it over. (*He grabs the paper from her. Frumele, crying, runs out. Pinchus screams at the frightened Tzalyeh and Chaim.*) Get out of here! I'll send for you if I need you. Get out! (*Tzalyeh and Chaim scurry out. Pinchus reads the note aloud.*)

You're so lovely, you're so sweet.
I'd spend my life at your feet.
You're so sweet, so very nice;
I'll give you my life more than twice.
I am yours and you are mine.
The world is great—everything is fine.
Yet my love must be secretly hid,
For your father won't let me marriage bid.
So we keep in touch with a letter or note.
I dream of your eyes, your hair, your throat.
Darling Frumele, beautiful, divine—
You will be, you are forever mine.
Write me, my love, when we may meet.
That day when we each other greet,
On your tender finger I'll place a ring,
And before witnesses I will sing
That we are one, now and forever.
Then let your father us try to sever.
I wait, I yearn for your welcome sign
That tells when you will be mine.

That scoundrel, that barefoot lout, I'll fix him. Tomorrow the first thing I'll go to the court. That miserable swine has the nerve, the gall to chase after my daughter, Reb Pinchus's Frumele. And with rhymes yet. I'll have that no-good dog simply whipped out of town. I can't believe the town will pardon such a beggar. I'll fix him, all right—the first thing in the morning, if I don't have a heart attack from aggravation. (*Reb Aaron Kluger enters.*)

AARON. Hello, Reb Pinchus. You see, I come as I promised to do. Did you come to any conclusion . . .

PINCHUS. I think I'm going out of my mind from aggravation . . .

AARON. Did I come at a bad time? Maybe I can help you. What's going on?

PINCHUS. Please excuse me, Reb Aaron. Such an honored guest. Please sit down. To my troubles, there's no end. Such a scoundrel, such a charlatan, that miserable, no-good tailor.

AARON. You mean that Nachman whatshis-name? Is that the one? You could only mean that imp of the devil. You mean we should send him as the recruit for our town?

PINCHUS. What a blessing that would be. (*Pinchus walks to the door and summons Frumele. Frumele enters.*) Frumele, come here. Bring in some tea and something to eat for Reb Aaron. (*Frumele exits.*) That ruffian. He's an only child. His mother let him have his way in everything. Now she can reap the whirlwind. She can take pride in her work. I see him on his way to perdition—a thief, a murderer, a highwayman.

AARON. Ah, these mothers! If they only knew the evil they bring about by giving in to children. They destroy the child and do harm to all of us, to the whole world. But, you know, it's a wonderful idea; I believe he would make a good soldier. What do you think? They'll discipline him; he'll settle down. Right?

PINCHUS. You mean it? Oh, if I could only bring this about! But, he's got all the luck, confound him—he's an only child. The Czar's law specially says that an only child is exempt from going as a recruit. I just can't stomach it—that low-life has the nerve to seek out my daughter, my Frumele.

AARON. Aha, now I get the drift. I heard a little about it in town. The gossip is that this Nachman is in love with your Frumele. Is this true? But how about Frumele? What does she say? You know, this was one of the things I came to see you about.

PINCHUS. What are you talking about, Reb Aaron? I wouldn't lie to you. After all, you're one of us. Just wait,

I'll fix her all right. (*Frumele enters with refreshments.*)

AARON. Just look, Frumele, how angry your father is. It's not good when a father wants only his own way, is it? A daughter needs some freedom; she has her longings, desires, her needs. But what can you do with a stubborn father who has old-fashioned ideas?

FRUMELE. Please, Reb Aaron, explain this to my father. I'll always be grateful to you and bless you. He'll understand if you'll explain it to him.

PINCHUS. Do you realize what you're saying, Reb Aaron? Just listen to this: (*Pinchus reads from Nachman's poem.*) ". . . we are one, now and forever/ Then let your father us try to sever!" (*Frumele weeps.*) Do you hear that? The nerve of him! Yet in rhyme he taunts me. That rat!

AARON. (*Takes the note and reads it to himself.*) Well, well. For an uneducated boy he doesn't do badly. This isn't bad at all. Now, Reb Pinchus, listen to my advice. Just consider the situation. Come, Frumele, stop weeping. Your father is not a scoundrel. Don't cry. From your father you will yet get your heart's desire. A father won't destroy his own child, condemn her to misery.

PINCHUS. I don't know what's going on here, Reb Aaron. All I know is that he's lucky he's an only child, otherwise I'd fix him—he'd be the first recruit. But he won't get away with all he's done. I'll have him whipped out of town. That beggar dares to think of my daughter! (*Frumele is again frantically weeping.*)

FRUMELE. Poppa—Reb Aaron—

AARON. You must make up with your daughter, Reb Pinchus. Nothing will be accomplished in anger, with fighting and bitterness. After all, she's your only daughter, your only child. Give in a little. It shouldn't be hard to indulge your only daughter, such a beautiful girl.

PINCHUS. Ha! All of you! And you, too, Reb Aaron. That miserable stitcher, that tailor, I'll have him horsewhipped and chased out of town if I have to do it myself . . .

AARON. Life could be so simple if we kept ourselves calm. Frumele, trust me, leave me with your father. Everything will turn out for the best. Go, dry your tears and have hope. Rest easy. A father won't harm a daughter. (*Aaron walks Frumele to the door. Frumele exits. Aaron turns to Pinchus.*) Ah, Reb Pinchus, how can you be so insensitive. You don't understand the romantic young. Now I have a plan that will certainly make your daughter, God bless her, have a happy and secure future with a decent husband—a plan that will help you solve the town's problems . . . (*He keeps talking as the* CURTAIN FALLS.)

SCENE 2

The street outside Pinchus's house. Late at night. Quite dark. Enter Tzalyeh, followed by Chaim.

TZALYEH. Here we are. They're coming, plain and simple.

CHAIM. But, eh . . . who's coming?

TZALYEH. Who? Nachman, of course. He together with the butcher's apprentice, simply.

CHAIM. Impossible. They're rough, I'm not exaggerating. We'd better beat it, right away.

TZALYEH. Wait. You want a share of the marriage brokerage fee? Then simply stay here, and you'll be a witness.

CHAIM. What, I should stay here with the wild one, Nachman? You yourself said, I'm not exaggerating, you said Nachman is coming with the butcher boy, didn't you?

TZALYEH. What about it? Stand here in the shadows and they won't see you. What is there to be afraid of?

CHAIM. Who's afraid? I'm not afraid. But if you want someone to stay here, you stay.

TZALYEH. Who, me afraid of that low-life tailor? But I think you'd better stay here instead of me.

CHAIM. Better if you stay.

TZALYEH. No. Better if you. (*Nachman and the butcher boy are seen approaching down the street.*)

CHAIM. Oh, here they come. I'm not exaggerating, I have no time now. I've got to run.

TZALYEH. (*Grabs hold of Chaim's jacket.*) Chaim, where are you running? You stay here; I'll be right back. I must see Reb Motele—it's very important. (*Chaim clutches Tzalyeh's coat.*)

CHAIM. Don't go. Wait. I'm not . . . (*They both pull at each other until each is released. They run off in separate directions. Nachman and butcher boy approach Pinchus's house. Nachman instructs the butcher boy.*)

NACHMAN. Stand here . . . at the corner. . . . Remember, if you see someone coming, whistle. (*Butcher Boy demonstrates whistle.*) Good. Now go stand over there. (*Butcher Boy goes to corner. Nachman moves into the shadows nearer Pinchus's house. He talks to himself.*) I must have come too soon. But for you, my Frumele, I will wait. Ah Frumele, I'll even wait till daybreak. Maybe I came too late. Maybe she was here already and left. That'll be some fix. What will she think of me! No, it can't be. Frumele, come out. Where are you, Frumele? (*Nachman throws some gravel up to a room over the porch. A light goes on, the door from the room leading to the terrace over the porch opens and Frumele comes forth. She stealthily looks around.*)

FRUMELE. He's not here. Oh dear, he must have been here already. It's so dark. It's cold. I'm afraid he didn't wait because it's cold. (*She calls.*) Nachman, Nachman, are you there? Oh no, he's not here. (*Nachman comes forth.*) Gracious, who's there?

NACHMAN. Frumele.

FRUMELE. Nachman.

NACHMAN. Your father's asleep?

FRUMELE. Yes, he's asleep.

NACHMAN. And the others?

FRUMELE. All are asleep.

NACHMAN. And you?

FRUMELE I couldn't sleep.

NACHMAN. Frumele, ah Frumele my own . . .

FRUMELE. Nachman, come up here. I'm so frightened.

NACHMAN. Don't be afraid, Frumele.

FRUMELE. Please come here. Why don't you come up here, Nachman?

NACHMAN. May I, Frumele?

FRUMELE. I told you I'm frightened. Please come up here to me. I want you close. (*Nachman finds a crude ladder alongside the house. He climbs up.*)

NACHMAN. When you ask me, I come, Frumele. Whenever you'll ask me, wherever it will be, I'll come.

FRUMELE. Ah, Nachman . . .

NACHMAN. I should come closer? You want me closer, Frumele?

FRUMELE. Please, Nachman, come sit here.

NACHMAN. Are you sure I should? May I really sit down here, Frumele?

FRUMELE. Why not? Of course. (*Nachman sits beside her.*) You're so . . . so handsome, Nachman. (*They are suddenly shy with each other.*) What do you have in your hand, Nachman? (*He opens a handkerchief out of which he pours some nuts into her hand.*)

NACHMAN. Here, Frumele, shell these. (*Frumele shells the nuts and pretends not to notice that he has put his arm around her. She sighs, then suddenly weeps.*) Why are you weeping, Frumele?

FRUMELE. Because I love you.

NACHMAN. I love you, too, Frumele.

FRUMELE. And we won't ever see each other again.

NACHMAN. Why not, Frumele?

FRUMELE. Because I am afraid of my father.

NACHMAN. Then come away with me. We'll run away, Frumele.

FRUMELE. Oh . . . oh, I'm so afraid of my father.

NACHMAN. But Frumele, what then shall I do?

FRUMELE. I am wicked, Nachman. I don't know what to do. (*A whistle is heard from the butcher boy. Nachman jumps up.*)

NACHMAN. We'll meet tomorrow. Come to the miller's . . .

FRUMELE. I won't . . . I can't . . . Oh Nachman.

NACHMAN. Frumele . . .

FRUMELE. I won't come. I'll never come to you.

NACHMAN. We love each other. Oh Frumele . . .

FRUMELE. My father . . . I'm so afraid of him . . . (*Whistle again. Frumele runs into her room. Nachman stands irresolute.*)

NACHMAN. Never again? (*Whistle again —more urgent. Nachman quickly descends the ladder, pulls it alongside the house, and runs away. Enter Tzalyeh and Chaim.*)

TZALYEH. Did you see?

CHAIM. What could I see? I ran away. Did you see?

TZALYEH. What could I see? If I wasn't here, what could I see? It's plain and simple . . .

CURTAIN

SCENE 3

At the tailoring shop of Reb Lazar Krivoshei.

Evening. At the work table are sitting Nachman and two apprentices; they are sewing. As they work, the apprentices sing.

APPRENTICES.

Outside it is raining,
Raining, raining, then a frost.
Then the snow is snowing
While my young years I have lost.
Ever sitting while I sew
White, white is the snow.

NACHMAN. Enough, already, with your whining like frightened brides.

FIRST APPRENTICE. Sing, Nachman. Please. Why are you so quiet?

SECOND APPRENTICE. Still water runs deep. Quiet, is he? You should hear what they say about him! Our Nachman is madly in love. (*Apprentices laugh.*)

NACHMAN. What are you laughing at, you smart alecks? If I wipe your nose, you'll first see your mothers-in-law.

FIRST APPRENTICE. (*To others.*) Ask him—does he have a mother-in-law yet?

NACHMAN. So-o-o-o, you're a couple of fresh ones, eh? I'll have to show you who is older here, who's in charge! (*Nachman chases after them. They run around the table and taunt him with song.*)

APPRENTICES.—Frumele mine, I am thine.
—Your Nachman is absolutely fine.
—Frumele mine, will always shine. (*Nachman grabs one and holds him down on the table.*)

NACHMAN. Hold on! (*Nachman catches the other and holds a firm grasp on both.*) Now sing! Darn you, get to work!

APPRENTICES.—Nachman, hold on . . .
—We're falling off the table . . .

NACHMAN. What? Did I hear you say something?

APPRENTICES.—Nachman, help us down . . .
—We're falling off . . .

NACHMAN. What, you're not singing? How come I don't hear you sing?

APPRENTICES.—Nachman, we promise we won't, honest.
—We should die if we ever sing again.
—Watch out, we're falling. (*Nachman releases them.*)

NACHMAN. Now get to work, you botchers.

FIRST APPRENTICE. Sing for us, Nachman. It makes the work easier. (*Nachman sings.*)

NACHMAN.

Nachman is the finest fellow,
He always sings a bright hello.
You won't find Nachman with a worry,
He has each day or his tomorrow.
Let the rich man have the worry
With all the money to lend or borrow;
Nachman has no debts to pay,
That is why he'll always say:
Nachman is the finest boy
In thought and deed he finds his joy.

(*Apprentices sing the refrain.*)

APPRENTICES.

Nachman is the finest boy
In thought and deed he finds his joy.

NACHMAN.

When Nachman has no place to stay,
No one to put him up for the night,
He makes his bed in a wagon of hay
And sleeps till noon, out of sight,
Better than in a feather-bed
There he rests his heart and head.
Sometimes Nachman's hungry and cold,
Sometimes people curse him and scold,

(*Apprentices join in each refrain.*)

Nachman is the finest boy,
In thought and deed he finds his joy.

(*Nachman sings alone.*)

I dance to music of my heart's desire
She arouses in me a glowing fire.
Frumele is mine, no ands, if, or but;
Yet her father won't let me into his hut.
I look at her with such a yen,
Like a rooster always looks at a hen.
She has such lovely, silken hair.
Till I see her again, I'm in despair.
Even the Rabbi makes love to his wife
(The funniest woman I saw in my life).

Nachman is the finest boy,
In thoughts and deed he finds his joy.

If I'm broke, no money have I,
You won't see me sit down and cry.
I have a good name, it shines like a light;
Nachman der Grosse treats everyone right,

Rich or poor, young or old, dumb or
  smart
Find the same place in Nachman's heart.
I don't care if a person is lah-de-dah
  nice,
From fanatic old sages I don't seek
  advice.
Big phonies with ease I make small,
And boot-lickers I don't like at all.
I can read and write, count without
  measure,
And taking a drink gives me much more
  pleasure.

Nachman is the finest boy,
In thought and deed he finds his joy.

No one dares to be boss over me.
A boss won't pay enough to buy tea.
Saloon-keepers take all my gelt,
When I'm broke I hock my pelt.
When Nachman has no shoes on his
  feet
Barefooted he can run much more fleet.
In my ragged outfit, when I go for a
  walk,
The Council's elders with me won't talk.
I had nice clothes, but what do you
  think?
I had to pawn it to buy me a drink.
If she keeps it for me for a while,
My needlework will stay in style.

(*Nachman and the apprentices sing
and dance the next refrain on the
work table.*)

Nachman is the finest boy,
In thought and deed he finds his joy.

(*Lazar Krivoshei, the boss, enters.*)

LAZAR. What's going on here! Is this
your idea of working? The devil take
your grandmothers. (*Apprentices
rush back to work, standing up on
the work table.*)

APPRENTICES.—We're working.
            —Look how quickly we
            sew.

LAZAR. What is this, a circus? How did
you get up there? It's your work,
Nachman. (*Then to the apprentices.*)
Was it Nachman?

APPRENTICES.—No, no.
            —We did it ourselves.

            —Watch out, we're fall-
            ing.

LAZAR. The devil take your fathers. The
work is long overdue, and you are
supposed to work—but you suck my
blood. The moment I go out, when
my back is turned, you stop working.

NACHMAN Ah, Reb Lazar, a pious Jew
like you, an official in the synagogue
yet, with a tongue like Satan—pugh!
(*To the apprentices, as he takes them
down one at a time.*) Well, come
down, children.

LAZAR. Of course I'm an official. You
think I'm like you!

NACHMAN. So, you're an official. Big
deal. But an official should have such
a vicious tongue, "The devil take
your fathers." Did you learn that in
the synagogue? They'd throw you
out. Fie.

LAZAR. The devil take your father! You
suck my blood and I'm not entitled
to curse you? I'll show them, the
vermin. (*He becomes very belligerent,
and makes as if to strike the apprentices.*) I'll kick them to kingdom
come. (*Nachman blocks him.*)

NACHMAN. Hold on. Curse with your
mouth all you want, but keep your
hands to yourself.

LAZAR. What? If he's my apprentice,
I've got the right to beat him to death
if I want to. Am I the boss or not?
If I take them as apprentices, to
teach them the trade, I'm allowed to
beat them all I like, to death even.
(*Lazar again tries to get at the apprentices.*)

NACHMAN. Of course you're allowed.
But let me see you just try to do it!
I'll put you up there from where I
took them down. That won't be nice
for an official of the synagogue. Fie.
That won't look nice, a boss and an
official of the synagogue stuck up
there on display like a dunce. What
will all the people say in the synagogue? What, our official is sitting
like a hen in a roost? (*Lazar, frus-
trated, outraged, sits.*)

LAZAR. You bastard, you just wait. The
devil will take you, too, you pirate.

You suck my blood—bah, you turn my stomach.

NACHMAN. That's a pity. That's real sad. Maybe I should quit. You don't need me.

LAZAR. (*Alarmed.*) Just look at him. You can't say a word, and he, right away he wants to quit.

NACHMAN. What? You really don't want me to leave? Honestly?

LAZAR. Oh, sit down already, and do your work. You scoundrels, you atheists; work, damn you. The devil take your fathers.

NACHMAN. That's the way I like you— when you talk like a dignified gentleman, when you use the sweet talk of an official of the synagogue, that's when I like you, then we get along in peace. Sing us your new song, and we'll sing with you. (*Nachman turns to apprentices.*) Sing along, you no-good bastards. (*Lazar starts singing.*)

LAZAR. Ahee, Ahee, the good king . . .

APPRENTICES AND NACHMAN. Ahee, Ahee . . . (*They sing a few choruses of this folk song. Chantze enters with a little boy. She stands shaking her head and moving her hands as though washing them. At the end of a refrain, she interrupts.*)

CHANTZE. Ah, Reb Lazar. How nice. Good evening, Reb Lazar; good evening, Reb Nachman.

LAZAR. (*Brusquely.*) A good evening to you and your old grandmother. What's on your mind, woman? You're Chantze the matchmaker, no? Your blessed husband, may he rest in peace, downed many a shot of whiskey with me at Lifshe's tavern. May he pray for us. Even Gavriel Shed can't drink as much as your late husband did. There was a man for you; I never saw anyone hold his liquor like that man—what a capacity. Come over here, my boy.

CHANTZE. What do you think, Reb Lazar? He's a poor orphan. Where can he go? I want you should take him on as a tailor's apprentice. You're known all over. Everyone will bless you.

LAZAR. Good. I could use him. He will be an apprentice for three years. After that I'll provide a cloak and a hat for him, together with all the garments that go with them. Come this way and I'll show you where you'll sleep. Tomorrow morning you start work. Meanwhile, get to bed; you'll need this night's sleep. (*Lazar and the boy exit. Chantze approaches Nachman. She feels the cloth he's working on.*)

CHANTZE. No wonder I recognized it. It's for Reb Pinchus's daughter. It's a vest for Frumele. (*Chantze lowers her voice and speaks secretly to Nachman.*) Nachman, I really came to have a few words with you. When I go out, follow me. Frumele sent me. Don't you think I'm a good marriage broker? You can depend on me. (*Lazar reenters.*)

LAZAR. Well, it's all settled. You may go now, woman.

CHANTZE. Take care, everybody. Good night. I earned a blessing. Why else do you suppose I came out so late at night. Bless you. Good night. (*Chantze exits. Quiet, as the men work. Soon Nachman rises, stretches, and walks toward the door.*)

LAZAR. Where are you going, Nachman? The devil take all your fathers and mothers. Just look at all the work we have yet to finish.

NACHMAN. Don't worry, Reb Lazar. I'll be back soon and I'll stay late. I'll make sure to finish all the work.

LAZAR. You bastard . . . you lout. Your father should be thrown out of his grave and thrown back in again. (*Nachman strolls out.*) He knows that he has golden hands, the best, so he takes advantage and does as he pleases. What can I do? He knows I won't fire him, because if I do he'll open his own business and compete with me. (*Lazar fumes as he walks up and down. Finally, he walks over to one of the apprentices and slaps him.*) Work, you vermin, work. (*Lazar sits down with them and works with them. He starts singing his song as the* CURTAIN FALLS.)

SCENE 4

Immediately following previous scene.

On the street. Chantze waits. Nachman enters.

CHANTZE. You're such a handsome youth, Nachman. So why shouldn't you appeal to her? Frumele is just pining away for you. She says she will marry only you.

NACHMAN. Who told you this?

CHANTZE. Who do you suppose? Frumele, of course. No wonder, you're so handsome.

NACHMAN. I know all about how handsome I am. Never mind all this talk. What did Frumele say?

CHANTZE. She agreed. "Nachman is the best," she said.

NACHMAN. She sent you to say this? Nothing more? Some marriage broker you turned out to be. (*Nachman starts to leave.*)

CHANTZE. Wait. Don't be in such a hurry. She told me that she is sending you a sign where to meet her.

NACHMAN. That's more like it. That's what she really said? Ah, Chantze, for that I will kiss you. Enjoy your old age with my kiss. (*He kisses her.*)

CHANTZE. What was that for? Wow! You almost burned me with your mouth. When I was a young girl, even though I'm much older now, I was really pretty.

NACHMAN. Good. You want another kiss? Then tell me more.

CHANTZE. My mother kept a store in those days. The nicest, high-class people used to come in. They'd see me and say, "Oh, how nice she is; oh, how pretty she is."

NACHMAN. Never mind all that. What else did Frumele say?

CHANTZE. She said that her father will surely agree. It won't do him any good to say no.

NACHMAN. She really said that, Chantze? Swear! It's really true?

She's so lovely, she's so sweet.
I'd spend my life at her feet.
She's so sweet, so very nice,
I'd give my life more than twice.
Frumele, Frumele, so divine.
Frumele, Frumele will be mine.

(*He dances for joy.*) Here's another kiss for you, Chantze. (*He kisses her.*) That should make you happy, too.

CHANTZE. Go to the devil, you scamp. God won't punish me for this. Listen to this. When I was a girl, a young Polish gentleman came into my mother's store. He grabbed me and gave me a kiss. I cried a whole day.

NACHMAN. Again you're telling me old wives' tales. I didn't kiss you for your memories. Where did Frumele tell you I was to meet her?

CHANTZE. My mother, may she rest in peace, scolded me with these words, "My child, pretend a dog licked you."

NACHMAN. What do all your dreams have to do with the case? Such a carcass even a dog won't lick. Where did Frumele tell you I was to meet her? (*They are interrupted by Gavriel Shed, who staggers in. He is drunk and mutters to himself.*)

GAVRIEL. Shloime, Shloime, the devil take you and your father. Bruche, the devil take you and your mother. Rochel is dead, the devil take her father. You idiot, Hirsh-Leib, the devil take your father. Gavriel, old boy, the devil take you, too. Hevreh Kaddisha (official mourners), the devil take all your mothers. Hit the road, Gavriel my boy. Who says I can't carry out a job? I can even undertake sour cream. If I could be a deputy for the

Council—I can do anything. Bah, that was terrible brandy. Ah, Lifshe you old hag. Lifshe, the devil take your father. Gavriel, you old drunk, the devil take your mother. Where is Lifshe's door; I hope I can find it, the devil take my mother. Ugh, what miserable brandy. The devil take your father. (*Gavriel kicks and bangs against the walls.*) You walls, the devil take your mothers. Where is Lifshe's door? (*Nachman and Chantze huddle out of Gavriel's sight.*)

NACHMAN. Oh boy, that sure is strong brandy that idiot drank. Where did he get such powerful stuff. Tomorrow I'll have to find out where he gets such strong brandy. Lifshe cuts hers with water, that bitch. You know what, Chantze, for Frumele's sake, I'll stop drinking. If my Frumele gives one hint, I'll absolutely take not even one drop, not a smell. But where did Frumele say I was to come?

CHANTZE. You'll never guess. It's really quite a place. Tomorrow night at Reb Aaron Kluger's!

NACHMAN. Now—at Reb Aaron Kluger's! That tycoon with his mirrored walls? To that crook? You sure you didn't make a mistake, or is Frumele playing a joke on me?

CHANTZE. God save us. You dare to say such things about a distinguished man like Reb Aaron? Frumele said this was the best plan. She will go to Reb Aaron tomorrow night. She'll tell her father she's going on a visit to Perele so her father won't have any suspicions.

NACHMAN. But Reb Aaron will see me, he'll see that I'm there—or has he gone blind already?

CHANTZE. Heaven forbid! He's not blind, but he knows the whole story. Frumele is really smart. Reb Aaron Kluger will make all arrangements. Everything will go like clockwork. Don't worry, he'll give you a proper welcome. Reb Aaron also doesn't like religious fanatics. He says that being in love is the most important, the dearest thing. He simply loathes the religious hypocrites who constantly invoke God.

NACHMAN. Ho ho, do I know he hates those religious thieves—he's a crook in his own right. But . . .

CHANTZE. What's with all these buts? He's very fond of your Frumele and feels sorry for her. He scorns that religious cant. He says that he, too, married for love and that Perele's father didn't approve. That's what Frumele wanted me to tell you.

NACHMAN. Wait a minute. What's going on here? Gosh, Frumele. It seems to me that Reb Aaron Kluger, damn him, knows his way around; he doesn't need God to be his partner. (*Gavriel comes to life.*)

GAVRIEL. The devil take the whole Council. They think I'm going to listen to them. The idea! Taking little children to be recruits! T'hell with them. T'hell with you, Reb Aaron and your money. If I'm going to kidnap anyone, it'll be a grown-up—not children—and they'll have to pay through the nose. The devil take the whole world. Whom can I kidnap? There isn't a soul around. Phew, what stinking brandy—the devil take its father. Where am I? Gavriel, you drunk, the devil take your mother. Lifshe, you spinster bitch, where the devil are you? So, I kidnap a recruit; so, what happens? Its mother weeps, she howls, she screams, she faints— "My child, my child!" she'll cry and tear her hair—cries—faints—tears her hair . . . I'm the kidnapper. I grab the child, I take a drink and laugh it off. The devil take it all. (*Gavriel bangs the walls and he falls.*) This is the end. Gavriel, you drunk, the devil take your father's, father's, father's father. Ugh, what terrible brandy. (*Gavriel continues to mutter in his drunken stupor.*)

NACHMAN. Pinchus, you red-headed bastard, the devil take your dog's soul. This is your idea—to take young children. You should burn in hell together with your Reb Aaron Kluger. No, Chantze, I won't go to Reb Aaron Kluger. You can tell Frumele that Reb Aaron Kluger is a swine just like her father, worse than swine. No, I won't go.

CHANTZE. Take it easy. Don't get so excited. I forgot to tell you that Frumele sent you this ring and told me to tell you, like something you wrote to her, "Please put on this ring in front of a witness, and after that no one can interfere with us." That's what she said. (*Chantze hands ring to Nachman, who seizes it.*)

NACHMAN. It's Frumele's ring, from her finger. (*He sings for joy.*)

I am yours and you are mine,
Frumele, you're mine, you're mine.
The world is great, everything's fine.

Oh well, if you need the thief, you take him even from the gallows. I'll save Frumele from those scoundrels. Let Reb Kluger go kiss himself in his mirrors. . . . And as for snatching children for recruits, we'll show him! We'll split the heads of the Council, with Reb Pinchus thrown in.

CHANTZE. What are you stewing about? It's late, I've got to go home. What shall I tell Frumele?

NACHMAN. Tell her—tell her—all right, tell her that tomorrow night I will come to meet her at Reb Aaron Kluger's. Tell her—well—good night.

CHANTZE. I'll tell her. Good night. (*Chantze leaves. Nachman approaches Gavriel and lifts him to his feet.*)

NACHMAN. Come on, you drunk. I'll take you home. Those swine are suddenly my buddies. They'll wait and see. They'll drink blood, by God.

GAVRIEL. Aaron Kluger, the devil take your father. Yes, you and the whole Council—the devil take your fathers' father—the whole pack . . . (*Gavriel staggers and falls. Nachman helps*

him up and struggles to help Gavriel along as the CURTAIN FALLS.)

SCENE 5

At Reb Aaron Kluger's. The following night.

Nachman, all dressed up in his pathetic idea of high style, is ushered in by a servant.

SERVANT. Reb Kluger said you should wait here. (*Servant exits. Nachman inspects his surroundings.*)

NACHMAN. The devil take his pocketbook. It's really not a bad set-up. Much nicer than Reb Lazar's. No wonder they call him Aaron the Wise. He's not just anybody. He knows how to live, that crook. (*Views himself in a mirror.*) If I had my buddies with me, those botchers, we'd really make a sight in that mirror. Frumele is no fool, Nachman is not a bad-looking buck. (*Views himself in another mirror.*) Nachman, bravo! You look swell, just like a bridegroom. Now just watch your step; don't do anything crude or gross. This is really big stuff—Reb Aaron Kluger, Aaron the tycoon, bah— Aaron the crook, Aaron the—but where is my Frumele? It's so quiet here. Did they all die on me? What's going on? (*A sound of voices and of someone approaching.*) Who's coming? It's about time. (*Reb Aaron enters.*)

AARON. Ah, Nachman. This is fine. We'll arrange everything just right to suit a good lad like you. You seem angry. What's wrong? You're usually so jolly.

NACHMAN. I'm not angry. Not really. It's just that I get impatient from waiting.

AARON. Don't worry. You won't have to wait much longer. Just wait, Frumele will arrive any moment.

NACHMAN. Frumele isn't here yet? I thought . . . I was told . . .

AARON. Exactly as you were told, that's how it will be. Frumele will be here any minute. My wife, Perele, has gone to fetch her.

NACHMAN. I don't get it. Why do you have to fetch her? I don't understand. What's going on?

AARON. What could be wrong? She's probably delayed. It's no easy job to get away from her father. He watches her every step. But with my Perele, there will be no problem. They'll let her go and she'll be here directly. You've waited so long, so just a little longer. I could understand your anxiety to see her. I know from experience . . .

NACHMAN. Reb Aaron, please tell me . . . how shall I say it . . .

AARON. What is it, Nachman?

NACHMAN. I just want to ask you something . . .

AARON. So ask. Don't be shy with me. Speak up.

NACHMAN. Did Frumele tell you everything?

AARON. Everything—that you are a great lad, that she loves you more than her father, and that she pines after every step of yours. (*Nachman is overjoyed.*)

NACHMAN. She actually said that! Reb Aaron, what do you say to that!

AARON. I say splendid, excellent! What if her father is so wealthy and you are only a poor tailor? As long as you love each other. The people in our town are gross, they're fanatics —they never ask their children whom they love. The parents simply arrange the weddings. Then the poor children are unhappy. But Frumele —ah, such a girl, such a gem— her father would probably make a match for her with some Chassidic fanatic, a student with his old-fashioned traditions and equally fanatical family.

NACHMAN. That's so right, Reb Aaron. But . . . you know . . . I'd like to ask you something . . .

AARON. Go right ahead. Don't be bashful.

NACHMAN. I know you are so right in what you say. But why are you so interested in us? Why is this meeting in your house?

AARON. I understand why you are puzzled. Why shouldn't I understand? It is simply that I am very fond of Frumele and I feel sorry for her. Why should her life be ruined with the wrong man? She's like my own daughter to me. I went through the same experience with my Perele. Her father was rich, just like Reb Pinchus, and he didn't want me for a son-in-law. You see, I was only a poor clerk. But, you see, I eventually married my Perele. You know why? How? Because some good, kind people helped us. Now you can understand. I like you. After all, you are a decent fellow, and I like what you did to that fanatic Rabbi. (*They both laugh.*) What a terrible thing they did to poor Rochel! And she was just out of bed from giving birth. They're murderers. You served them right. That Rabbi had a lesson coming to him. They call him a saint, but the truth is he's no better than other charlatans who pose as holy men. They're no good and they're not pious Jews. They scrounge out the last groshen from the poor, ignorant masses. (*Aaron laughs again.*) Serves him right. He was so frightened, he forgot to make the miracle they expected from him. Well, let me go see if Perele and Frumele have come in yet. I can see that Frumele is no fool. You're handsome and bright, and I heard you have golden fingers in your work. (*Aaron exits.*)

NACHMAN. Whew! That was some speech. He sure can talk—a seven-year curse on him. Just let me get my Frumele—I think her father will have a stroke. (*He listens intently.*) I think they're coming. I'll hide. (*He hides. Perele enters. Nachman does not see her face and mistakes her for Frumele. He comes behind her and puts his hand over her eyes, and his other arm around her.*)

PERELE. Oh . . . who is it? (*Nachman is confused, releases her.*)

NACHMAN. Oh . . . oh . . . who are y . . y . .

PERELE. It's you, Nachman. You frightened me to death.

NACHMAN. Excuse me, please. I didn't know. I thought . . .

PERELE. . . . that I was Frumele? So you see, I am not Frumele. She will be here right away. I rushed in to tell you. Don't be so upset. You made a mistake, that's all. No harm done. Just look at him, how embarrassed he is. (*Perele laughs.*) My goodness, but you are a handsome young man, a gem! (*Nachman is more at ease. He laughs with her.*)

NACHMAN. Wait till I tell Frumele. She'll have a good laugh.

PERELE. Do you regret it? Am I so bad looking?

NACHMAN. Oh no! . . .

PERELE. Oh no? But your Frumele is prettier? Well, she'll be here right away. I'll go to hurry her. Just be sure you don't frighten her like you did me. You mustn't grab so quickly. (*Perele exits.*)

NACHMAN. I think I like her better than her husband. But I wish I were already out of here. (*Views himself in mirror.*) Ah Nachman. God help you. You will become a richer man than Reb Aaron and probably a bigger thief. How long will you suffer, Nachman? If I thought you will turn out that way, I'll choke you to death while you're young. (*He hears someone at the door.*) Oh-h-h-h . . . (*Frumele enters. Nachman sees her in the mirror. He rushes to her, embraces her, and dances her around the room.*) Frumele, Frumele—I'll never let you go—no, never.

FRUMELE. Oh, Nachman . . .

NACHMAN. (*Kissing her.*) No, don't say a word. A maiden should be quiet, a maiden should not be late. (*Releases her and gazes fondly at her.*) Frumele, is this all really true? Is it real?

Frumele, say something.

FRUMELE. First you tell me I should be quiet, then you tell me to speak. You don't know your own mind. (*Holds his hands.*) Yes, Nachman, it's true. Thanks to Reb Aaron. He arranged it. He says it's a tricky world and you get what you want only through trickery. He says you must be smart and grab your chance.

NACHMAN. I always said he was a crook, the devil take him. I can't look at that sneak. Frumele, let's leave this place now. (*He embraces her. Frumele eagerly responds.*)

FRUMELE. Yes, oh yes . . .

NACHMAN. Just a minute. Wait a moment. Why are you so anxious? What's the hurry, Frumele? (*Reb Aaron enters. He smiles as he observes the lovers. Perele enters. Nachman and Frumele become aware of the others; they release each other.*)

NACHMAN. Oh . . .

FRUMELE. Oh . . . (*Nachman and Frumele are confused. Reb Aaron jests with them.*)

AARON. Just wait, Frumele, I'll tell your father.

PERELE. Look how the brave young man is blushing.

AARON. Well, enough of that for the present.

PERELE. Save some affection for later.

AARON. Sit down, my children. I expect a few neighbors to be here soon to be the witnesses. Meanwhile, let's have a snack, some refreshments. (*They seat themselves at the table as two servants bring in drinks and food* [cakes]. *Aaron pours drinks and hands them around.*) L'chaim, Nachman. L'chaim, Frumele. (*As they drink, Aaron addresses one of the servants.*) Go tell the neighbors we're ready. (*As the servant exits, Chaim Platt rushes in; while kissing the mezuzah, he drops his hat; then he drops his walking stick. He is constantly unable to manage his coat, hat, and stick all at the same time.*)

CHAIM. Good evening. I'm in such a hurry, I'm not exaggerating, I haven't any time. But when Reb Aaron sends for me, oh well, it's no small matter when Reb Aaron sends, I'm not exaggerating—after all, Reb Aaron . . . !

AARON. Sit down, Reb Chaim. We'll need you as a witness. (*Chaim eyes the refreshments.*) Here, make a L'chaim with us. (*Chaim helps himself.*)

CHAIM. I see. I can just imagine. What? You think I forgot? It's no exaggeration, with all I have to do . . . Well, L'chaim. (*Chaim drinks and follows it with some cake. Looks at Nachman.*) And who is this young man, long should he live? (*As Chaim sits open-mouthed gazing at Nachman, Gavriel Shed enters.*)

GAVRIEL. The devil take me. When Reb Aaron sends for me—even though I'm not an actual member of the Council, I'm not just an anybody. They think I'm going to kidnap children to be recruits . . .

AARON. Sit down, Reb Gavriel. Have some brandy.

GAVRIEL. The devil take me—who ever heard of not accepting brandy when it's offered! L'chaim, Reb Aaron, L'chaim. (*Gavriel sees Nachman. He is stunned. Aaron covers up.*)

AARON. Drink, drink up, Reb Gavriel.

GAVRIEL. The devil take me, it's you, Nachman?

AARON. Have another drink, Reb Gavriel. And don't forget some food with it. You will be one of the witnesses. (*To Nachman.*) I have a marriage license all ready so that everything will be in order exactly according to our Jewish laws. You understand. You will sign first, then they will sign as witnesses. Here, Reb Chaim will read the license. What do you say, Nachman? Good, no?

CHAIM. Huh, the license? Really, I must leave—it's no exaggeration. I must hurry, I've got to go.

AARON. Wait, Reb Chaim. You're not finished. Wait! (*Chaim tries to leave.*)

CHAIM. Yes, I understand. But I have to leave, it's no exaggeration.

NACHMAN. What's there to read? A li-

cense is a license. We just have to see where to sign. (*Aaron places document in front of Nachman and hands Nachman a pen. Nachman whispers to Frumele while Aaron shows him where to sign.*)

AARON. Maybe you're right, Nachman. All licenses are the same. You don't have to read it. (*Nachman signs.*) Now, neighbors, look closely and remember. Nachman signed here. You are witnesses, so please sign here. You first, Reb Chaim.

CHAIM. When I was a bridegroom, I wrote the whole story on a pin cushion. It's no exaggeration. (*Chaim signs.*)

AARON. And now you, Reb Gavriel.

GAVRIEL. The devil take me. Who can write? My Rabbi couldn't write either. And what use is it to know how to write? Rabbi Motele says that he who knows how to write is on an evil path. (*Aaron humors him.*)

AARON. Reb Mottele? Is that right? Come now, put your finger to it. Like this, put your finger in the ink and make your mark here. Our poor Jews are so foolish that they can be told all kinds of lies and fantasies and they swallow it . . . Right here, Reb Gavriel. (*Aaron guides Gavriel's finger.*) He who knows nothing thinks the Rabbi knows everything. But this Rabbi is more ignorant than the foolish mob. The pious fanatics prattle like parrots, and the poor fools believe and repeat the same nonsense. . . . Reb Gavriel, finished? Good. (*Aaron takes the document aside as though to study it. He then beckons Gavriel to him. They have a whispered conversation, the last part of which is:*) . . . Do you understand?

GAVRIEL. Why shouldn't I understand? Finished is finished.

AARON. (*Quietly.*) But hurry. (*Then loudly.*) You can go now, Reb Gavriel. Have another drink of brandy. (*Gavriel drinks, then runs out.*)

CHAIM. You reminded me. I'm late, it's no exaggeration. Good night.

AARON. Wait, Reb Chaim. What's your

hurry all the time? We're not through yet. Nachman, I hear you have a beautiful ring. Is that right, Nachman? (*Nachman produces the ring. Nachman speaks quietly and tenderly to Frumele.*)

NACHMAN. Frumele, give me your hand.

AARON. Let's see it. (*Aaron takes the ring.*) It is really a fine ring. Let's all have a toast. And you, Reb Chaim, you're something of a minstrel and entertain wonderfully at joyful occasions. How about a few choruses? Give us a song. (*Aaron hands Chaim a few coins.*) Come, spill it out, just like you do at weddings.

CHAIM. (*Chants.*)

Listen, my friends, to my rhymes.
Specially composed for such times.
I sing this song for a bride and groom.
Pretty in her youthful bloom,
The bride is chaste and full of charm.
But he's so big, she feels alarm:
Will he be gentle, will he be kind?
Too late now, they're intertwined.
So clap your hands and let's all dance
While the lovebirds coo in their trance.

NACHMAN. Good, real good. It's getting late. What do you say, Reb Aaron. (*Nachman takes the ring from Aaron, approaches Frumele and takes her hand. Nachman says the Hebrew Prayer of the Ceremony of Giving the Marriage Ring.*) Harai Att, Battabas Zu, K'das Moishe b'Isroel. (*The front door bursts open. The Manager of the Count's estate bursts in, accompanied by Shloime, Velvel, Gavriel, others, and two cossacks.*)

MANAGER. Where is he? (*Gavriel approaches and points at Nachman.*)

GAVRIEL. Here he is.

MANAGER. Are you Nachman der Grosse?

NACHMAN. Yes. That's me.

MANAGER. (*Signaling to the cossacks.*) Take him. (*Cossacks seize Nachman.*)

NACHMAN. What's this all about? Take me where?

MANAGER. What are you trying to do? Are you joking? They'll take you to the government barracks, to the Czar's army. Where do you think we send a recruit? To the army of course.

NACHMAN. Me? A recruit? Oh no. You've made a mistake, you peasant!

MANAGER. (*Addresses the Council Members.*) Is he the recruit the Council selected?

SHLOIME. Yes. One recruit is due from our town. The Council . . .

VELVEL. For example, how does the saying go—one, but a good one.

PERELE. Aaron, what's going on here? Tell them . . .

AARON. Perele, please go to your room. You don't belong here in this business.

PERELE. Aaron . . .

AARON. (*Angry.*) Go, Perele. I'm asking you to do as I say. (*Perele, frightened, runs out.*)

NACHMAN. They're liars. Pshyakref—dog's blood. I'm an only child. You are not allowed to take an only child. You'll all rot in jail; I'm an only child.

MANAGER. Don't get so excited, you. Even though you're an only child, if you volunteer, you're taken and you go. If you volunteer, you're the recruit for the Council, for this town's Jewish community.

NACHMAN. So that's what the Council wants here? I should volunteer? Well, I don't want to volunteer. Forget it.

MANAGER. (*Producing the paper Nachman has signed. Reads.*) Listen, "I, Nachman der Grosse, of my own free will, wish to be the recruit for the levy on our Jewish Council of the town of Nibyvalle." Signed, Nachman der Grosse, witnessed by Chaim Platt, a finger-mark witness by Gavriel Shed.

NACHMAN. What! When! Tonight? Listen you, they fooled you. It's false. They swindled me. Now I get it, now I see. Frumele, they cheated us . . . Frumele . . . Frumele! (*Frumele swoons away.*) Ha, it's he . . . the monster . . . you dog's blood . . . (*Nachman hurls himself at Aaron.*)

MANAGER. (*To cossacks*) Take him away. (*Cossacks seize Nachman. Chains are put on Nachman's hands. The cossacks rush him to the door. Frumele comes to; she starts running after Nachman.*)

FRUMELE. Wait, please, please. Oh Nachman . . . (*Aaron blocks her path as the struggling Nachman is dragged out.*)

AARON. Frumele . . . you mustn't. God will help you. Calm yourself. (*Frumele struggles to get away from Reb Aaron's grasp.*)

FRUMELE. A father doesn't kill his child. . . . So, Frumele should be calm, Frumele should be quiet. (*Frumele beats at him. Aaron tears himself away from her. Enter more townspeople. Nachman's blind mother enters. She screams at all and holds her arms aloft as though to destroy them.*)

NACHMAN'S MOTHER. My son! Where is my Nachman! Give me back my son, my shining star. . . . My only child. Where is he, my Nachman? Where is Reb Aaron, you false snake, where are you, you angel of death! I'll tear you to pieces . . . Where is his bride . . . (*Frumele comes to her.*) He was the brightest of sons . . . I would have been proud . . . (*The agonized Frumele falls to her knees and puts her arms around the blind mother.*) Give me back my son . . . (*The scene turns into a tableau.* [Can be cinematically projected.] *From one side of the stage, soldiers cross; they are in chains and are being whipped on by cossacks. From the other side of the stage come groups of limping crippled soldiers.*)

THE END

HAMAN'S DOWNFALL

by

Chaim Sloves

(1905-   )

Son of a leather worker, Chaim Sloves was born in Bialystok, Poland, in 1905. Growing up in the city, he never actually experienced the life of the shtetl except vicariously, for "while the other boys of my acquaintance were studying a chapter of the Bible or a page of the Gemara, we were fervently studying a chapter of Mendele, or Sholem Aleichem, and a page of Peretz."* Young Chaim attended a Russian school for a short time and then entered a Yiddish school (as distinguished from the customary religious Hebrew heder and yeshiva), one of the earliest such schools in Europe.

His earliest ambition was to be an actor and eventually an opera singer. With a passionate interest in the theatre, he began writing dramatizations from Yiddish literature when he was in his teens. At the age of 21, Sloves moved to Paris, where he attended the Lyceum and the university. Developing a proficiency in French, he started a career in that language of writing plays and novels, some of which were gratifyingly well received by eminent critics. As he records it,

> By this time it was 1936, and the songs of the spilling of Jewish blood were starting to come from across the Rhine. One fine morning I dried the ink from my French pen and with my whole heart and body and soul I threw myself into Yiddish cultural activity. Then it was 1939 and The War.
>
> After the panic of the first war days . . . Paris was suddenly enveloped in an eerie stillness. In the extinguished "City of Lights," waiting for my mobilization list, at blacked-out windows and a turned-down table lamp, I began to write. Naturally, a play. This time, in Yiddish. The name of the play—"Haman's Downfall."
>
> An evil Haman, the most evil of all times, undertook to destroy a defenseless people. His power was tremendous, he rolled from one victory to another. But in that people glowed an optimistic faith which made it unconquerable. This historic folk optimism forced itself upon the writer precisely in the hour of greatest danger.

195

In quite a natural way, the Haman theme led to the *purim-shpil* form, to this oldest and most original Jewish theatre form, which had been luring me for a long time.*

Chaim Sloves continues his distinguished career as an author and journalist in Paris, where he lives with his wife near the Place de la Bastille. Among his critically acclaimed works are the Yiddish plays *Avengers, The Jonahs and the Whale, Baruch of Amsterdam, The War of God, We Were Ten Brothers,* and his play in this collection, *Haman's Downfall.*

In addition to translating *Haman's Downfall,* Max Rosenfeld devoted himself to translating and adapting important prose and poetry from the Yiddish. Among his successful works are *Pushcarts and Dreamers* (Thomas Yoseloff, 1969), a volume of short stories from the Yiddish on American themes; and *The Prophets: Their Times and Their Social Ideas,* by Shmuel Eisenstadt (YKUF, 1971).

---

* Chaim Sloves, *In and Around* (in Yiddish), (New York: Yiddisher Kultur Farband, 1970), pp. 306–7.

HAMAN'S DOWNFALL

A Purim-shpil
in Four Acts

by

Chaim Sloves

Translated from the Yiddish
by Max Rosenfeld
Edited by David S. Lifson

The musical score for *Haman's Downfall* is available from the composer.
Maurice Rauch, 115 East 9 St., N. Y. C. 10003, or from the
Jewish Music Alliance, 1 Union Square West, N. Y. C. 10003.

CAST OF CHARACTERS

HERALD
KING AHASUERUS
MEMUCAN)
MEZUMEN) King's Advisors
KAPARTI)
MORDECAI
HAMAN
QUEEN VASHTI
QUEEN ESTHER
SOOTHSAYER
PARSHANDATA, KING'S OFFICER
TERESH)
BOGATIN) Conspirators
KING'S ANNOUNCER
FIELD MARSHAL MARSANA
GENERAL PARSANA
KING'S HORSE
GUARDS AND ATTENDANTS
LADIES, MAIDENS, COURTIERS AND NOBLES

PROLOGUE

HERALD.
A good Good-evening to you all, dear folks!
God bless you if you chortle at our jokes.
Good evening, Princes, Nobles, Cavaliers,
Listen to our tale with both your ears.
And you may listen too, O highborn dames,
Especially you, you set my heart in flames!
I love you all so very much (somewhat)
It makes no difference, beautiful or not.
So ladies, gentlemen, please to listen well
It's not a fairy tale I have to tell.
It's true and comical as anything,
And starts out with a Persian king.
But wait—I hear the players in the wings—
It's time for me to pull the curtain-strings!

(*sings.*)

Chidibim chidibim chidibim
Fellow actors, please come in!

Chidibim chidibim chidibim
Purim-shpielers, all come in!

CAST. (*Behind curtain, sings.*) Chidibim chidibim chidibim. (*Curtain rises. All come forward singing, and form a semi-circle.*)
HERALD. Introducing—His majesty the King, the Wise and Illustrious King— Hail Ahasuerus!
AHASUERUS. (*Steps forward, bows, sings.*)

I'm King Ahasuerus, Ahasuerus my name.
My wisdom is my claim to fame!

CAST. His wisdom is his claim to fame!

HERALD.
Introducing—The Scholar, the Teacher, the Seer,
Reb Mordecai the Righteous, son of Ya-eer!

MORDECAI.
I'm Mordecai the Righteous, I scotched the plot—
For which I'll never be forgot!

CAST. For which he'll never be forgot!

HERALD.
Introducing—A brave little lady, Vashti the Ex-queen
Refused to do a dance obscene!

VASHTI.
Vashti's my name, I no longer rule.
Refused to listen to this poor old fool!

CAST. She refused to listen to this poor old fool!

HERALD.
Introducing—The beautiful, the modest, the serene—
Esther the Queen!

ESTHER.
I'm Esther the Beautiful, Esther the Queen.
To be married to a fool is a terrible thing!

CAST. To be married to a fool is a terrible thing!
HAMAN. (*Running forward out of the line.*) What kind of Jewish hanky-panky is this, friend Herald—leaving Prince Haman for last? I won't stand for it! (*Brandishes his sword.*)

HERALD.
Patience, patience, friend Haman. For you I've left the best part, the longest introduction:
Introducing—The Glorious, the Bully, the Bane—
of the Jews; Haman ben Hamdata, cursed be his name!

HAMAN.
I'm Haman the Agagi, fearless knight,
My sword put the world in a terrible fright!
Mordecai the Righteous is not so brave,
Soon he'll be my obedient slave!

CAST. First he'll dance around your grave!

HERALD.
Players, soldiers, generals, pages,
Jews and Persians, knaves and sages,
Wives and maidens, youth and age,
Please, I beg you, leave the stage.
Reb Conductor, I mean you too—
Start up a march and play it through!
All you Purim-shpielers, come join hands
Show the people how you dance!

(*Orchestra plays joyfully, cast joins hands, dances.* CURTAIN.)

ACT 1

HERALD. (*Front of curtain, reading from a scroll.*) ". . . And it came to pass in the days of Ahasuerus, the same Ahasuerus whose kingdom extended from India to Ethiopia over 127 provinces. And the capital of his kingdom was Shushan-Habira . . ."

And now, my fine ladies and gentlemen I'll take you to Shushan as Shushan was then!

Chidibim chidibim chidibim
Let Shushan-Habira come in!

(*Curtain rises. A space in front of Ahasuerus's palace. In the background, a tower and a sentry booth. It is a dark night. From behind the curtain are heard occasional drunken shouts and laughter. The space is bare. From the sentry booth comes a noisy snoring.*) (*Enter Mordecai in a rush of words, chanting loudly, a little tipsy.*)

MORDECAI.
Where's a Jew hail from, hail from?
Where's a Jew hail from?
From Shushan, from Shushan, from Shushan-Habira!
What do they do in Shushan-Habira?
What do they do in Shushan-Habira?

They drink and get tight
They dance all night
In Shushan, in Shushan-Habira . . .
(*Warbles like a virtuoso cantor testing his voice.*)

PARSHANDATA. (*from the sentry booth.*) What the devil! Who goes there?

MORDECAI.
A man, my friend. A man of worth!
There's no one like him on all the earth!

PARSHANDATA. What're you straining your tonsils like that for in the middle of the night? You think this is a saloon?

MOREDCAI. Pearls of wisdom drop from your mouth, my friend! All of Shushan is now one big saloon! Our King has decreed that everyone must be happy, so the wine has been flowing night and day . . .

PARSHANDATA. Beat it, you old drunk, and let me sleep!

MORDECAI. The ground I walk on belongs to the Almighty first and then to our great King Ahasuerus. Here I stand whether you like it or not. And if you don't like it, I'll lie down. (*Stretches out on ground.*) Neither Haman nor all his dogs will chase me away from this spot tonight!

PARSHANDATA. What! What's that you're jabbering!

MORDECAI. Whoever has ears can hear. Haman and his dogs, I say again— his dogs; you hear me, his dogs!

PARSHANDATA. Hold on a minute! I'm putting on my boots. Don't make a break for it!

MORDECAI. Me? Make a break for it? Make a break for what? Don't kid me, friend! What am I, a convict,—or a general? Why should I run?

PARSHANDATA. We'll soon see. (*Comes out of booth, carrying a lantern.*) Hey now, where the devil are you?

MORDECAI. (*Still lying on ground.*) In Shushan-Habira—

PARSHANDATA. What's your name?

MORDECAI. What's your game?

PARSHANDATA. Where were you born?

MORDECAI. In my mother's bed—ha!

PARSHANDATA. Oho! You're afraid to tell me what they call you!

MORDECAI. When they need me, they call me! Go back to sleep, old buddy!

PARSHANDATA. Don't buddy me! What's your name, you damn Jew! Show me your fake identity papers!

MORDECAI. Sha, sha, listen to him bark! What a hullaballoo! (*Rises slowly, yawns, stretches, scratches himself. Parshandata yawns too, loudly.*) When they call me up to read the Toyreh they announce: Ya-moyd! Reb Mordcha b'reb Ya-eer!

PARSHANDATA. Mordecai ben Ya-eer?

MORDECAI. Ben Ya-eer, ben Shammai, ben Kish . . .

PARSHANDATA. A man of Benjamin?

MORDECAI. You got it right, buddy.

PARSHANDATA. From Jerusalem?

MORDECAI. Where else? From the moon?

PARSHANDATA. (*Runs up, shines lantern on Mordecai's face.*) Mordcha the Tsaddik, as I'm a Jew!

MORDECAI. (*Lifts lantern to Parshandata's face.*) Parshandata, you old son-of-a- —

PARSHANDATA. Well, I'll be—! Let me shake your hand! Sholem Aleichem! Mordcha the Tsaddik! Gimme five! (*Squeezes Mordecai's hand.*)

MORDECAI. Ai! Well, I'll be! I see you still have the paws of a bear! Let's see your mug! Ha! the same—

PARSHANDATA. You too! Haven't changed a hair! What brings you to Shushan-Habira?

MORDECAI. Ai, brother, it's a long story. (*Grows solemn, sighs.*) Just got out of Jerusalem by the skin of my teeth.

PARSHANDATA. Eh? How come?

MORDECAI. Haman's dogs, God damn them all to hell! I escaped by a miracle.

PARSHANDATA. Is that so?

MORDECAI. Me and my niece. Nobody else left. Nobody. (*Sighs.*) I brought her here—my niece. Maybe the Lord will take pity on her. You ought to see her—so pretty, so clever, such a capable girl. Only one thing wrong with her—she's Jewish.

PARSHANDATA. What are you living on?

MORDECAI. Better you didn't ask. Haman's decrees have ruined me. All I have left is the shirt on my back. So, in my old age I had to turn to matchmaking. What else can I do?

PARSHANDATA. (*Scratches his head.*) I don't remember reading in the Megilah that Mordecai the Righteous was a matchmaker.

MORDECAI. So what? There's a lot of things going on that our sages never even dreamed of. (*Livelier.*) Understand me now, Parshandata. Now that I'm a matchmaker, Haman can go to the devil! Let him try to get married! Just let him! And by the way, a shadchan sees and hears a lot, and can put in a good word—or a bad one—in the right places. Who knows? God willing, Mordecai ben Ya-eer may match Haman up with a witch.

PARSHANDATA. Amen! But do you make a living?

MORDECAI. Such a living only Haman should make!
(*Sings.*)

A little from the groom, a little from the bride.
On Sabbath and the holidays a cantor on the side.
The way I earn my bread
A curse on Haman's head
We'd all be better off if he were good and dead!
On Sabbath day no bread or fish
For Mordecai ben Ya-eer ben Kish.
You really can believe me
I haven't got it easy
Scrimping for a piece of bread
A curse on Haman's scurvy head!

(*Shines lantern on Parshandata's sleeve.*) Well, Parshandata, what's new with you? Looks to me like you've earned yourself a few more stripes.

PARSHANDATA. (*Proudly.*) Officer of the Royal Guards!

MORDECAI. Pu-pu-pu! You don't say! Tell me something, Parshandata, didn't they investigate your Jewish grandmother?

PARSHANDATA. Sh! Quiet! For God's sake, have a heart! The walls have ears around here! (*Looks around furtively.*) That's a damn lie!

MORDECAI. What's a damn lie?

PARSHANDATA. My grandmother, my Jewish grandmother, wasn't even my real grandmother. She was my step-grandmother!

MORDECAI. You don't say!

PARSHANDATA. Sure! My grandfather, olov hasholem, had three wives: One from Persia, one from India, and one from Eretz Yisroel, her name was Zalpha. And when Haman decreed against Jewish grandmothers, we proved with witnesses that Zalpha had been childless.

MORDECAI. And who were the witnesses?

PARSHANDATA. All of Zalpha's children! Including my father. So my grandmother didn't come from Eretz Yisroel but from Persia and we all belong to the race of purest Aryans.

MORDECAI. You don't say!

PARSHANDATA. But just between you and me, things are not so hotsy-totsy around here anyway. (*Lowers his voice.*) They're planning a war. Against the Greeks. I'll tell you a secret. Three weeks ago Haman ordered all the armies of Persia and Media to sharpen up their swords and grease them with goosefat. That's a sure sign. (*Sighs, moves closer to Mordecai.*) I hear that our battle-ships are closing in on the Greek coasts. Haman does whatever he pleases and doesn't bother to get anybody's permission.

MORDECAI. And what about the Royal Signet Ring?

PARSHANDATA. Who gives a damn about that? When he has eveything lined up, Haman prepares a big feast—listen, there's one going on now—and he loads the King up with booze and then he sticks the paper under the King's nose and makes the King a pretty speech and that's the end of it. (*spits.*) Tfu! My own throat is dry just thinking about it! Be a good fellow, Mordecai, stand guard for me a few minutes while I go wet my whistle.

MORDECAI. A new recruit in the Royal Guards!

PARSHANDATA. What's the difference? There's nobody to guard anyway. They're all dead drunk, the pigs! Do me a favor, Mordecai. Here, take my sword.

MORDECAI. I hope nobody ever finds out, for *your* sake.

PARSHANDATA. Forget it. I'll be back before you get the sword buckled on. And I won't come back empty-handed . . . (*Exit.*)

MORDECAI. (*Alone.*) Never mind your favors. (*Sighs.*) I shouldn't have taken that last drink. These days, you have to keep your wits about you. Lucky for me it was him I stumbled on. (*Goes into booth, yawns, hums. For a moment all is quiet. No action on stage. Then enter Teresh and Bogatin.*)

BOGATIN. Teresh!

TERESH. What's the matter?

BOGATIN. I think there's somebody else here—over there, in the corner—(*Points to dark corner.*)

TERESH. Where?

BOGATIN. There—look—

TERESH. (*Goes to look; finds no one.*) You're drunk, Bogatin! You're seeing things!

BOGATIN. I haven't had a drop all day, so help me!

TERESH. Then listen—and pay attention!

BOGATIN. No. Wait a minute. Who's the officer of the guard tonight?

TERESH. Parshandata. He's sleeping like an ox.

BOGATIN. Better take a look and make sure.

TERESH. (*Goes to booth.*) Parshandata! (*Sound of snoring from booth.*)

TERESH. He's asleep, can't you hear?

BOGATIN. Parshandata! Come out and have a drink with us! Come on out, we have a bottle here!

TERESH. He's asleep, I tell you.

BOGATIN. Yeah, I guess he really is, if he won't come out for a free drink.

TERESH. Well, put the bottle away! What

are you playing with it for?

BOGATIN. I'm not playing with it, Teresh. My hands are shaking.

TERESH. Be a man, Bogatin!

BOGATIN. Easy to say, but my teeth are chattering . . .

TERESH. Get hold of yourself, man, and listen. Tomorrow night at supper, we'll be on guard at the King's dining-room. When the Wine Steward brings you the wine for his Majesty, you take this stuff (*takes vial out of his pocket*) —and pour it into the wine-bottle. Then you hand me the bottle and I take it in to the King. Then you throw this vial into the lake below the window? Understand?

BOGATIN. I hear you.

TERESH. You hear me, but do you understand me? Get rid of that vial immediately! We don't want it found! If they trace the poison it's all up with us!

(*A noise in the booth, as though someone had knocked something over.*)

BOGATIN. (*Frightened.*) My God, Teresh, we're caught already!

TERESH. Take it easy, you yellow-livered chicken! (*Moves cautiously to the booth.*) Hey, Parshandata! (*Sound of snoring from booth.*) Hey, Parshandata! (*To Teresh.*) He must have turned over on the other side and knocked something over— Hey! Where the hell are you going?

BOGATIN. They won't catch me here!

TERESH. My God, Bogatin, when will you ever get some guts?

BOGATIN. I'm scared, Teresh! (*Runs off stage, Teresh after.*)

MORDECAI. (*Sticks his head out of booth, looks around, slips carefully out of booth.*) God have mercy! Murderers in the King's palace! Snakes in the royal grass! Who could be putting them up to it? Maybe Haman? What a spot for *me* to be in! First thing you'd better do, Mordecai ben Ya-eer, is get your carcass out of here! If these gangsters ever get wind that you were here, your life isn't worth a plugged drachma!

(*Runs across stage, then stops thoughtfully.*) Now wait a minute, Mordcha, wait one minute! It's beginning to dawn on me that this whole business is a sign from heaven. (*Exit. Haman and Soothsayer enter from other side.*)

HAMAN. Soothsayer, ask the stars if this is my lucky night.

SOOTHSAYER. I'm asking them, my lord.

HAMAN. Make sure you hear their answer right and tell me exactly what they say.

SOOTHSAYER. Yes, my lord.

HAMAN. Well, what do you see?

SOOTHSAYER. In the Seventh Heaven of the Fifth Constellation, bounded in the triangle of Purnius, I see the Star of Orion. He is beginning to glow.

HAMAN. What does that mean, Soothsayer?

SOOTHSAYER. It can mean many things, my lord. Unlucky love or an upset stomach, a plague of the cattle or triplets for some poor woman, angry winds, wars—

HAMAN. Wars! Yes, there will be a war. The swords of the Medes and the Persians will soon ring over the fields of Greece. Soothsayer, doesn't Orion say that the land of the Greeks is inside our *lebensraum?*

SOOTHSAYER. All the stars of all the heavens say, O Prince, that any place where there's room to live is our *lebensraum.*

HAMAN. Well said, Soothsayer. For that you get a gold drachma. And what else do you see?

SOOTHSAYER. In the 19th Constellation I see the tenth star. It is surrounded by the hectagon of greatness.

HAMAN. And what is the meaning of that?

SOOTHSAYER. Many weddings and a good crop of jackasses, a few lottery winners and a thousand sentimental verses, military victories—

HAMAN. Military victories! Great victories! In what constellation does the 10th star lie, Soothsayer?

SOOTHSAYER. In the constellation of the Lion, my lord. And its symbol is a leopard killing a sheep. The leopard —that is you. The sheep—that is the land of the Greeks, which you will destroy.

HAMAN. No, I will not destroy it. I will make it part of the great empire of the Persians. Soothsayer, doesn't the 10th star say that the Greeks are only waiting for me to bring them glory?

SOOTHSAYER. All the stars of all the heavens, Prince Haman, say that wherever there is a people in this world, it only yearns to bow to your mighty will, just as every maiden waits and yearns for her lover.

HAMAN. And do the generals of Greece know this?

SOOTHSAYER. Does the earth know that it yearns for the dew of the morning or the rain of the evening? Your mighty will is like the rain from heaven which revives the parched earth.

HAMAN. True, Soothsayer, true. Here's another drachma. Tell me—is tonight a lucky night to dance the war dance against the Greeks? What do the stars say?

SOOTHSAYER. The Polar Star has risen in the constellation of the Arrow. Its symbol is an archer piercing the heart of his enemy. You may stretch out your strong right arm, my lord. All the heavenly bodies are in your favor!

HAMAN. Soothsayer, here are three more ducats. Now go quickly and ask permission for me to speak with the King and his advisors.

SOOTHSAYER. I go, my lord. (*Exit.*)

HAMAN. (*To audience.*) Do you all know Haman, son of Hamdata? No? You don't know him? You will! You will soon know him! The sons of India tremble when they hear my name. The Persians and the Egyptians, the Babylonians and the Assyrians, all bow to me. Unto the edges of the earth, even to far-off Ethiopia, I am revered or I am feared. I swallow countries like beans. I drive away kingdoms like fleas. Haman ben Hamdata! Heaven is with you and the

earth will be yours! (*Exit. Enter Soothsayer.*)

SOOTHSAYER. (*Calling.*) Friend Herald, Friend Herald! (*Herald comes out of wings.*)

HERALD. What's up, Soothsayer?

SOOTHSAYER. I've been looking all over for you.

HERALD. You should have asked the stars.

SOOTHSAYER. Don't make fun of an old man.

HERALD. Don't make fun of the world.

SOOTHSAYER. You don't realize what you're saying, friend Herald. I have a wife and kids to support. Be a good fellow and bring in the Royal Court.

HERALD. The whole Royal Court! Oh well, for your wife and kids I'll do it. Go home and leave it to me. (*Exit Soothsayer.*)

HERALD.
chidibim chidibim chidibim
Let the Royal Court come in!

(*Singing backstage. Ahasuerus is carried in on a golden throne. Accompanying him, his three advisors and a number of lords and ladies. All are drunk. Haman enters and bows ceremoniously to the King.*)

AHASUERUS. Haman, open your mouth like Baalam's ass and tell us what's botherin' you.

HAMAN. If it please the King, request the company to leave.

AHASUERUS. Wine Steward—out! Ladies —raus! All of you—scram! (*All exit except advisors.*) All right, Haman, now speak your piece! You have the floor, but I don't know how you can stand on it, it's spinning like a merry-go-round! (*Laughter.*)

HAMAN. Your Majesty the King—

AHASUERUS. Let's dance around and sing!

MEMUCAN. The elephants are pink!

MEZUMEN. Let's have another drink!

HAMAN. Your Majesty, I think—

AHASUERUS. Think thunk, I think you're drunk!

KAPARTI. Yeah. Go to bed.

MEZUMEN. Go soak your head!

MEMUCAN. Your brains are dead!

HAMAN. Your Majesty the King—

AHASUERUS. Let's dance around a ring!

KAPARTI. Yeah. Whiskey's better than wine!

MEMUCAN. But both of them are fine!

HAMAN. (*Screaming.*) Your Majesty! Persia is in danger! We're being attacked.

ALL. (*Sobering.*) Attacked? Who? Who's attacking us?

HAMAN. The Jews and the Greeks!

ALL. Whom are they attacking?

HAMAN. Us—the flower of the Aryans!

ADVISORS. Aryans sharyans!

HAMAN. The world belongs to us, nation of glorious heroes, nation of victors! The Jews tried to encircle us with hostile countries, but we foiled them! 127 provinces are ours! Our fleets are in the Black Sea, the Green Sea, and the Hellespont!

ADVISORS. The hell you say!

HAMAN. But to the north of your kingdom, my liege, is the Great Sea. And the Great Sea we must have! Mare Nostrum! So we go to Greece!

AHASUERUS. Eh? Are the Greeks Jews too?

HAMAN. No, your Majesty, they are kosher Aryans, but they have let themselves be deceived by the Jews and are a willing tool in their hands. But Greece is only the beginning. North of the Great Sea are other lands, rich in silver and gold, grain and cattle, and a thousand fruits. All will be yours, Great King! All will be yours—the world we know now, plus the islands that Columbus will one day discover. We will rule the world and the world will be our slaves! (*Bows servilely.*) If it please your majesty, put your seal to this document—

AHASUERUS. Eh? What does it say, anyway?

HAMAN. It's an order from the all-powerful King Ahasuerus to his glorious soldiers to go and occupy the land of the Greeks.

AHASUERUS. Eh? What? (*Suddenly understands.*) War?

MEMUCAN. (*Quite sober.*) War? Again? We just finished one!

HAMAN. My lord, you know how Prince Haman wages war. The Greeks are waiting for us with the keys to the city. They are only waiting for your Majesty to sign the decree.

ADVISORS. (*Quietly.*) No, your Majesty . . .

HAMAN. Put your ring to the paper, King Ahasuerus!

ADVISORS. No—with a capital N!

AHASUERUS. Eh? Maybe we ought to have a conference?

ADVISORS. Certainly, certainly, a conference! Splendid idea!

AHASUERUS. Eh—the Queen, bless her, doesn't like wars. Maybe we ought to ask her opinion?

MEMUCAN. (*Rushes to second the idea, speaks quickly.*) Yes, yes, a custom, your Majesty, an old Persian custom —to take counsel with the Queen before declaring war—

MEZUMEN. Yes, let everyone hear the opinion of the Queen!

HAMAN. Very well, if it please the King. But if you wish our people to listen to their dearly-beloved Queen, you must first save her honor.

AHASUERUS. Her what?

HAMAN. Her honor. The heart of this faithful servant is being broken by the slanderous lies that enemies of the throne are spreading about Queen Vashti. They say our Queen not only has a horn on her head but that she is pigeon-toed too—

AHASUERUS. Pigeon-toed?

HAMAN. And that's not all! They say that her royal body is covered with canary feathers—

AHASUERUS. (*Beside himself.*) Lies! All lies!

HAMAN. Your Majesty, I beg you in the name of our Empire—summon your queen, let her appear in the same clothes she was born in. Let the whole world see that Queen Vashti is still the most beautiful woman in the kingdom!

ADVISORS. But—but—

HAMAN. Button your lip! Do what the

king says! Isn't it so, my liege, that you wish the Queen to appear before you to disprove all those lies?

AHASUERUS. Eh—yes, let her come here —

HAMAN. Obey the king's command! Kaparti, go summon the Queen! Mezumen, bring in the guests! (*Exit Kaparti and Mezumen. Guests, musicians enter.*)

MEMUCAN. And suppose the Queen refuses to come here?

HAMAN. She must! A queen who disobeys our mighty sovereign is no queen! (*Enter Herald.*)

HERALD. Is this really your wish, friend Ahasuerus—what these lamebrains have just told me?

AHASUERUS. Really, friend Herald, it is.

HERALD. Okay, it's your funeral. Haman's leading you up the creek!

AHASUERUS. Eh—no—it's really my own wish—

HERALD. Well—don't say I didn't warn you—

chidibim chidibim chidibim
Let Queen Vashti come in!

(*Music. Enter Vashti and her ladies-in-waiting.*)

VASHTI. My dearly beloved husband, king and sovereign, be greeted eternally and forever . . . (*Bows.*)

AHASUERUS. Welcome to the court, Vashti my dear!

VASHTI. Beloved husband and ruler! I come to make complaint against this churlish knave, this stupid lout, your advisor Kaparti. How dare he propose such an obscene joke to me, your loyal and devoted wife, Queen of the Medes and Persians and 127 provinces?

KAPARTI. My lord, I only carried out your wish.

AHASUERUS. Eh—Vashti, my dear, he only carried out my wish—

VASHTI. No, oh no, honored sir! Mine ears have surely failed me. Wherefore wouldst thou subject me to such shame and dishonor? Why must I expose myself to this assemblage of —drunken bums? In God's name, I am a decent woman!

AHASUERUS. Eh—we know that, Vashti, but it won't hurt you—

VASHTI. Merciful God, look down upon me! Protect my honor! Almighty King, beloved husband, I beseech thee on bended knee—

AHASUERUS. Eh—that's enough—take off your clothes!

VASHTI. Oh my God! To this have we been brought! A queen—and no more than a slave-girl, a strip-teaser! Let this be a lesson to you, all ye women of the kingdom!
(*Sings.*)

O wives and maidens, all my friends
This is how my story ends.
My soul is torn, my heart is broken
Since this nasty king has spoken.
Now he orders me to pose
Indecently without my clothes!
O Friends, before it is too late
Save me from this bitter fate!
Help me, tell me what to do—
I think the king has gone cu-ckoo!

(*All the ladies weep, even some of the men.*)

AHASUERUS. (*Blowing his nose.*) Oh, all right, all right, Vashti, that's enough! You know I'm not cuckoo. A little silly, maybe, but not cuckoo. What can I do? I have no other choice. All right, take off only your shoes and stockings; that will be sufficient.

VASHTI. Thank God in heaven! (*Starts to take off her shoes.*)

AHASUERUS. Eh—Vashti, my dear, somebody's been spreading rumors that besides your horn—

VASHTI. (*Her manner of speech changes suddenly.*) My what!

AHASUERUS. I didn't mean anything—

VASHTI. You dare talk about a horn!

AHASUERUS. Eh—God forbid—not me, Vashti—

VASHTI. My horn! And how many horns are *you* wearing, and don't even know who hung them on you! (*Laughter.*)

AHASUERUS. Eh—Vashti, my pet—

VASHTI. Sits there loaded to the gills like a pig and babbles like a nut, that old rumpot! So Queen Vashti has a horn, has she! How do you like that!

AHASUERUS. Vashti, let me get a word in edgewise. Not a horn, but—pigeon toes—

VASHTI. Pigeon toes! May all the bad dreams I dreamed last night and the night before come down upon your empty head, you old lummox! God in heaven! Where did I ever find such a stupid jerk!

AHASUERUS. That's what they're saying, Vashti—pigeon toes and feathers—

VASHTI. Feathers too! You dirty old whiskey-guzzling excuse for a king! Wait till I get you home! I'll give you feathers you'll remember in your grave!

AHASUERUS. Eh—Vashti, you're forgetting who I am—

VASHTI. How can I ever forget who you are? You're a blockhead, that's who you are! A dumb cluck, that's what you are! A shlemiel, that's what you are!

AHASUERUS. I command it—it's a royal order—

VASHTI. Royal order my behind! You dare give me orders? (*Laughs hysterically*.) Look at him—that genius of mine! Have you forgotten who *you* were? Have you forgotten what you were in my grandfather Nebuchadnezzar's house, may he rest in peace? A stable boy, that's what you were! You cleaned the horses in my grandfather's stables, that's what you did, you stupid oaf!

AHASUERUS. That's not true, Vashti—

VASHTI. Don't call *me* a liar, you old simpleton! If it weren't for me, you'd have been as much a king as I'm a rebbetsin! You wouldn't be sitting up there on that throne—you'd have been six feet under, where you'll yet be one of these days, God willing and amen! You better go sleep off your package, you old drunk, and then I'll really give you what-for! My God, what an awful mess! (*Stamps out in a huff, her attendants behind her.*)

HAMAN. Your Majesty, Vashti has disobeyed the king—

AHASUERUS. Eh—yes, disobeyed—

HAMAN. She has put your royal authority to shame—

AHASUERUS. Oy vey!

MEMUCAN. Dear me! Now we'll really never hear the end of it from our wives—

MEZUMEN. They'll make life miserable for all of us!

HAMAN. We can't permit it! Your majesty must decree that Queen Vashti, for her crime, should have her head chopped off!

ADVISORS. Feh! Feh!

MEMUCAN. Divorce her—

MEZUMEN. Correct. A divorce is the best thing—

KAPARTI. Check and double-check!

AHASUERUS. Eh—a divorce, you say? Yes. I so order.

MEMUCAN. (*Writing*.) Okay, your Majesty, all written out. Put your seal to it.

AHASUERUS. Poor Queen Vashti!

HAMAN. No more queen, your Majesty, no more queen. And now, if it please the king, put your seal to this order for the Greek War.

MEMUCAN. Not so fast, Prince Haman. We must observe the traditions.

HAMAN. (*Menacingly*.) Again with your traditions!

MEMUCAN. So long as the King is divorced, without a wife, he is not permitted to proclaim a war—

HAMAN. Aha! So that's why you advised the King to divorce—

MEMUCAN. And why did you advise him to chop her head off?

HAMAN. You think Vashti's horn is going to keep us out of Greece?

MEMUCAN. Ten plagues on you and your Greece together! The chancellor of the Medes and Persians must observe the laws, customs, and traditions of our land!

HAMAN. Is there a law, custom, or tradition that permits a chancellor to oppose the king's advisor?

MEMUCAN. No—no such law.

HAMAN. Is there maybe a law that prevents a king from getting married right after he's been divorced?

MEMUCAN. No, no such law.

HAMAN. If so, Lord Advisor, take your pen and write: "Be it known: To all the King's satraps, all the King's princes throughout the kingdom—

MEMUCAN. Take it easy, Agagi, I'm not a stenographer—

HAMAN. "Queen Vashti has been deposed and sent back to her village to feed the pigs—"

MEMUCAN. P-i-g-s—as in Haman the Agagi—

HAMAN. (*Incensed.*) Cut it out, Memucan! (*Continues.*) "A replacement is being sought for ex-Queen Vashti. Must be young, pretty, of Aryan blood on both sides, and a virgin—"

MEMUCAN. Is it necessary to put that in? What else would you get for a king?

AHASUERUS. Well, really, gentlemen— it isn't necessary—it might take too long—

HAMAN. All right. Make 127 copies and send them out at once! Memucan, what's taking you so long? Stop stalling!

MEMUCAN. Hold your horses! I must follow the traditional form and it must be in five copies. Five times 127 is—

HAMAN. Cut it out! Now, your Majesty, put your seal to it. Royal Announcer —read the King's decree to the people.

ANNOUNCER. (*Roll of drums.*) Official decree of the all-powerful Ahasuerus, praise his name, Emperor of the Medes and Persians. Whereas the King has found it necessary to divorce his unworthy Queen Vashti and send her back to feeding the pigs; and whereas however, such a sacred personage as the good and pious Ahasuerus may not be without a wife; therefore be it decreed, by royal order and command, that every young maiden of Aryan blood, beautiful of face and form, shall at once and forthwith be brought to the Royal Palace in Shushan-Habira, or shall come willingly of her own accord, and that the maiden who finds favor in the eyes of the King shall become Queen of Media and Persia and the 127 provinces. It has been ordered. (*Long roll of drums.*)

HERALD. Your Majesty, the famous and renowned matchmaker Mordecai ben Ya-eer the Shadchen has come to Shushan with a proposition.

AHASUERUS. What—already? Let him come in. (*Enter Mordecai, in a hurry.*)

MORDECAI. My goodness, why all the fuss? Why didn't you come right to me? I'll bring you the best selection you ever did see! The biggest assortment, without a doubt; you'll have a hard time picking one out!

AHASUERUS. Eh—what are you jabbering about? Assortment of what?

MORDECAI. The best, your Majesty. Big as a mountain or small as a minute. Dark as a burnt kugel or blond as apple-tsimmis. Fat as the olives of Judea or skinny as the twigs of the willow tree—

MEMUCAN. (*Amazed.*) You came at precisely the right moment, sir!

MORDECAI. Of course! Why not? As soon as I heard that the poor king was wifeless, I came flying over hill and vale, across seas and deserts, to rescue him from boredom. Your Majesty, you've only to look at my prospects and you'll cheer up. May our dear Prince Haman go as quickly to Paradise, amen.

ALL. Amen!

MORDECAI. Your Majesty, it says in the Holy Writ: V'tichya— he shall live. And the meaning is: May our all-powerful King Ahasuerus live to a hundred-and-twenty. But, says Rashi: With a wife! Because, naturally, what kind of a life is it without a wife?

True, your Majesty, *with* a wife it can also be bitter as gall, but without her is it any better? What do you say to that, your Majesty?

AHASUERUS. Eh—beh—

MORDECAI. Golden words! King Solomon himself couldn't have done better. And the Toyreh says: "In haste." A marriage must not be put off. You dare not procrastinate. Therefore, your Majesty, I have sent letters to all your 127 provinces and ordered them to send here, at once, by special delivery, several parties of prospective brides for the King. (*Listens.*) In fact, I think they're arriving now. Pick one out yourself. Friend Herald, invite them in, please.

HERALD. With pleasure!

chidibim chidibim chidibim
Let the brides come in!

(*Music. Procession. First girl enters.*)

AHASUERUS. Eh—what's the matter with her hair?

MORDECAI. She was caught in a storm. Let the next one come in.

AHASUERUS. Why is she dragging her feet like that?

MORDECAI. Poor child, she has big feet and can't find shoes to fit—let the next one come in—

AHASUERUS. Look at her face! Why is she so pale?

MORDECAI. Just went through a long confinement. Triplets—

AHASUERUS. Eh—what sort of trick is this, Mordecai? You take me for a fool?

MORDECAI. God forbid! I just wanted to show you what kind of girl NOT to marry. Now feast your eyes on the beauties coming in now—each one is prettier than the other. Strike up the band! A real beauty pageant! Your Majesty—choose the Queen! (*Enter several girls, Esther last. Oohs and aahs. Ahasuerus is transfixed by her beauty. Points to her with his sceptre.*)

ALL. Hail the new Queen!

CURTAIN

ACT II

HERALD. (*Reading from a scroll.*)
"So Esther was taken unto King Ahasuerus into his royal house in the seventh year of his reign. And the King loved Esther above all the women, and she obtained grace and favor in his sight . . ."

And now, my friends, here is the beautiful setting
For the King's and Esther's beautiful wedding!

chidibim chidibim chidibim
Let the Royal Palace come in!

(*Curtain opens. A room in the palace. Mordecai and Haman on stage, with wine glasses in their hands.*)

HAMAN. L'chaim, Mordecai ben Ya-eer!

MORDECAI. (*Aside.*) He won't last out the year!

HAMAN. (*Sighs.*) Ai, Mordecai. You think I have no worries? Who is like unto Prince Haman? Who is so famous? So mighty? So rich? And yet—all is vanity, nothing plus nothing. I'll tell you a secret. For years I've been planning this war against the Greeks, and now, when our glorious armies are finally in Greece teaching the Greeks a lesson, I can't enjoy the victory! Instead of celebrating, I sit here with a headache.

MORDECAI. (*Aside.*) He doesn't even know yet the headache he's going to have! (*to Haman.*) That's a real shame, Ben Hamdat. The war, however, is one thing; that's your business, and may you go bankrupt, God willing. But on the day of our King's wedding you might at least wear a smile on your face.

HAMAN. Don't say it, Mordecai. Every word is a knife in my heart!

MORDECAI. (*Aside.*) If it only were!

HAMAN. Don't you even want to know why?

MORDECAI. I'll tell you frankly, Prince Haman. I'm not a very inquisitive man.

HAMAN. You're not kidding me, you dumb fox! All you Jews are clever and full of hanky-panky, but you're the hankiest of the pankiest, a smooth article, a smart operator, a real finagler, a slippery customer—l'chaim, friend, I wish you well!

MORDECAI. (*Aside.*) He should live to roast in hell!

HAMAN. Why don't you like me, Mordcha? What have you got against me?

MORDECAI. Me? Something against you? Whatever gave you *that* idea? Only a tenth of what I wish you should come true!

HAMAN. For instance, what difference would it make to you if you bowed down to me once in a while?

MORDECAI. (*Aside.*) I'd much rather see him bow to me once and not be able to straighten up again!

HAMAN. Everybody else bows down to me—everybody but you, Motya Ha-Yehudi. You'll be sorry, Motya! It would be better if we were friends.

MORDECAI. Well, all right, I don't mind being friends. But we have a parable about that. A wolf once said to a sheep: Let's be friends. So the sheep said: Reb Wolf, what can you possibly gain out of our friendship? I'm a poor skinny sheep, nothing but skin and bones—

HAMAN. Stop with your wisecracks, Motya! Let's not argue! L'chaim! (*Getting drunker all the time.*) A toast—whatever you wish—

MORDECAI. A Judgment Day on you and all the Hamans, today and forever-more—

HAMAN. Amen! Mordecai, I think you and I will yet be good friends—yes, Motya? (*Maudlin.*) Come closer, Motya, and I'll tell you the secret of my success. (*Opens his mouth wide.*) Look, Motya, look inside!

MORDECAI. Your beautiful white teeth?

HAMAN. Only a front!

MORDECAI. Your long tongue?

HAMAN. Only good for small talk!

MORDECAI. What, then? Your tonsils?

HAMAN. You're getting warm. My voice, Motya, my voice! How do you think I became the greatest statesman of all time? How do you think I got next to Alexander of Macedonia, or Hannibal of Carthage, or Caesar of Rome, or Napoleon of Josephine? How do you think I won the greatest battles of history without a single shot? With my voice! A lion's roar! (*Roars.*) A tiger's scream! (*Screams.*) A jackal's wail. (*Wails.*) The enemy gets scared to death. Then my army marches in and just blows—poof!—and it's all over. That's how I built the biggest empire in the world. That's how I took Assyria and Babylonia and Egypt and—that's what will happen to Greece. You don't believe me?

MORDECAI. Why shouldn't I believe you?

HAMAN. I'll show you. Listen. Where is he, that son of a dog who refuses to bow down to Haman ben Hamdata? (*Roars.*) Where are they—the heathen who oppose the gods of mighty Prince Haman? Tremble, you scoffers, you wisenheimers, you eggheads, you intellectuals! My patience is at an end! I'll step on you like cockroaches, you worms, you traitors, you pinkos! (*Bellows, smiles smugly.*) Well, Mordecai?

MORDECAI. That's all there is to it?

HAMAN. Don't be a wiseguy, Motya! You can do better?

MORDECAI. Maybe. I never tried it.

HAMAN. Well, here's your chance. Go ahead and try.

MORDECAI. If you wish, I'll do you the favor. But remember, don't complain to me afterwards. (*Assumes pose, clears his throat, takes a deep breath, roars.*) Haman you louse, a horrible end to you! Haman, you hyena, you mangy son-of-a-horse-thief! How much longer do you think you're going to play around with us? We have a great God in heaven and he'll soon put you six feet under to meet your ancestors! You'll bow from the gallows—and the crows will feast on you! (*Roars.*)

HAMAN. (*Frightened.*) Enough! Enough!

MORDECAI. (*Innocently.*) Well? How did I do? Was it bad?

HAMAN. Bad enough. You scared the daylights out of me. I'm so nervous these days, Motya, I can't stand it. I can't eat, I can't sleep. Worry, worry, all the time.

MORDECAI. Poor Prince Haman! (*Aside.*) May we continue to hear the same, amen.

HAMAN. I'll confide something else to you, Motya, something I haven't told anybody else—I'm in love!

MORDECAI. Lord have mercy—

HAMAN. Terribly in love. Dying of love.

MORDECAI. (*Aside.*) From your mouth to God's ear! (*To Haman.*) And who's the lucky girl?

HAMAN. Esther.

MORDECAI. Who?

HAMAN. Esther.

MORDECAI. (*Incredulous.*) Esther the Queen?

HAMAN. Esther! Esther! Esther!

MORDECAI. You must be out of your mind!

HAMAN. If I'm not now, I soon will be —

MORDECAI. What are you saying? The King's bride!

HAMAN. Mordecai, you have no idea what's going on inside me! But Esther must be mine—she will be mine! And you will help me!

MORDECAI. Me? Me?

HAMAN. You, you. She listens to you. Don't deny it. My spies know everything. Tonight, when Ahasuerus falls asleep, let Esther slip out of the palace and go out into the royal garden. She won't be stopped—I'll tip off the guards. Let her meet me at the fountain.

MORDECAI. Come on now, Haman! Why send *me* on such an errand?

HAMAN. Why not? Aren't you my friend? Don't contradict me, Motya! And remember what I told you, friend! (*Glares menacingly, then controls himself.*) As I told you, Mordecai— without Esther, my life isn't worth living. Under those circumstances you

should be able to figure out how much *your* life is worth. And if that isn't clear enough, let me make it plainer —if Esther doesn't show up at the fountain tonight, all the Jews in all the 127 provinces will pay for it! The rest is up to you. (*Exit.*)

MORDECAI. That double-damned—no wonder they named him Haman! He's going to ruin the whole wedding —(*Enter Esther. She runs to Mordecai, throws her arms around him, and weeps.*)

ESTHER. Uncle Mordecai!

MORDECAI. Esther my child! What's the matter?

ESTHER. I can't help crying, Uncle— I'm so unhappy!

MORDECAI. Unhappy! But why? Because you'll soon be Queen?

ESTHER. No. Because I'll soon be Ahasuerus's wife!

MORDECAI. Ahasuerus is ruler of 127 countries—

ESTHER. Ahasuerus is old and ugly and I don't love him—

MORDECAI. Oh, he's not so bad. All the girls in the kingdom envy you.

ESTHER. Because I'm Queen, not because I'm Ahasuerus's wife.

MORDECAI. A throne doesn't come along every day—

ESTHER. The throne is my cell and the palace is my prison—

MORDECAI. Now see here, Esther! If it wasn't so close to your wedding day I'd *really* tell you a few facts of life! Do you know what you want, or don't you?

ESTHER. What I want? What every normal girl wants! (*Sings love song.*)

MORDECAI. All right, child, stop crying. Can't you see it's God's will? (*Comforts her.*) I understand. It hurts to bid farewell to childhood years and youthful dreams. But don't make things worse for me than they already are. So many terrible things are happening, so many cruel and unjust decrees . . . and if that's not enough, now along comes Haman—

ESTHER. What, Uncle?

MORDECAI. Nothing, nothing. Whatever

God has decreed will come to pass. Wipe your eyes, my child, today you must look your prettiest. Maybe through you will come our salvation. Maybe because of you, Jewish children will no longer have to hide their names to stay alive. God be with you always, Esther the Queen. (*Kisses her.*) I hear the King approaching. Be a brave girl. (*Exits.*)

AHASUERUS. (*Entering.*) My angel! My Queen!

ESTHER. (*Bows.*) Your grace—

AHASUERUS. Eh—I'd rather you called me sweetheart—

ESTHER. I would not be so bold, your majesty—

AHASUERUS. I's asking you to do so—

ESTHER. (*Softly.*) Sweetheart . . .

AHASUERUS. Oh my dear—tell me you love me!

ESTHER. I blush to do so, your majesty—

AHASUERUS. Call me Chatskl—

ESTHER. Chatskl my sweetheart—

AHASUERUS. (*Ecstatically.*) Eh, my dear, since I first saw you I've become a new man! No more pains in my back, no more heartburn, no more headaches, even my old cough has disappeared. A miracle! (*coughs long and loud.*) You'll be the happiest queen in the world! Tell me, my Queen, tell me your slightest wish, and I'll grant it, even if it's half my kingdom.

ESTHER. Thank you, thank you, your majesty. There's nothing I wish.

AHASUERUS. Eh—maybe you'd like me to send away the 365 wives in my harem and devote myself completely —

ESTHER. (*Hastily.*) No, no, it's really not necessary! Don't send them away, poor things—

AHASUERUS. Bless you for a kind heart.

ESTHER. Better yet, why don't you take another hundred wives to celebrate the occasion?

AHASUERUS. If it please the Queen—

ESTHER. Yes, sweetheart, do that.

AHASUERUS. Anything to please you, my dear! Anything to please the Queen!

(*Tries to embrace her.*)

ESTHER. (*Eludes him.*) Your majesty my dear! I hear the musicians coming. I must go put on my wedding dress. (*Runs out.*)

AHASUERUS. (*Pleased with himself; sits down at a table laden with food.*) Still time before the wedding supper. Something to hold me over. (*Stuffs himself.*)

MORDECAI. (*Entering.*) Your majesty— good appetite! The guests are beginning to arrive.

AHASUERUS. (*His mouth full.*) Come here, Mordecai, join me in a little drink.

MORDECAI. If we must drink, make it a big one. Nu, l'chaim, your majesty, God grant you long years with the Queen in honor and in wealth and in good health and may all of Israel benefit from the union—yes, God bless the union—

AHASUERUS. L'chaim, l'chaim—

HAMAN. (*Entering.*) Your majesty, good appetite! (*Takes Mordecai aside.*) Did you give Esther my message?

MORDECAI. Not exactly. I haven't seen her yet.

HAMAN. You lie!

MORDECAI. Maybe after the ceremony—

HAMAN. You're lying! You did see her! You talked with her! You'll pay for this! I'll show you all! And now, damn Jew, bow down to me—at once!

MORDECAI. Now listen, you—

HAMAN. (*Enraged.*) Bow down!

MORDECAI. Me—Mordecai—bow down to Haman?

HAMAN. Remember what I said!

MORDECAI. Drop dead!

AHASUERUS. Eh—what's going on here?

MORDECAI. Ask Haman—let *him* tell you what he's howling about. (*Exit.*)

HAMAN. Your majesty, listen to what I'm sayin'—

AHASUERUS. Can't it wait, Haman? I'm hungry.

HAMAN. He's hungry, and I'm eating my heart out! I've had enough! (*slams table with his fist. From stage rear,*

Memucan pokes his head out, cries Oy! From right stage, Mezumen cries Oy; from left stage Kaparti cries Oy! Haman continues bellowing)—Enough, enough.

ADVISORS. (*Rush on stage.*) Gevald! Help! Police!

HAMAN. I'll destoy them all! Put an end to it!

ADVISORS. Who? Why?

HAMAN. (*To King.*) Your majesty, it is written in the Megilah: "There is a people, scattered and dispersed among the nations in all the provinces of your kingdom, and their ways are different, and they do not observe the laws of the King . . ."

AHASUERUS. Eh—they don't?

HAMAN. No. And they don't eat our food, either.

AHASUERUS. Eh? What do they eat, then?

ADVISORS. Bulbes!

HAMAN. On the sixth day of the week, while we are toiling in sweat and blood for our livelihood, they rest, just to spite us.

ADVISORS. Shabbes in an-novineh a bulbe-kugeleh—

HAMAN. And on the seventh day, while we go piously to pray, they bang away with their shears and irons—

ADVISORS. Zuntik veiter bulbes—

HAMAN. And this people, your majesty, are the Jews. Now I ask you—what benefit do you get out of them alive? They are a bother to all the nations and a misfortune to themselves. If you want to earn the thanks of the world, let them all be exterminated. We'll take over their property—they are almost as rich as me. What do you say, majesty?

ADVISORS. (*Softly.*) No . . . no . . . no . . .

AHASUERUS. Eh, I don't know, maybe you're right, but—

HAMAN. Your majesty, never have I asked a favor for myself—

AHASUERUS. You haven't?

HAMAN. (*Excited.*) But now I'm demanding it!

AHASUERUS. Take it easy, Hamdata,

you'll spoil my digestion. All right, take my signet ring and do what you like. And now, my esteemed advisors, come with me and help me get dressed for my wedding. (*Exit with advisors.*)

HAMAN. (*Barely able to control himself.*) Ha! Ha! Finally and at last— revenge! Your end is near, damn Jews! Mordecai will get a special lesson! And Esther will be mine! But that is not my purpose. (*Postures.*) My sacred cause is to liberate the world from the Jewish yoke. I shall cut out this cancer of humanity. I shall be known as the greatest man that ever lived. The world will remember me forever!

HERALD. (*Entering.*) Prince Haman, have you finished your Jew-baiting speech?

HAMAN. Finished, friend Herald. Now you can bring in the lousy wedding, tfui! (*Exit.*)

HERALD.
chidibim chidibim chidibim
Let the wedding come in!

(*A happy crowd comes on stage from all sides. Jewish wedding music. Esther is led on stage and seated on a high-backed chair. The women surround her.*)

HERALD.
Make room, make room
For bride and for groom!
Welcome every friend and guest—
Eat and drink with gusto and zest!

(*Advisors enter with Ahasuerus and seat him next to Esther.*)

HERALD.
A tune for the groom!
A royal tune!
chidibim chidibim chidibim
Let the canopy come in!

(*Enter canopy.*) Who leads the bride to the chupah? (*Esther's attendants lead her to the canopy.*) Come forward Mordecai ben Ya-eer ben Shammai ben Kish!

MORDECAI. Well, friend Herald, what's your wish?

HERALD. Please to perform the ceremony!

MORDECAI. The ceremony too?

HERALD. What else can we do? These foreigners don't know any Hebrew!

MORDECAI. All right, so I'll have another mitzva. Your majesty, repeat after me, word for word, and say it loud, so you can be heard. Say after me—HARAY

AHASUERUS. HARAY—

HERALD. No reservations in what you say!

MORDECAI. OT—

AHASUERUS. OT—

HERALD. What a prize you got!

MORDECAI. MEKUDESHESS LEE—

AHASUERUS. MEKUDESHESS LEE—

HERALD. Listen to her and don't disagree!

MORDECAI. B'TABAT ZUHUV ZOO—

AHASUERUS. B'TABAT ZUHUV ZOO —

HERALD. And the servant, your majesty, will be you!

MORDECAI. KE-DOT—

AHASUERUS. KE-DOT—

HERALD. You're tying a permanent knot!

MORDECAI. MOSHE V'YISROEL—

AHASUERUS. MOSHE—what?

MORDECAI. V'YISROEL—

AHASUERUS. V'YISROEL—

HERALD. Soon, we hope, you'll have need for a mohel!

ALL. Amen! O-mayn!

MEMUCAN. Your majesty, I, counsellor of the Medes and Persians, do hereby certify that everything has been done in accordance with the rules and regulations of the royal nuptial code. You may now crown your wife, Mrs. Esther Ahasuerus, Queen of Media and Persia and all the 127 provinces.

AHASUERUS.
My angel, my sweetheart, how your eyes shine!
Fill me a cup of this sparkling wine!

My dearest, my treasure, my everything —

Wear upon your finger this royal ring!
My fairest lady of world renown,
Wear upon your head this royal crown!

ALL. Long live Esther the Queen! Mazl-tov! Mazl-tov!

HERALD.
Musicians, play with all your might!
We'll sing and dance throughout this night!

CURTAIN

ACT III

HERALD. (*Reading from Megilah.*) "And it came to pass that on that night the King could not sleep and he ordered brought to him the Chronicles of the Kingdom. . . ."

chidibim chidibim chidibim
Let the Chronicles come in!

(*Curtain opens on a room in the palace. Memucan, Mezumen, and Kaparti poke their heads in cautiously from three sides of the stage, then tiptoe in.*)

MEZUMEN. They say—

MEMUCAN. What do they say?

MEZUMEN. They say that of the 600 battleships that sailed away to the land of the Greeks, 590 are already at the bottom of the sea—

ADVISORS. Ai-Ai-Ai—

KAPARTI. They say—

MEMUCAN. What else do they say?

KAPARTI. They say that of the 800,000 soldiers who went off to Greece, 750,-000 are kaput—

ADVISORS. Ai-Ai-Ai—

MEMUCAN. Sha! They say—

ADVISORS. What do they say?

MEMUCAN. They say that the women are starting to grumble from India to Ethiopia. The women are saying that if their men stay away much longer they'll forget how to have children—

ADVISORS. Ai-Ai-Ai—

MEZUMEN. The Soothsayer told me that General Parsana is ready to start a putsch against Haman the Agagi.

KAPARTI. Field Marshal Marsana, too. The whole army hates Haman's guts.

MEMUCAN. So what are we waiting for? Gevald! What are we waiting for?

ADVISORS. You speak up, Memucan!

MEMUCAN. No, you speak up, Mezumen.

MEZUMEN. Me? I'm so sick I can hardly move. No, Kaparti, you are the one. We'll be right in back of you.

KAPARTI. Why me? What's the matter with you? You speak up, if you're so tired of living!

MEZUMEN. Ai, if we could only find somebody to talk. Somebody with a fearless tongue.

MEMUCAN. Wait a minute—I think I know the very man!

ADVISORS. Who, for goodness sake?

MEMUCAN. Yes, gentlemen, exactly the right man—the royal shadchan!

MEZUMEN. A splendid idea, 'pon my soul!

KAPARTI. But will he agree?

MEMUCAN. It won't hurt to ask him. He's right outside the gate. Call him in, Kaparti.

MEZUMEN. He's a Jew, you know.

MEMUCAN. So what? That's as good a recommendation as any. (*Enter Mordecai and Kaparti.*)

MORDECAI. I'd wish you good morning, gentlemen, but it's still dark. Good evening? It's almost dawn. So what should I say, gentlemen?

MEMUCAN. Say sholem-aleichem!

MORDECAI. Aleichem sholem, gentlemen!

MEMUCAN. How's business?

MORDECAI. Thanks for asking. Could always be better. Thank God it's not worse. What can I do for you, gentlemen?

MEMUCAN. We want you to arrange something—

MORDECAI. For you, Lord Memucan?

MEZUMEN. Why only for *him*?

MORDECAI. Okay—for both of you?

KAPARTI. For all of us!

MORDECAI. Well, I've never done a wholesale business before, but I'll try my best. For all three of you. With whom?

MEZUMEN. With the whole empire.

MORDECAI. K'n'hora! And to whom shall I go first?

MEMUCAN. To King Ahasuerus.

MORDECAI. To King Ahasuerus for a bride for *you*?

ADVISORS. A bride? Phui! What are you talking about?

MORDECAI. Maybe you'd better tell me what *you* are talking about.

MEZUMEN. Listen, Mordecai, you're the royal shadchan—yes or no?

MORDECAI. So?

MEZUMEN. So I ask you. What good does it do you? Does it earn you a living?

MORDECAI. Don't rub it in!

MEZUMEN. So why do you stay there?

MORDECAI. I have a reason.

MEZUMEN. For instance?

MORDECAI. Ask Haman.

KAPARTI. You can tell us, Mordecai, don't be afraid.

MORDECAI. Ai, gentlemen, an ox has a long tongue, but he still can't blow shofar. What does a shadchan do for a living? A shadchan is the right hand of God—he helps to bring couples together. A shadchan is like a good angel—he arranges engagements and weddings, brisses and pidyan habens, mazeltovs and kiddushes—but gentlemen, we have a wicked Haman in our midst, so instead of births we have deaths, instead of weddings we have funerals, instead of peace we have wars, and instead of celebrations we have yortseit—

MEMUCAN. Golden words!

MORDECAI. How do you expect people to be happy when that Agagi has drowned all of Persia in a sea of sorrow? How do you expect young fellows to even think of marriage when Haman ben Hamdata is dragging them off to war?

MEZUMEN. Brilliant words!

MEMUCAN. That's exactly what we want, Mordecai, we want you to talk—

MEZUMEN. We'll tell you a secret, Mordecai. Everybody in the kingdom is Haman's enemy, not only the soldiers and sailors—

MEMUCAN. The only trouble is, nobody speaks up—

KAPARTI. The people are like a baby, you have to teach them how to talk—

MEZUMEN. Just let somebody say the first word—

MORDECAI. Aha! Now I get it! You want me to be the spokesman—in other words, to stick my neck out—

MEZUMEN. Yes. You are the one, Mordecai the Righteous.

MEMUCAN. Mordecai the Wisest of the Jews—

KAPARTI. We wouldn't even know the right words to use—

MORDECAI. Against Haman?

MEMUCAN. Not *against* Haman—*for* the country!

MORDECAI. No, gentlemen. Why me? Who am I and what am I? A poor little Jew, Mordecai ben Ya-eer, and from the provinces at that. You want me to stand up to Prince Haman ben Hamdata and his gorillas? What do you see in me, gentlemen? At least if the Almighty had given me two heads, I'd gamble one. But to go and stick my neck under the axe deliberately? That would be a sin! Even God Himself wouldn't want that. I really appreciate the honor, gentlemen, but you'll excuse me—

MEZUMEN. Come, come, Mordecai— whom else do we have?

MORDECAI. It's a big country—you'll find another candidate. (*enter announcer.*)

ANNOUNCER. Prince Haman has this day ordered—

MEMUCAN. Now what has that dog ordered? Out with it!

ANNOUNCER. (*Roll of drums.*) Official decree of King Ahasuerus, praise his name, emperor of the Medes and Persians. Hear ye! Whereas the accursed Jews are disobeying the laws of the King and conspiring to corrupt our youth and destroy our beloved Fatherland, therefore do we

order and decree that on the 13th day of Adar all the Jews shall be taken out and executed—old and young, men and women and children, and their possessions shall go to the Royal Treasury. Hear ye! Good night, Lord Advisors. Good night, Lord Shadchan.

MORDECAI. So now I've become Lord Shadchan! God in heaven! My poor people! (*Wrings his hands.*) Bring me ashes for my head and sackcloth for my loins—

MEZUMEN. Well, Mordecai, what do you say now?

MORDECAI. I will die with the Philistines, like Samson! That's what I say. I'll do your bidding, gentlemen, come what may!

MEMUCAN. Lord be praised!

MEZUMEN. And now that you are the leader of his majesty's opposition—

MEMUCAN. You will be the Assistant to the King—

KAPARTI. When the Opposition comes to power—

MEMUCAN. May that day come soon!

MEZUMEN. Amen! With God's help!

MORDECAI. God will help, gentlemen. He must help. What other choice does He have? Will He let his people die? We can leave it to Him. And you gentlemen leave it to me. Now fetch the Queen—

MEZUMEN. You don't think we're risking too much?

MORDECAI. Don't worry. I have a plan. Go ahead, Kaparti, go get the Queen. Leave me alone with her, gentlemen. (*They exit. Enter Esther.*)

ESTHER. What in heaven's name is wrong, Uncle, that you wake me up in the middle of the night?

MORDECAI. Esther, my child, I don't want to frighten you, but your people are in mortal danger.

ESTHER. What's wrong, Uncle Mordecai? For God's sake tell me!

MORDECAI. Your Ahasuerus has sold our people to Haman for a bowl of soup. Three days from now all the Jews in the kingdom will be killed— by royal decree. All of us, young and old, rich and poor, all of us—

ESTHER. No! We can't let that happen! What can we do?

MORDECAI. You can do something, Esther. You must speak to the king now, immediately!

ESTHER. (*Frightened.*) Uncle! You know that going to the King without his permission is like going to your death!

MORDECAI. I know it, my child. I know it. But perhaps the King will grant you his grace at the last moment. And God forbid, if not—Esther, do you think that you, alone of all Jews, will escape by hiding in the King's house?

ESTHER. Would you rather I go voluntarily to my death, like a sacrifice upon an altar? I'm still young, I have much to live for! Even here, like a bird in a cage, life is worth living. Is this the end, Uncle Mordecai?

MORDECAI. Perhaps not, my child. No, not necessarily. Maybe you were born for just such a moment as this. Perhaps it was destined by Providence that you be the salvation of your people. You dare not be silent in this hour of peril, that's all we can be sure of now. You must not think of your own life when your whole people is tied to the stake!

ESTHER. (*Softly.*) Go, Uncle. Go out and gather together all the Jews of Shushan. Let them fast and pray that Esther's days may not be cut down. At dawn I shall go to seek an audience with the King.

MORDECAI. Bless you, my child. He who is in heaven will guide you. But don't tell the King the whole story all at once. He can understand only a little bit at a time. Invite him and his advisors to your chambers for a banquet tonight. And invite Haman, too. But ask Haman to arrive earlier than the others. (*Esther starts to object.*) Do as I tell you, Esther. Trust me.

ESTHER. Very well, Uncle, I'll do as you wish. (*Moves to leave, but Mordecai detains her.*)

MORDECAI. Esther, be brave, don't tremble so. Haman will pass. Trouble will pass. Like a bad dream. The world will again be at peace. And Jewish children will laugh again— in Jerusalem, in Babylon, in Shushan, and everywhere on earth. Jewish mothers will name their daughters after you. And when many generations have passed, when the evil memory of Haman will have disappeared, Jewish writers will still be writing plays about Haman's downfall, and Jewish actors will still play the wonderful story of Queen Esther and Mordecai the Righteous— (*Esther kisses him.*)

HERALD. (*Rushing in.*) What the devil's the matter with you, Mordecai? What's come over you?

MORDECAI. (*Startled.*) Eh?

HERALD. You've let your imagination run wild and you're holding up the play. The cast is waiting in the wings. Even the King is awake—

MORDECAI. Ist that so? Forgive me, friend Herald. (*Exits with Esther.*)

HERALD. He's a good man, but he gets carried away sometimes—Memucan —Mezumen—bring the King in! (*enter advisors, leading King.*)

AHASUERUS. Whew, it's hot! No breeze anywhere tonight! Can't sleep! My eyes are closing and still I can't sleep! Eh—let's have a schnapps—

MEMUCAN. Your majesty, perhaps it would be better for you if we read you to sleep? We haven't been keeping up with the Chronicles—

AHASUERUS. The Chronicles? You're right, they do put me to sleep. Anyway, it can't hurt—

MEMUCAN. Royal Guard! Bring me the latest volume of the Chronicles. (*Guard comes in with huge book. Memucan takes it and hands it to Mezumen with a broad wink.*)

MEZUMEN. (*Clears throat.*) "In the third year of his reign, King Ahasuerus made a feast unto all his princes and nobles and he showed them the riches of his glorious kingdom. . . . And the feast was in the court of the garden of the Royal Palace, where there were hangings of white, fine cotton, bordered with cords of the finest linen of blue and purple . . . the couches were of gold and silver upon a pavement of green and white —

AHASUERUS. (*Groans.*) Oh no! You're not going to read me the whole megilah? Find something else—

MEMUCAN. (*Turns pages.*) "A servant-girl was brought to the Royal Magistrate by her mistress, who made the following complaint: She came home one afternoon and examined her provisions and found that two pounds of butter were missing. She accused the servant-girl of stealing the two pounds of butter, but the girl denied it and said that the cat had eaten it. The mistress then put the cat on a scale and weighed it and the cat weighed two pounds. The woman asked the magistrate to decide: If the two pounds is the butter, then where is the cat? The Royal Magistrate referred the case to the Royal Court—"

AHASUERUS. Eh—she has a good point there. Let me know how it comes out. What else do we have there?

MEZUMEN. (*Stage whisper to Memucan.*) Read about (*spells*)—M-O-R-D-E-C-A-I—

MEMUCAN. (*Doesn't understand.*) Another Chronicle, your majesty?

MEZUMEN. Certainly! Can't you see the King is not sleepy yet? (*Winks frantically to Memucan, spells "Mordecai," then impatiently yanks book out of Memucan's hands.*) Here's an interesting one, your majesty. Listen to this. "It came to pass in Shushan Habira that two royal servants, Bogatin and Teresh, conspired to assassinate the King by poison. The plot became known to the Jew, Mordecai ben Ya-eer, who reported it to the proper authorities. An investigation was thereupon conducted and the existence of the conspiracy was substantiated. The two conspirators were then hung upon the gallows and the king's life was saved—

AHASUERUS. Oh! I feel sick!

MEMUCAN. Your majesty!

KAPARTI. Give him some spirits!

AHASUERUS. Spirits—right! Give me spirits. Memucan!

MEMUCAN. Yes, your majesty?

AHASUERUS. Pour me another one. Were those two scoundrels really hung?

MEMUCAN. (*Checks the record.*) Yes, it's marked in the book.

KAPARTI. Mordecai the Righteous saved the king from certain death.

AHASUERUS. Eh, yes. What kind of reward did we give him?

MEMUCAN. None, your majesty, none at all.

MEZUMEN. Not even a tiny bit of recognition.

KAPARTI. Haman refused to okay it.

AHASUERUS. That wasn't nice. We should have done something—

MEMUCAN. It's not too late, your majesty. We could—

GUARD. (*Entering.*) Your majesty. Prince Haman requests an audience.

AHASUERUS. Let him come in.

MEMUCAN. If it please the King, let Haman himself say what reward should be given to Mordecai. Let *me* ask him.

AHASUERUS. Eh—yes, sure, Memucan.

HAMAN. (*Entering.*) Greetings, your majesty.

AHASUERUS. Greetings, ben Hamdata. Can't you sleep either?

HAMAN. This is no time to talk about the weather, your majesty. I come with an urgent request. I have sent out the order that all the Jews within our borders be destroyed. But there is one Jew in Shushan who is insolent to me and I want him taken care of first. The gallows is all ready—

MEMUCAN. Leave your request for later, Prince Haman. The King wants your advice on a matter of greater importance. You are the Assistant to the King—

MEZUMEN. The princeliest of all the princes—

KAPARTI. The richest and most esteemed of all the nobles—

MEMUCAN. Advise the King, Prince

Haman. What should be done with a man whom the King wishes to honor?

HAMAN. Whom the King wishes to honor? (*Struts like a peacock.*)

AHASUERUS. Yes, Haman, tell us—

HAMAN. A man whom the King wishes to honor—hm-m—he should be dressed in a royal robe that the King himself has worn, and should be given a horse that the King himself has ridden, and he should be given into the hands of one of the King's trusted lieutenants and led in parade down the main street of Shushan, and the Royal Announcer should proceed at the head of the procession and call out: Thus is done with the man whom King Ahasuerus has chosen to honor!

MEMUCAN. Splendid, Prince Haman! Couldn't have thought of a better plan myself! Please be so good as to take a royal robe and put it around Mordecai's shoulders, and take a royal horse and seat Mordecai upon it on a royal saddle and lead him through the streets of Shushan Habira—because Mordecai is the man whom the King wishes to honor!

AHASUERUS. Eh, yes—he's the one.

HAMAN. Your imperial majesty! How could you? How can I? Mordecai the Jew!

AHASUERUS. Eh—that's my royal wish, Haman—

HAMAN. The Assistant King—a servant to Mordecai the Shadchan!

ADVISORS. It is the will of our incomparable ruler—

AHASUERUS. That's me—(*beams.*) (*Enter Mordecai.*)

MEZUMEN. Mordecai ben Ya-eer, for the deed you did of saving the king from death, you are now to be given your reward. Prince Haman will dress you up in a royal robe and lead you on a steed through the royal streets of Shushan. That's the King's wish.

MORDECAI. Your majesty, if I may be so bold, it would please me more if you did something for my fellow-Jews, but since you wish to honor me, then honor me. God knows that Mordecai

ben Ya-eer is no glory-seeker, but if it pleases your majesty—

MEMUCAN. Haman! Put the robe on Mordecai!

MORDECAI. Okay, Haman, let's try on the King's kimona—

HAMAN. (*Putting robe on Mordecai.*) Don't look so smug, Motya—the gallows is all ready.

MORDECAI. I think you and the gallows will go steady!

HAMAN. Motya, you'll never get away!

MORDECAI. Agagi, the hell you say!

AHASUERUS. Bring in my royal white horse! (*It is brought in.*) Haman, help the shadchan get on board! (*Haman leads Modecai toward the horse, but the horse pulls the reins out of Haman's hands and races over to the king.*)

AHASUERUS. What's wrong, friend horse?

HORSE. (*Bows and sings.*)
Your majesty, to thee I bow.
Who is going to ride me now?

AHASUERUS.
Horsie, my horsie, why do you neigh?
Mordecai ben Ya-eer will ride you today!

HORSE.
Kingie, my kingie, spare my pains.
Who will lead me by the reins?

AHASUERUS.
Horsie, my horsie, careful what you say.
Haman will hold your reins today!

HORSE.
Kingie, my kingie, how could you do it?
That son of a prince will never live through it!

AHASUERUS.
Horsie, my horsie, that will do!
We've enough advisors without adding you!
Take friend Mordecai upon your back—
Or else you'll get the royal sack!

HORSE. I hear and I obey, your majesty. (*Horse, Mordecai, and Haman exit.*)

AHASUERUS. Herald! Bring in the main

street of Shushan. I'd like to see this part of the play myself!

HERALD.

> chidibim chidibim chidibim
> Let Main Street come in!

(*Enter men, women; they form two rows; between them Haman leads the horse carrying Mordecai, who greets the crowd like a visiting celebrity.*)

CROWD. Look at the stable-boy—Haman the Drayman!

HAMAN. (*Mumbling*)—the King wishes to honor—

CROWD.

> Mordecai, Mordecai, all will be well
> And Haman the Wicked will go to hell!

CURTAIN

ACT IV

HERALD. (*Reading from Megilah.*) "And it came to pass, when the King returned home, he found Haman sprawled upon a couch, forcing his attentions upon Esther the Queen. And the King said: What! Mauling the Queen in my own house!"

And now, ladies and gentlemen— (*breaks off, as he notices approaching from left stage two men in tattered military uniforms. They move as fast as they can, but they are weary and footsore.*)

Well, well, look who's here! General Parsana and Field Marshall Marsana, home from the wars! Wait a minute, gentlemen, what's your hurry?

MARSANA. We've got to see King Ahasuerus right away!

PARSANA. We've got to tell him—

BOTH. Our glorious army is kaput! (*Weeping.*)

HERALD. What! After so many victories —kaput?

MARSANA. There was a terrible snow—

PARSANA. And a freezing frost—

MARSANA. And our army is lost! (*Tears his hair.*)

HERALD. Wait a minute! Take it easy! Is it possible they weren't fighting so good?

BOTH. You dog! You insulting dog! (*Pull out their swords.*)

MARSANA. The generals—

PARSANA. And the colonels—

BOTH. Fought like lions!

ADVISORS. (*Poke heads out of curtain.*)

> The generals went to war, to war
> 'Cause warring is their habit.
> But then they met the enemy's sword—
> And ran like a frightened rabbit!

HERALD. (*Shushing advisors.*) What happened to the soldiers?

MARSANA. Shot to pieces!

PARSANA. Haman's to blame!

MARSANA. Curse his name!

PARSANA. What business did we have in Greece?

MARSANA. Strutting like the silly geese!

PARSANA. Now we're down to the very dregs—

MARSANA. With our tails between our legs—

ADVISORS.

> The generals went to war, to war
> And now they've come a-running.
> So powerful smart they were before
> But now they've lost their cunning!

HERALD. (*Waving advisors back.*) Don't worry, my brave heroes—Haman will get his. And very soon. In this act Mordecai gets his revenge.

MARSANA. Who is this Mordecai?

HERALD. You don't know Mordecai the Tsaddik? You poor ignoramus! Never read the Megilah? No? Well, take it from me—you can depend on Mordecai. At sundown tonight, gather all your soldiers in front of the Queen's palace. But first you'd better disarm Haman's bodyguards. Go in peace, glorious heroes. The audience is getting impatient. I have to raise the curtain. (*Generals exit.*)

And now my friends, we'll see Haman's end!

chidibim chidibim chidibim
Let Haman's end come in!

(*Curtain rises. A room in the palace. The Soothsayer is gazing intently at the sky through a telescope. Haman paces feverishly back and forth.*)

HAMAN. Search them, Soothsayer, search all the heavens diligently, all the 120 galaxies! Well, what do you see? Why don't you say something, goddammit!

SOOTHSAYER. The stars are silent, my lord.

HAMAN. Tell me the truth, you nincompoop! Is the silence a sign of defeat?

SOOTHSAYER. Not necessarily, my lord. It may be a sign of rain. Too many clouds up there.

HAMAN. Don't be funny with me! Get rid of the clouds! Drive them away! Use your magic!

SOOTHSAYER. I'll try, Prince Haman, I'll try. (*Chants incantation.*)

Breezes cold, breezes hot
Breezes here and breezes not
Chase the clouds, black and gray
Chase them all away, away
Blow ye winds from far and near
Make the clouds to disappear!

HAMAN. Nu?

SOOTHSAYER. One cloud has moved over —

HAMAN. And what do you see?

SOOTHSAYER. Nothing. Another cloud took its place.

HAMAN. Look through it with your spyglass!

SOOTHSAYER. (*Staring into glass, sighs, groans, wipes his brow.*)

HAMAN. Well? What do you see?

SOOTHSAYER. The Star of Orion. It's very pale. Hardly visible.

HAMAN. Under what sign? In what constellation?

SOOTHSAYER. The constellation of the Virgin.

HAMAN. Does that mean trouble?

SOOTHSAYER. Doesn't it always?

HAMAN. Keep looking! Make the stars answer! What happened to my 600 ships? Why don't we hear from them? Ask the stars!

SOOTHSAYER. The stars are dark, my lord.

HAMAN. (*Alarmed.*) Dark? All dark?

SOOTHSAYER. Not a spark!

HAMAN. Maybe if you read my palm?

SOOTHSAYER. My eyes are old and feeble, Prince Haman.

HAMAN. Do what I tell you! Read my palm!

SOOTHSAYER. (*Takes Haman's palm, looks up startled.*) You are in great danger, my lord!

HAMAN. What is it?

SOOTHSAYER. A woman. A Jewish woman—or maybe an Aryan—it's all mixed up—

HAMAN. Will I get out of it safely? Will I?

SOOTHSAYER. I can see nothing more—

HAMAN. Try again! I'll give you ten ducats!

SOOTHSAYER. It's no use. Everything is dark. Every path is blocked. Run away, Prince Haman, run away from this place! (*Runs off stage.*)

HAMAN. The stars are dark! He's afraid to tell me the truth! I am lost! (*Pauses.*) No! Haman ben Hamdata is not one of those spineless jellyfish! I know those damned stargazers! Greece will be ours! I'll send more armies! His majesty's Opposition—ha! Jews! I'll show them! War to the death! I'll not be scared off! The Queen will be at my side! Nothing can stop me now! Herald! Herald!

HERALD. (*Entering.*) What's all the rantin' and ravin', Haman?

HAMAN. Never mind! Bring in the Queen's palace! I've been invited to a banquet! You'll soon be hearing great news about me!

HERALD. I hope so. The sooner the better. This play is beginning to drag. However, one good turn deserves another. Do me a favor. Save me a piece of the rope they hang you with.

HAMAN. Don't tell me you still believe in those fairy tales!

HERALD. Who knows? People say it's good luck. Is it agreed?

HAMAN. Agreed. (*Exit.*)

HERALD.
    chidibim chidibim chidibim

SOOTHSAYER. (*Pokes his head in.*) Psst! Friend Herald!

HERALD. What's up, Friend Soothsayer? You have some special extra news?

SOOTHSAYER. No, no. Just save me a piece of that rope too, will you? I need it in my work.

HERALD. What will you give me for it?

SOOTHSAYER. I'm sure we can make a deal—

HERALD. (*Sharply.*) No!

SOOTHSAYER. But why not?

HERALD. I don't fancy the stars doing Haman's will!

SOOTHSAYER. What! You haven't heard? (*whispers.*) I've gone over to the Opposition. The wheel of fortune turns—and whoever doesn't turn with it is a fool. We have to make a living, colleague, we have to make a living. (*Sighs, exit.*)

HERALD. (*Shrugs.*)
    chidibim chidibim chidibim
    Let the Queen's palace come in!

ESTHER. (*Entering, nervously.*) How my heart beats! God help me!

SERVANT. Prince Haman has arrived.

ESTHER. Show him in.

HAMAN. (*Entering.*) O beautiful Queen —

ESTHER. Prince Haman—

HAMAN. This is the happiest moment in my life!

ESTHER. Indeed?

HAMAN. Say the word and I'll be your slave—

ESTHER. You say slave but you mean master—

HAMAN. No! I adore you, Queen Esther! I need you!

ESTHER. I can imagine . . .

HAMAN. Tell me at once—I need your help—will you give it to me?

ESTHER. My help? For what?

HAMAN. My enemies grow bolder. The eagle has broken one of his talons and already the crow proclaims himself King of the Birds! But they'll never live to see the day! Tonight I shall wipe out the entire Opposition! And I'll start with Mordecai the Jew—tonight he hangs!

ESTHER. You won't do that!

HAMAN. I won't? Why not?

ESTHER. Because—because I ask you not to, Prince Haman.

HAMAN. You ask me? And may I know why?

ESTHER. Because—

HAMAN. What does that Jew have to do with you, Queen Esther?

ESTHER. He—he—

HAMAN. He what? Tell me!

ESTHER. He's my shadchan—

HAMAN. Is that all? Then why worry about him? (*tries to embrace her.*)

ESTHER. Don't touch me!

HAMAN. So that's the way it is? Then my informers are right. They tell me this Mordecai is a frequent guest of yours. There's even talk that he's your lover—

ESTHER. That's a lie!

HAMAN. We could have an investigation, but I'd prefer to take your word for it. If you're telling me the truth, don't mention his name to me again!

ESTHER. If you promise me—

HAMAN. Enough! I promise you only that Mordecai will hang—and it's nothing to do with you! You're mine, Esther, mine and no one else's! (*Embraces her.*)

ESTHER. (*Struggling.*) Leave me alone!

HAMAN. I am Prince Haman! You hear me? You invited me here! What kind of games are you playing? Nobody plays games with Haman, not even the Queen! (*Kisses her.*)

ESTHER. (*Turns her head in disgust.*) No! No!

HAMAN. Don't turn away from me, Esther! (*Frenzied, tosses her violently onto the couch.*)

ESTHER. Go away! Help! Help!
    (*Mordecai rushes in, followed by Advisors and Ahasuerus.*)

MORDECAI. Help! Gevald! Haman is attacking the Queen! (*Tries to pull Haman away.*)

AHASUERUS. (*Stunned.*) What—what's going on here?

MORDECAI. Haman attacked the Queen! Call the guards!

AHASUERUS. Help! Call the guards! (*Guards rush in, subdue Haman.*)

MORDECAI. Tie his hands with a stout rope!

HAMAN. Wait till my bodyguards hear about this!

MORDECAI. Don't hold your breath! They've all surrendered to the army —or what's left of it.

HAMAN. Ai—ai—I'm finished!

MORDECAI. Dig a grave for somebody else and you end up in it yourself!

HAMAN. What a time for proverbs! (*Groans.*)

AHASUERUS. (*Comforting Esther.*) Don't cry, my angel, I can't bear it. Did he hurt you, that scoundrel, that evil man, that—that—Guards! Put the hood on him! To the gallows with him! Mordecai, once you saved my life. Now you've saved more than my life. Memucan!

MEMUCAN. Yes, your majesty?

AHASUERUS. Call in the Royal Magistrates. We'll have a trial, right here and now! (*Enter Magistrates.*) Advisors, nobles, magistrates! Your grateful sovereign has been rescued from a horrible plot. Haman is the villain! He must be sentenced according to the laws of the Medes and Persians. Lord Advisor, ask the two legal questions.

MEMUCAN. (*Chanting.*) What must be done to a man who has caused the death of 750,000 sons of Media and Persia and who tried to violate the Queen right in her own house?

MEZUMEN. Hang him!

KAPARTI. On a gallows 50 cubits high!

ALL. True! True and just!

MEMUCAN. What must be done to a man who has twice saved the King's life and who has saved the Queen's honor?

MEZUMEN. Raise him higher than all the nobles of the kingdom!

KAPARTI. The All-Powerful King should appoint him Chief Royal Assistant!

ALL. True! True and just!

MEMUCAN. The villain is Haman! (*Sound of groggers.*)

MEMUCAN. The hero is Mordecai! (*Cheers.*)

AHASUERUS. From this day forward, Mordecai ben Ya-eer, you are the right hand of the King. Guards, remove my signet ring from Haman's hand and put it on Mordecai's. (*Guards attempt to remove the ·ring but Haman roars like a lion. The crowd laughs.*)

ESTHER. (*Pointing to Haman.*) And to such a villain, your majesty gave permission to slay me—me and my people—

AHASUERUS. Your people?

ESTHER. Yes. Me and my people. Your Queen is a Jewish daughter—

ALL. Oh—ah—

ESTHER. And the King's Assistant is my uncle—

MORDECAI. For these brave words, my child, you will be held up forever as an example for all the Jewish daughters of the world.

MEMUCAN. Mordecai, maybe you can set me up as an example too? My grandfather was a Jew—

MEZUMEN. And my great-grandfather—

VOICES IN CROWD. My father! My mother-in-law! My wife!

AHASUERUS. And how about me? My own grandmother, may she rest in peace, was half-Jewish—

ALL. Oh—ah—

HAMAN. My god! Look at the company I've been keeping! Motya, if it is my fate to die among Jews, then let me at least say the Videh—maybe things will be better for me in the next world than they were in this one. Say my last confession with me, Mordecai—

MORDECAI. You're a paskudnyak and a no-good anti-Semite, Haman ben Agagi! Nevertheless, I'll do you the favor. You want to say your confession, say it. (*chanting.*) You wickedest of the wicked, you sinner against humanity—what did you do last Pesach at the seder?

HAMAN. (*Same chant.*) Last Pesach at the seder—I ate bread, and pork later.

ALL. Oy vey!

MORDECAI. You wickedest of the wicked, you sinner against humanity—what did you do on Rosh Hashona?

HAMAN. On Rosh Hashona I sinned with a woman who didn't wanna.

ALL. Oy vey!

MORDECAI. You wickedest of the wicked, you sinner against humanity—what did you do on Purim?

HAMAN. On Purim I gave the Jews the Megilah! (*Backstage there is a sudden commotion.*)

AHASUERUS. Guards! What's going on out there?

MARSANA. (*Rushing in.*) Your majesty, your glorious army is storming the palace! The men are raving mad—

PARSANA. (*Rushing in.*) They're waving their swords like lunatics!

GUARD. The people are up in arms! They're coming with sword and shield, hammer and tongs, pick and axe, mortar and pestle, knife and fork—

MORDECAI. What do they really want, my friends?

ALL. They want Haman hanged!

MORDECAI. Is that all? Then give them Haman and may it be the end of all our troubles, amen!

MEMUCAN. Guards! Take Haman to the gallows! (*Guards try to move Haman, but he stands firm.*)

HERALD. Friend Haman, if you please—it's time for the rope.

HAMAN. (*Angry.*) Take your time! I'm in no hurry!

HERALD. Don't make trouble, Haman. You know we have everything timed to the last second. We're running on a schedule. It's time for the hanging.

HAMAN. (*Tears away from the guards, throws his sword down.*) No! This is as far as I go and no further! What kind of business is this, anyway? Why must I be hanged—and in the middle of the Act yet? Didn't I do a good job with my role? Didn't I?

HERALD. God forbid! You did a wonderful job! The audience really hates you! But all those good people out there are anxious to celebrate Purim, and how can Jews celebrate when Haman is still walking around with his head on his shoulders? I beg you, Haman—do it for your public—

HAMAN. Oh, for my public? That's something else. (*Places himself dramatically between the two guards.*) Now let the Jews celebrate! *Zeit gezunt,* your majesty! Goodbye, Queen Esther, I'm sorry things couldn't have been different between us. Farewell, everybody! God grant a real Haman's end to all the Hamans of all times!

ALL. Amen! Amen! (*Haman is led out. Tumultuous noise backstage.*)

MEMUCAN. Mordecai, say a few words to the people.

MEZUMEN. You are the Assistant King—speak!

ALL. Speech! Speech!

MORDECAI. (*Clears throat.*) People of Media and Persia and all the 127 provinces! Citizens of Shushan-Habira! This is the new Assistant King, Mordecai ben Ya-eer! (*Cheers.*) Mordecai ben Ya-eer, ben Shammai, ben Kish, a man of Benjamin. (*Cheers.*) Citizens! Our wise and good King Ahasuerus has decided to make Haman the Wicked a head shorter. (*Cheers.*) May that be the fate of all Hamans now and forevermore, amen! (*Wild cheers.*)

From this moment forward, in all the King's provinces from India to Ethiopia, there is no superior race! All are equal! Anyone caught mistreating a Hebrew will follow Haman to his ancestors! I promise our glorious armies—you will never again go out to war! (*Cheers.*) Citizens! Our country will again be a land of milk and honey, dates and figs, bread and meat, and plenty to eat! Roast duck and beer and good wine to fill you with cheer! No trouble and no fights, sunny days and peaceful nights! (*Stormy applause. Shouts of "Long Live Mordecai."*)

MEMUCAN. That's what I call a speech!

MORDECAI. (*Wiping his brow.*) Friend Herald, I can't think of anything else to say. Maybe you could give somebody else the floor?

HERALD. Correct, Motya. Introducing the Wise, the Illustrious, the Benevolent King Ahasuerus!

AHASUERUS.
Your king is hereby proclaimin'
What a relief to be rid of Haman!

ALL. To be rid of Haman!

HERALD. Introducing the Fair, the Modest, the Virtuous Queen, Esther the Beautiful!

ESTHER.
I'm Esther the Beautiful, Esther the Queen,
Almost the victim of Haman the Mean.

ALL. Oy vey! Almost the victim—

HERALD.
Introducing Haman the Knave—
May the earth toss him out of the grave!

(*Enter Haman.*)

HAMAN. She already did, Friend Herald, she already did.

I'm Haman the Agagi, once a hero—
Now a zero.

ALL. Once a hero and now a zero!

HERALD.
In that case, colleague players,
Soldiers, generals, Jews, Persians, wives, maidens—
Everyone! Take a bow—the play is done!

Our Purim-shpil is finished
It's come to an end—
And may we hear the same
From all the Hamans—Amen!

ALL.
The play is over, without a doubt.
So give us our money—and throw us out!

THE END